ROMANTICISM AND THE BIOPOLITICS OF MODERN WAR WRITING

Military literature was one of the most prevalent forms of writing to appear during the Romantic era, yet its genesis in this period is often overlooked. Ranging from histories to military policy, manuals, and a new kind of imaginative war literature in military memoirs and novels, modern war writing became a highly influential body of professional writing. Drawing on recent research into the entanglements of Romanticism with its wartime trauma and revisiting Michel Foucault's ground-breaking work on military discipline and the biopolitics of modern war, this book argues that military literature was deeply reliant upon Romantic cultural and literary thought and the era's preoccupations with the body, life and writing. Simultaneously, it shows how military literature runs parallel to other strands of Romantic writing, forming a sombre shadow against which Romanticism took shape and offering its own exhortations for how to manage the life and vitality of the nation.

NEIL RAMSEY is Senior Lecturer in English Literature at the University of New South Wales, Canberra. His interests include the literary, cultural and biopolitical responses to warfare during the eighteenth century and Romantic eras, with a particular focus on the representations of personal experience and the development of a modern culture of war. He is the author of *The Military Memoir and Romantic Literary Culture, 1780–1835* (2011) and co-editor, with Gillian Russell, of *Tracing War in British Enlightenment and Romantic Culture* (2015) and, with Anders Engberg-Pedersen, of *War and Literary Studies* (2022).

CAMBRIDGE STUDIES IN ROMANTICISM

This series aims to foster the best new work in one of the most challenging fields within English literary studies. From the early 1780s to the early 1830s, a formidable array of talented men and women took to literary composition, not just in poetry, which some of them famously transformed, but in many modes of writing. The expansion of publishing created new opportunities for writers, and the political stakes of what they wrote were raised again by what Wordsworth called those 'great national events' that were 'almost daily taking place': the French Revolution, the Napoleonic and American wars, urbanization, industrialization, religious revival, an expanded empire abroad, and the reform movement at home. This was an enormous ambition, even when it pretended otherwise. The relations between science, philosophy, religion, and literature were reworked in texts such as *Frankenstein* and *Biographia Literaria*; gender relations in *A Vindication of the Rights of Woman* and *Don Juan*; journalism by Cobbett and Hazlitt; and poetic form, content, and style by the Lake School and the Cockney School. Outside Shakespeare studies, probably no body of writing has produced such a wealth of commentary or done so much to shape the responses of modern criticism. This indeed is the period that saw the emergence of those notions of literature and of literary history, especially national literary history, on which modern scholarship in English has been founded.

The categories produced by Romanticism have also been challenged by recent historicist arguments. The task of the series is to engage both with a challenging corpus of Romantic writings and with the changing field of criticism they have helped to shape. As with other literary series published by Cambridge University Press, this one will represent the work of both younger and more established scholars on either side of the Atlantic and elsewhere.

See the end of the book for a complete list of published titles.

ROMANTICISM
AND THE BIOPOLITICS
OF MODERN WAR WRITING

NEIL RAMSEY

University of New South Wales, Canberra

CAMBRIDGE
UNIVERSITY PRESS

CAMBRIDGE
UNIVERSITY PRESS

University Printing House, Cambridge CB2 8BS, United Kingdom

One Liberty Plaza, 20th Floor, New York, NY 10006, USA

477 Williamstown Road, Port Melbourne, VIC 3207, Australia

314–321, 3rd Floor, Plot 3, Splendor Forum, Jasola District Centre, New Delhi – 110025, India

103 Penang Road, #05–06/07, Visioncrest Commercial, Singapore 238467

Cambridge University Press is part of the University of Cambridge.

It furthers the University's mission by disseminating knowledge in the pursuit of education, learning, and research at the highest international levels of excellence.

www.cambridge.org
Information on this title: www.cambridge.org/9781009100441
DOI: 10.1017/9781009118798

First published 2023

A catalogue record for this publication is available from the British Library.

Library of Congress Cataloging-in-Publication Data
NAMES: Ramsey, Neil, author.
TITLE: Romanticism and the biopolitics of modern war writing / Neil Ramsey.
DESCRIPTION: [New York] : Cambridge University Press, [2022] | Includes bibliographical references and index.
IDENTIFIERS: LCCN 2022018428 | ISBN 9781009100441 (hardback) | ISBN 9781009118798 (ebook)
SUBJECTS: LCSH: English literature – 19th century – History and criticism. | War in literature. | Biopolitics in literature. | War and literature – Great Britain. | Romanticism – Great Britain. | LCGFT: Literary criticism.
CLASSIFICATION: LCC PR468.W37 R36 2022 | DDC 820.9/3581–dc23/eng/20220722
LC record available at https://lccn.loc.gov/2022018428

ISBN 978-1-009-10044-1 Hardback

Contents

v

Acknowledgements

This book has taken a while to write and, in that time, has benefitted enormously from conversations with some wonderful thinkers. I would especially like to acknowledge the advice and encouragement of Gillian Russell, Russell Smith, Ben Dibley, Peter Otto, Anders Engberg-Pedersen, Brecht de Groote, Phil Shaw, Will Christie, Jon Mee, Alan Bewell, Jane Gleeson-White and Tom Ford. My thanks to the huge support from my colleagues and friends at the University of New South Wales, Canberra, David Stahel, Ned Dobos, Michael Austin, Nicole Moore, Christina Spittel, Heather Neilson, Morgan Burgess, and Peter Balint. I have also benefitted enormously from several reading groups and would like to thank Tony Simoes da Silva, David Cribb, Carlos Morreo Boada, Trang X Ta, Sandeep Singh, Gayani Ranawake and Priyanka Shivadas.

I have received considerable support from associates of the Australian Research Council Centre for the History of Emotions, and would especially like to thank Andrew Lynch, Katrina O'Loughlin, Bob White and Stephanie Downs. I am also grateful for lively discussions and encouragement from members of the British Association for Romantic Studies and the Romantic Studies Association of Australasia, especially Ian Haywood, Sharon Ruston, Matt Sangster, Jeremy Davies, Rachel Hewitt, Ildiko Csengei, Tom MacLean, Elias Greig, Alexandra Hankinson, Sarah Comyn and Amelia Dale.

Thanks to my editor at Cambridge University Press, Bethany Thomas, to my editorial assistant, George Laver, and to the editors of Cambridge Studies in Romanticism Series, especially James Chandler and Mary Jacobus for her early encouragement. My thanks also to the staff at the British Library, the National Library of Scotland and the Australian Defence Force Academy Library.

This project was supported by an Australian Research Council Australian Postdoctoral Fellowship DP1097164. Funding was also provided by the Australian Research Council Centre for Excellence in the History of

Emotion, Associate Investigator Grant and Research-to-Publication Grants.

Some material from two chapters in this study has formerly appeared in an altered form in other places. Chapter 1 draws on 'Wartime Reading: Romantic Era Military Periodicals and the *Edinburgh Review*', *Australian Literary Studies* 29 (2014): 28–40. Chapter 5 uses material from '"To Die as a Soldier": The Vital Romance of the Military Novel', *Journal for Eighteenth-Century Studies* 41 (2018): 579–96.

Finally, my most especial thanks to Esther, who has been for me a constant source of encouragement and support.

Introduction
Romanticism and the Bio-aesthetics of the Military Literary World

Although Romanticism has long been understood as a reaction to the political conflict of the French Revolution, it has only been more recently that Romantic texts have been read in close relation to the era's wars.[1] British Romanticism is now widely regarded as a body of writing that was deeply troubled by news of distant military violence and suffering.[2] Britons lived during what Mary Favret defines as a modern wartime, the experience of those 'living through but not in a war'.[3] This wartime experience was, therefore, primarily formed by the circulation of information within Britain's daily journalism that reported on wars fought in distant locations. Each day brought fresh news of the conflicts that profoundly shaped the emotional life of the nation, whether through shared celebrations of victory, commiseration of defeat or, more commonly, the apprehensive or at times simply tedious activity of waiting for further clarity or confirmation of events. Romantic Britain was subject to what Dominick LaCapra describes as a 'structural trauma', in which war's absent or remote violence came to be felt as an anxious disturbance of national history.[4]

But, despite giving rise to a modern culture of war spectatorship, Romantic writing was nonetheless thoroughly entangled with the

---

[1] See Gillian Russell, *The Theatres of War: Performance, Politics and Society, 1793–1815* (Oxford: Clarendon Press, 1995); Philip Shaw, *Waterloo and the Romantic Imagination* (New York: Palgrave Macmillan, 2002); Simon Bainbridge, *British Poetry and the Revolutionary and Napoleonic Wars* (Oxford: Oxford University Press, 2003); Mary A. Favret, *War at a Distance: Romanticism and the Making of Modern Wartime* (Princeton: Princeton University Press, 2010); Neil Ramsey, *The Military Memoir and Romantic Literary Culture, 1780–1835* (Farnham: Ashgate, 2011); Jeffrey N. Cox, *Romanticism in the Shadow of War: Literary Culture in the Napoleonic War Years* (Cambridge: Cambridge University Press, 2014); and Lily Gurton-Wachter, *Watchwords: Romanticism and the Poetics of Attention* (Stanford: Stanford University Press, 2016).

[2] Favret, *War at a Distance*, 52; Jan Mieszkowski, *Watching War* (Stanford: Stanford University Press, 2012).

[3] Favret, *War at a Distance*, 9.

[4] Favret, *War at a Distance*, 161.

logistical and strategic requirements of conflicts that formed the first total wars of history.[5] In his wide-ranging analysis of war and its media technologies, Paul Virilio has argued that to wage war it is as vital to master and control perceptual fields as it is to conquer on fields of battle.[6] To fully understand Romantic literature as a body of wartime writing therefore means that we must pay attention to the vast military republic of letters that also formed in these years. The period from the 1760s to the 1830s gave rise to a wealth of books on modern military thought, from drill manuals to works of military history, strategy, policy and discipline, with an associated network of military authors, booksellers, publishers, journals and even a nascent imaginative war literature of military memoirs and novels.[7] One correspondent in *The British Military Library; or Journal* (1798–1800) responded to this outpouring of material by declaring that 'the æra of military literature' had taken hold of Britain.[8] Overturning long-established classical traditions of military thought, this material was critical to the formation of a modern security state with the capacity to mobilise its population for war. It formed a body of writing that enabled a nation to undertake, in the words of the military author Jacques Antoine-Hippolyte, Comte de Guibert, 'conquests upon itself' through its prescriptions for the regulation of behaviours, habits, perceptions, bodies and actions that could militarise the very fabrics of daily life.[9]

If a central focus of Romantic studies has been the 'symbiotic relationship' that formed in the period between literature and science (whether the natural or social sciences), there has nonetheless been almost no concern

---

[5] On the French Revolutionary and Napoleonic Wars as total wars, see David A. Bell, *The First Total War: Napoleon's Europe and the Birth of Modern Warfare* (London: Bloomsbury, 2007).

[6] Paul Virilio, *War and Cinema: The Logistics of Perception*, trans. Patrick Camiller (London: Verso, 1989).

[7] For historical research into this material, see Ira D. Gruber, *Books and the British Army in the Age of the American Revolution* (Chapel Hill: University of North Caroline Press, 2010); Donald E. Graves, *'Reading Maketh a Full Man': British Military Literature in the Napoleonic Wars: An Annotated Bibliography of the Titles Published by the London Firm of Egerton, 1782–1832* (Godmanchester: Ken Trotman Publishing, 2007); Mark Danley, 'Military Writings and the Theory and Practice of Strategy in the Eighteenth-Century British Army' (PhD diss., Kansas State University, 2001); and John Houlding, *Fit for Service: The Training of the British Army, 1715–95* (Oxford: Oxford University Press, 1981).

[8] 'Letter to the Editor', *British Military Library; or Journal*, vol. 1, revised ed. (1802): 67.

[9] Jacques Antoine Hippolyte, Comte de Guibert, *A General Essay on Tactics. With an Introductory Discourse upon the Present State of Politics and the Military Science in Europe. To which is Prefixed a Plan of a Work, Entitled, The Political and Military System of France. Translated from the French of M. Guibert. By an Officer* (London: printed for J. Millan, opposite the Admiralty, Whitehall, 1781), xii.

with the era's military science.[10] This neglect of military thought is surprising given that war, empire, science and literature were fundamentally entangled in this era. Naval voyages and military campaigns not only attracted enormous public attention but also played a prominent role in the production of knowledge.[11] Moreover, military science was widely considered to be of immense significance, the first edition of the *Encyclopaedia Britannica* proposing that the study of war was not only 'the most necessary and useful of all the sciences', but the most complex and difficult to master.[12] Yet the limited concern with the cultural status of this body of thought speaks to a continuing uncertainty surrounding the very idea that it is possible to fully conceptualise a coherent military science. A long tradition of Western thought has insisted that truth belongs to the realm of peace, not the brutality and chaos of war.[13] For cultural theorists of war such as Elaine Scarry, Hannah Arendt and Simone Weil, violence renders us speechless and so represents the antithesis of language, thought and rationality.[14] Language is debased by war, rendered into a tissue of lies that hover above and beyond physical bodies and the traumatic pain of combat. The peculiar difficulty in conceptualising military thought was compounded with the rise of a modern military science and the simultaneous appearance of a separate civilian sphere at the end of the eighteenth century, the term civilian first coming into its modern usage in the 1790s.[15] War's status as a field of knowledge was left uncertain and fragmented, war seemingly remaining entirely aesthetic, absolute or sublime.[16]

---

[10] John Holmes and Sharon Ruston, eds, *The Routledge Research Companion to Nineteenth-Century British Literature and Science* (New York: Routledge, 2017), 9.

[11] *The Routledge Research Companion*, 4.

[12] *Encyclopaedia Britannica; Or, a Dictionary of Arts, Sciences, and Miscellaneous Literature on a Plan Entirely New*, 18 vols (Dublin: printed by James Moore, 1790–98), XVIII, 703. *Eighteenth Century Collections Online*, www.gale.com/intl/primary-sources/eighteenth-century-collections-online, accessed 15 April 2022.

[13] See Tarak Barkawi and Shane Brighton, 'Powers of War: Fighting, Knowledge, and Critique', *International Political Sociology* 5, no. 2 (2011): 126–43; Michel Foucault, *Society Must Be Defended: Lectures at the Collège de France, 1975–1976*, ed. Mauro Bertani and Alessandro Fontana, trans. David Macey (London: Penguin Books, 2004), 173.

[14] Elaine Scarry, *The Body in Pain: The Making and Unmaking of the World* (Oxford: Oxford University Press, 1985); Hannah Arendt, *On Violence* (San Diego: Harcourt Brace, 1970); Simone Weil, '*The Iliad*, or the Poem of Force', *Chicago Review* 18, no. 2 (1965): 5–30.

[15] The term 'civilian' formerly referred to an expert in civil as opposed to ecclesiastical law, see Bell, *The First Total War*, 11.

[16] On how war has been defined in relation to the aesthetic, see Nick Mansfield, 'Destroyer and Bearer of Worlds: The Aesthetic Doubleness of War', in *Tracing War in British Enlightenment and Romantic Culture*, ed. Neil Ramsey and Gillian Russell (Basingstoke: Palgrave Macmillan, 2015), 188–203. See also Favret, *War at a Distance*, 40–43.

Arendt proposes that modern political and cultural theory has largely abandoned any serious consideration of war or military thought, leaving its analysis to be undertaken by mere military 'technicians' whose knowledge of war is inseparable from its practice.[17]

This book argues that Romantic-era military literature is worthy of attention as more than a simply technical body of writing. Military thought influenced Romantic cultural life as extensively as nearly any of the other proto-scientific disciplines that formed in this period because it was pivotal to the violence that defined Romantic wartime culture. An anxiogenic age beset by the fear and alarm of imminent invasion and revolutionary upheaval, Britain in the Romantic period may have remained distant from war, but the nation nonetheless lived under the shadow of war's perpetual threats and enduring obligations for national service. Jerome Christensen reminds us that for all British Romanticism was distant from war, it was also shaped by the far-reaching demands of national wartime mobilisation, meaning that Romantic literature 'was written under the threat of imminent invasion, during the state's emergency suspension of dailiness, amidst the din of official exhortations to unity, and in the face of brutal and systematic repression'.[18] Research into the rise of Britain's fiscal-military state reveals how the nation's extensive wartime military bureaucracy, administration and propaganda constituted a veritable revolution of social and political life almost as far reaching in its implications as the revolution in France.[19] For Michel Foucault, military disciplinary practices were foundational to a new, disciplinary society that found its 'full blossoming' at the time of the Napoleonic Wars.[20] This was a time when Jane Austen delighted in the military policy of Captain Charles Pasley, while William Wordsworth and Samuel Taylor Coleridge were branded alongside Pasley as amongst the nation's leading military authors.[21] Radicals from William

---

[17] Hannah Arendt, *On Revolution* (London: Penguin, 1965), 19.

[18] Jerome Christensen, 'The Detection of the Romantic Conspiracy in Britain', *South Atlantic Quarterly* 95 (1996): 603–27, 603.

[19] Anthony Page, *Britain and the Seventy Years War, 1744–1815: Enlightenment, Revolution and Empire* (London: Palgrave Macmillan, 2014), 98; John Brewer, *The Sinews of Power: War, Money, and the English State, 1688–1783* (Cambridge, MA: Harvard University Press, 1990); Yuval N. Harari, *The Ultimate Experience: Battlefield Revelations and the Making of Modern War Culture, 1450–2000* (Basingstoke: Palgrave Macmillan, 2008), 180–81.

[20] Michel Foucault, *Discipline and Punish: The Birth of the Prison*, trans. Alan Sheridan (New York: Vintage, 1991), 217.

[21] Timothy Fulford, 'Sighing for a Soldier: Jane Austen and Military Pride and Prejudice', *Nineteenth-Century Literature* 57, no. 2 (2002): 153–78; John Stoddard, letter to Charles Pasley, 1 September 1811, cited in 'Introduction' to Charles Pasley, *The Military Policy and Institutions of the British Empire*, ed. and intro. B. R. Ward, 5th ed. (London: W. Clowes and Sons, 1914), 10.

Cobbett to Percy Bysshe Shelley were, conversely, united by their antipathy towards military disciplinary practices such as flogging and pressgangs.[22] Post-Waterloo Romantic culture was hardly free of its entanglements with militarised conflict, as is evident in Shelley's response to Peterloo or Lord Byron's involvement with the Greek War of Independence (1821–32).

Notwithstanding the demands of war, there has been little consideration of how such military elements permeated Romantic cultural life. This is in striking distinction to studies of early modern literature that have demonstrated a detailed understanding of the extensive associations between the era's military books and its drama and poetry.[23] Gert Geoffrey Langsam observes that the discourses on war originating in early modern military books extended into 'every conceivable literary form of the day'.[24] In stark contrast, Robert Gordon has observed that Ian Watt's foundational *The Rise of the Novel* documents the emergence of modern literature as a demilitarisation of society or a veritable 'civilian revolution' that displaced an earlier culture concerned with martial conflict, Gordon concluding '[it] was in the eighteenth century that fictional man, like social man, abandoned the sword'.[25] Romanticism is epistemologically distant from war because it is, fundamentally, a civilian body of writing. Given that the definition of the civilian dates from the 1790s, one of the defining characteristics of Romanticism is surely that it constitutes the first body of writing to be produced by authors who could conceptualise themselves as civilians. At the same time, however, a new and distinct body of military writing also acquired its modern form. This was a body of work formed out of military technical, professional, disciplinary and, notably, a fictional knowledge of war that assumed the task of documenting, interpreting and representing war for the modern nation. The demilitarisation of society or the civilian revolution that Watt documents went hand in hand with the 'militarisation' of war by the state's military apparatus and an emergent military science.[26] Encompassing hundreds of titles, this body of modern war writing admittedly constituted an enormous range of topics and

---

[22] Paul Foot, *Red Shelley* (London: Bookmarks, 1984), 57.

[23] For an overview of these studies, see Patricia Cahill, *Unto the Breach: Martial Formations, Historical Trauma, and the Early Modern Stage* (Oxford: Oxford University Press, 2008).

[24] Gert Geoffrey Langsam, *Martial Books and Tudor Verse* (New York: King's Crown Press, 1951), 1.

[25] Robert C. Gordon, *Arms and the Imagination: Essays on War, Politics, and Anglophone Culture* (Lanham: Hamilton Books, 2009). Despite his focus on the civilian, Watt was himself a veteran whose wartime service profoundly affected his literary criticism, see Marina MacKay, *Ian Watt: The Novel and the Wartime Critic* (Oxford: Oxford University Press, 2018).

[26] As David Bell argues, militarism is dependent upon this separation of the military from a civilian sphere that is in need of being remilitarised, Bell, *The First Total War*, 11–12.

approaches. Yet however much a 'military literary world' was composed of a diverse and distinct body of writing, it nonetheless emerged at the same moment and in parallel with its civilian wartime counterpart.[27] As Nick Mansfield has proposed, war cannot be fixed into a stable identity but can only be thought through 'aporetic entanglements' with its 'others', however that other of war is conceived.[28] This book proposes that the military thought of the Romantic era has just such a set of 'aporetic entanglements' with the broader wartime culture that we know as Romanticism.

Examining the cultural significance of military writing in Romantic-era Britain, this study is founded on Jacques Rancière's theorisation of indisciplinarity.[29] Adopting a radically new approach to the spectacular politics of modernity, Rancière has insisted that rather than unmask spectacle by revealing its basis in suffering we must seek to understand how politics is itself aesthetic. This means examining how politics operates through an underlying 'distribution of the sensible' concerned with questions of who can and cannot speak with authority. Rancière has thus enacted what Gabriel Rockhill terms a 'Copernican revolution' in approaches to the politics of aesthetics because he refuses to see politics and aesthetics as separate categories.[30] All politics is aesthetic because all politics is intrinsically concerned with questions of how we can see and understand the world.[31] Rancière broadens our idea of literature from fiction to the operation of the sensible within any and all fields of knowledge.[32] He advances an idea of a 'poetics of knowledge' that is concerned with untangling the literary effects by which a science is able to develop itself as a science, with finding beneath the formation of a science the operation of writing and its quests for signification and meaning.[33] He directs attention to a 'new regime of writing' and its formulation of a 'symptomology of society' that

---

[27] Houlding, *Fit for Service*, 168.

[28] Nick Mansfield, *Theorizing War: From Hobbes to Badiou* (New York: Palgrave Macmillan, 2008), 98. For an account of modern literature's aporetic relationship with war, see Sean Gaston, *Derrida, Literature and War: Absence and the Chance of Meeting* (London: Continuum, 2009).

[29] Jacques Rancière, 'Jacques Rancière and Indisciplinarity', interview by Marie-Aude Baronian and Mireille Rosello, trans. Gregory Elliot, *Art and Research: A Journal of Ideas, Contexts and Methods* 2, no. 1 (2008), n.p.

[30] Gabriel Rockhill, *Radical History and the Politics of Art* (New York: Columbia University Press, 2014), 163.

[31] Jacques Rancière, *Disagreement: Politics and Philosophy*, trans. Julie Rose (Minneapolis: University of Minnesota Press, 2000), 57–58.

[32] Rancière, 'Jacques Rancière and Indisciplinarity', 5.

[33] Jacques Rancière, *The Names of History: On the Poetics of Knowledge*, trans. Hassan Melehy, with a foreword by Hayden White (Minneapolis: University of Minnesota Press, 1994), 8.

underpinned the human sciences as much as imaginative literary texts in the Romantic age.[34]

Rancière distances his thought from Walter Benjamin's earlier theorisation of the 'aestheticization of politics', which, for Benjamin, was inextricably linked to war.[35] Nonetheless, not only does Rancière carry forward Benjamin's earlier concerns with modern media by elaborating the a priori forms of aesthetics, but there are also innumerable ways that Rancière's understanding of the aesthetics of politics circles back to concerns with war, strategy and what he terms the 'war machine' of disciplinary thought.[36] He has proposed with regards to the aesthetics of Romanticism that 'the conditions for the creation of this new art world were first and foremost political – and even military'.[37] Developing much further Foucault's analysis of modern disciplinary societies, Rancière insists that discipline must be understood as encompassing more than simply the exercise and coercion of bodies because discipline also conditions the language and knowledge that surrounds bodies.[38] For Rancière, indisciplinary thought means looking past disciplinary boundaries of knowledge to rethink the 'context of the war' by which bodies are made to conform to discourse.[39] Hence, while this study is deeply informed by Foucault's analysis of military disciplinary practices and their foundational role in the dawning of a disciplinary society during the Romantic era, it also follows Rancière's efforts to read the aesthetic and political alongside one another in order to explore in more detail the full flourishing of military power as a vast discourse concerned with the force and power of life. This study offers a history or poetics of knowledge that examines how military thought developed out of the massive expansion of print of the latter half of the eighteenth century.[40] In the

[34] Jacques Rancière, 'The Politics of Literature', *SubStance* 33, no. 1 (2004): 10–24, 18; Jacques Rancière, *The Politics of Aesthetics: The Distribution of the Sensible*, trans. and intro. Gabriel Rockhill, with an afterword by Slavoj Žižek (London: Continuum, 2004), 33.

[35] Rancière, *The Politics of Aesthetics*, 13.

[36] Jacques Rancière, 'Thinking between Disciplines: An Aesthetics of Knowledge', trans. Jon Roffe, *Parrhesia* 1 (2006): 1–12, 7.

[37] Jacques Rancière, 'Aesthetics and Politics Revisited: An Interview with Jacques Rancière', interview by Gavin Arnall, Laura Gandolfi and Enea Zaramella, *Critical Inquiry* 38 (Winter 2012).

[38] Jacques Rancière, *Disagreement and Philosophy*, trans. Julie Rose (Minneapolis: University of Minnesota Press, 1999), 29.

[39] Rancière, 'Thinking between Disciplines', 8.

[40] On the history of knowledge, see Johan Östling, David Larsson Heidenblad, Erling Sandmo, Anna Nilsson Hammar and Kari Nordberg, 'The History of Knowledge and the Circulation of Knowledge: An Introduction', in *Circulation of Knowledge: Explorations in the History of Knowledge*, ed. Johan Östling, Erling Sandmo, David Larsson Heidenblad, Anna Nilsson Hammar and Kari

context of this study, an indisciplinary approach means seeing how, in the modern era, a new kind of military writing attained a privileged status for articulating what we can know and say about war.

The central argument of this book is that military writing was deeply informed by an elementary feature of Romantic wartime: the intensification of military disciplinary regimes in line with the period's embryonic biopolitical thought.[41] Biopolitics has received considerable attention from a large and growing body of cultural theory as one of the most incisive ways of conceptualising modern power, but the concept has not been extensively examined in relation to Romantic culture.[42] The precise meaning of biopolitics is widely debated and there is little settled agreement beyond the obvious reference to the role of 'life' in modern political power and government. While the term can be traced back to the early twentieth century, the word biopolitics was coined by Rudolph Kjellén to refer to vitalist ideas of the state (Kjellén, not coincidentally, also coined the term geopolitics), the modern usage of the term is indebted to the work of Foucault.[43] Foucault argues that biopolitics first emerged as a response of government to the demographic explosions of the eighteenth century.[44] Where disciplines targeted the individual bodies of workers, prisoners or patients, thus developing as an anatamo-politics of the body, biopolitics developed as a means for acquiring power and knowledge over entire populations. Biopolitics arose from new conceptions of the population as a living entity, governed by its own laws and regularities, and so complements

Nordberg (Lund: Nordic Academic Press, 2018), 9–33. For a general overview of the growth of print and its impact upon fields of knowledge in this era, see Clifford Siskin and William Warner, eds, *This Is Enlightenment* (Chicago: University of Chicago Press, 2010).

[41] On the role of life in Romantic aesthetics, see Denise Gigante, *Life: Organic Form and Romanticism* (New Haven: Yale University Press, 2009). See also Catherine Gallagher, *The Body Economic: Life, Death, and Sensation in Political Economy and the Victorian Novel* (Princeton: Princeton University Press, 2009); and Maureen McLane, *Romanticism and the Human Sciences: Poetry, Population, and the Discourse of the Species* (Cambridge: Cambridge University Press, 2000).

[42] For an overview, see Alastair Hunt and Matthias Rudolf, eds, *Romanticism and Biopolitics*, Romantic Circles Praxis Series (December 2012), www.rc.umd.edu/praxis/biopolitics. For studies addressing aspects of Romanticism and biopolitics, see Ron Broglio, *Beasts of Burden: Biopolitics, Labor, and Animal Life in British Romanticism* (Albany: State University of New York Press, 2017); Sara Guyer, *Reading with John Clare: Biopoetics, Sovereignty, Romanticism* (New York: Fordham University Press, 2015); Georgina Green, *The Majesty of the People: Popular Sovereignty and the Role of the Writer in the 1790s* (Oxford: Oxford University Press, 2014); and Robert Mitchell, *Infectious Liberty: Biopolitics between Romanticism and Liberalism* (New York: Fordham University Press, 2021).

[43] Roberto Esposito, *Bios: Biopolitics and Philosophy*, trans. Timothy Campbell (Minneapolis: University of Minnesota Press, 2008), 16.

[44] Michel Foucault, *The History of Sexuality*, vol. 1: *An Introduction*, trans. Robert Hurley (New York: Penguin Books, 1981), 140–45.

earlier disciplinary practices by targeting the collective life of the population. Taken in its entirety, however, a modern biopower encompasses these two poles of life, which it co-ordinates by imposing a series of norms that can align individual behaviour with the biological needs of the collective.[45] Biopower targets life in its totality, from the individual through to the collective. Reflecting on these developments, Giorgio Agamben goes so far as to propose that the modern world can be defined by the failure of all 'historical tasks' for humanity so that only life, the animality or biological existence of the human, is able to still hold meaning and significance.[46] Life is coming to be the most important and elementary source of modern power.

Theorists of biopolitics have insisted, however, that it is imperative to understand how the modern politics of life always risk reversion to racism, war and death.[47] If the Romantic era gave rise to a biopolitics that sought to administer the health and productivity of a living population, this was nonetheless matched with what Foucault terms a 'thanatopolitics' that sought to marshal the population for war.[48] In his classic study of military professional power, *The Soldier and the State*, Samuel Huntington adapted Harold Lasswell's work on the modern 'garrison state' to encapsulate how war has today come to be waged through ideals of military professionalism and national service by the 'managers of violence'.[49] This study takes such thought further, however, by examining how military professionalism has been implicated with the disciplinary management and control of bodies

---

[45] Thomas Lemke notes that Foucault does not consistently maintain this distinction between the terms biopolitics and biopower, after having first elaborated the difference in volume one of the *History of Sexuality*, and the two terms essentially become synonymous in his later work, Thomas Lemke, *Biopolitics: An Advanced Introduction*, trans. Eric Frederick Trump (New York: New York University Press, 2011), 34. Rancière believes that Foucault's work must be understood as a theory of power, a biopower, but rejects the idea that there might also be a positive or emancipatory biopolitics, or politics based on an 'ontology of life'. See Jacques Rancière, *Dissenus: On Politics and Aesthetics*, ed. and trans. Steven Corcoran (London: Continuum, 2010), 93–94.

[46] Giorgio Agamben, *The Open: Man and Animal*, trans. Kevin Attell (Stanford: Stanford University Press, 2004), 75–77. Agamben is primarily concerned with twentieth-century totalitarianism, Foucault however finds the roots of that totalitarianism in the biopolitics that first formed in the nineteenth and eighteenth centuries, see Foucault, *The History of Sexuality*, 149–50.

[47] See Foucault, *The History of Sexuality*, 135–59; Giorgio Agamben, *Homo Sacer: Sovereign Power and Bare Life*, trans. Daniel Heller-Roazen (Stanford: Stanford University Press, 1998); and Roberto Esposito, *Bios: Biopolitics and Philosophy*, trans. Timothy Campbell (Minneapolis: University of Minnesota Press, 2008).

[48] On the relationship between biopolitics and thanatopolitics, see Michel Foucault, 'The Political Technology of Individuals', in *Power: Essential Works of Foucault, 1954–1985. Volume 3*, ed. James D. Faubian, trans. Robert Hurley (London: Penguin, 1994), 416.

[49] Samuel P. Huntington, *The Soldier and the State: The Theory and Politics of Civil-Military Relations* (Cambridge, MA: Harvard University Press, 1957).

and lives. The specialist knowledge of the professional soldier is inseparable from the forms of knowledge derived from military disciplinary power, as a new body of military literature transformed the mechanical approach of neo-classical military thought by cultivating quasi-medical concerns with the vitality of disciplinary subjects.[50] A new disciplinary regime began to conceptualise the disciplined subject in terms of what Foucault describes as the 'natural body', a biopolitical body of vital, living forces, a body informed by inner depths and potentials that resist the imposition of 'mechanical' authority.[51] While modern military thought undoubtedly encompasses many diverse topics, at its heart it shares a new-found set of mechanisms for developing the basis of all military power in the living body. No longer was war fought as the basic right of the sovereign, war was fought to protect and foster the purity, health and vitality of the nation, meaning that an increasingly professionalised military began to wage wars not simply as the managers of violence, but as the 'managers of life'.[52]

Cultural and media theorists such as Christoph Menke and Friedrich Kittler have insisted, however, that the natural body revealed by Foucault stands at the intersection of both new kinds of disciplinary practices and new forms of aesthetics that governed Romanticism.[53] As a growing number of studies have shown, it is far from a coincidence that biopolitics emerged at the same moment that an Aristotelian poetry of 'action' was superseded by a Romantic poetics grounded in the ordinary details of human life, a poetics 'dedicated to the repetition and reproduction of unadorned life'.[54] If Romantic aesthetics is underpinned by an organic model, a similar organicism was deeply implicated in the development of modern military thought. The eighteenth-century language of aesthetics paralleled the rise of a language of military discipline, Alexander Gottlieb Baumgarten theorised the cultivation of aesthetic taste by likening the

---

[50] On the distinction between the study of professionalisation and disciplinarisation, see Jan Goldstein, 'Foucault among the Sociologists: The "Disciplines" and the History of the Professions', *History and Theory* 23, no. 2 (1984): 170–92.

[51] Foucault, *Discipline and Punish*, 155. On a new conception of life in the modern era, see Davide Tarizzo, *Life: A Modern Invention*, trans. Mark William Epstein (Minneapolis: University of Minnesota Press, 2017), 3–5.

[52] Foucault, *The History of Sexuality*, 137.

[53] Christoph Menke, *Force: A Fundamental Concept of Aesthetic Anthropology*, trans. Gerrit Jackson (New York: Fordham University Press, 2012); Friedrich Kittler, *The Truth of the Technological World: Essays on the Genealogy of Presence*, trans. Erik Butler (Stanford: Stanford University Press, 2014), 1–17.

[54] Jacques Rancière, *The Politics of Literature*, trans. Julie Rose (Cambridge: Polity Press, 2011), 9–11. See also Hunt and Rudolf, eds, *Romanticism and Biopolitics*.

practice to the exercises of soldiers.[55] Harvie Ferguson observes that war can even be understood as 'a kind of applied aesthetics' because it is concerned with structuring, and deforming, the world of the senses.[56] Virilio similarly contends that military command is essentially aesthetic in its operation, '[s]ince the battlefield has always been a field of perception, the war machine appears to the military commander as an instrument of representation, comparable to the painter's palette and brush'.[57] Ferguson and Virilio echo and extend Azar Gat's definitive study of how military thought is culture-bound and so always develops within a specific aesthetic milieu. No matter how much aesthetics developed in the Romantic era within its own, distinct terms, its development was paralleled by the growth of wide-ranging disciplinary practices that sought to govern and control life, modes of control that were intensely elaborated and informed by military thought.

Rancière places such tensions at the heart of the 'new regime of writing' that formed at the end of the eighteenth century as writing became detached from an earlier, neo-classical representative regime of art concerned with the living speech of aristocratic masters.[58] Modern writing perpetually oscillates between freedom and materiality, producing either a 'democratic literarity' that lays the foundations for anyone to say anything, or else forming as the 'war machine' of human scientific, sociological or disciplinary knowledge that establishes coincidence between bodies and words.[59] This tension within writing is reflected in the enormous expansion of war writing that grappled with the unprecedented power and political significance of mass armies. While modern war writing collapses the neo-classical military world, it also decisively reorients the vast democratic potential unleashed by mass armies into the theorisation and control of the biological. Menke, in a similar manner to Rancière, reads this tension in writing as a conflict between conceptions of life developed by aesthetics and bio-aesthetics.[60] If the aesthetic attempts to liberate life by freeing it of any teleology or biological destiny, bio-aesthetics,

---

[55] Menke, *Force*, 27.

[56] Harvie Ferguson, 'The Sublime and the Subliminal: Modern Identities and the Aesthetics of Combat', *Theory, Culture and Society* 21, no. 3 (2004): 1–33, 9.

[57] Virilio, *War and Cinema*, 26.

[58] Jacques Rancière, *Aesthetics and its Discontents*, trans. Steven Corcoran (Cambridge: Polity Press, 2009), 1–15.

[59] Rancière, 'The Politics of Literature', 16; Rancière, 'Thinking between Disciplines', 7.

[60] Christoph Menke, 'Aesthetic Nature: Against Biology', *The Yearbook of Comparative Literature* 58 (2012): 193–95, 194.

conversely, perpetually seeks to conflate the aesthetic with the biological in efforts to foster and direct the productive forces of the natural body. This bio-aesthetic in effect constitutes disciplinary knowledge, the disciplinary imposition of discursive meanings and truth onto the senses, actions and self-understanding of bodies. Where democratic literarity is definitive of the emancipatory poetics of High Romanticism, a converse process of writing's capacity to materialise itself into bodies is epitomised by modern forms of war writing.[61] There are striking yet inverted parallels, in other words, between Romantic concerns with the living body and the sublimity, genius, organicism, perceptions and force of war that place the state's war machine in a strangely transposed relationship with Romantic aesthetics.

The concept of bio-aesthetics also elucidates the new aesthetics of imaginative war writing that came into being during the Romantic era. As much as other forms of military literature, this imaginative writing of military memoirs, biography and novels took shape in relation to a Romantic aesthetics of life that overturned earlier classical narratives concerned with the actions and speech of the great men of history. Instead, a new kind of story of the soldier's personal experience came to the fore, giving rise to what Kate McLoughlin terms a 'veteran poetics' concerned with the suffering and trauma of war.[62] While this aesthetics of military service is characterised by a 'democratic literarity' as it allowed any and all soldiers to speak on war, there was nonetheless a concomitant reduction of war stories to the physical experiences and suffering of the body and its 'revelation' that life is constituted above all by our biological existence.[63] A body of imaginative writing by military veterans, therefore, emerged in conjunction with other elements of the era's military war writing concerned with understanding the violent forces surrounding the natural body in ways that perpetually conflate the aesthetic with the biological. Understood as a version of aesthetics, modern war writing can be associated as much with the counter-Enlightenment of Romanticism as with the other proto-sciences forming in the Romantic era, but it appears as a sombre shadow

---

[61] Although Rancière seldom addresses biopolitical theory directly, his thought does carry some discernible traces of the concept. On this point, see Arne De Boever, 'The Politics of Realism in Rancière and Houellebecq', in *Rancière and Literature*, ed. Grace Hellyer and Julian Murphet (Edinburgh: Edinburgh University Press, 2016), 226–48, 230.

[62] Kate McLouhglin, *Veteran Poetics: British Literature in the Age of Mass Warfare, 1790–2015* (Cambridge: Cambridge University Press, 2018).

[63] Harari, *The Ultimate Experience.*

of counter-Enlightenment thought in its concerns with the manipulation and brutal suffering of the body.[64]

Manuel De Landa has described the transformations in military power during the era of the French Revolutionary and Napoleonic Wars as a shift away from clockwork towards motorised warfare.[65] Where the clockwork mechanism aligns with the early modern era's neo-classical assumptions that soldiers should be treated as though they were clockwork automatons set in motion by their commander, the idea of a motor implies that the soldier possesses an internal mechanism of control and orientation, epitomised not by the wound-up clock but the internalised mechanisms of the steam engine.[66] While agreeing with his general outline of a shift from a clockwork to an internally motivated soldier, this study offers a conception of motorisation less in strictly mechanical terms than in terms of living beings, of the vital interiorities and souls that a new regime of biopower inaugurated.[67] The soldier ceases to be perceived merely as an automaton and appears instead as a living organism possessed of autonomous, inner forces and affects.[68] What is more, this study shifts its focus away from De Landa's stress on the materiality of machines to emphasise instead the mediality of writing, seeing the latter as essential to the formation of a new era of warfare.[69] If a 'new regime of writing' was concerned with the historical forces that lie within domains of knowledge, those forces could be seen to reveal themselves as the living forces, the disciplinary lives that actually constituted military power. Catherine Gallagher has argued that life became a regulating principle of knowledge at this time – that political economy as much as literature was delineated as a 'kind of life science'

---

[64] On German military writing and the counter-Enlightenment, see Anders Engberg-Pedersen, *Empire of Chance: The Napoleonic Wars and the Disorder of Things* (Cambridge, MA: Harvard University Press, 2015).

[65] Manuel De Landa, *War in the Age of Intelligent Machines* (New York: Zone Books, 1991), 67. He believes that motorised warfare would in turn be displaced by a new paradigm of network warfare in the mid-twentieth century.

[66] De Landa, *War in the Age of Intelligent Machines*, 67.

[67] For related views on the internal motivation of the soldier in the modern era, see Harvie Ferguson, 'The Sublime and the Subliminal: Modern Identities and the Aesthetics of Combat', *Theory, Culture and Society* 21, no. 3 (2004): 1–33, 2–3; and Philip K. Lawrence, 'Enlightenment, Modernity and War', *History of the Human Sciences* 12, no. 1 (1999): 3–25, 8.

[68] Foucault, *Discipline and Punish*, 155.

[69] De Landa was keenly aware of the importance of media, but he only focussed on technical media, proposing that machinic warfare gave way to network warfare because of the medial transformations of the radio that generated what was, in effect, a 'wireless nervous system' for the military. De Landa, *War in the Age of Intelligent Machines*, 74–75.

concerned with understanding 'vital human energy'.[70] So too, however, military knowledge developed as a 'kind of life science' equally concerned with the vital powers of human lives and their energies.

Attending to the bio-aesthetics of military thought and teasing out its aporetic entanglement with Romantic wartime culture, this study reconceptualises the relationships between aesthetics, life, history, and warfare that formed in the Romantic era. It seeks to show how military thought shaped elementary questions about the visibility of political conflict and its suffering. Romanticism may have elided its violent contemporary history, but this was in large part because military literature, a modern war writing of military technicians, had become tasked with shaping a new understanding of history's violence. Although largely ignored by Romantic studies, this writing nonetheless profoundly shaped how British culture approached war. Moreover, it established the intellectual foundations for our own contemporary perceptions of war and its strategies and violence. If war today is governed by complex entanglements of militarised entertainments, strategic power and modern media forms, whether defined as 'the logistics of perception', 'the military-entertainment complex', 'virtuous war', 'netwar', 'militainment' or even more broadly 'the liberal way of war', Rancière's thought invites us to examine more foundational, even a priori, questions about the intersection of aesthetics and politics that can be seen to lie behind the militarisation of modern media technologies.[71] A study of the formation of modern war writing reveals a far longer and more complex history to war's relationship to capitalist or liberal modernity and the militarised control over the productive forces of the living body. Foucault posits that by 'elaborating procedures for the individual and collective coercion of bodies', the writing of junior military officers played as central a role in the formation of modernity as the great work of Enlightenment jurists and philosophers, perhaps even poets.[72] If the modern episteme was inaugurated by the immense epistemological shocks

---

[70] Gallagher, *The Body Economic*, 22, 33–34.

[71] Virilio, *War and Cinema*; Tim Lenoir and Luke Caldwell, *The Military-Entertainment Complex* (Cambridge, MA: Harvard University Press, 2018); James Der Derian, *Virtuous War: Mapping the Military-Industrial-Media-Entertainment Network* (Boulder: Westview Press, 2001); Michael Hardt and Antonio Negri, *Multitude: War and Democracy in the Age of Empire* (New York: Penguin Press, 2004), 55; Roger Stahl, *Militainment, Inc.: War, Media, and Popular Culture* (New York: Routledge, 2010); Michael Dillon and Julian Reid, *The Liberal Way of War: Killing to Make Life Live* (Abingdon: Routledge, 2009). On Rancière view of the a priori of aesthetics, see Jacques Rancière, 'From Politics to Aesthetics?' *Paragraph* 28, no. 1 (2005): 13–25, 13.

[72] Foucault, *Discipline and Punish*, 168–69.

of the French Revolutionary and Napoleonic Wars, this rupture could also be seen as a result of military power's discovery of the natural body.[73] Yet if Romantic era military writing provided a decisively new discursive framework for representing war, so too the disciplinary instability of writing on war means that this material remains highly open to new readings. This study thus offers its own redistribution of the sensible as it examines the underlying generic forms and assumptions of military thought to reveal how they first established a hold over war knowledge in the Romantic era.

Chapter 1 outlines the growth of military writing in Britain during the Romantic period. It does so by situating this growth in relation to the far more extensive expansion of print that occurred in the late eighteenth century and, in particular, the expansion of the era's periodical writing. Periodicals were not only one of the main products of an expanding realm of print but were also central to the task of making sense of this expansion by reviewing, cataloguing and organising the burgeoning world of print. It is significant, then, that there was also a rapidly growing number of military journals. Seeking to develop an intellectual culture out of the increasingly daily experience of wartime, the military journals played a foundational role in the formation of a new kind of deep but narrow field of military disciplinary knowledge. The appearance of military journals reflects how knowledge in this era was undergoing what Michel Foucault terms a process of 'disciplinarisation', as the localised and fragmentary forms of earlier technical knowledges were variously disqualified or else centralised, normalised and hierarchicised into a set of modern disciplinary fields that formed the basis of modern science.[74] The military journals were pivotal to this process because they supplied an institutional home and voice to the military that allowed modern military thought to first coalesce as a unified discipline of knowledge. The chapter reveals how an increasingly professionalised military acquired a totalising, scientific authority on war.[75]

This chapter also considers, however, how this disciplinarisation of knowledge gave rise to counter-histories of war's sublime shock and brute force. There is a tension in military writing that can be traced to the formation of military disciplinary knowledge out of the corresponding military

---

[73] See Engberg-Pedersen, *Empire of Chance*, 4–5. On Foucault's speculations as to how the idea of the population may have given rise to the modern episteme, see Foucault, *Society Must be Defended*, 190 and Michel Foucault, *Security, Territory, Population: Lectures at the Collège de France, 1977–1978*, trans. Graham Burchell (New York: Palgrave Macmillan, 2007), 75–79.

[74] Foucault, *Society Must be Defended*, 184.

[75] Foucault, *Society Must be Defended*, 184.

disciplinary control of bodies, actions and lives. Although studies of early modern war writing have built upon Foucault's account of the formation of modern disciplinary practices, his thought has had little impact upon studies of modern war writing since the Romantic era.[76] Studies of modern literature have shown a far greater concern with his work on sexuality while discounting his related concerns with war.[77] Addressing the subjective side of disciplinarity, the formation of self-writing and what Ian Hacking has theorised as memoro-politics, this chapter concludes by examining how literature and science appear as twinned elements within the disciplinary knowledge of war. It details how we can read the full extent of military writing in relation to an emergent biopower or, in Thomas Lemke's terms, a 'vital politics' that extended discipline ever more deeply into the control of life.[78]

The following two chapters examine the evolution of military thought during the Romantic era by delineating its relation to evolving military disciplinary practices. The two chapters are far from being exhaustive of this material, but concentrate on two foundational texts of a new military biopolitical thought. Chapter 2 looks at the formation of an exceedingly influential genre of modern war writing, the critical-military history that can be traced to the Welsh military officer Henry Lloyd and his *History of the Late War in Germany, Between the King of Prussia, and the Empress of Germany and Her Allies* (1766–90). Recent criticism has challenged traditional views of Lloyd as a merely neo-classical author with little relevance to modern conceptions of war, his work most notably encompassing the characteristically Romantic impulse of generic experimentation.[79] Building on this new research, this chapter shows how Lloyd's approach to military history not only helped introduce concerns with the aesthetics of genius and sublimity into military thought but that it also established a new way of conceptualising the historical conditions of war. His writing decisively broke with past efforts to teach history by example

---

[76] See, for example, Patricia A. Cahill, *Unto the Breach: Martial Formations, Historical Trauma, and the Early Modern Stage* (Oxford: Oxford University Press, 2008).

[77] Marco Formisano, 'Introduction: Stuck in Panduria: Books and War', in *War in Words: Transformations of War from Antiquity to Clausewitz*, ed. Marco Formisano and Hartmut Böhmep (Berlin: Walter de Gruyter, 2011), 1–9, 4.

[78] Thomas Lemke, 'Beyond Foucault: From Biopolitics to the Government of Life', in *Governmentality: Current Issues and Future Challenges*, ed. Ulrich Bröckling, Susanne Krasmann and Thomas Lemke (New York: Routledge, 2010), 165–84, 174.

[79] Patrick Speelman, *Henry Lloyd and the Military Enlightenment of Eighteenth-Century Europe* (Westport: Greenwood Press, 2002).

to instead conceptualise strategy around an emergent historical consciousness, a consciousness that Reinhart Koselleck associates with the momentous challenges to historical representation posed by the Seven Years War (1756–63).[80]

This chapter also argues that by turning military thought away from traditions of memoir and maxims, Lloyd's writing was critical for breaking down a neo-classical view of the commander as a figure of authority, command and action. As it transformed the history of war from a storehouse of examples to an object to be studied, it simultaneously reimagined the commander in relation to the quasi-natural 'life' of the army. A new conception of strategy altogether emerges from Lloyd's history as he attempts to comprehend the army as, in effect, an organism that lies outside the general's complete control. Military science comes to focus on the 'space of campaigns' concerned with the strategic movements or circulation of the living collective of the army.[81] Although many of Lloyd's ideas would be superseded by subsequent military thinkers, his thought operated in a similar fashion to Burke's theorisation of the sublime because it enabled the study of war to branch into diverse yet hierarchically ordered areas of military knowledge, whether of strategy, tactics, military policy or the human passions.[82] His work signalled how war in the Romantic era was coming to be conceptualised as a human science concerned with understanding and harnessing the vital power and force of life, what Lloyd describes as a new and sublime philosophy of war.

Chapter 3 considers in more detail the evolution of military disciplinary practices as military thought became ever more akin to a human science. It does so by focussing on a key work in the theorisation of military discipline, Robert Jackson's *A Systematic View of the Formation, Discipline, and Economy of Armies* (1804). Described by the military theorist J. F. C. Fuller as the first scientific account of war, with a status comparable to the writing of Antoine-Henri Jomini and Clausewitz, Jackson's ideas also informed Sir John Moore's revolutionary experiments in military training that are today seen as having inaugurated the first truly

---

[80] Reinhart Koselleck, *Futures Past: On the Semantics of Historical Time*, trans. and intro. Keith Tribe (New York: Columbia University Press, 2004), 244.

[81] Michel Foucault, *Power/Knowledge: Selected Interviews and Other Writings, 1972–1977*, ed. Colin Gordon, trans. Colin Gordon, Leo Marshall, John Mepham and Kate Soper (New York: Pantheon, 1980), 151.

[82] Clifford Siskin, *The Work of Writing: Literature and Social Change, 1700–1830* (Baltimore: Johns Hopkins University Press, 1998), 70.

modern soldiers.[83] Undoubtedly prompted by the mass volunteering of early nineteenth-century Britain, while developing much further ideas first adumbrated by Guibert, exemplified by Foucault as a founder of the modern disciplinary society, Jackson's book elaborates the enormous military and political power of the revolutionary era soldier.[84] An overlooked text, it nonetheless represents the first fully realised expression of the modern disciplinary regime in relation to war and offers a set of crucial correctives to Foucault's account of the development of modern military disciplinary practices.

With Jackson drawing on his extensive experience as a surgeon in the British army, *Systematic View* places the medicalised body at the heart of military discipline. Jackson insisted that the soldier must be viewed as a living organism, possessed of a complex and self-governing interiority that determines how tactics operate, in which 'instinctive movements and innate energy ... overturn the calculations of systematic tacticians, and humble the pride of the disciples of the mechanical school'.[85] In Jackson's conception, the soldier appears as a self-governing figure who functions independently and at a distance from disciplinary sites, a figure who more closely resembles the modern subject than the mechanical automatons associated with Frederick the Great's military drill practices. More than this, however, Jackson's book reveals how an emergent Romantic aesthetics penetrated deeply into the era's military thought to reconceptualise how the soldier functioned within the field. The military's concern with the imagination was undoubtedly a 'shock' to poets, Clausewitz surmised, but was nonetheless central to emergent aesthetic concerns with perception and interiority that suggest an unexplored context of wartime media surrounding a Romantic poetics and its formation of subjectivity.[86] Jackson's book represents a key shift in the conceptualisation of military discipline.

The final two chapters of the book consider the formation of new genres of military literature that were written by military authors for a predominantly non-military reading public. Reflecting a thoroughgoing militarisation of writing about war in this period, the two chapters examine the emergence of new forms of aesthetic expression surrounding war

[83] John Frederick Charles Fuller, *The Foundations of the Science of War* (Fort Leavenworth: US Army Command and General Staff College Press, 1993), 18. Fuller has been described as second only to Clausewitz for the significance of his military thought on modern warfare; see Franklin D. Margiotta, ed., *Brassey's Encyclopedia of Military History and Biography* (Washington: Brassey's, 2000), 352.

[84] Foucault, *Discipline and Punish*, 155 and 169.

[85] Robert Jackson, *A Systematic View of the Formation, Discipline, and Economy of Armies* (London: printed for John Stockdale, 1804), 145.

[86] Clausewitz, *On War*, 109.

that were fundamentally concerned with the vigour, health and organicism of the nation and the individual soldier. Chapter 4 examines one of the most politically influential books to appear in Britain during the years of the Napoleonic Wars, Charles Pasley's *Essay on the Military Policy and Institutions of the British Empire* (1810).[87] One of the first titular uses of the phrase 'military policy', Pasley's *Essay* concerns itself with the military capacities of Britain in ways that carry striking echoes of Lloyd's conception of a philosophy of war concerned with the management of collective, living forces. Many political commentators held the *Essay* to be decisive in bringing the wars to a conclusion, and it was even considered at the time to have had an impact on the political life of the nation second only to Burke's *Reflections on the Revolution in France* (1790). Pasley also received a surprisingly positive reception from his contemporary poets and novelists, including William Wordsworth, Samuel Taylor Coleridge, Robert Southey, Walter Scott, Maria Edgeworth and Jane Austen, all of whom applauded his manly and inspiring writing even as they recoiled from his call for imperial conquest.[88]

As Pasley imagines the expansion of a British empire of liberty, so he argues the need for aggressive conquest to be brought home to Europe if Britain is to resist Napoleonic France. He outlines a programme of endo-colonisation, or a return of the military-colonial project to the metropole, that seeks to remodel Britain itself in relation to far reaching demands of military security. He thereby shifts concerns with national identity away from the warlike relations that might prevail between nations and into the institutional management of the population and its potentiality, what Pasley calls its inherent 'vigour'.[89] Pasley's writing stands at the roots not only of new conception of empire but equally of what Hannah Arendt saw as the most dangerous idea in political theory – the organic view of the nation that links killing to the necessary preservation and expansion of life.[90] Considering, finally, why he was so widely praised as a writer, more a poet than a statesman in Wordsworth's view, this chapter draws on work into the relation between culture and the state to propose that military

---

[87] Charles Pasley, *Essay on the Military Policy and Instructions of the British Empire* (London: printed by D. N. Shury, Berwick Street, Soho; For Edmund Lloyd, Harley Street, 1810).

[88] On the reception of Pasley, see Neil Ramsey, "'A Question of Literature": The Romantic Writer and Modern Wars of Empire', in *Stories of Empire: Narrative Strategies for the Legitimation of an Imperial World Order*, ed. Christa Knellwolf and Margarete Rubik (Trier: Wissenschaftlicher Verlag Trier, 2009), 49–68.

[89] Pasley, *Essay on the Military Policy and Instructions of the British Empire*, 466.

[90] Arendt, *On Violence*, 75.

policy can be conceptualised as the aesthetic realisation of the nation as a living organism. In Pasley's writing, the military author displaces and reorients the traditional patriotic functions of the poetic bard to establish a new kind of national wartime narrative, a sublime liberal epic founded on the nation's traumatic confrontation with war.

In the post-Waterloo era, a large body of military tales were published in Britain that recounted veterans' experiences of the Napoleonic Wars for the general reading public.[91] Chapter 5 examines Thomas Hamilton's *The Youth and Manhood of Cyril Thornton* (1827), a fictionalised treatment of the author's military service in the Peninsular War (1808–14) and a book for which the *Quarterly Review* first coined the term 'military novel'.[92] Henry Crabb Robinson described it as one of the most lifelike novels he had read, one that contained 'much Wordsworthism'.[93] Hamilton himself was a key writer for *Blackwood's Edinburgh Magazine* and a close associate of Scott, from whose *Waverley* (1814) Hamilton clearly took inspiration. This chapter argues for the central importance of *Cyril Thornton* not only in inaugurating the genre of military novel, but equally for its formative role in the rise of modern war novels and, indeed, modern war literature more broadly. While war novels are traditionally associated with soldier-authors of the First World War, Hamilton's novel was nonetheless the first to offer what Paul Fussell views as the basis of all modern war stories – the reformulation of the romance of war around the physical survival of the soldier.[94] By mapping contemporary war onto the framework of the his-torical romance, with its capacity to align individual *Bildung* and national growth, so Hamilton's novel established a key generic form by which war is rendered accessible to the modern nation.

This study also contextualises *Cyril Thornton* in relation to the focus of previous chapters by demonstrating how it participates in the biopolitics that invests other forms of military writing of this period. The novel over-turns a traditional association of the aristocracy with war by aligning the military officer not only with an emergent discourse of sexuality but also with a related set of concerns around wounding, patriotism and military

---

[91] Ramsey, *Military Memoir and Romantic Literary Culture, 1780–1835*; McLoughlin, *Veteran Poetics*; and Harari, *The Ultimate Experience*.

[92] Thomas Hamilton, *The Youth and Manhood of Cyril Thornton* (Edinburgh: William Blackwood; and London: T. Cadell, 1827); *Quarterly Review* 37, no. 73 (1828), 521.

[93] *Henry Crabb Robinson on Books and their Writers*, ed. Edith J. Morley, 3 vols (London: Dent, 1938), II, 577.

[94] On the modern romance of the war memoir, see Paul Fussell, *The Great War and Modern Memory* (Oxford: Oxford University Press, 2003), 140–41.

honour. By following Menke and Rancière's concerns with the critical role of the aesthetic in the completion of the disciplinary subject, this chapter also suggests that the aesthetic rendition of the body in the military novel represents the culmination of military discipline's transformation into a form of biopower.[95] It reconceptualises the trauma of war literature by revealing how the novel enacts a fundamentally biopolitical operation of bringing bare life, the death in life of trauma, into the centre of British politics. By narrating the traumatic tale of the junior military officer, the novel may have quite literally enabled a subaltern to speak, but the novel also simultaneously reduces the officer to a suffering body in ways that reveal the total hold of a militarised biopower over discourses of war, a bio-aesthetics that has continued to reverberate across modern war writing.

By investigating the development of a proto-disciplinary field of military thought, this book documents the rise of militarism as a sombre shadow across British Romantic culture. It concludes, however, by taking a different perspective on the potentialities and instabilities that can also be located within this field of thought. Fredric Jameson has recently offered a strikingly original view of the emancipatory potential of the military when he argues for a universal military enlistment that could establish the military as a dual power alongside the state. The military, he proposes, could form what amounts to a counter-government to act as a source of national solidarity and welfare in an age of globalised, financial capitalism.[96] Although his apparent support for militarism has attracted considerable criticism, Jameson nonetheless reflects a broader turn to war and the military in recent critiques of the historical origins and progress of capitalist modernity. Drawing on Foucault's work on biopolitics and war, Jacques Bidet has observed that while war and class struggle cannot simply be equated, neither can they be isolated from one another. Although considerable work has been undertaken on populations in relation to modes of production, far more remains to be done to understand their relationship to territory and the biopolitics of war.[97] Éric Alliez and Maurizio Lazzarato have, in a related manner, proposed a new critique of capitalism

---

[95] Christoph Menke, 'A Different Taste: Neither Autonomy Nor Mass Consumption', in *Cultural Transformations of the Public Sphere: Contemporary and Historical Perspectives*, ed. Bernd Fischer and May Mergenthaler (Oxford: Peter Lang, 2015), 183–202; Jacques Rancière, 'The Aesthetic Dimension: Aesthetics, Politics, Knowledge', *Critical Inquiry* 36, no. 1 (Autumn 2009): 1–19.

[96] Fredric Jameson, *An American Utopia: Dual Power and the Universal Army*, ed. Slavoj Zizek (New York: Verso Books, 2016).

[97] Jacques Bidet, *Foucault with Marx*, trans. Steven Corcoran (London: Zed Books, 2016), 176–77.

in which military conflict and its biopolitical practices play a central role, and in which they argue that not only are we engaged in real wars but that we must also respond to these wars by drawing on the counter-strategic thought of French theory.[98]

Taking inspiration from this emergent work on the relationship between capitalist modernity, war and emancipation, this book ends with a short afterword to consider how the 'wartime poetry' of Romanticism could itself be seen to align with the counter-strategic thought of French theory. Indeed, where Marx developed his ideas in response to the earlier political economy of thinkers such as Adam Smith, Thomas Malthus and David Ricardo, French theorists such as Foucault, Raymond Aron, Gilles Deleuze and Michel de Certeau constructed their thought out of a very real recovery of Clausewitz.[99] But the enormous interest in the history of political economy that spreads out past Smith, Malthus and Ricardo has not been met with a similar level of critical interest in Clausewitz, and, as discussed here, the vast body of military thought that surrounds, informs and enables Clausewitz. Read in relation to modern war writing, Romantic wartime literature could be understood not simply through theories of trauma, therefore, but as representing an earlier version of this counter-strategic thought that finds its roots in the Romantic era.[100] Romantic counter-strategic thought can be seen to turn strategic military thought back against itself as it obstructs, problematises and renders inoperative the strategic modes for ordering and managing life that we have inherited from the Napoleonic era.

---

[98] Éric Alliez and Maurizio Lazzarato, *Wars and Capital*, trans. Ames Hodges (South Pasadena: Semiotext(e), 2016), 37.

[99] Julian Reid, 'Re-appropriating Clausewitz: The Neglected Dimensions of Counter-Strategic Thought', in *Classical Theory in International Relations*, ed. Beate Jahn (Cambridge: Cambridge University Press, 2006), 277–95.

[100] For an overview of historically inflected approaches to trauma, see Lisa Kasmer, ed., *Traumatic Tales: British Nationhood and National Trauma in Nineteenth-Century Literature* (New York: Routledge, 2017).

CHAPTER I

Writing and the Disciplinarisation of Military Knowledge

The latter half of the eighteenth century was a time of almost constant warfare between the major European powers. Not only did the fighting give rise to increasingly massive armies and an unprecedented mobilisation of state resources, but these conflicts were also dependent upon a rapidly growing body of military writing. The period was also, therefore, witness to a military enlightenment concerned with understanding the manifold issues at stake in waging war.[1] The idea of a military enlightenment has traditionally been considered an oxymoron because the rationality of Enlightenment thought appears antithetical to the brutality of military violence. Madeline Dobie has proposed that a defining principle of the Enlightenment could be found in the widely shared antagonism towards warfare amongst Enlightenment thinkers.[2] Yet the thinkers who constituted a military enlightenment were concerned with the same spirit of philosophy and the same humanist ideals as major philosophers of the Enlightenment, who were, moreover, far from being wholly critical of war.[3] Moving beyond a neo-classical inheritance, the military enlightenment fostered a new kind of war knowledge that radically transformed how war was conceptualised.

New approaches to the Enlightenment have begun to examine how Enlightenment thought materialised out of the rapid expansion of print during the latter half of the eighteenth century.[4] Just as the Enlightenment was utterly dependent upon this medial infrastructure of writing, so a military enlightenment can be seen as having formed in relation to the rapid growth of military writing between the 1760s and the 1830s. A wholly new

---

[1] For an overview, see Christy Pichichero, *The Military Enlightenment: War and Culture in the French Empire from Louis XIV to Napoleon* (Ithaca: Cornell University Press, 2017).
[2] Madeline Dobie, 'The Enlightenment at War', *PMLA* 124, no. 5 (2009): 1851–54, 1852.
[3] Pichichero, *The Military Enlightenment*, 4.
[4] For a general overview, see Clifford Siskin and William Warner, eds, *This Is Enlightenment* (Chicago: University of Chicago Press, 2010).

system for military thought developed in these years with the proliferation and consolidation of new genres of military writing, the emergence of dedicated military publishers, booksellers and military authors, the formation of military journals and, by the 1820s, a branching of military books into separate scientific and popular imaginative forms. Britain has traditionally been deemed almost wholly peripheral to major developments of military thought, which were centred on the military enlightenment of France and a subsequent military counter-enlightenment originating in Germany.[5] Yet historical research by Ira Gruber, Michael Danley, Patrick Speelman, Huw Davies, John Houlding and others has revealed that there was an extensive and significant military republic of letters in Britain by the end of the eighteenth century.[6] The country witnessed a steady publication of military books in these years, both through translations of continental and classical writing and the publication of original English language texts. This research into Britain's contribution to modern military thought aligns with burgeoning interest in the formation of the British fiscal-military state and the role of militarism more generally in the industrial revolution and Britain's hegemonic ascendancy in this era.[7]

Building on this research, this chapter examines the British military enlightenment in relation to what Jacques Rancière has described as a 'new regime of writing' that arose at the end of the eighteenth century.[8] Not only was there far more writing in this period, an accelerating increase in the rate of publication of printed materials, but this expansion can be associated

[5] See Azar Gat, *A History of Military Thought: From the Enlightenment to the Cold War* (Oxford: Oxford University Press, 2001).

[6] Ira D. Gruber, *Books and the British Army in the Age of the American Revolution* (Chapel Hill: University of North Caroline Press, 2010); Patrick Speelman, *Henry Lloyd and the Military Enlightenment of Eighteenth-Century Europe* (Westport: Greenwood Press, 2002); Michael Danley, *Military Writings and the Theory and Practice of Strategy in the Eighteenth-Century British Army* (PhD diss., Kansas State University, 2001); Huw Davies, 'Networks of Knowledge Mobility Within Eighteenth Century British Imperial Militarism', www.academia.edu/12359005/Networks_of_Knowledge_Mobility_Within_Eighteenth_Century_British_Imperial_Militarism, accessed 15 April 2022. John Houlding, *Fit for Service: The Training of the British Army, 1715–95* (Oxford: Oxford University Press, 1981); and Gavin Daly, *The British Soldier in the Peninsular War: Encounters with Spain and Portugal, 1808–1814* (Basingstoke: Palgrave Macmillan, 2013), 27–30.

[7] On the fiscal-military state, see John Brewer, *The Sinews of Power: War, Money and the English State, 1688–1783* (New York: Alfred A. Knopf, 1989). For an updated view, that emphasises the role of the British navy, see Anthony Page, 'The Seventy Years War, 1744–1815, and Britain's Fiscal-Naval State', *War and Society* 34, no. 3 (2015): 162–86. On the significance of militarism to the British industrial revolution, see Giovanni Arrighi, *Adam Smith in Beijing: Lineages of the Twenty-First Century* (London: Verso, 2007), 268; and Priya Satia, *Empire of Guns: The Violent Making of the Industrial Revolution* (New York: Penguin, 2018).

[8] Jacques Rancière, 'The Politics of Literature', *SubStance* 33, no. 1 (2004): 10–24, 18.

with the proliferation of new genres, protocols, systems and literary forms that sought to make sense of the growing mass of information. The overall effect was the birth of a fledgling modern science that organised knowledge into a set of deep but narrow proto-disciplinary fields. Military writing conformed with this expansion of writing as it came to itself take shape as a proto-disciplinary field of modern military thought. To track the role of print in this development, this chapter concentrates on the earliest emergence of military journals as a key form underpinning the development of a military enlightenment. Exemplary of this process by which a discipline first took shape, the journals not only allowed a distinctive military science to cohere, but they also established a corporate, institutional voice behind scientific military authority. But this chapter also considers the complexity behind the formation of modern military knowledge and the ongoing ambivalence as to whether military thought could ever attain the status of a science. The chapter therefore concludes by turning to a concern that lies at the heart of a new body of military writing – the management of life. If the defining element of the Enlightenment was the application of rational thought to the human world, the formation of a 'science of man', so the military enlightenment can be understood in terms of its analysis of the human and hence as something akin to a life science or human science of war.[9] Life complicates military science, however, because it exemplifies war's simultaneous relation to other human sciences and to the brute physicality, conflict and strategic calculation that stand outside even as they support and structure military thought. Military knowledge was premised on new insights into the disciplining of the soldier that also gave rise to an awareness of the soldier's brutalisation and traumatic bodily experience. The two elements together shaped the new proto-disciplinary field of military thought.

The Formation of a Military Literary World

Military books were central to the military revolution of early modern Europe. Michael Roberts first formulated the concept of the military revolution by proposing that warfare was profoundly transformed from the mid-sixteenth century by gunpowder weapons and the concomitant rise of the modern state system and military institutions.[10] Few concepts in

---

[9] Christopher Fox, Roy Porter and Robert Wokler, eds, *Inventing Human Science: Eighteenth-Century Domains* (Berkeley: University of California Press, 1995), 1.

[10] Michael Roberts, *The Military Revolution, 1560–1660: An Inaugural Lecture Delivered before the Queen's University of Belfast* (Belfast: M. Boyd, 1956).

military history have been more highly debated than the nature and timing of the military revolution. Responses to Roberts' original thesis have variously contended that the revolution could be dated anywhere from the invention of the *trace italienne* fortress in the fifteenth century to the widespread adoption of uniforms, muskets and socket-bayonets at the end of the seventeenth century.[11] Although gunpowder can be considered a revolutionary innovation, it triggered changes that were largely incremental in their progression, meaning that the development of the military revolution cannot be wholly ascribed to a solitary technological development nor to a single period.[12] Most notably, the revolutionary effects of gunpowder cannot be fully understood without also recognising the effects of the printing press on early modern warfare. Marshall McLuhan has even suggested that the rise of print was crucial to modern war because it was here that the forms of thought necessary for modern war and industry were first pioneered, or as he argues, '[t]he linear, sequential, fragmented, and mechanized operation of the printing press also prepares the way for the "technological meat grinder" of modern industrialism and its ways of making war and wealth'.[13]

The initial influence of the printing press on warfare largely occurred via the publication of classical military texts such as Sexust Julius Frontinus' *The Strategems of War*, Caius Julius Caesar's *Commentaries* of *Caesar* and, notably, Vegetius' *De Re Militari*, which was itself a neo-classical text written at some point between AD 383 and 450 that sought to recover the wisdom of an earlier epoch of Roman military dominance.[14] Alongside the publication of classical texts, however, a growing body of writing also appeared that adapted this classical inheritance to the study of contemporary

[11] See Geoffrey Parker, *The Military Revolution: Military Innovation and the Rise of the West, 1500–1800*, 2nd ed. (Cambridge: Cambridge University Press, 1996); Jeremy Black, *A Military Revolution?: Military Change and European Society, 1550–1800* (Atlantic Highlands: Humanities Press, 1991) and David Eltis, *The Military Revolution in Sixteenth-Century Europe* (London and New York: Tauris Academic Studies, 1995).

[12] There have even been calls to abandon the concept entirely in favour of understanding military change in the early modern period as an ongoing evolutionary development; see, for example, Frank Jacob and Gilmar Visoni-Alonzo, *The Military Revolution in Early Modern Europe: A Revision* (London: Palgrave Macmillan, 2016).

[13] Quoted in Michael MacDonald, 'Martial McLuhan I: Framing Information Warfare', *Enculturation: A Journal of Rhetoric, Writing and Culture* 12 (2011), http://enculturation.net/martial-mcluhan.

[14] Gruber, *Books and the British Army*, 36; Catherine Nall, *Reading and War in Fifteenth-Century England: From Lydgate to Malory* (Cambridge: D. S. Brewer, 2012), 11–12; Henry J. Webb, *Elizabethan Military Science* (Madison: University of Wisconsin Press, 1965), 6.

warfare.[15] The roots of the military enlightenment lay with seventeenth-century neo-classical writers such as Raimondo, Count of Montecuccoli, who sought to construct a systematic account of the diverse elements of military thought, and Sébastien le Prestre de Vauban, who revolutionised siege operations through his system of military engineering.[16] War was, however, most clearly revolutionised through the application of classical military drill practices to the use of gunpowder weapons, a process originating with Maurice of Nassau's reorganisation of the army of the Dutch Republic during the Dutch War of Independence (1568–1648) and the development of the first illustrated drill manuals.[17] Of the ninety military books published in early seventeenth-century England, almost half were drill manuals or what contemporaries termed 'analytical treatises' that examined the drilling of foot soldiers alongside related issues of encampments or fortifications.[18] Even though the English army was not nearly as large or as frequently engaged in combat as its continental European counterparts, military thought was as influenced by neo-classical military books as elsewhere in Europe.[19]

Dependent on the rise of print culture, military books also intersected with the incipient scientific inquiry of the seventeenth century. The era saw the adoption of mechanistic approaches to science that correlated with Descartes' rationalistic philosophy and, eventually, an application of Newtonian physics to nature and the human world that suggested the operation of a universal clockwork mechanism. Louis Dupre observes that if mechanism had begun as the basis of scientific theory, it rapidly expanded to a controlling schema of early modern thought, a point that has been developed at more length in Stephen Gaukroger's multi-volume study of the history of science during the early modern era.[20] Manual De

---

[15] In his study of military books possessed by British officers in the eighteenth century, Gruber proposes that the most popular books concerned histories, engineering, drill and discipline, laws and regulations, art of war, maps and dictionaries, and medicine, Gruber, *Books and the British Army*, 294.

[16] Gat, *A History of Military Thought*, 15–26 and 37–38.

[17] David R. Lawrence, *The Complete Soldier: Military Books and Military Culture in Early Stuart England, 1603–1645* (Leiden: Brill, 2009), 137; Geoffrey Parker, 'The "Military Revolution," 1560–1660 – a Myth?', *Journal of Modern History* 48, no. 2 (1976): 195–214, 202.

[18] Lawrence, *The Complete Soldier*, 195.

[19] Webb, *Elizabethan Military Science*, 3.

[20] Louis Dupre, *The Enlightenment and the Intellectual Foundations of Modern Culture* (New Haven: Yale University Press, 2004), 25; Stephen Gaukroger, *The Collapse of Mechanism and the Rise of Sensibility: Science and the Shaping of Modernity, 1680–1760* (Oxford: Oxford University Press, 2010); Stephen Gaukroger, *The Natural and the Human: Science and the Shaping of Modernity, 1739–1841* (Oxford: Oxford University Press, 2016).

Landa, Antoine Bousquet and Francis Gros have outlined this schema in relation to early modern warfare, which, they argue, conformed to a clockwork approach that shifted war away from an earlier world of chivalric nobility to a military world shaped by planning and rationality that, in its ideal form, produced soldiers as highly drilled as machinic automatons.[21] This governing schema surrounding war took shape within what Foucault termed the classical episteme that arranged knowledge into tables of identities and differences based in representation.[22] Central to the classical episteme was the formation of a shared taxonomy that located a place for everything within an overarching ideal of order.

With war able to be conceptualised within a shared tabula of knowledge, military books not only formed a crucial infrastructure for war making, but they also intersected closely with other literary forms as part of a shared neo-classical engagement with war. Henry Webb suggests that military books likely circulated right across the reading public of the day.[23] As much as print facilitated the spread of new ideas about war, however, so the waging of war encouraged the wider expansion of print. The voluminous reporting of war in the period's pamphlets, gazettes and newspapers was critical to the expansion of the market for printed materials, and possibly contributed to the development of scientific methods via demands for veracity and confirmation of news.[24] Given its widespread diffusion, however, writing on war was seldom free of anxieties about the morality of war or even about war's legitimacy as a science. The end of the feudal age and the rise of the absolutist state was tied to a new discourse on peace as the state and its military institutions began to assume their monopoly of violence, meaning that justifications for war were of enormous importance and even appeared as a prominent feature of the era's military manuals.[25] Authors ranging from Shakespeare to Milton, and on to Joseph Addison, George Farquhar and Samuel Richardson in the eighteenth century, all

---

[21] Manuel De Landa, *War in the Age of Intelligent Machines* (New York: Zone Books, 1991); Antoine J. Bousquet, *The Scientific Way of Warfare: Order and Chaos on the Battlefields of Modernity* (New York: Columbia University Press, 2009); Francis Gros, *States of Violence: An Essay on the End of War*, trans. Krysztof Fijalkowski and Michael Richardson (London: Seagull Books, 2010), 47–79.

[22] Michel Foucault, *The Order of Things: An Archaeology of the Human Sciences* (London: Routledge, 2005). For a summary of Foucault's thought on the episteme, see David R. Shumway, *Michel Foucault* (Boston: Twayne Publishers, 1989), 75–76.

[23] Webb, *Elizabethan Military Science*, 170–71.

[24] Frank Bösch, *Mass Media and Historical Change: Germany in International Perspective, 1400 to the Present*, trans. Freya Buechter (New York: Berghahn Books, 2015), 48; David Randall, *Credibility in Elizabethan and Early Stuart Military News* (London: Routledge, 2015), 153.

[25] Mark Neocleous, *War Power, Police Power* (Edinburgh: Edinburgh University Press, 2014), 26–29.

drew extensively on ideas about war and its relationship to social life, their writing making extensive use of material published in their contemporary military texts.[26] Ros King, for example, argues that William Garrard's *The Art of Warre* (1591) provided source material for at least three of Shakespeare's plays, while Simon Barker proposes that we examine dramatic literature of the period alongside military books, because 'as far as we know, they were immensely popular at the time – the prose widely read and the drama widely seen'.[27] Paul A. Jorgensen similarly concludes that Shakespeare made a 'real, perhaps urgent' use of military ideas found in 'numerous military treatises and newsbooks'.[28] Despite the civilising influence of print and its emphasis on polite conversation and rationality, war continued to serve across the early modern era as a site for the performance of gentlemanly virtue, honour and service.[29] Neither is it a coincidence that military books were closely associated with history plays and epic poetry. War played a critical role in art of the early modern era, particularly through concerns with dynastic lineages and crises of political authority that are central to what Rancière defines as the era's neo-classical representative regime of arts.[30] Understood by Rancière as the set of rules and assumptions that governed a hierarchical genre system, the representative regime of art elaborated appropriate forms of expression for the portrayal of speech and action. Concerned above all with recounting the actions of great men, classical poetics found its archetype of action in the military general.[31]

---

[26] Nick de Somogyi, *Shakespeare's Theatre of War* (Aldershot: Ashgate, 1998); James A. Freeman, *Milton and the Martial Muse: Paradise Lost and European Traditions of War* (Princeton: Princeton University Press, 1980); Andrew Lincoln, 'War and the Culture of Politeness: The Case of *The Tatler* and *The Spectator*', *Eighteenth-Century Life*, 36, no. 2 (2012): 60–79; Kevin J. Gardner, 'George Farquhar's *The Recruiting Officer*: Warfare, Conscription, and the Disarming of Anxiety', *Eighteenth-Century Life* 25, no. 3 (2001): 43–61; M. John Cardwell, 'The Rake as Military Strategist: Clarissa and Eighteenth-Century Warfare', *Eighteenth Century Fiction* 19, nos 1 and 2 (2006): 153–80.

[27] Ros King, '"The Disciplines of War": Elizabethan War Manuals and Shakespeare's Tragicomic Vision', in *Shakespeare and War*, ed. Ros King and Paul J. C. M. Franssen (Basingstoke: Palgrave Macmillan, 2008), 15–29; Simon Douglas, *War and Nation in the Theatre of Shakespeare and His Contemporaries* (Edinburgh: Edinburgh University Press, 2012), 8.

[28] Paul A. Jorgensen, *Shakespeare's Military World* (Berkeley: University of California Press, 1956), viii.

[29] Christy Pichichero, *Battles of The Self: War and Subjectivity in Early Modern France* (PhD diss., Stanford University, 2008), 18–19; Andrew Lincoln, 'The Culture of War and Civil Society in the Reigns of William III and Anne', *Eighteenth-Century Studies* 44, no. 4 (2011): 455–74.

[30] On the affinity of war with history in the era, see Patricia A. Cahill, *Unto the Breach: Martial Formations, Historical Trauma, and the Early Modern Stage* (Oxford: Oxford University Press, 2008), 18; Ros King and Paul J. C. M. Franssen, 'War and Shakespearean Dramaturgy', in *Shakespeare and War*, ed. Ros King and Paul J. C. M. Franssen (Basingstoke: Palgrave Macmillan, 2008), 1–11, 1–2.

[31] Jacques Rancière, *Mute Speech*, trans. James Swenson, with an intro. by Gabriel Rockhill (New York: Columbia University Press, 2011), 47–48.

Nonetheless, this neo-classical aesthetics came under pressure from developments in warfare that gradually displaced the significance of individual heroic action.[32] As military educational texts circulated knowledge of war, so they also supplanted the natural right to command of the aristocracy.[33] War was becoming a mass experience with a massive growth in the size of armies in line with the development of an expanding fiscal-military state.[34] War was no longer associated with a feudal nobility but with the military institutions of the nation state, which was, in turn, assuming centrality in an evolving international system of war.[35] This 'statification of war' was, at least in Britain, met with a corresponding fear of the standing army as an instrument of tyranny following Britain's bloody experience of the English Civil War (1642–51). With a series of restraints accordingly placed on military power, this process was not complete in Britain until the late eighteenth century as the widespread use of contractors and mercenaries finally gave way to a fully state-run army financed through taxation and national debt. Growing bureaucracies meant that the state, too, was increasingly militarised.[36] This massification of war was deeply entangled with the intellectualisation of the military and hence the growth of ever larger masses of writing about war. A military enlightenment has even been identified by Azar Gat as a four-fold increase in the annual publications of military themed books, a 'sharp upsurge in the volume of military literature', that occurred from the mid-eighteenth century and which, in turn, inspired the counter-Enlightenment critiques of military theorists such as Carl von Clausewitz.[37] The increase in military writing is supported by the *English Short Title Catalogue*, which reveals a five-fold increase in annual publication rates from the first half of the eighteenth century to the 1790s in titles concerned with war and the military.[38]

---

[32] For an account of how we might read these great men of action in relation to war's trauma, see Cahill, *Unto the Breach*. On the relationship between the failure of strategy and the emergence of aesthetics, see Jacques Rancière, 'The Reality Effect and the Politics of Fiction', Public Lecture at ICI Berlin, accessed 23 July 2019, www.ici-berlin.org/videos/jacques-ranciere/part/2/.

[33] John R. Hale, *Renaissance War Studies* (London: Hambledon Press, 1983), 225.

[34] Brewer, *The Sinews of Power*.

[35] Charles Tilly, *Coercion, Capital, and European States, AD 990–1990* (Cambridge, MA: Basil Blackwell, 1990).

[36] For an overview of these changes, see David Parrott, *Business of War: Military Enterprise and Military Revolution in Early Modern Europe* (Cambridge: Cambridge University Press, 2015), 260–61. On the 'statification of war', see Éric Alliez and Maurizio Lazzarato, *Wars and Capital*, trans. Ames Hodges (South Pasadena: Semiotext(e), 2016), 83–95. On the militarisation of the state, see Gros, *States of Violence*, 62–3.

[37] Gat, *History of Military Thought*, 27.

[38] *English Short Title Catalogue*, http://estc.bl.uk/F/?func=file&file_name=login-bl-estc, accessed 13 August 2019.

The rapid expansion of military writing can be associated with the late eighteenth-century transformation of a classical into a modern episteme.[39] Gat's quantitative analysis of the birth of the military enlightenment, in other words, corresponds with an emerging body of work that similarly explores the material basis of Enlightenment knowledge and its dependence upon protocols, genres and forms of communication. Focussing on such elements as the rise of newspapers and periodicals, this new approach to the Enlightenment has not only drawn attention to the rapid expansion of printed materials in these years, but has also sought to theorise how this expansion underpinned the shift towards a new approach to knowledge concerned with analysis of the historical forces that shape and inform objects of scientific inquiry.[40] Rather than see print progress in a consistent evolutionary manner from the fifteenth century, Clifford Siskin and William Warner suggest that there are three distinct phases in this history that match key phases in the development of Enlightenment thought.[41] First, they trace an initial development of genres, infrastructure and protocols in the sixteenth and seventeenth centuries, from the growth of coffee houses and postal services to widespread publication and distribution of newspapers, that collectively formed the grounds for the Enlightenment to occur. Secondly, they identify the historical Enlightenment of the mid-eighteenth century with the proliferation of print from the second quarter of the eighteenth century and the related emergence of a range of genres and forms designed to encompass the massive increase in knowledge, from the growth of philosophical systems to dictionaries and encyclopaedia projects. They propose that in a final phase, however, the Enlightenment 'ends' as a period in the late eighteenth century not because of a generalised counter-Enlightenment reaction but because print had proliferated to such an extent that it saturated society. This process of saturation meant that the efforts to systematise all knowledge that characterised the Enlightenment gave way to a fragmentation of knowledge into increasingly diverse proto-disciplinary fields of an embryonic science by the end of the eighteenth century. Print, and with it the new forms of knowledge that it enabled,

---

[39] For an overview, see James Chandler, *England in 1819: The Politics of Literary Culture and the Case of Romantic Historicism* (Chicago: University of Chicago Press, 1998), 100–05.

[40] See Clifford Siskin, 'The Problem of Periodization: Enlightenment, Romanticism and the Fate of System', in *The Cambridge History of English Romantic Literature*, ed. James Chandler (Cambridge: Cambridge University Press, 2009), 101–26.

[41] Clifford Siskin and William Warner, 'This Is Enlightenment: An Invitation in the Form of an Argument', in *This Is Enlightenment*, ed. Clifford Siskin and William Warner (Chicago: University of Chicago Press, 2010), 1–33, 8.

had come to be naturalised as the goals of the Enlightenment were confirmed in the enduring progress of rational thought.

Siskin and Warner echo a number of thinkers who have, in a related manner, proposed that a new culture of writing dawned in Europe at the end of the eighteenth century. While, as Raymond Williams argues, modern, industrial societies have naturalised writing, rendering it virtually invisible, there was nonetheless a complex history behind the rise of writing and the formation of what William St Clair describes as the 'reading nation'.[42] A focus on writing, Williams claims, can help us recognise critical links between the more formal study of writing as literature and, conversely, the study of the 'political, military, economic and generalized social facts' that we take to constitute history.[43] McLuhan goes so far as to claim that print structured nationalism and industrialism because it enabled the universalisation of repeatable precision, while allowing for the fragmentation and delegation that structured new fields of disciplinary knowledge.[44] Walter Ong similarly identifies the shift from orality to writing at the end of the eighteenth century with a new-found ability to engage in close scrutiny of objects of knowledge, an approach that engendered both Romantic literature and the technological sciences.[45] Developing much further this medial approach to writing and its movement beyond classicism and rhetoric, Friedrich Kittler insists that the sheer quantity of printed material available forced the use of hermeneutic reading practices:

> As a result literature and science had to revamp their transmission and receiving techniques: away from the literalness of quotes from the scholarly elite, and rhetorical mnemonics, towards an interpretative approach which reduced the quantity of printed data to its essence, in other words to a smaller quantity of data.[46]

Developing as a way to make sense of the expansion of writing, modern practices of interpretation and hermeneutics assumed priority over the earlier classical rhetoric. Kittler's thought approximates Jacques Rancière's

---

[42] Raymond Williams, *Writing in Society* (London: Verso, 1983); William St Clair, *The Reading Nation in the Romantic Period* (Cambridge: Cambridge University Press, 2004).

[43] Williams, *Writing in Society*, 7. On the arbitrary distinction between such different genres of writing, see John Guillory, 'The Memo and Modernity', *Critical Inquiry* 31, no. 1 (2004): 108–32, 111.

[44] Marshall McLuhan, *Understanding Media: The Extensions of Man* (London: Routledge, 2001), 188.

[45] Walter Ong, *Orality and Literacy: The Technologizing of the Word* (London: Routledge, 2002), 106, 125.

[46] Friedrich Kittler, 'The History of Communication Media', https://journals.uvic.ca/index.php/ctheory/article/view/14325/5101, accessed 24 July 2019.

analysis of how an older culture of speech and rhetoric was displaced by a 'new regime of writing' in which knowledge no longer operated through a received authority that imposed one will upon another, but was reformulated as an act of presenting and deciphering symptoms.[47] Jacques Derrida had similarly observed that science emerges within and is defined by an epoch of writing, and that there is thus a critical need for a grammatology that can further our understanding of the influence, forms and structures of writing.[48] Rancière, however, does not follow Derrida to regard the structure of writing as the essence of logos or reason itself, but instead offers an historical analysis in which new forms of writing came to define a break or rupture with an earlier representative regime of art.[49] Writing establishes a 'symptomatology' that is revealed as much through new scientific regimes such as geology or sociology as through literary texts that explore the underlying depths of society, or which, conversely, allow language to be understood as itself a dense field of symbols set free from reference and possessed of its own, intransitive forms.[50]

A historicist approach to knowledge came to guide and shape Enlightenment as much as Romantic thought, as authors within a new regime of writing sought to discern the dynamic secrets or evolutionary truths that lay behind represented facts.[51] As Gary Gutting explains:

> A thing is what it is not because of its place in the ideal classification system but because of its place in real history. The order of concretely existing things is from now on determined not by ideal essences outside them but by the historical forces buried within them.[52]

A fundamental rupture occurred in the surface distribution of knowledge, as its foundation in representation and the taxonomic world of order and categories gave way to a concern with the evolutionary foundations or underlying forces and histories that reside within objects of knowledge. Systematic accounts of all knowledge were no longer feasible, resulting in

---

[47] Rancière, 'The Politics of Literature', 18.

[48] Jacques Derrida, *Of Grammatology*, trans. Gayatri Chakravorty Spivak (Baltimore: Johns Hopkins University Press, 1997), 27.

[49] Hector Kollias, 'Taking Sides: Jacques Rancière and Agonistic Literature', *Paragraph* 30, no. 2 (2007): 82–97, 82.

[50] Jacques Rancière, *The Politics of Aesthetics: The Distribution of the Sensible,* trans. and intro. Gabriel Rockhill, with an afterword by Slavoj Žižek (London: Continuum, 2004), 33.

[51] For an overview, see Mark Bevir, 'Historicism and the Human Sciences in Victorian Britain', in *Historicism and the Human Sciences in Victorian Britain,* ed. Mark Bevir (Cambridge: Cambridge University Press, 2017), 1–20, 4.

[52] Gary Gutting, *Michel Foucault's Archaeology of Scientific Reason* (Cambridge: Cambridge University Press, 1989), 181.

a movement away from a classical inheritance, with its focus on universal systems and overarching reason, as knowledge became splintered into disciplinary divisions.[53] If a neo-classical approach to knowledge continued to rely, as Rancière intimates, on the quotation and interpretation of established authorities, now multiple authors began to participate in the constitution of knowledge via the rapidly expanding realm of print.[54] Writing was not only changing the form of knowledge, but was also contributing to the overarching Enlightenment perception of continual scientific progress.

The formation of this 'new regime of writing' is of critical importance to the massive expansion of writing on war that constitutes the military enlightenment. There was not simply more military writing being published at the end of the eighteenth century, but this writing was moving beyond its neo-classical inheritance to produce a distinct, modern disciplinary field of military thought. If, gradually, the study of war literature has been expanding into the study of a more broadly conceived 'war writing', there has for the most part been limited effort to consider exactly what is meant by writing and the broader relationships that exists between war and writing.[55] Where exactly do the borders lie between literary and other forms of war writing? How can forms of war writing be located within a history of writing more generally and, therefore, within a history or poetics of knowledge? How did the evolution of war writing disrupt the close relations that had earlier existed between military books and more obviously literary forms of writing? If modern literature since the Romantic age has seemingly progressed with little need for military books, there remains a question as to what happened to produce this break and how we should understand the resulting relationship that formed between literature, a modern military science and a modern body of war writing. This chapter draws on work into the history and formation of modern writing and disciplinarity to reconceptualise both imaginative war literature and the science of war by treating these less as oppositional developments than as twinned elements within a new 'regime of writing'. Christy Pichichero has argued that the decisively interdisciplinary character of the military enlightenment, its existence across multiple fields of

---

[53] Siskin and Warner, *This Is Enlightenment*, 16.
[54] Siskin and Warner, *This Is Enlightenment*, 11.
[55] See, for example, Samuel Hynes, *On War and Writing* (Chicago: University of Chicago Press, 2018); Kate McLoughlin, ed., *The Cambridge Companion to War Writing* (Cambridge: Cambridge University Press, 2009); and Margot Norris, *Writing War in the Twentieth Century* (Charlottesville: University Press of Virginia, 2000)

knowledge, requires the use of techniques of literary analysis to tease out shared thematic concerns.[56] Adopting an approach informed by the history of knowledge, Anders Engberg-Pedersen adapts Rancière to similarly propose that military writing in this era must be understood through a 'poetics of war' that examines the literary techniques by which military science assumed the status of a science.[57] The massification of military writing not only broke with classical traditions but also generated enormous efforts to contain, harness and understand that expansion by establishing war as an object of study possessed of its own internal forces and historical depths.

Daily Life and the Proto-Disciplinarity of Military Journals

Siskin and Warner propose that the effects of the saturation of culture by writing are apparent in the distinction between the French *Encyclopédie* (1751–72) and the subsequent *Encyclopaedia Britannica* (1768). The *Encyclopédie* epitomises the Enlightenment ambition to organise all knowledge through an overarching classificatory system, as it featured nearly 72,000 articles in an effort to universally cover all known topics. The *Encyclopaedia Britannica* progressed beyond this earlier effort to systematise knowledge by combining the framework of the dictionary with a series of separate articles or 'discrete treatises' on select topics that can be read as prototypes of modern disciplinary knowledge.[58] This shift in the constitution of knowledge is exhibited in the contrasting ways that the encyclopaedias approached the topic of war. Where the *Encyclopédie* encapsulates war as part of the totality of knowledge, offering a brief definition of war as a type of geometrical science, the *Encyclopaedia Britannica* featured a lengthy treatise on war by the military theorist Lancelot Turpin, Comte de Crissé (although it appeared anonymously in the encyclopaedia). The *Encyclopédie's* understanding of war as geometry reflects a classical view of war that can be traced back to Plato and which readily associates war with other forms of knowledge.[59] Although Enlightenment philosophers were notoriously hostile to the practice of war, the *Encyclopédie* still included nearly 1,250 articles classified by the editors as belonging to subjects of

---

[56] Pichichero, *The Military Enlightenment*, 22.
[57] Anders Engberg-Pedersen, *Empire of Chance: The Napoleonic Wars and the Disorder of Things* (Cambridge, MA: Harvard University Press, 2015), 5.
[58] Siskin and Warner, 'This Is Enlightenment', 20.
[59] Bousquet, *The Scientific Way of Warfare*, 55.

'Art militaire'.[60] Spread throughout the *Encyclopédie*, military themed articles are arrayed in ways that suggest military knowledge is as familiar as geometry, that it sits comfortably within and alongside a generalised order or table of knowledge. Turpin de Crissé's treatise in the *Encyclopaedia Britannica*, conversely, not only distinguishes war as a separate topic but also describes it as 'the most necessary and useful of all the sciences', while claiming the greatest generals were the 'most sublime'.[61] Although Turpin de Crissé has been considered an archetypal military thinker of the French Enlightenment, the redeployment of his writing in the pages of the *Encyclopaedia Britannica* also represents an emergent shift away from the taxonomic organisation of knowledge to a recognition of war as occupying its own deep but narrow proto-discipline that formed a discrete element within a fragmented field of scientific knowledge.[62]

The formation of such proto-disciplinary fields of knowledge is most clearly delineated, however, in the rapid expansion of periodicals, an expansion that included military journals. The 'new form' of the eighteenth-century periodical played a primary role in the formation of a modern culture of writing.[63] Immanuel Kant explicitly defined the Enlightenment in relation to periodicals, his essay 'What is Enlightenment?' appearing in a periodical, a 1784 issue of *Berlinische Monatsschrift*; he also portrayed the Enlightenment as a public sphere 'composed of a vast population of readers of periodicals'.[64] Foucault points out that knowledge in the eighteenth century was primarily advanced by periodicals, which organised the public as a realm of reading and writing.[65] The underlying philosophical

---

[60] John A Lynn, 'The Treatment of Military Subjects in Diderot's *Encyclopédie*', *Journal of Military History* 65, no. 1 (2001): 131–65, 133.

[61] *Encyclopaedia Britannica; Or, a Dictionary of Arts, Sciences, and Miscellaneous Literature on a Plan Entirely New....* vol. 18 (Dublin: printed by James Moore, 1790–98), 703. *Eighteenth Century Collections Online*, www.gale.com/intl/primary-sources/eighteenth-century-collections-online, accessed 15 April 2022.

[62] Gat, *History of Military Thought*, 38.

[63] Adrian Johns, 'Print and Public Science', in *The Cambridge History of Science: Volume 4: Eighteenth-Century Science*, ed. Roy Porter (Cambridge: Cambridge University Press, 2008), 536–60, 536; Adrian Johns, 'The Piratical Enlightenment', in *This Is Enlightenment*, ed. Clifford Siskin and William Warner (Chicago: University of Chicago Press, 2010), 301–20, 309. On the significance of genres such as periodicals in the history of mediation, see Clifford Siskin, *System: The Shaping of Modern Knowledge* (Cambridge: MIT Press, 2016), 69–70. For an overview of scientific journals in this era, see David A. Kronick, *A History of Scientific and Technical Periodicals: The Origins and Development of the Scientific and Technological Press, 1665–1790* (Metuchen: Scarecrow Press, 1962).

[64] Johns, 'The Piratical Enlightenment', 316.

[65] Michel Foucault, *The Government of Self and Others: Lectures at the Collège de France, 1982–1983*, ed. Frédéric Gros, trans. Graham Burchell (Basingstoke: Palgrave Macmillan, 2010), 8.

question of the Enlightenment, who are we today, is at the centre of both philosophy and of journalism.[66] It is notable, therefore, that the proliferation of periodicals in the eighteenth century included a number of military themed journals (while the Seven Years War was a watershed for the spread of periodicals across Europe more generally).[67] The military journals represent an elementary mechanism by which military thought formed as a distinct proto-disciplinary field of knowledge.

Although the earliest military journal published in Europe was the *Kriegsbibliothek* (1755), they only appeared with any regularity from the 1770s with such titles as the French *Encyclopédie Militaire* (1770–71) and, in Germany, the *Magazin für Ingenieurs und Artilleristen* (1777–89). They primarily flourished in Germany with the emergence of *Militarische Monatssch* (1785–87), *Genaalogischer Miliarischer Calendar* (1784–90) and *Berliner Military Kalendar* (1797–1803), amongst other publications.[68] Featuring an array of military themed articles, the content of these journals ranged from descriptions of new tactical formations, to historical accounts of battles and an assortment of military anecdotes. While prominent in Germany, military journals took some time to appear in Britain and were not published until the 1790s, with the *Military Magazine* (1793) and, by the end of the decade, the *British Military Library; or, Journal* (1798–1800), the *Soldiers' Pocket Magazine* (1798) and the *Monthly Military Companion* (1801–02). Following a similar pattern to their continental counterparts, they included articles that ranged from histories of campaigns and battles to accounts of military regulations, and the maxims and biographies of famous generals. Although publication of Britain's first military periodicals had ceased by the conclusion of the peace of Amiens in 1803, they were revived during the Napoleonic wars with the *Royal Military Chronicle* (1810–17), the *Military Panorama* (1812–14) and the *Military Register* (1814–22). The related *Naval Chronicle* (1798–1818) ran throughout the period. While the cessation of hostilities in 1815 saw the demise of all extant

---

[66] Helge Jordheim, 'The Present of Enlightenment: Temporality and Mediation in Kant, Foucault and Jean Paul', in *This Is Enlightenment*, ed. Clifford Siskin and William Warner (Chicago: University of Chicago Press, 2010), 189–208, 199.

[67] Will Slauter, 'Periodicals and the Commercialization of Information in the Early Modern Era', in *Information: A Historical Companion*, ed. Ann Blair, Paul Duguid, Anja-Silvia Goeing and Anthony Grafton (Princeton: Princeton University Press, 2021), 128–51, 145. On the more general politics of periodicals, see Jon P. Klancher, *The Making of English Reading Audiences, 1790–1832* (Madison: University of Wisconsin Press, 1987); and Kevin Gilmartin, *Print Politics: The Press and Radical Opposition in Early Nineteenth-Century England* (Cambridge: Cambridge University Press, 1996).

[68] Pichichero, *The Military Enlightenment*, 58–59; Gat, *A History of Military Thought*, 66–67.

military journals, the post-war period saw the publication of the *Naval and Military Magazine* (1827–28) and the *United Service Journal* (1828–41). Continuing the form of earlier military periodicals, including descriptions of battles and tactical arrangements, the *United Service Journal* also featured a range of soldiers' tales, or 'personal Histories' of war, supplied for the interest of both a military and a public audience.[69]

One of the leading developments in the way periodicals functioned during the Romantic era is represented by the *Edinburgh Review* (1802–1929). Where earlier eighteenth-century journals were characterised by their expansive efforts to review all published material, the *Edinburgh Review* instead supplied fewer but far more in-depth articles that intensively interpreted select texts.[70] In doing so, the *Edinburgh Review* was not necessarily the first journal to offer a more critical approach, but it was instrumental in establishing the periodical as a major conduit for interpreting and shaping, rather than merely reflecting, public taste and opinion.[71] It elaborated a conception of an intellectual culture that could guide national life, and which found full expression in the corporate identity of the journal itself.[72] Characteristic of this development was the way that the *Edinburgh Review* expanded upon the frameworks of Scottish Enlightenment political economic thought. Drawing on stadial views of historical progress and modernisation, in which commerce, rather than war, serves as the driver of modern civilisation, political economy developed as the science of 'common life'.[73] For Jon Klancher, the *Edinburgh Review* can be defined by its embrace of political economy and the attention it gave to decoding and interpreting common or daily life.[74] Using the frameworks of political

---

[69] Advertisement featured in John Blakiston, *Twelve Years' Military Adventure in Three Quarters of the Globe; or, Memoirs of an Officer Who Served in the Armies of His Majesty and of the East India Company between the Years 1802 and 1814, in which are Contained the Campaigns of the Duke of Wellington in India, and his Last in Spain and the South of France*, 2 vols (London: Henry Colburn, 1829), II, 382.

[70] Kim Wheatley, 'Introduction: Romantic Periodicals and Print Culture'. *Prose Studies: History, Theory, Criticism* 25, no. 1 (2002): 1–18, 2.

[71] Mark Schoenfield, *British Periodicals and Romantic Identity: The Literary 'Lower' Empire* (Basingstoke: Palgrave Macmillan, 2009), 1–2; Ina Ferris, 'The Debut of *The Edinburgh Review*, 1802', *BRANCH: Britain, Representation and Nineteenth-Century History*, ed. Dino Franco Felluga. Extension of *Romanticism and Victorianism on the Net*, https://branchcollective.org/?ps_articles=ina-ferris-the-debut-of-the-edinburgh-review-1802, accessed 22 August 2019. On the earlier 'more actively critical strategies' of the *Monthly Review* and *Critical Review*, both first established in the mid-eighteenth century, see Siskin and Warner, *This Is Enlightenment*, 15.

[72] Schoenfield, *British Periodicals and Romantic Identity*, 6–7.

[73] Ian Duncan, *Scott's Shadow: The Novel in Romantic Edinburgh* (Princeton: Princeton University Press, 2007), 119.

[74] Klancher, *The Making of English Reading Audiences*, 39–41.

economic thought to instruct and guide its readers in the nature of the social world, it set out to 'interpret daily life' by lifting the encounter with daily life to the level of a philosophy.[75] Marilyn Butler hazards that the review periodicals inaugurated with the *Edinburgh Review* could be regarded as providing the very medium of culture.[76]

A related concern with daily life was also, as Mary Favret has persuasively argued, characteristic of Romantic era cultural responses to war. Britons lived during what Favret defines as a modern wartime, the experience of those 'living through but not in a war'.[77] This wartime experience was, therefore, a primarily mediated experience dependent upon British journalistic reporting of distant wars. The constitution of war via print meant that the British public apprehended war on an inherently daily basis as fresh news arrived each day about the progress of the war. War news itself circulated as a source of affect as it generated expectant, hopeful, belated, anxious and uncertain emotional responses to distant suffering.[78] War had become, in Jerome Christensen's phrasing, a 'condition of eventfulness', constructed from the 'simulation of dailiness' by war journalism.[79] To an extent, reporting on the wars thereby worked to redistribute pain to the home front, where it could be either suffered as fear and horror or, far more commonly, placated by maternal consolation for loss or the idealisation of national heroes, or imagined as a vital restorative for the nation's own moral unease.[80] War news could even, as many feared, simply be ignored or dismissed as remote, unimportant, even a source of boredom.[81] No matter how it was imagined, though, war did not form part of the immediate sensible experience of the nation because it appeared, instead, as a matter of reading.[82]

It is, however, in relation to the expansion of daily wartime writing and reading that a new kind of military intellectual culture crystallised in Britain.

---

[75] Klancher, *The Making of English Reading Audiences*, 51.

[76] Marilyn Butler, 'Culture's Medium: The Role of the Review', in *The Cambridge Companion to British Romanticism*, ed. Stuart Curran (Cambridge: Cambridge University Press, 1993), 120–47.

[77] Mary A Favret, *War at a Distance: Romanticism and the Making of Modern Wartime* (Princeton: Princeton University Press, 2009), 9.

[78] Favret, *War at a Distance*, 74, 77–81.

[79] Jerome Christensen, *Romanticism at the End of History* (Baltimore: Johns Hopkins University Press, 2000), 4.

[80] Mary A. Favret, 'Writing, Reading and the Scenes of War', in *The Cambridge History of English Romantic Literature*, ed. James Chandler (Cambridge: Cambridge University Press, 2009), 314–34, 322–31.

[81] See Jan Mieszkowski, *Watching War* (Stanford: Stanford University Press, 2012), 15–19.

[82] Favret, *War at a Distance*, 144. See also Favret's discussion of the changing meaning of the term war in eighteenth century dictionaries that increasingly defined war as something intellectual, rather than physical, 173–84.

The experiential distance of war from civilian society was counterbalanced with an increasing military professionalism and far-reaching efforts by military authorities to analyse the nation's wars. While the military journals were obviously quite distinct from Britain's review periodicals, they first appeared in Britain only a few years before the *Edinburgh Review* and share its elementary concern with interpreting and directing the daily life of the wartime nation. Indeed, if in its inaugural issue the *Edinburgh Review* had unequivocally established its support for modern political economy, it also announced the critical importance of a 'scientific military system' that, similarly to political economy, enabled 'a constant superintendence and controul [*sic*]' over a nation's feelings, feelings that otherwise fostered constant revolutions amongst 'barbaric nations'.[83] Responding to war's sensory distance from the nation, along with a growing perception of the vulgarisation and unruliness of patriotic culture over the course of the 1790s, military periodicals sought to make sense of war by establishing this very military intellectual culture or 'scientific military system' for the nation.[84] This is not to suggest that the major periodicals entirely neglected the nation's wars. The nation's daily reading, as Benedict Anderson argues, was central to the formation of a national 'imagined community' characterised by a fraternity of individuals who would 'willingly' die for national survival.[85] Both the *Quarterly Review* (1809–1967) and the *Edinburgh Annual Register* (1808–26) were in part established to counter what their editors saw as the *Edinburgh Review*'s increasingly defeatist attitude towards the war.[86] But the military journals developed their response to war in a far more professional manner. In part reflecting the *Anti-Jacobin Review*'s (1798–1821) similar efforts to instruct the nation in counter-revolutionary politics, the military periodicals took upon themselves the task of superintending and controlling the nation's response to war.[87]

Moreover, it is no coincidence that military periodicals appeared in Britain under the threat of imminent invasion and at a time of massive volunteering.[88] Although military periodicals were clearly professional

---

[83] The *Edinburgh Review* 1, 2nd. ed (1803) 347; on the importance of its inaugural issue, see Christensen, *Romanticism at the End of History*, 107; and Ferris, 'The Debut of *The Edinburgh Review*, 1802'.

[84] Timothy Jenks, *Naval Engagements: Patriotism, Cultural Politics, and the Royal Navy 1793–1815* (Oxford: Oxford University Press, 2006), 142.

[85] Benedict Anderson, *Imagined Communities: Reflections on the Origin and Spread of Nationalism*. Revised ed. (London: Verso, 2006), 7.

[86] Kenneth Curry, *Southey* (London: Routledge, 2016), 47.

[87] The *Edinburgh Review* 1, 2nd ed. (1803): 347.

[88] See Linda Colley, *Britons: Forging the Nation, 1707–1837* (New Haven: Yale University Press, 1992).

journals targeting military and naval officers, they were also consciously disseminating their professional knowledge to the nation at large as they sought to interpret the nation's experience of war. The military publications were eager to admonish the public about the threats of invasion and the urgency of national mobilisation, the *Soldiers' Pocket Magazine* going so far as to claim that '[i]n the history of mankind, there never was a greater necessity for every individual capable of bearing arms, becoming a Volunteer for the defence of the country, than at the present moment'.[89] Although Britain was not subject to a fully fledged militarism in these years, notably resisting conscription during the wars, a new kind of military intellectual culture was taking shape that could direct how the nation responded to war.[90] As David Bell notes, modern forms of militarism can only emerge in relation to a separation of civilian and military worlds, because militarism comes into existence as the imposition of military ideals upon a non-military realm.[91] The military periodicals facilitated both the growth of militarism and its imposition upon the civilian British reading public as they set out to circulate, organise and interpret knowledge of war. By drawing together military news and analysis, the periodicals simultaneously contributed to the construction of the daily or common experience of wartime and offered a military interpretation of that wartime experience.

Through the journals, therefore, the military were able to assume a daily presence within the British calendar, landscape and social life, a presence that was reflected in the regular publication schedule of the journals themselves. The *Naval Chronicle*, for example, included a 'Monthly Register of Naval Events' and a 'Plymouth Report' that supplied information about the ongoing arrivals and departures of naval vessels from the port of Plymouth.[92] The *Monthly Military Chronicle* and *British Military*

---

[89] Philip Woodfine, "'Unjustifiable and Illiberal": Military Patriotism and Civilian Values in the 1790s', in *War: Identities in Conflict, 1300–2000*, ed. Bertrand Taithe and Tim Thornton (Stroud: Sutton Publishing, 1998), 73–93, 85; *The Soldiers' Pocket Magazine* (1798): 3.

[90] While Bell focusses on the rise of militarism in the United States and France, the conditions for militarism were also established in Britain; see Alan Forrest, Karen Hagemann and Michael Rowe, 'Introduction: War, Demobilization and Memory in the Era of Atlantic Revolutions', in *War, Demobilization and Memory: The Legacy of War in the Era of Atlantic Revolutions*, ed. Alan Forrest, Karen Hagemann and Michael Rowe (Basingstoke: Palgrave Macmillan, 2016), 3–29, 14–15.

[91] Bell, *The First Total War*, 12. For an extended discussion of the emergence of militarism in these years, see David A. Bell, 'The Birth of Militarism in the Age of Democratic Revolutions', in *War, Demobilization and Memory: The Legacy of War in the Era of Atlantic Revolutions*, ed. Alan Forrest, Karen Hagemann and Michael Rowe (Basingstoke: Palgrave Macmillan, 2016), 30–47.

[92] *The Naval Chronicle* 2 (1799): 75, 79.

Library both similarly featured a regular column of, respectively, 'Military Occurrences' and 'Military Transactions' that provided regular accounts of important military activities.[93] This military news covered a range of topics, the *British Military Library* primarily reporting on the army's military operations in Europe and Ireland, with the *Monthly Military Companion* documenting military activities within the nation such as the movements of regiments, court martials and military inspections. For example, the British Military Library observed of joint British and Russian operations in the Low Countries at the end of 1799:

> On the 1st of September the British took post with their right to Perren, and their left to Oude Sluves; the head-quarters being at Schager Brug … His Royal Highness the Duke of York sailed with the second division for Holland on the 9th, and arrived at the Helder on the evening of the 13th, at which time 7,000 Russians were debarking.[94]

The *Monthly Military Companion* similarly posed its military transactions as a dated sequence of events:

> Dec. 26. The remains of the gallant 42d, or Royal Highlanders are arrived at Spithead, last from Gibraltar, in good health and high spirits. Col. Mames Stewart, with three companies, are on board the Ceres frigate…
>   Dec. 28. The Hon. Col. Meade, brother to the Earl of Clanwilliam, has arrived from Egypt, where he has been for some time with the army in the service of his country.[95]

Such information was not unique to the journals; military occurrences were commonly reported in the national newspapers. But by concentrating and condensing information about the daily routines and movements of the military, the journals introduced a distinctly militarised perspective to the nation's reading. Anderson argues more generally that by the nineteenth century the daily newspapers had come to embody a modern national identity because they reflected and encouraged the shared sense of simultaneity that constitutes a nation.[96] Not only circulating a shared language, newspapers also invoke a shared temporality and spatiality by uniting disparate elements of national life on the basis of their simultaneous occurrence within the borders of the nation. The military journals were in effect recasting this shared simultaneity from a national and into a

[93] *The Monthly Military Companion* 1, no. 1 (1801): 79–84; *The British Military Library; or, Journal* 1, no. 1 (1798): 38–39.
[94] *The British Military Library* 2, no. 13 (1799): 40.
[95] *The Monthly Military Companion* 1, no. 4 (1801): 321.
[96] Anderson, *Imagined Communities*, 33–36.

more specifically military perspective as they brought their readers into an intimate relation with the temporalities, locations and personalities of the nation's military institutions. In this recasting of simultaneity, the nation itself appears to assume a more mobile or fluid form as the contours of a shared national experience are defined by the movements of the military.

This militarisation of national dailiness was matched with the journals' extensive efforts to make sense of that dailiness. The *Naval Chronicle*, for example, published letters from the Admiralty Office describing the daily movements and engagements of the navy alongside articles offering scientific analysis of defence from French invasion, the history of navigation or the development of naval mines.[97] The *British Military Library* and the *Monthly Military Companion* similarly combined their reportage on of the daily movements and locations of Britain's military forces with wide-ranging analysis, including histories of campaigns and battles along with essays on military theory and technology. The *British Military Library*, for example, published essays on recent military campaigns that could contextualise and refine knowledge of current conflicts, such as the 'Action fought on the 19th of September, 1799, between the Anglo-Russian and the Gallo-Batavian Armies', which analysed military operations the journal had listed in its military transactions only two issues previously.[98] The journal also provided a miscellany of analytical essays on a variety of scientific developments, ranging from the 'new Military-System of the French', to recent innovations such as the 'newly-invented Night Telegraph' and 'Aerostatic Machines, or Air-Balloons'.[99] It also supplied a 'Military Dictionary' compiled from the 'best and latest Authorities' that was serialised across the issues and defined military terms used in the daily reporting of war.[100] The *Monthly Military Companion* likewise combined its reportage of military occurrences with a variety of analytical tools, including essays on military history, such as on the 'Battle of Rosbach', a serialised dictionary of key terms related to military 'Fortification' (including illustrations) and information and advice on military tactics or 'Short Considerations on War'.[101] Through the journals, the daily movements, occurrences and events of the war could be read via a scientific military perspective that sought to

---

[97] The *Naval Chronicle* 2 (1799): 52, 69, 56.
[98] The *British Military Library; or, Journal* 2, no. 15 (1798): 86–90.
[99] The *British Military Library; or, Journal* 1, no. 2 (1798): 57; *British Military Library; or, Journal* 1, no. 1 (1798): 12, 14.
[100] The *British Military Library; or, Journal* 1, no. 2 (1798): 78.
[101] The *Monthly Military Companion* 1, no. 1 (1801): 34, 25; *The Monthly Military Companion* 1, no. 3 (1801): 210–15.

articulate the present war in theoretical terms and in relation to the latest military innovations.

If the journals were helping to construct what the *Edinburgh Review* saw as a 'military scientific system', they were also ensuring that this military system could exercise close scrutiny and control over the daily or ordinary experience of war. One prominent element is the way that the journals included a range of articles on the organisation or management of the daily life of soldiers. The *British Military Library* carried articles such as the 'Situation of the British Soldier', concerned with questions about his pay, clothing, food and living arrangements, and on 'the inadequacy of the present establishment of surgeons in the army', addressing the need for adequate medical services.[102] The two articles reflected a growing concern with managing the overall life and health of the soldier. The *Monthly Military Companion* carried similar articles, such as on the correct completion of 'Returns' to eliminate administrative delays and any possible corruption and 'Analytical Hints' on such topics as the 'hazards of wet clothing' for soldiers' health.[103] The journals envisioned military discipline as extending past drill routines and superintendence of regulations to a far more complete disciplinary structuring of the entirety of the soldiers' living arrangements, behaviour and health, a point to which this chapter returns.[104] By drawing such regulation into the regular reading of the nation, the journals in effect lifted military regulation and procedure from their institutional housing and into a more pervasive structure of experience. The *Monthly Military Companion* concluded that inattention to the routines of discipline had enormous consequences far beyond the military; their neglect would mean that 'the country suffers'.[105] What is more, it is no coincidence that the military assumed their quotidian presence in print in conjunction with the militarisation of other elements of British national life, including the Ordnance Survey's comprehensive mapping of the nation, a national census, a national income tax to fund the war and, remarkably, the establishment across Britain of a network of permanent barracks.[106] Formerly feared as a veritable imposition of martial law, by the

---

[102] *The British Military Library; or, Journal* 1, no. 9 (1799): 417; *The British Military Library; or, Journal* 1, no. 2 (1798): 55.

[103] *The Monthly Military Companion* 1, no. 4 (1801): 249, 276.

[104] *The Monthly Military Companion* 1, no. 1 (1801): 9.

[105] *The Monthly Military Companion* 1, no. 1 (1801): 22–23.

[106] On the establishment of barracks in the 1790s, see Neil Ramsey, 'De Lancey's Tour: Military Barracks and the Endo-Colonization of England in the 1790s', *English Language Notes* 54, no. 1 (2016): 27–41.

end of the 1790s barracks were commonly accepted as a normal and even desirable institution.

The journals also featured a miscellany of individualised forms of writing concerned with the personal comportment, experience and even feelings of the officer. This included advice on moral conduct, such as warnings about gaming, biographical essays, letters to the editor from readers, expostulations about officer's education, military schools and reading, and material on officers' promotions, court-martials and military deaths. The *Monthly Military Companion* went so far as to include military themed lyric poetry in what it termed a 'Parnassian Column'.[107] The journals encouraged the reader to see the military officer as something more than a merely institutional role and rather as an all-encompassing way of life that demanded extensive reading and devotion to service. Biographies were particularly significant in this regard because they supplied exemplary action for other officers to follow, or as one correspondent observed: 'Biography may be placed among the most useful parts of literature. It enables us to pay a just tribute to characters which have deserved well of their country, excites emulation, enlarges our knowledge of mankind, and stimulates us to attain similar excellence and praise'.[108]

What is more, the journals featured biographies of a diverse range of commanders, including obscure military figures, and even histories of regiments that supported an institutional view of the military. The *British Military Library* opened with the memoirs of the Duke of York but proceeded with the lives of far less prominent military personalities such as the Earl of Moira.[109] The *Monthly Military Companion* similarly featured short biographies of less imposing figures such as Lieutenant General Hutchinson, who took over command of the British Egyptian campaign in 1801 following the death of General Abercromby, and General Lord Rossmore, who served as commander in chief of the British forces in Ireland in the 1790s.[110] At times the journals also included biographies of junior and entirely unknown military officers, such as 'The Journal of Captain Benjamin Hill, formerly of the Fifth Regiment of Foot, and now Adjutant to the Northumberland Militia'.[111] Hill accomplished little and eventually sold his captain's commission because of financial

---

[107] The *Monthly Military Companion* 1, no. 1 (1801): 60.
[108] The *Monthly Military Companion* 1, no. 5 (1802): 353.
[109] The *British Military Library; or, Journal* 2, no. 16 (1799): 121–31.
[110] The *Monthly Military Companion* 1, no. 3 (1801): 200–02 and 216–20.
[111] The *British Military Library; or, Journal* 2, no. 18 (1800): 197–98.

difficulties; his biography is deemed significant simply because it exemplifies a 'whole life … devoted to the service of his King and Country'.[112] This intensification of the officer's duties was further reflected in the notices of 'Deaths of Military Men', which extended a degree of biographical recognition to all officers solely on the basis that they had committed their life to military service, irrespective of their achievements, rank or actions.[113]

Military life was not only coming to be framed by the journals as a totalising daily experience, then, it was also being recast in accord with a modern military scientific thought. The journals undertook to explain battles, explicate the skills and decisions of generals and admirals, announce new technologies and procedures, and explain regulations in ways that allowed this diverse assemblage of materials to cohere as a unified body of thought. A military perspective on war began to assume its own form in distinction to the broader national experience of war, while the daily life of the military was also subjected to intense scrutiny. Biographies and personal advice sought to foster greater levels of commitment and service, to refashion the subjectivity of the officer and encourage an intimate and exacting attention to military regulations and the intellectual culture encouraged by reading. The journals were, in effect, saturating the military life in the information and analysis of a new regime of writing. The journals lent an intellectual seriousness and coherence to the military as they articulated a military scientific overview of war. A form of military 'critique' developed in the military journals' approach to daily life that corresponds with Foucault's insistence on the shared approach of Enlightenment philosophy and journalism to understanding the historical roots of the contemporary. Military periodicals oversaw the formation of an intellectual culture that could engage daily wartime life at the level of a philosophy or a sublime knowledge – which could even be seen as one of the first expressions of modernity's characteristic effort to heroicise the present.[114] The journals embodied the military enlightenment's quest to understand who we are today, to investigate a 'historical ontology of ourselves', from a military perspective.[115]

[112] *The British Military Library; or, Journal* 2, no. 18 (1800): 198.
[113] *The Monthly Military Companion* 2, no. 8 (1802): 162.
[114] Michel Foucault, 'What Is Enlightenment?', *Ethics: Subjectivity and Truth. The Essential Works of Michel Foucault, 1954–1984*, ed. Paul Rabinow, trans. Robert Hurley and others, vol. 1 (New York: The New Press, 1997), 303–19, 310.
[115] Foucault, 'What Is Enlightenment?', 315.

Military Knowledge and Its Counter-Histories

Although the military journals played a primary role in establishing an intellectual culture of war, they were only one part of an expanding 'military literary world' of print.[116] The journals even at times sought to review, condense and re-present this other military writing.[117] When the *British Military Library* was republished as a two volume book, the editors announced in an advertisement that they had drawn extensively on earlier military writing, and so 'spared no expense to procure the most respectable Military Journals, and other works published upon the Continent; and the selections and translations have been made by gentlemen of experience in the German service, and that of the late French monarchy'.[118]

Britain was no exception to this explosion of military writing at the end of the eighteenth century. Each of Britain's major wars during the latter half of the eighteenth century was accompanied by a flurry of military books, and the British military experiences of these wars contributed enormously to the overall evolution of modern military thought. Although much of what was published in Britain were translations of French and German material, there was also a steady stream of original English publications.[119] While the present study concentrates on the formation of a theoretical knowledge of war rather than the histories of campaigns, it will address aspects of British responses to the Seven Years War in Chapter 2, of the American and French Revolutionary Wars in Chapter 3 and the Napoleonic Wars in Chapters 4 and 5. Henry Lloyd's efforts to make sense of Frederick the Great's unprecedented success is of particular importance for the history of military writing, and is discussed in detail in Chapter 2.

However, military writing expanded most rapidly with the increased scale and intensity of the French Revolutionary and Napoleonic Wars. Hundreds of titles were published in Britain during these years, many coming from Thomas Egerton's Military Library. Egerton began publishing military writing after the death of the publisher John Millan in 1782, who had dominated publication of military titles in the mid-eighteenth

---

116 Houlding, *Fit for Service*, 168.
117 Timothy Jenks, *Naval Engagements: Patriotism, Cultural Politics, and the Royal Navy 1793–1815* (Oxford: Oxford University Press, 2006), 162.
118 *The British Military Library* 1 (1804): iii–iv.
119 Danley, *Military Writings and the Theory and Practice of Strategy in the Eighteenth-Century British Army*, 10.

century.[120] Taking over many of Millan's titles and selling from Millan's former bookshop in the middle of Whitehall, and hence a short walk from the headquarters of both the British army and the navy, Egerton quickly became the nation's leading publisher of military texts. He had also been involved with publication of the *British Military Library* and adopted the title of this periodical for his publishing business.[121] His materials ranged from the government's drill regulations to books on artillery training, military engineering, histories of military campaigns, the character of different nation's armies, medical advice and accounts of court martials. Egerton's publications, however, only composed a fraction of all the material noticed by the *Monthly Review, or Literary Journal* (1749–1845) in its 'Monthly Catalogue' under the heading 'Military and Naval Affairs'.[122] Military writing was prominent in Romantic Britain, involving numerous titles, authors, publishers, genres and a readership that while clearly military in character may have extended to much the same readership as that of the major review periodicals.

As had been the case in the early modern era, military writing continued to be dominated by drill manuals. One of the most widely read books in Britain may well have been the government's *Rules and Regulations for the Formations, Field-Exercise, and Movements, of His Majesty's Forces* (1793) that formed the basis of the army's standardised government drill regulations (which were themselves based on the equally significant *Principles of Military Movements, Chiefly Applied to Infantry* (1788) by Sir David Dundas). The regularisation of drill in turn led to the publication of a plethora of guidebooks designed to help officers make sense of the regulations, a particular concern at this time given the proliferation of officers in Britain's newly formed volunteer and militia regiments. In turn, the widespread publication of drill regulations and manuals prompted the publication of books seeking to analyse the foundations of drill and training. Significant amongst these was Robert Jackson's *Systematic View of the Formation, Discipline and Economy of Armies* (1804), examined in Chapter 3, whose underlying ideas may have influenced the drill regimes of Sir John Moore at his famous Shorncliffe training camps in the early 1800s. The rise of Britain's volunteer units, however, also point to the ongoing

---

[120] Donald E. Graves, *'Reading Maketh a Full Man': British Military Literature in the Napoleonic Wars: An Annotated Bibliography of the Titles Published by the London Firm of Egerton, 1782–1832* (Godmanchester: Ken Trotman Publishing, 2007), 7–8.

[121] Graves, *'Reading Maketh a Full Man,'* 4. The *British Military Library* was itself re-published in a second edition that took the form of a book.

[122] See, for example, *Monthly Review, or Literary Journal* 38 (1802): 104–06.

fear of military invasion. There was a proliferation of military books during the Napoleonic Wars concerned with questions of national defence and the nature of military service that were responding, like the military journals, to the demands for service of a wartime nation. Charles Pasley, examined in Chapter 4, was a highly prominent author in this national debate and one of the first thinkers to theorise a modern military policy for how a nation should be organised for war.

There was a clearly gendered dimension to military writing, which was almost exclusively written by, for and about men. The era's military writing reflected what has been described as an increasing rigidification of ideas about gender from the mid-eighteenth century, which was at least in part a response to the rise of nationalism and the era's ongoing warfare.[123] Admittedly, armies on campaign in this era were still accompanied by large trains of camp followers, including non-combatant men, women and even children, that made warfare far from a wholly masculine or exclusively military venture. The inherent theatricality of eighteenth-century warfare had also occasioned a degree of transgressive sexuality and gender performance.[124] To a certain extent, the advent of total warfare created an expectation that women must be involved with the nation's military efforts. The French *levée en masse* exhorted women to make clothing and serve in hospitals, an ideal of feminine support for the national war effort that was duplicated across Europe. But as the declaration reveals, women were also circumscribed to a wholly supportive capacity. The advent of a near total war saw an unequivocal gender distinction emerge between a feminised civilian culture in need of defence and masculinised military culture that placed obligations on all men to defend the nation.[125] This gender division was further reinforced with the rise of a serious intellectual military culture that gradually displaced the populist and theatrical ideas of volunteering and national defence that had risen to prominence in the 1790s. The more flexible set of gender associations that had earlier circulated around war were superseded by professionalised forms of militarism and warfare.

---

[123] Karen Hagemann, 'The Military and Masculinity: Gendering the History of the Revolutionary and Napoleonic Wars, 1792–1815', in *War in an Age of Revolution, 1775–1815*, ed. Roger Chickering and Stig Förster (Cambridge: Cambridge University Press, 2010), 331–52, 339.

[124] On war's theatricality in the eighteenth century, see Gillian Russell, *The Theatres of War: Performance, Politics and Society, 1793–1815* (Oxford: Clarendon Press, 1995)

[125] Alan Forrest, 'Society, Mass Warfare, and Gender in Europe during and after the Revolutionary and Napoleonic Wars', in *The Oxford Handbook of Gender, War, and the Western World since 1600*, ed. Karen Hagemann, Stefan Dudink and Sonya O. Rose (Oxford: Oxford University Press, 2020), 159–76. See also Karen Hagemann, Gisela Mettele and Jand Rendall, eds, *Gender, War and Politics: Transatlantic Perspectives, 1775–1830* (Basingstoke: Palgrave Macmillan, 2010), 20.

The development of a professionalised military intellectual culture also gradually displaced classical knowledge about war. It is true that classical knowledge about war continued to shape military thought during the eighteenth century, contributing to a geometric approach to the era's warfare. British officers, for example, frequently read and recommended works by Caesar, Polybius and Vegetius, along with the neo-classical texts by the Marquis de Vauban, Marquis de Feuquières and Maurice de Saxe.[126] Yet the unprecedented scale and nature of warfare in the latter half of the eighteenth century was defying previous experience and pushing military writing far beyond its classical precedents. This writing now began to attempt to discern something of the essence, depth or foundation of war and its histories. Azar Gat observes in his compendious study of military strategic thought there has been a consistent effort since the Enlightenment to formulate a 'general theory of war'.[127] Henri Jomini and Carl von Clausewitz were the leading theorists at this time, their writing elaborating foundations of modern strategic thought that have continued to this day. While they each took a distinctive approach to the core concepts of military strategy, a divergence that is explored in Chapter 2, they nonetheless contributed to a growing perception of the complex inner workings and historical forces of warfare. So too, military writers also began to develop theories about the underlying historical development of warfare itself from antiquity to the far more complex conditions of modern war.[128] Departing from classical traditions, war was coming to be understood in terms of its historical depths and specificity as a modern discipline.

That Egerton styled his publishing firm a 'military library' also evinces the burgeoning infrastructure that had grown up around the publishing and dissemination of military writing. Military writing was finding its own disciplinary home in a distinct 'library' or 'catalogue' of materials, which marked its separation from other fields of knowledge while offering a degree of homogeneity to the divergent topics associated with military thought. Although the military periodicals were central to this development, they nonetheless appeared alongside books that similarly republished extracts from earlier war writing, suggesting an emergent hierarchy of works and

---

[126] Gruber, *Books and the British Army in the Age of the American Revolution*, 35; Danley, *Military Writings and the Theory and Practice of Strategy in the Eighteenth-Century British Army*, 70–1.

[127] Azar Gat, *A History of Military Thought: From the Enlightenment to the Cold War* (Oxford: Oxford University Press, 2001), vii.

[128] Richard Nicholson Magrath, *An Historical Sketch of the Progress of the Art of War* (Dublin: William Curry, Jun. and Company, 9 Upper Sackville-Street, 1838).

the need to condense and organise a growing mass of material.[129] In the mid-eighteenth century, Thomas Simes had published numerous compilations of earlier military material, which if somewhat hastily put together were nonetheless republished by Egerton and so must have retained some value.[130] The prominence of a figure such as Simes further points to the appearance of specialist military authors such as Thomas Reid and Charles James.[131] This study centres on four of the leading military authors writing in Britain during the Romantic era. There was, of course, also a large body of naval writing, albeit this was not as extensive as military writing. The present study will discuss aspects of naval writing in Chapter 4, but it focusses on military writing as by far the most influential martial material from this era and the most directly concerned with the transformation of warfare into a totalising national experience.

Taken together, these developments in military writing reflect the more general disciplinarisation of knowledge occurring at the end of the eighteenth century as knowledge was taken up and administered by the state.[132] Foucault's work has been enormously significant for questions about the historical foundations of knowledge, especially through his archaeological investigations that attempted to articulate the discursive basis of cognitive structures. But he also revisited his archaeological approach in his later work by proposing a 'genealogy of knowledges' that was informed by his reflections on the role of war in shaping modern institutions and modes of thought.[133] He contends that we can account for the changing structure of knowledge at the end of the eighteenth century by turning away from the traditional approaches of the history of science that regards the Enlightenment as a battle between truth and ignorance to instead examine the battles being waged between contending forms of knowledge.[134]

---

[129] *The Military Cabinet; Being a Collection of Extracts from the Best Authors, Both Ancient and Modern; Interspersed with Occasional Remarks, and Arranged under Different Heads. The Whole Calculated to Convey Instruction in the Most Agreeable Manner, and to Give to Young Officers Correct Notions in Regard to Many Subjects Belonging to or Connected with the Military Profession. In Three Volumes. By Capt. T.H. Cooper, Half Pay 56th Regt. Infantry, Author of a Practical Guide for the Light Infantry Officer* (London: Printed by R. Wilks, Chancery Lane, for T. Egerton, Military Library, Whitehall; Sherwood, Neely, & Jones, Paternoster-Row; and B. Crosby & Co. Stationer's Court, 1809).

[130] Danley, *Military Writings and the Theory and Practice of Strategy in the Eighteenth-Century British Army*, 80–1; and Houlding, *Fit for Service*, 218.

[131] Graves, '*Reading Maketh a Full Man*,' 6.

[132] Michel Foucault, *Society Must be Defended: Lectures at the Collège de France, 1975–1976*, ed. Mauro Bertani and Alessandro Fontana, trans. David Macey (London: Penguin Books, 2004), 184–85.

[133] Foucault, *Society Must Be Defended*, 178.

[134] Foucault, *Society Must Be Defended*, 178–79.

Foucault postulates that the state prevailed in this conflict by undertaking a disciplinarisation of knowledge that recalibrated localised and dispersed forms of knowledge into more clearly defined disciplinary knowledge. It did so through four elementary operations; selection, normalisation, centralisation and hierarchisation.[135] First, divisions were made between what counts as knowledge and what counts as non-knowledge, a process that led to the dismissal or eradication of what was seen as irrelevant, marginal or spurious. Extending this first step in the disciplinarisation of knowledge were a series of further steps that normalised and homogenised accepted knowledge by making knowledge not only widely accessible, but also by creating a range of standardised approaches to classifying, producing and disseminating knowledge. This process in turn had the effect of centralising and hierarchising knowledge – creating a universalised system of knowledge that could account for multiple domains of knowledge and which could integrate more particular or material forms of knowledge with those that were more general and all encompassing. Dispensing with the older organisational devices of mathesis and philosophy and removing knowledge from its former shrouds of secrecy, censorship and received ideas of authority, a modern science instead formed via the distribution of knowledge into discrete disciplines.

Military thought was developing along such lines as it was centralised by a state-sponsored institutional military science. Disdaining a shared classical inheritance, a germinal military science operated by normalising military knowledge across an expanding body of print. Military journals were an essential part of this process because they enabled the diverse and localised elements of military power to be conceptualised as a unified body of knowledge and assembled in ways that began to form a normalised, hierarchised and far more homogeneous totality, one that came to be governed by its own publishing infrastructure of booksellers, translations, compilations, authors, genres and journals. A far more consistent approach was adopted to key concepts within military thought, the term strategy, for example, taking on its modern meaning and distinction from other, subordinate knowledges, such as of tactics or military policy.[136] Writing in the first decades of the nineteenth century, Clausewitz was able to declare that an established distinction between strategy and tactics 'is now almost

---

[135] Foucault, *Society Must Be Defended*, 180–81.
[136] The term strategy first appearing in English its modern sense in 1810, see Danley, *Military Writings and the Theory and Practice of Strategy in the Eighteenth-Century British Army*, 66–7.

universal'.[137] Ultimately, however, what defines modern science is that it does not rely on the orthodoxy of statements but on the 'dispersal' of knowledge, the 'orthology' of the correct use of words.[138] What is critical is the correct authority or qualification of the speakers and the modes by which information is circulated and debated, an authority that functions in the last instance in relation to the state and its university system.[139] It was the military periodicals, however, that first enabled an institutionally separate military to gain a national 'voice' through the formation of the periodical's corporate editorial persona. The growing disciplinarisation of military knowledge was epitomised by the military journals that elevated and legitimated the military as a scientific authority on war.

But even if it is possible to recognise a rationality of violence, knowledge about war was never able to completely form into a discrete scientific discipline within the modern university.[140] There are, undoubtedly, many reasons for this failure. Military knowledge perhaps remained too secretive or already too close to the state and its authority to be able to form into a separate discipline. So too, it could be argued that it is difficult to identify a central uniting element behind the full range of military knowledge, leaving it splintered between related forms of disciplinary knowledge such as ballistics, metallurgy or psychology. But as military knowledge condensed into a proto-disciplinary field, there were repeated attacks on the very idea that military thought could be conceptualised as knowledge at all.[141] War knowledge remained suspended between Enlightenment accounts and counter-Enlightenment reactions that consistently attacked rational knowledge with an awareness of war's chaos and pain, or, in Clausewitz's terms, of war's 'friction'.[142] The idea that British officers could improve themselves by reading was, moreover, both widely encouraged and yet perpetually met with countervailing views of the inadequacy of reading for the practice of war.[143] The period certainly witnessed the appearance of military scientific institutions and training colleges, but

---

[137] Carl Von Clausewitz, *On War*, ed. and trans. Michael Howard and Peter Paret (Princeton: Princeton University Press, 1984), 128.

[138] Foucault, *Society Must Be Defended*, 184–85.

[139] Foucault, *Society Must Be Defended*, 183.

[140] On the rationality of violence, see Michel Foucault, *Foucault Live (Interviews, 1961–1984)*, ed. Sylvère Lotringer, trans. Lysa Hochroth and John Johnston (New York: Semiotext(e), 1996), 299.

[141] Dennis E Showalter, 'Information Capabilities and Military Revolutions: The Nineteenth-Century Experience', *Journal of Strategic Studies*, 27, no. 2 (2004): 220–42, 222.

[142] Clausewitz, *On War*, 119–21.

[143] Daly, 27.

there was simultaneously a lack of clarity as to whether there was a science of war at all. The United Service Institute, which began life as a military library and museum in 1832, failed to establish a fully institutionalised military science along the lines of other scientific institutions or societies such as the Royal Geographical Society. The institute's museum collections comprised items that officers had located on foreign travel that were far from wholly military in character, while the few military items chosen for display were typically 'trophies and relics' rather than objects of scientific importance.[144] To this day, debate remains as to whether and how the academy might conceptualise something like war studies because war never formed as a foundational discipline within the modern university.[145]

Associated with brute physicality, conflict and strategic calculation, war failed to fully conform to the universalism of knowledge that underpinned the rise of modern scientific disciplines. In his genealogy of modern historicist knowledge, Foucault uncovers a history of political and racial struggles that leads him to conclude that historicism is entirely complicit with war.[146] Unlike technical forms of knowledge, modern historicist thought, he argues, first appeared as an anti-state body of knowledge, a historical memory of conflict that was initiated in the sixteenth century from the nobility's reaction to increasing sovereign power. As the state lifted war out of the social realm and into its military institutions, eliminating social conflict and appropriating the nobility's former role in war, it also adapted this historicist memory of conflict into its own state knowledge.[147] History may eventually have been turned into a law governing the production of knowledge more generally in the modern episteme, but the state's pacification of the social also had the effect of transforming real social wars into discursive conflicts that strengthened memories of counter-histories while turning history itself into the general form or tactic of political struggle. However much military science came to be reduced to a mere tool of the

[144] Neil Ramsey, 'Exhibiting Discipline: Military Science and the Naval and Military Library and Museum', in *Tracing War in British Enlightenment and Romantic Culture*, ed. Neil Ramsey and Gillian Russell (Basingstoke: Palgrave Macmillan, 2015), 113–31, 123.

[145] Tarik Barkawi and Shane Brighton, 'Powers of War: Fighting, Knowledge, and Critique', *International Political Sociology* 5, no. 2 (2011): 126–43.

[146] Foucault, *Society Must Be Defended*, 173. Reinhart Koselleck also drew attention to the alignment of war and historicism, see Mary A. Favret, 'Field of History, Field of Battle', *Romantic Circles* (Sept 2011). https://romantic-circles.org/praxis/frictions/HTML/praxis.2011.favret.html, accessed 15 April 2022.

[147] Foucault, *Society Must Be Defended*, 185–90.

modern state, therefore, war could not be fully disciplinarised because it remained entangled within this historical matrix of conflict and struggle. Historical knowledge of war cannot eliminate the counter-histories that speak of underlying struggle and uncertainty, of counter-heroics and glories, of bodies and horror, of truths that are suppressed and rationalities that serve their own, strategic purposes. War also contains the archaic and chaotic, a necessity of violence and its brutal assault of the body that can never fully subsume itself into the peace of the state's efforts to encompass a universalised knowledge. War thought came to be characterised by its sublimity, as Turpin de Crissé observed, because it represents an effort to master this other dimension of physical terrors and violence. But if this discourse of war's sublimity can be seen as an appropriation of the nobility of war for the modern state, it also underlines how war exists as a sublime excess that stretches beyond the rationality of disciplinary knowledge and complicates how the military assumed authority over war.[148]

The Sublime Poetics of the Military Body

One place in which this sublime counter-history of war can be seen is in the personal forms of military writing that also appeared in the military journals. The *New Monthly Magazine* (1814–84) proposed in 1829 that there were two distinct kinds of 'military work', those for 'military men of science' and those of 'personal adventure'.[149] Describing soldiers' personal adventures and their sublime experiences of war, this material constituted what McLoughlin describes as a 'veteran poetics' that first appeared in the 1790s.[150] Such stories could range from accounts of heroic adventure to tales of unimaginable horror, but collectively they came to constitute a new art and literature of war associated with the traumatic witness of combat experience in an age of mass warfare. Where books of military instruction had in the early modern era been widely read and even left traces across all forms of writing, now there was a growing perception of a divide between military scientific texts and the materials found interesting

---

[148] Robert Doran, *The Theory of the Sublime from Longinus to Kant* (Cambridge: Cambridge University Press, 2015), 288; Foucault, *Society Must be Defended*, 190.

[149] *New Monthly Magazine*, 27 (1829): 94.

[150] Yuval Noah Harari, *The Ultimate Experience: Battlefield Revelations and the Making of Modern War Culture, 1450–2000* (Basingstoke: Palgrave Macmillan, 2008); Kate McLoughlin, *Veteran Poetics: British Literature in the Age of Mass Warfare, 1790–2015* (Cambridge: Cambridge University Press, 2018).

to the ordinary, civilian, reader. So too, such stories displaced an earlier aesthetics formed out of the speech of the great generals and their heroic action with accounts of the common and inherently embodied experience of soldiering.[151] Military thought was not only divided from other fields of knowledge, therefore, but it also appears as itself divided along two distinct lines of scientific and imaginative, literary work.

McLoughlin intimates that this veteran poetics must be placed in the context of the late eighteenth-century print revolution, a development she reads in relation to Walter Benjamin's analysis of modern information. Benjamin argues that the modern mass media displaced traditional wisdom, or '*erfahrung*', with the shock and uncertainty resulting from the widespread circulation of information. The result was a reconception of experience itself in terms of sensation or '*erlebnis*'.[152] Benjamin had first developed these ideas in relation to the shell shock of the First World War, but he identified this shock as much with the trauma of battle as with a far reaching social trauma of war news as it reported on the unprecedented violence of the war.[153] Although the news to some extent protects the reader from being entirely overwhelmed by information, it does so by dating and hence isolating events within a particular moment and thereby foreclosing any possibility of integrating this news into a meaningful experience of history.[154] The lived experience of war, he thus supposes, is regrounded in a new kind of information that could not be integrated into a life as a whole and which could not contribute to the '*erfahrung*' of individual memory, wisdom or tradition. While Benjamin focussed on the First World War, McLoughlin draws attention to a much longer history behind the rise of information and its social effects that stretches back to the advent of mass warfare in the Romantic era. These are effects that can also be associated with the era's military journals and their integration of war news and analysis. Reimagining wartime life in terms of regulations, abstractions and innovations, along with the dated regularity of war news and their own regular publication schedule, the journals recast wartime life in terms of isolated military information.

---

[151] On the progression of war literature away from myth and heroic action to the modern low mimetic or ironic forms of stories concerned with ordinary individuals, see Paul Fussell, *The Great War and Modern Memory* (Oxford: Oxford University Press, 2013).

[152] McLoughlin, *Veteran Poetics*, 190.

[153] Walter Benjamin, 'The Storyteller', in Hannah Arendt (ed.) *Illuminations*, trans. Harry Zorn (London: Fontana, 1973), 83–109.

[154] Walter Benjamin, 'Some Motifs in Baudelaire', in Hannah Arendt (ed.) *Illuminations*, trans. Harry Zohn (London: Fontana, 1973), 157–202.

If this had the effect of intensifying the officer's personal commitment to war by more closely uniting him with the military institution, it also foreclosed the broader relevance of personal wisdom and classical tradition. The journals helped open the way for the personal experience of war to be understood in terms of sensation, adventure and shock, to become the *'erlebnis'* of the modern war story.

This new poetics of shock appears in military accounts of personal adventure published in the *United Service Journal,* such as a pair of sketches of the 'Storming of Ciudad Rodrigo' and 'Storming of Badajoz', published in the journal's first volume in 1829. The anonymous narrator, an officer who was witness to the events, tells of the appalling loss of life during the British assault on the two fortifications. He describes in graphic detail the horrifying sight of his unrecognisable comrade after the battle:

> I went towards the large breach, and met Uniacke of the 95th; he was walking between two men. One of his eyes was blown out, and the flesh was torn off his arms and legs. I asked who it was; he replied Uniacke, and walked on. He had taken chocolate with our mess an hour before.[155]

From the shock of this encounter, the narrator proceeds to describe the abysmal aftermath of the combat where the ground is covered in the mutilated bodies of dead British soldiers, including General McKinnon who has been stripped nearly naked following his death. The narrator ponders the cause of his fate, concluding that it must not have been from an explosion or his face should have been 'scorched'.[156] The narrator recounts meeting two friends, Madden and Merry, who had been desperately wounded in the assault of Badajoz. The first lies dying covered in his own blood while the second insists he will soon die from a knee shattered by grapeshot. The story not only foregrounds the officers' familiarity with the shocking experience of suffering and misery, highlighted by the radical disjunction between the sociability of Uniacke taking chocolate with the narrator and the brutal violence of military combat that tears, scorches and shatters flesh and bone, but it also equally signals the officer's unparalleled fortitude and courage in meeting such horrors. It is a courage that effaces all marks of rank and distinction by reducing soldiers to their naked, vulnerable and suffering bodies. The sketches conclude with reflection on the noble qualities that found their expression in the sacrifices of the soldiers at Badajoz, the narrator demanding of the reader '[l]ook on those blood

[155] *The United Service Journal* 1, no. 1 (1829): 63–64.
[156] *The United Service Journal* 1, no. 1 (1829): 65.

stained uniforms; gaze on these noble forms stretched on the earth, and think on their agonies!'.[157]

In this account of battle, the general is, notably, not a subject of speech or heroic action, as in a former representative regime of art that was epitomised by the great speech of the general haranguing his troops. The general is, instead, simply identified as a silent and naked body who lies amidst the corpses of his fellow British soldiers. In a basic sense, therefore, such stories conform to, while inverting, an emergent discourse of imaginative literature as a discourse of the universal human.[158] Just as literature, via the modern novel, began to speak of a shared common nature at the same moment that knowledge of the human world was splintering into discrete scientific disciplines, so a new kind of war story depicts each soldier via a shared bodily experience, a common nature, rather than in relation to command and heroic achievement. But the war story also orients its vision of the universal human around a specific figure of bodily suffering that contrasts sharply with the domestic focus that came to define the universality of the human in the wider field of literature. If the novel itself can be defined by the shock of modernity, it is nonetheless typified by the shocks of modern urban life rather than the shock of war's violent horror. It is as though these emerging military tales matched literature's focus on domestic life, the realms of marriage, maturity and social standing, with a concern for the common physical experiences of military suffering, wounds and death. Rather than such stories simply taking a place within the discourse of a common or shared life, therefore, they assume an inverted form as a militarised mirror image of literature because they focus on the uncommon yet shared military experience of military death and horror. The reader can only gaze on in wonder at the agonies represented.

This represented the birth of a new kind of war literature that expanded dramatically beyond the journals in the years following the end of the Napoleonic Wars. Emerging somewhat later than other developments in military writing, this material no doubt rose to prominence in the wake of the wars because it served a commemorative function for a modern, civilian society.[159] By the 1830s, dozens of military memoirs had been published in Britain that recounted the stories of ordinary soldiers and officers who had

---

[157] *The United Service Journal* 1, no. 1 (1829): 169.
[158] Ian Duncan, 'Literature', in *Historicism and the Human Sciences in Victorian Britain*, ed. Mark Bevir (Cambridge: Cambridge University Press, 2017), 105–27, 106–07.
[159] Neil Ramsey, *The Military Memoir and Romantic Literary Culture, 1780–1835* (Farnham: Ashgate, 2011), 51–77.

fought in the wars. In part this work still displayed its roots in earlier generic forms. The memoirs continued the more expansive approach to biography that had earlier characterised the military journals, which recorded the lives of ordinary officers and so functioned as stories of embodied life and service rather than as stories of command and heroic action. So too, the memoirs had roots in travel narratives that were published with increasing regularity by the end of the eighteenth century and which at times reflected on the events of military campaigns, as seen with the outpouring of travellers' writing on the Battle of Waterloo (1815). But such stories also documented the daily travails of a soldier's life, an approach dominated in the immediate post-war era by private soldiers who apprehended war in terms of despair and a nascent class awareness. Officers began to compose memoirs in increasing numbers by the 1820s, transforming the genre into accounts of adventure that evoked stoical courage and good humour. Such stories were in turn adapted into military and naval novels by the end of the 1820s. The leading author of this new genre was Frederick Marryat, a veteran naval officer long acclaimed as the most significant British novelist between Austen and Dickens. Yet it was Thomas Hamilton who originated the military novel, when he adapted his memoirs of war to the form of historical romance originated by Sir Walter Scott. His work represents a militarised sublime poetics of war, which, as discussed in Chapter 5, founded a subsequent tradition of the novel defined not by domestic life and sexuality but by imperial adventure and its racialised violence.[160]

During the Romantic era, military writing came to be conceptualised in relation to two diverging ideas of sublimity: of sublime command and of sublime suffering. How might we understand both elements as forming together into a modern war writing? However much stories of war's horror can be seen to function as a counter-discourse to military strategic thought, they still appeared in the pages of the *United Service Journal* in tandem with other forms of military writing. Representative of a new 'veteran poetics', in effect a nascent modern war art of suffering and trauma, such stories can be understood as being as much a product of a new regime of writing as other works of military science, bound as they are by the circulation of *erlebnis* and its shocked 'silences'. They result from the saturation of war in writing, the remodelling of traditional wisdom and experience surrounding war into information, instruction, analysis, regulation,

---

[160] For an overview of how imperial adventure emerges alongside domestic literature, see Patrick Brantlinger, *Rule of Darkness: British Literature and Imperialism, 1830–1914* (Ithaca: Cornell University Press, 1988).

sensation and discipline. To fully understand these developments, however, we might take a cue from Clausewitz's insistence that while war is more like an art than a science, it can neither be entirely resolved into a science nor an art because at heart it is a 'conflict of living forces'.[161] Writing as a strategist, Clausewitz posits this conflict as one between generals, as though they were two duellists or card players or even two traders interacting via 'commerce'.[162] Yet there is another conflict of living forces that does not occur between commanders but between those who command and those who are commanded. Clifford Siskin observes that as new disciplines emerged at the end of the eighteenth century, they each took shape through their share of knowledge about the human.[163] Disciplines, in other words, united the two modern meanings of discipline: a disciplinary knowledge about the human with the disciplinary techniques necessary to regulate and control the human. If we understand war writing as a broad category beyond either the science or art of war, it is towards the body and its life, towards a bio-aesthetics, that we need to turn.

Writing and the Transformations of Military Discipline

In the wake of Foucault's pioneering studies there has been enormous interest in the historical development of disciplinary power as a set of techniques for regulating behaviour within disciplinary institutions, ranging from workshops to schools, hospitals, prisons and barracks. As is well known, Foucault proposes that while power was traditionally related to sovereign authority and its spectacular display of supremacy through public execution, pageants and courtly displays, discipline came to the fore in the early modern period as a micro-physics of power based on the surveillance and regulation of bodily practices. The new techniques of discipline were no longer extractive, a form of taxation or a spectacular imposition of fear and awe. Rather, they worked by developing an individual's productive capacities while simultaneously producing ever greater levels of obedience and docility. As Foucault argues, 'discipline produces subjected and practised bodies, "docile" bodies. Discipline increases the forces of the body (in economic terms of utility) and diminishes these same forces (in political terms of obedience)'.[164]

---

[161] Clausewitz, *On War*, 149.
[162] Clausewitz, *On War*, 149.
[163] Clifford Siskin, *System: The Shaping of Modern Knowledge* (Cambridge: MIT Press, 2016), 149.
[164] Michel Foucault, *Discipline and Punish: The Birth of the Prison*, trans. Alan Sheridan (New York: Vintage, 1991), 138.

Widely deployed in response to the demographic explosion of the eighteenth century and hence the need to control ever growing populations, discipline points towards the fundamental importance in the modern era of the accumulation of labour alongside the accumulation of capital.[165] However, disciplinary practices were not only integral to the worker obedience and productivity necessary for capitalism to flourish, but were also just as critical for the waging of mass warfare. In Foucault's account of the lineage of modern disciplinary practices, military disciplinarians from Frederick the Great to Jacques Antoine-Hippolyte, Comte de Guibert play a crucial formative role.

Foucault's initial work on discipline was further developed in his own subsequent writing on sexuality and in the writing of Giorgio Agamben, Robert Esposito and others, all of which has extended into the related concepts of biopolitics and biopower.[166] There is much debate about the nature of biopolitics and the modern usage of the term, instigated by Foucault, has shifted dramatically from its earliest roots in vitalist conceptions of the state that were first formulated in the 1920s.[167] Broadly speaking, Foucault used the concept to expand his earlier work on discipline into a concern with questions of population and, ultimately, the force and power of life. Biopower developed around two complementary poles – an anatamo-politics of the body governed by disciplinary techniques and a biopolitics of the population that drew on a range of statistical data and governmental forms of intervention to regulate the social and biological processes inherent to populations.[168] Sovereignty had always ruled over the people, but traditionally the people were understood as a collection of individual subjects who were ruled in accord with their personal rights and obligations. Biopolitics describes how the people came to be understood as a population, an entity possessing its own organic characteristics and natural processes, such as rates of birth and death, or the prevalence of disease and criminality.[169] The characteristics of the population, this 'kind of thick natural phenomenon', cannot be worked upon directly through laws

---

[165] Michel Foucault, *Psychiatric Power: Lectures at the Collège de France, 1973–1974*, ed. Jacques Lagrange, trans. Graham Burchell (Basingstoke: Palgrave Macmillan, 2006), 71.

[166] Giorgio Agamben, *Homo Sacer: Sovereign Power and Bare Life*, trans. Daniel Heller-Roazen (Stanford: Stanford University Press, 1998). For a historical summery of how the concept of biopolitics has developed, see Roberto Esposito, *Bios: Biopolitics and Philosophy*, trans. Timothy Campbell (Minneapolis: University of Minnesota Press, 2008), 13–44.

[167] Esposito, *Bios*, 16.

[168] Michel Foucault, *The History of Sexuality. Volume One: An Introduction*, trans. Robert Hurley (London: Penguin Books, 1981), 139.

[169] Foucault, *Society Must Be Defended*, 244–45.

or moral injunctions, in the same manner that sovereign power directly targets the behaviour of an individual via juridical prohibitions or obligations.[170] Rather, biopolitics depends upon forms of governmental regulation or security that seek to influence these natural processes or collective behaviours via various public health initiatives or campaigns designed to increase the health and well-being of the population. Sovereignty in the modern era is governmentalised, forced to account for the natural properties and collective identity of those over whom it rules so that it is unable to simply rule by law and decree.

The modern era thus saw the transformation of the neo-classical tradition of sovereign rule that was characterised by a 'symbolics of blood' associated with sovereign power, alliances, nobility and lineage. Nineteenth-century government appropriated these older noble ideals of inheritance and heredity by adapting them to a wide ranging concern with the management of life and, above all, an 'analytics of sexuality' that sought to make life proliferate by developing mechanisms for increasing its sexual purity, productivity and well-being.[171] Foucault regards sexuality as indispensable to the development of biopower because it forms at the intersection between regulations surrounding the body and those surrounding the population, meaning that sexuality united 'the two axes along which developed the entire political technology of life'.[172] Sexuality not only served as a vital mechanism for developing an individual's personal beliefs, attitudes and approaches to sexual conduct, but it also aligned the individual with procreativity and so helped to regulate optimum rates of fertility for the overall health of the population. But sexuality was, Foucault insists, only one of a range of 'concrete arrangements' that co-ordinated power between individuals and populations.[173] The expanding population in the late eighteenth century led to increasing demands for control as too many elements were escaping the attention of sovereign authority.[174] What required attention were, on the one hand, the endless details of individual comportment and behaviour, and, on the other hand, the overarching phenomenon and mass characteristics of the populations. Biopower describes the manifold set of responses to the

---

[170] Foucault, *Security, Territory, Population*, 71.
[171] Foucault, *The History of Sexuality*, 148.
[172] Foucault, *The History of Sexuality*, 145.
[173] Foucault, *History of Sexuality*, 140.
[174] Michel Foucault, 'Truth and Juridical Forms', in Michel Foucault, *Power: The Essential Works of Michel Foucault, 1954–1984*, ed. James D. Faubian, trans. Robert Hurley and others, vol. 3 (London and New York: Penguin Books, 1994), 1–89, 62.

perceived 'strategic urgency' of controlling this growing population and ensuring the productive regulation of individuals with the collective.[175] As with the formation of disciplinary knowledge more generally, this was a process by which disparate forms of knowledge were gradually concentrated and utilised in a more systematic fashion. A set of diverse and localised elements coalesced, through a series of extensions, inflections, developments, and transformations, into a more general mechanism of control that Foucault describes as a new dispositive or apparatus of power concerned with understanding and governing life. A modern conception of life was born at this juncture that saw life as something interiorised and obscure, a hidden force, resistance and will that must be studied and understood to govern effectively.[176]

Although biopower targets the natural phenomenon of life, therefore, it rejects the overt and crude violence of sovereign forms of rule and operates as much through knowledge and discourse, 'symbolic forms', as it does through the physical regulation of bodies and populations.[177] Uniting truth and government, biopower was wholly dependent upon writing. It was the 'power of writing' that transmuted disciplinary practices into biopower by allowing a 'total and continuous' observation of the living human.[178] The constant oversight of writing was critical to the permanent and complete investment of the individual disciplined life that allowed earlier disciplinary mechanisms to extend beyond enclosed institutions and into a social field characterised by 'an indefinitely generalisable mechanism of "panopticism"'.[179] Disciplines intensified their grip as they adapted the cataloguing techniques of libraries and botanical gardens to ever more fully individualised, categorised and regulated human behaviour.[180] As knowledge of the body increased, mechanical forms of discipline gave way to forms that conceptualised the body as organic and living, possessed of depth, drives and interiority as a natural body. While much attention has been directed at the architecture of the panopticon as a key to how

---

175 See Michel Foucault, 'The Confession of the Flesh', interviewed Alain Grosrichard, Gerard Wajeman, Jaques-Alain Miller, Guy Le Gaufey, Dominique Celas, Gerard Miller, Catherine Millot, Jocelyne Livi and Judith Miller, in *Power/Knowledge: Selected Interviews and Other Writings, 1972–1977*, ed. Colin Gordon, trans. Colin Gordon, Leo Marshall, John Mepham and Kate Soper (New York: Pantheon, 1980), 194–228, 194–98.

176 Davide Tarizzo, *Life: A Modern Invention*, trans. Mark William Epstein (Minneapolis: University of Minnesota Press, 2017), 3–5.

177 Thomas Lemke, *Foucault, Governmentality, and Critique* (New York: Routledge, 2012), 29–31.

178 Foucault, *Discipline and* Punish, 189, Foucault, *Psychiatric Power*, 48.

179 Foucault, *Psychiatric Power*, 48; Foucault, *Discipline and* Punish, 216.

180 Foucault, *Psychiatric Power*, 50.

disciplinary surveillance operated, Foucault had originally been clear that it is writing that enables this panoptic effect:

> Disciplinary power is individualizing because it fastens the subject-function to the somatic singularity by means of a system of supervision-writing, or by a system of pangraphic panopticism, which behind the somatic singularity projects, as its extension or as its beginning, a core of virtualities, a psyche, and which further establishes the norm as the principle of division and normalization, as the universal prescription for all individuals constituted in this way.[181]

The effect of writing is a centralised individualisation, a 'pangraphic panopticism', wherein disciplinary institutions produce individuals by identifying and normalising bodies through the 'disciplinary gaze' that is enabled by 'continual writing'.[182] The subjectivity of the disciplined individual is woven from such webs of writing, which produce an individual's 'body-psyche' or 'soul' by relating him or her to the norms of a population.[183]

Yet writing also contributed to the cultivation of individual subjectivity beyond the disciplinary institution.[184] In part this is reflected in the psychological interventions directed at maladaptive, ignorant or abnormal individuals who failed to fully conform to disciplinary structures, what Foucault terms the Psy-functions, or psychologically based sciences, that evolved from the Romantic era onwards by expanding the confessional practices originally rooted in the revelations of self-writing.[185] This subjective dimension can also be associated, however, with the flourishing of self- or life-writing in the Romantic era, the rise of memoir and autobiography along with more extensive letter writing, journal keeping and even the rise of lyric poetry.[186] Resembling earlier confessional practices, such writing cultivates subjectivity by adapting and extending the writing techniques developed in the governmental and institutional administration of individuals, with their bureaucratic maintenance of vast registers of writing about individual comportment and capacities.[187] Life-writing can

---

[181] Foucault, *Psychiatric Power*, 55.
[182] Foucault, *Psychiatric Power*, 56.
[183] Foucault, *Psychiatric Power*, 56; Foucault, *Discipline and Punish*, 174.
[184] For an overview of this relationship, see Jan Goldstein, 'Foucault's Technologies of the Self and the Cultural History of Identity', in *Cultural History After Foucault*, ed. John Neubauer (New York: Aldine de Gruyter, 1999), 37–54, 43–44. This issue is discussed at more length in Chapter 3.
[185] Foucault, *Psychiatric Power*, 85–6.
[186] Rancière, *The Politics of Literature*, 181; Ransom, *Foucault's Discipline*, 65.
[187] Michel Foucault, 'On the Genealogy of Ethics: An Overview of Work in Progress', in *Ethics: Subjectivity and Truth. The Essential Works of Michel Foucault, 1954–1984*, ed. Paul Rabinow, trans. Robert Hurley and Others, vol. 1 (New York: The New Press, 1997), 253–80, 272.

be understood, in this sense, as an adjunct to the disciplinary norms of a living body, with their assumption that the body is not a mechanical entity but possesses interiority, appetite, self-consciousness and drives in ways that disrupt any simple distinction between mind and body.[188] Aesthetics itself emerges in no small part from this discovery of the natural body and hence the awareness that the individual is determined by unconscious elements that resist even as they demand elucidation. While the aesthetic can be associated with freedom and the transcendent Kantian idea, it can also be subsumed into a bio-aesthetics that conflates the aesthetic with the teleological unconscious or biological drives of the organism.[189] In its confessional conflation of the body with the self, the era's self-writing could be seen to grow out of and extend the broader disciplinary cultivation of the natural body.

Writing, however, also operates at the level of the population and in relation to social and biological norms. The instigation of statistical methods in the eighteenth century gave rise to a wealth of writing about the population that facilitated a new understanding of its underlying natural qualities and processes. Rancière proposes that the rise of statistics underpinned a new poetics of knowledge because numbers played a critical role in bringing visibility to the masses.[190] Command over life was essential to the formation of modern disciplinarity as disciplines expanded their knowledge across the full domain of the human – biopower serving as an essential component in the disciplinarisation of knowledge of the era more generally. Foucault would eventually speculate that a modern episteme concerned with the historical forces buried within objects of knowledge may have been entirely dependent upon this emergent understanding of the population.[191] Through writing, an interplay formed between administration and knowledge about individuals and populations that produced what Foucault viewed as the 'epistemological "thaw"' of the human sciences.[192] John Guillory asks why writing has remained so central today in our own age of technological media. The answer can be found in the

[188] Christoph Menke, 'Force: Towards an Aesthetic Concept of Life', *MLN* 125, no. 3 (2010): 552–70, 553.

[189] Christoph Menke, 'Aesthetic Nature: Against Biology', *The Yearbook of Comparative Literature* 58 (2012): 193–95, 195.

[190] Jacques Rancière, *The Names of History: On the Poetics of Knowledge*, trans. Hassan Melehy; foreword Hayden White (Minneapolis: University of Minnesota Press, 1994), 8–9.

[191] Foucault, *Security, Territory, Population*, 76–9.

[192] Foucault, *Discipline and* Punish, 224. For a discussion of the role of writing in this process, see Jan Goldstein, 'Foucault among the Sociologists: The "Disciplines" and the History of the Professions', *History and Theory* 23, no. 2 (1984): 170–92, 182.

intimate relationship that historically formed between writing and the development of power over life.[193] That Britain became saturated in writing from the latter part of the eighteenth century cannot, in other words, be untangled from the ways in which disciplinary and biopolitical practices emerged over the course of the century as the primary sources of governmental power.

If military journals were central to the disciplinarisation of military knowledge, they also played a formative role in producing a new kind of knowledge about life in relation to war. Foucault acknowledges that war was subsumed by biopolitical imperatives in this era, that there is a necessary thanatopolitics accompanying biopolitics, but it was not something he pursued in detail beyond his speculative reflections on state racism.[194] The intersection of biopolitics and war remained paradoxical in ways that he felt required further explanation:

> if we think about the way in which the modern state began to worry about individuals—about the lives of individuals—there is a paradox in this history. At the same moment the state began to practice its greatest slaughters, it began to worry about the physical and mental health of each individual. The first great book on public health in France was written in 1784, five years before the Revolution, and ten years before the Napoleonic wars. This game between death and life is one of the main paradoxes of the modern state.[195]

This paradox of life and death is deeply etched into the formation of biopower. In *Recherches et Considérations sur las Population de la France* (1778), one of the first texts that can be associated with a modern biopolitics, Jean-Baptiste Moheau had already announced that it is not wealth but population 'that decides the great quarrels of nations'.[196] William McNeill gives further weight to such views in his historical investigations of how war in this era was driven by the necessity of managing rapidly expanding populations.[197] This is not to deny that finance played an enormous role in wars, as witnessed by the central importance in European political power of the

---

[193] Guillory, 'The Memo and Modernity', 132.
[194] Foucault, *The History of Sexuality*, 136–37; On the link between war, regeneration and sexuality, see Bell, 'The Birth of Militarism in the Age of Democratic Revolutions', 41.
[195] Foucault, *Foucault Live*, 299.
[196] Jean-Baptiste Moheau, *Recherches et Considerations sur la Population de la France, 1778. Public Avec Introduction et Table Analytique par Rene* Gonnard (Paris: Libraire Paul Geuthner, 13, Rue Jacob, 13, 1912), 10, author's translation. On Moheau and biopolitics, see Foucault, *Security, Territory, Population*, 22.
[197] William H. McNeill, *The Pursuit of Power: Technology, Armed Force, and Society since A.D. 1000* (Chicago: University of Chicago Press, 1982), 185–87; See also Giovanni Arrighi, *Adam Smith in Beijing: Lineages of the Twenty-First Century* (London: Verso, 2007), 243–44 and 268.

fiscal-military state.[198] But this was also an increasingly professionalised, bureaucratic state dependent upon adequate taxation, which administered its economy and population in accord with the natural properties of the economic life of the people. The military journals were integral to this regulation of national life in relation to war because their association of discipline with the management and study of daily life enabled discipline to be rendered 'national' or extended across the social sphere.[199] The journals transformed disciplinary practices surrounding soldiers' bodies into a more general disciplinary knowledge of war and its living forces, a shift that underpinned the development of the 'immense tactical knowledge that had its effect in the period of the Napoleonic wars'.[200]

Military journals, in other words, were vital to the 'epistemological "thaw"' of military disciplinary knowledge because they established an interplay between techniques of disciplinary control and fields of knowledge that together allowed the militarised body to be directed and understood in its full complexity. By investigating and interpreting the daily operation of the military, the journals enabled the trivial details and regulations of military practice to coalesce into homogeneous frames of military thought. The disparate practices associated with military training and regulation could be understood as a total and continuous operation that echoes the emergent discourse on sexuality in its increasing intensity of concern with the entire life of the soldier. As military discipline extends beyond the mechanical imposition of bodily regulation it was increasingly concerned with the total conduct of an individual, so that '[m]ilitary discipline begins to be the general confiscation of the body, time, and life; it is no longer a levy on the individual's activity but an occupation of his body, life, and time'.[201] The journals reflected the more general rise of total war and the elevation of soldierly self-sacrifice as military power intensified its hold over the entirety of an individual's life and soldiering came to be understood in terms of 'a moral and political conduct, a sacrifice, and devotion to the common cause and common salvation'.[202] This increasing

---

[198] Brewer, *The Sinews of Power*.
[199] Foucault, *Discipline and* Punish, 169.
[200] Foucault, *Discipline and Punish*, 187.
[201] Foucault, *Psychiatric Power*, 47.
[202] Foucault, *Security, Territory, Population*, 198. See, also, Linda Colley, *Britons: Forging the Nation, 1707–1837* (New Haven: Yale University Press, 1992); and Stefan Dudnik and Karen Hagemann, 'Masculinity in Politics and War in the Age of Democratic Revolutions, 1750–1850', in *Masculinities in Politics and War: Gendering Modern History*, ed. Stefan Dudnik, Karen Hagemann and John Tosh (Manchester: Manchester University Press, 2004), 3–21. On biopolitics as an intensification of disciplinary power, see Jeffrey T. Nealon, *Foucault Beyond Foucault: Power and Its Intensifications Since 1984* (Stanford: Stanford University Press, 2008), 46–7.

totalisation of control over the soldier was hardly complete by the start of the nineteenth century, but it can be seen with the introduction from the late eighteenth century of new concerns about soldiers' pensions, barracks, desertion, volunteering and education, and, as noted earlier, new theories about military discipline.[203] By addressing diverse elements of the soldier's life through their expansive concerns with personal regulations, advice and biography, the journals underpinned an emergent organic or even vitalist understanding of the soldier. The body was understood as an increasingly complex totality that presents latent capacities and internal resistance to forms of manipulation and training. In turn, the living or natural body demands ever more complete forms of training, control and government that extended far beyond anything imagined in the earliest military journals. Yet the import of the journals is that they provided an underlying infrastructure that allowed these elements to first develop.

But it is also critical to understand how new approaches to interiority and vitalism in turn shaped the subjectivity of soldiers and the related growth of autobiographical forms of military writing. Criticism of Foucault's account of military disciplinary practices have argued that he ignored the importance of pastoral care and attention to personal conduct and civic values in the training of soldiers.[204] Agamben regards this tension between domination and subjectivity as the essential 'blind spot' or 'zone of indistinction' in Foucault's thought, prompting Agamben's own turn to the study of sovereignty as the intersections of law and violence.[205] Foucault had, however, gestured towards this alternative dimension of subject formation in his subsequent work on 'governmentality' as the encounter between 'technologies of domination of others', typified by the disciplines, and what he termed 'technologies of the self', those mechanisms by which individuals worked to transform themselves.[206] Foucault proposes that we always locate these elements together because discipline always orients itself towards a degree of voluntary willingness to conform. Thomas Lemke argues that the governmental approach developed in Foucault's latter work requires us to pay equal attention to bodily and symbolic forms in the analysis of biopolitical power.[207] It is reading and

---

[203] Foucault, *Discipline and* Punish, 217.
[204] See Berkovich, *Motivation in* War and Guinier, *L'Honneur du Soldat.*
[205] Agamben, *Homo Sacer*, 6. For a discussion of Agamben's position on Foucault, see Catherine Mills, *Biopolitics* (New York: Routledge, 2018), 162.
[206] Michel Foucault, 'Technologies of the Self', in *Ethics: Subjectivity and Truth. The Essential Works of Michel Foucault, 1954–1984*, ed. Paul Rabinow, trans. Robert Hurley and others, vol. 1 (New York: The New Press, 1997), 223–51, 225.
[207] Thomas Lemke, *Foucault, Governmentality, and Critique* (New York: Routledge, 2012), 29–31.

writing that enables individuals to work on themselves, whether through reading conduct manuals, writing journals or even through the cultivation of taste and aesthetic experience.[208] Discipline thus evolves less through its institutional settings than it does by directing an individual to wholly embrace disciplinary power through the complete subjective experiences of sexuality or national service that links the individual with the surrounding socius.[209] It is, then, no coincidence that the development of disciplinary power coincides with the rise of military autobiographical writing more generally in this period. The military journals drew together disciplinary regulations with autobiographical writing to fully extend military power over life.

This concern with the self and the body highlights what Ian Hacking termed memoro-politics that he believes forms a 'third pole' in the techniques of power surrounding life and which explains the ways in which trauma develops out of the normalising or biopolitical society.[210] Originating as a military term that referred to soldiers' wounds, trauma functions like other dimensions of biopower as a shift away from a classical understanding of the human. It reflects the rise of a newly embodied science of memory that superseded an earlier *ars memoria* or the cultivation of memory that had stemmed from Plato and Aristotle to the eighteenth century.[211] Trauma refers to wounds that are not experienced consciously but, rather, have a somatic dimension that is only experienced via the unconscious through forms of repetition, flashbacks and nightmares.[212] Trauma, then, assumes its modern form as a concern with the abnormality of memory and a mechanism by which the growth of the disciplined individual can be controlled or manipulated via the body and its unconscious.[213] Although the psychological study of trauma did not properly commence until the late

---

[208] Christoph Menke, 'Two Kinds of Practice: On the Relation between Social Discipline and the Aesthetics of Existence', *Constellations* 10. No. 2 (2003): 199–210, 201.

[209] Jeffrey T. Nealon, 'The Archaeology of Biopower: From Plant to Animal life in *The Order of Things*', in *Biopower: Foucault and Beyond*, ed. Vernon W. Cisney and Nicolae Morar (Chicago: The University of Chicago Press, 2016), 138–57, 139.

[210] Ian Hacking, 'Memoro-politics, Trauma and the Soul', *History of the Human Sciences* 7, no. 2 (1994): 29–52, 35. On the biopolitics of trauma, see also Pieter Vermeulen, 'The Biopolitics of Trauma', in *The Future of Trauma Theory: Contemporary Literary and Cultural Criticism*, ed. Gert Buelens (New York: Routledge, 2014), 141–56.

[211] Hacking, 'Memoro-politics, Trauma and the Soul', 39, 46–7.

[212] On trauma, see Cathy Caruth, *Unclaimed Experience: Trauma, Narrative, and History* (Baltimore: Johns Hopkins University Press, 1996).

[213] For a discussion of Hacking that further examines the relationship between trauma and biopolitics, see Jenny Edkins, *Trauma and the Memory of Politics* (Cambridge: Cambridge University Press, 2003), 51.

nineteenth century, in line with other elements of the psy-sciences, there are earlier roots to the experience of trauma in the Romantic era concerns with soldiers' nostalgia and diffusion of mechanisms of fear and security.[214] Pieter Vermeulen proposes that the modern understanding of trauma is underpinned by the findings of the statistical surveys that were integral to the emergence of biopolitics.[215] The possibility of conceptualising trauma grew out of efforts to calculate the hidden risks that inhered within populations, as the nineteenth century saw a series of 'quasi-military' interventions into urban life that both increasingly prevented accidents and yet made accidents appear ever more cataclysmic and omnipresent when they did occur.[216] A version of this structural trauma typifies Britain during the French Revolutionary and Napoleonic Wars, as the mediation of war both underscored the conflict's distance from daily life and yet constantly subjected daily life to the fear and anxiety of imminent invasion.[217] A new veteran poetics may have emerged as a nascent literature of trauma that reveals the shock of war's pain, but read in relation to the natural body and memoro-politics, the writing of war's trauma nonetheless can also be seen to remain bounded by disciplinary concerns with governing life and its norms. Trauma shares a direct lineage with military power's burgeoning knowledge and authority over life.

Rancière proposes that disciplinary knowledge always operates by fixing an ethos upon a body to thereby establish what can be known and said about that body. Disciplines, he insists, do not simply allow thought to address a given object; they constitute that object and so operate via a partitioning of the sensible world. Disciplinary knowledge, therefore, must also disqualify other knowledge; it must ceaselessly wage a 'war' as it seeks to determine how we understand the world. The disciplined bodies that are produced through human sciences cannot freely enter into discourse to

---

[214] See Kevis Goodman, 'Romantic Poetry and the Science of Nostalgia', in *The Cambridge Companion to British Romantic Poetry*, ed. James Chandler and Maureen N. Mclane (Cambridge: Cambridge University Press, 2008), 195–216; Mary A. Favret, *War at a Distance: Romanticism and the Making of Modern Wartime* (Princeton: Princeton University Press, 2010); Lily Gurton-Wachter, *Watchwords: Romanticism and the Poetics of Attention* (Stanford: Stanford University Press, 2016).

[215] Pieter Vermeulen, 'The Biopolitics of Trauma', in *The Future of Trauma Theory: Contemporary Literary and Cultural Criticism*, ed. Gert Buelens (New York: Routledge, 2014), 141–56, 146–47.

[216] Roger Luckhurst, *The Trauma Question* (New York: Routledge, 2008), 25. Foucault argues that liberalism could only establish its concerns with freedom in conjunction with the diffusion of dangers and hence strategies for ensuring security, Michel Foucault, *Birth of Biopolitics: Lectures at the Collège de France, 1978–1979*, ed. Michel Senellart, trans. Graham Burchell (Basingstoke: Palgrave Macmillan, 2008), 65–69.

[217] Favret, *War at a Distance*, 161.

challenge the ways in which they are shaped and structured by disciplinary knowledge. Those disciplines can only perceive the subjective experience of disciplined bodies through expressions of pleasure and pain. Disciplines, in other words, can only encompass their own institutional knowledge of bodies while reducing all other speech to a simple, biological voice – an expression of the natural life of the body.[218] They cannot understand these voices as having equal claims to authority, as constituting counter-strategic discourses that could offer their own conceptions of the conduct and tele-ology of a life. By reading from this disciplinary perspective, a modern war literature that began to give voice to the pain of combat, the revelation of shock and trauma of war's suffering, nonetheless appears to simply con-firm ever more completely the military disciplinary control over war and the lives of soldiers. The expression of trauma, as Rancière intimates, can also be understood as a product of the disciplinary intervention into a life that ceaselessly reduces the power of speech to the mere, embodied voice of pain. Where we see disciplinary knowledge emerging, as Rancière notes, we always hear the 'rumble of battle' within the social arena – a battle in which discipline perpetually seeks to fix bodies to forms of knowledge and which suppresses alternative experiences by only hearing cries of pleasure and pain in those whose lives it structures.[219]

Military writing of the Romantic era wages this disciplinary war as part of an overarching apparatus of biopower that appeared in response to the demands of a nascent total war. Military writing contributed to the strategic urgency of managing the population for war, and in doing so reconceptualised the very nature of strategy, tactics and military poli-cies. The revolutions in warfare of these years may well have stood behind the sudden shift in knowledge that Foucault understands as the birth of the modern episteme of knowledge concerned with making sense of chance and complexity.[220] We can also follow Foucault's more speculative thought, however, that the modern episteme resulted from the discovery of the population and hence is intimately linked to a new apparatus of power concerned with governing life. Developing Foucault's understanding of the apparatus, Agamben defines the apparatus as 'literally anything that has in some way the capacity to capture, orient, determine, intercept, model,

---

[218] Jacques Rancière, *Disagreement: Politics and Philosophy*, trans. Julie Rose (Minneapolis: University of Minnesota Press, 2000), 22–23.
[219] Jacques Rancière, 'Thinking between Disciplines: An Aesthetics of Knowledge', trans. Jon Roffe, *Parrhesia* 1 (2006): 1–12, 9.
[220] On war, chance and complexity, see Engberg-Pedersen, *Empire of Chance*.

control, or secure the gestures, behaviors, opinions or discourses of living beings'.[221] Uniting the two elements of apparatus and living beings are subjects, which result from the 'relentless fight' by which apparatuses seek to capture and control living beings.[222] Military writing formed a central element in an emergent military apparatus of Romantic Britain because it played a key role in establishing the violent rationalities required for targeting living beings and constructing the militarised subjectivity of the soldier. As Rancière supposes, however, this subject formation must be resisted if we are to think about how to achieve emancipation from disciplinary efforts to control the ethos of a body. Modern war is also about the war that unfolds within the social body because it is first and foremost a disciplinary war of managing bodies and lives. The traumatic pain of war literature has presented this 'distant roar of battle' by giving voice to the pain of battlefield experience.[223] But examining war writing in its entirety reveals another roar of battle, the 'relentless fight' that lodges in the contests and conflicts that work within and alongside the military control of lives. It is in relation to disciplinary control over war and the resulting 'conflict of living forces' that indisciplinary work can reveal a different kind of battle beneath the surface of military writing, a battle over the formation and contestation of disciplinary knowledge and its composition of bodies and lives in line with modern rationalities of violence. This study seeks to analyse this other dimension of Romantic era war knowledge, to interrogate the formation of a biopolitics of modern war writing.

---

[221] Giorgio Agamben, *What Is an Apparatus? and Other Essays*, trans. David Kishik and Stefan Pedatella (Stanford: Stanford University Press, 2009), 14.
[222] Agamben, *What Is an Apparatus?* 14.
[223] Rancière, 'Thinking between Disciplines', 9.

CHAPTER 2

Strategy in the Age of History
Henry Lloyd's Sublime Philosophy of War

In his history of modern military thought, Azar Gat proposes that we can not only see a series of efforts to construct a 'general theory of war' since the Enlightenment, but also that this theorisation of war has been fundamentally 'culture-bound' in its conceptions.[1] What writers in the eighteenth century commonly termed the 'art of war' was, like any other art, bound by culturally specific contexts, approaches and rules of composition. Gat identifies two basic aesthetic outlooks that have informed military thought since the mid-eighteenth century. On the one hand, rationalist Enlightenment military theories developed out of eighteenth-century French neo-classical thought, primarily with the writing of Paul-Gédéon Joly de Maïzeroy, Jacques Antoine-Hippolyte, Comte de Guibert, the German theorist Dietrich Heinrich von Bülow and the most important military theorist of the nineteenth century, Antoine-Henri Jomini. Alongside this military enlightenment, however, there also emerged a set of Romantic or counter-Enlightenment military theories epitomised by the work of Carl von Clausewitz, who drew on the intellectual climate of German Romanticism through his acquaintance with August Wilhelm Schlegel and familiarity with Kant's aesthetic theories to call into question the rule bound nature of military thought.[2] Enlightenment thinkers, Gat argues, drew on neo-classical conceptions of order, rules and principles, while counter-Enlightenment thought insisted that dogmatic concentration on rules was simplistic and misguided because military genius, to follow Kant, must be free to create its own rules. Although Gat's history accounts for nearly three hundred years of military thought since the eighteenth century, he

---

[1] Azar Gat, *A History of Military Thought: From the Enlightenment to the Cold War* (Oxford: Oxford University Press, 2001), vii.

[2] Sibylle Scheipers, *On Small War: Carl von Clausewitz and People's War* (Oxford: Oxford University Press, 2018), 62–65; Peter Paret, 'The Genesis of On War', in Carl Von Clausewitz, *On War*, ed. and trans. Michael Howard and Peter Paret (Princeton: Princeton University Press, 1984), 3–25, 14.

believes that subsequent military thought remains tied to its origins in these twinned developments of the Enlightenment and Romanticism.

While there has been general agreement with Gat's view of military writing as an art form or cultural practice shaped by an aesthetic milieu, there has been little effort to analyse these cultural dimensions or to interrogate Gat's understanding of the broader Enlightenment and Romantic contexts.[3] Recent approaches to Romanticism have, notably, sought to historicise Romantic texts by revealing wide ranging shifts in historical consciousness at the end of the eighteenth century that underpinned both Enlightenment theories of progress and Romantic concerns with the hidden vitality of life.[4] Indeed, the Romantic era can be situated within a much longer development across the eighteenth century from mechanical to naturalised modes of thought associated with vitalism and sensibility.[5] Such an approach is apparent in Manuel De Landa's efforts to reconceptualise the history of military thought in relation to a broad epistemic shift from the earlier mechanistic or clockwork paradigm and towards a modern motorised paradigm associated with depth and interiority (in part he does so by re-orienting Foucault's thought on the episteme around Gilles Deleuze and Felix Guattari's analysis of the war machine).[6] If De Landa only offers a relatively brief sketch of the origins of military thought, his underlying concerns have been addressed in more recent and historically detailed studies. Anders Engberg-Pedersen offers an expansive reading of German Romantic era military authors that argues for their contribution to the underlying epistemic shift of modernity, while Christy Pichichero concentrates on the French military enlightenment and draws on recent work on the Enlightenment and print to call into question the stark divide between Romantic and Enlightenment military thought.[7]

---

[3] See, for example, John Lynn, *Battle: A History of Combat and Culture from Ancient Greece to Modern America* (New York: Westview Press, 2003).

[4] See in particular, James Chandler, *England in 1819: The Politics of Literary Culture and the Case of Romantic Historicism* (Chicago: University of Chicago Press, 1998). For an overview of this work, see Damian Walford Davies, ed., *Romanticism, History, Historicism: Essays on an Orthodoxy* (New York: Routledge, 2009).

[5] Catherine Packham, *Eighteenth-Century Vitalism: Bodies, Culture, Politics* (Basingstoke: Palgrave Macmillan, 2012); Robert Mitchell, *Experimental Life: Vitalism in Romantic Science and Literature* (Baltimore: Johns Hopkins University Press, 2013); Ildiko Csengei, *Sympathy, Sensibility and the Literature of Feeling in the Eighteenth Century* (Basingstoke: Palgrave Macmillan, 2011); Clifford Siskin and William Warner, eds, *This Is Enlightenment* (Chicago: University of Chicago Press, 2010).

[6] Manuel De Landa, *War in the Age of Intelligent Machines* (New York: Zone, 1991).

[7] Anders Engberg-Pedersen, *Empire of Chance: The Napoleonic Wars and the Disorder of Things* (Cambridge, MA: Harvard University Press, 2015); Christy Pichichero, *The Military Enlightenment: War and Culture in the French Empire from Louis XIV to Napoleon* (Ithaca: Cornell University Press, 2017).

This chapter continues such lines of thought by focussing on the most significant British author to contribute to the military enlightenment, the Welsh military officer Henry Lloyd. Although he has traditionally held only a marginal role in the history of military writing, reappraisals of Lloyd have revealed much greater complexities to his writing and demonstrated his considerable influence on subsequent military thought.[8] If in many respects his writing retains neo-classical features he nonetheless introduced an entirely new generic framework into military thought via his didactic or critical approach to military history. Developments within genres were critical to the formation of Romantic aesthetics, yet the study of genre has seldom figured in discussion of military thought. This chapter will address Lloyd's contribution by drawing on Jacques Rancière's analyses of art regimes in relation to shifting theories of genre. In particular, Rancière is concerned with what he terms the 'poetics of knowledge', an analysis of those literary forms and techniques by which a science or field of knowledge takes shape and hence is 'constituted as a specific genre of discourse'.[9] Rancière follows a traditional view of Romanticism as a break with the rigid genre system of neo-classicism, but he interprets this break in terms of the far reaching consequences of the collapse of mimesis and its representational strategies.[10] New aesthetic approaches abandoned older ideals of decorum and order as they turned attention to the hidden depths of social and historical worlds. Establishing fundamentally new relations between the visible and the sayable, the aesthetic regime is intimately associated with the appearance of new ideas about democratic politics focussed on the ordinary, mass details of life in what Rancière terms the 'age of history'.[11]

The generic innovations of Lloyd's history were of foundational importance for modern conceptions of strategy. Providing something distinct from the established form of the general's maxims and memoirs, his work broke with an earlier regime of art that found its exemplary form in the great

---

[8] Patrick Speelman, *Henry Lloyd and the Military Enlightenment of Eighteenth-Century Europe* (Westport: Greenwood Press, 2002); For recent discussions of Lloyd in relation to aesthetic concerns, see Catherine Gallagher, *Telling It Like It Wasn't: The Counterfactual Imagination in History and Fiction* (Chicago: University of Chicago Press, 2018), 29–36; and Philip Shaw, 'Longing for Home: Robert Hamilton, Nostalgia and the Emotional Life of the Eighteenth-Century Soldier', *Journal of Eighteenth-Century Studies* 39, no. 1 (2016): 25–40, 30–31.

[9] Jacques Rancière, *Names of History: On the Poetics of Knowledge*, trans. Hassan Melehy, foreword Hayden White (Minneapolis: University of Minnesota Press, 1994), 8.

[10] Jacques Rancière, *Mute Speech,* trans. James Swenson, intro. Gabriel Rockhill (New York: Columbia University Press, 2011), 8.

[11] Jacques Rancière, *Figures of History*, trans. Julie Rose (Cambridge: Polity, 2014), 21–24.

general's speech and wisdom. Undertaking, instead, an analysis of command, Lloyd develops a 'military semiology' to account for the hidden, empirical knowledge that suffuses war and its histories.[12] He moves beyond the older tradition of teaching history by example to instead interrogate the structural elements that condition and shape history. But his effort to understand the hidden details of war can also be understood as an effort to understand a newly vitalised idea of the army as a collective life. Lloyd concluded that the general's understanding of the hidden depths of collective life constituted the true philosophy of war, or what he saw as the sublime management and conduct of the military collective. Such thought on war and life would not reach its apogee until Clausewitz's concerns with the 'moral and living forces' of war, but if we are to examine the formation of military thought historically rather than transcendentally we need to examine the books that surround and lead up to *On War*, the 'great book' that defines the study of war.[13] Clausewitz clearly drew upon an intellectual environment informed by German Romanticism and Kantian aesthetic theories, but he was also in dialogue with a far broader set of developments surrounding aesthetics, vitalism and history that stretched back into the eighteenth century.[14] Lloyd represents an equally significant figure in the long development of what Rancière terms the 'silent revolution' that, this chapter argues, established the aesthetic milieu of modern military thought.[15]

The Military Enlightenment and Orders of Knowledge

As a military writer, Lloyd enjoyed a considerable prominence during the latter half of the eighteenth century and was widely acclaimed as the leading British author on war. Born in Wales in 1718, the son of a clergyman, he was unable to afford a commission in the British army after being defrauded of his inheritance and so embarked upon a career as a soldier of fortune in European armies.[16] He went on to serve with the French,

---

[12] Jacques Rancière, *The Flesh of Words: The Politics of Writing*, trans. Charlotte Mandell (Stanford: Stanford University Press, 2004), 115.

[13] Carl Von Clausewitz, *On War*, ed. and trans. Michael Howard and Peter Paret (Princeton: Princeton University Press, 1984), 86; Michel Foucault, 'Titre et Travaux', *Dits et Ecrits, vol. 1: 1954–1969*, ed. Daniel Defert and François Ewald (Paris: Gallimard, 1994), 842–46, 845.

[14] On the diversity of influences upon Clausewitz, see Sibylle Scheipers, *On Small War: Carl von Clausewitz and People's War* (Oxford: Oxford University Press, 2018), 18.

[15] Rancière, *Mute Speech*, 7.

[16] James Jay Carafano. 'Lloyd, Henry Humphrey Evans (c. 1718–1783), Army Officer and Military Writer', *Oxford Dictionary of National Biography*. 23 September 2004, https://doi-org.rp.nla.gov .au/10.1093/ref:odnb/16836, accessed 20 June 2021.

Prussian, Austrian and Russian armies, having first entered the French army staff under the patronage of the French marshal Maurice de Saxe. He also acted for a time as military tutor to Lord John Drummond, whom he accompanied on the unsuccessful Jacobite rebellion in 1745 when Drummond brought across French reinforcements from the continent. Serving as a captain in the Jacobite army and tasked with raising Welsh support for the rebellion, Lloyd was captured by the English as a spy and only released on Drummond's intercession.[17] Lloyd concluded his military career by attaining the rank of general in the Russian army, although as he was not an aristocrat he was denied the order of merit. Nonetheless, being possessed of enormous military experience and influenced by the ideas of de Saxe and the Italian Enlightenment philosopher Pietro Verri, with whom Lloyd had become acquainted after they both served together in the Austrian army, Lloyd would go on to make a considerable contribution to eighteenth-century military thought.[18] While his writing extended to essays on the English constitution, a theory of money and even an unpublished philosophical study of human nature, his reputation as a thinker rested on his military publications. This included a plan for the defence of England from French invasion and, more importantly, his *History of the Late War in Germany* on Frederick the Great's campaigns during the Seven Years War, the first volume of which was published in two parts in 1766 and 1781, while the second volume was published posthumously in 1790, several years after Lloyd's death in 1783.[19]

Widely read by other military theorists, his history prompted numerous reactions and considerable criticism. Most prominent amongst his interlocutors were Georg Friedrich von Tempelhoff and Antoine-Henri Jomini, both of whom composed histories of the Seven Years War in

---

[17] Patrick Speelman, *War, Society and Enlightenment: The Works of General Lloyd* (Leiden: Brill, 2005), xiv.

[18] *Sophus A. Reinert*, "'One Will Make of Political Economy ... What the Scholastics Have Done With Philosophy': Henry Lloyd and the Mathematization of Economics', *History of Political Economy* 39, no. 4 (2007): 643–77, 647.

[19] Henry Lloyd, *The History of the Late War in Germany; Between the King of Prussia, and the Empress of Germany and Her Allies*, vol. I (London: printed for the author; and sold by R. Horsfield, in Ludgate Street; L. Hawes and Co. in Pater-Noster Row; J. Dodsley, in Pall Mall; J. Walter, Charing Cross; T. Davies, in Covent Garden; W. Shropshire, New Bond-Street; and E. Easton, at Salisbury, 1766); Henry Lloyd, *Continuation of the History of the Late War in Germany, between the King of Prussia, and the Empress of Germany and Her Allies. Illustrated with a Number of Maps and Plans*, vol. I, Part ii (London: printed for the author, and sold by S. Hooper, the Corner of May's Buildings, St. Martin's Lane, 1781); and Henry Lloyd, *The History of the Late War in Germany, between the King of Prussia, and the Empress of Germany and Her Allies: Containing the Campaigns of 1758 and 1759*, vol. II (London: printed for T. and J. Egerton, at the military library, Whitehall, 1790). All references to Lloyd's history are featured in the body of the text.

response to Lloyd's. The Duke of Wellington and Napoleon also both read Lloyd, although Napoleon disagreed with much of what he found in the history – his copy being heavily annotated, as John Shy has noted, 'Ignorance ... Ignorance ... Absurd ... Absurd ... Impossible ... False ... Bad ... Very bad ... How absurd ... What absurdity!'.[20] Despite such criticism, Lloyd nonetheless introduced several concepts that would prove to be pivotal in the development of modern military thought.[21] His main theoretical contribution was his concept of the army's *'Line of Operation'*, his elaboration of how an army's manoeuvring forms the basis for understanding military campaigns (I.ii. 134). Lloyd did not develop the concept at great length, yet its underlying premises proved foundational for subsequent military thought, principally via Jomini's conception of strategy as a concentration of forces at a critical point.[22] Napoleon himself, for all his stated hostility, may well have employed Lloyd's theories and frequently referred to concepts such as the line of operations or lines of communication that appear derived from Lloyd.[23]

Lloyd can be understood as a highly influential military theorist of the era. His work on the threat of a French invasion of Britain was republished multiple times in Britain during the 1790s, and appeared in both French and Italian editions.[24] His history of the Seven Years War went through ten editions prior to 1808, a total that included a number of German and French translations, including five French language editions between 1784 and 1803.[25] Captain Hamilton republished Lloyd's history in 1808, because of what he felt to be its continuing relevance to the British army, the work notably being published under the authority of the Duke of York, then Commander in Chief of Britain's forces. Hamilton claimed of the book:

> Among the moderns, England may justly boast, that Lloyd was the first who wrote on war with an enlarged view of the great combination of the science. Possessing the intuitive spirit of a philosopher, and the practical knowledge of a soldier, the plan of his work is conceived with superior skill, and his reflections abound with many profound observations on the

---

[20] On Wellington's reading, see Huw J. Davies, *Spying for Wellington: British Military Intelligence in the Peninsular War* (Norman: University of Oklahoma Press, 2018), 47; Napoleon's comments on Lloyd are quoted in John Shy, 'Jomini', in *Makers of Modern Strategy from Machiavelli to the Nuclear Age*, ed. Paret Peter, with contributions from Gordon A. Craig and Felix Gilbert (Princeton: Princeton University Press, 1986), 143–85, 149.

[21] See Speelman, *Henry Lloyd and the Military Enlightenment*, 110–11.

[22] Speelman, *War, Society and Enlightenment*, 6–7.

[23] Speelman, *Henry Lloyd and the Military Enlightenment*, 114.

[24] Speelman, *War, Society and Enlightenment*, 329.

[25] Speelman, *War, Society and Enlightenment*, 7–8.

principles of war, and the causes of success and misfortune. He was the first who displayed great views on lines of operations and strategical movements; but his genius appears most conspicuous in his system of battles. Unfortunately for those who study the profession, he has not minutely developed nor generalized his ideas; and his judgment, upon particular facts, is sometimes in seeming contradiction with his own maxims. But, notwithstanding these defects, his reflections on the battle of Leuthen bespeak the superiority of his talents; and while his chapter on the philosophy of war, adorns the memory of his moral qualifications; the discovery of the important truth, that the operations of war can be reduced to simple and incontestable principles, will remain a lasting monument of his genius.[26]

Lloyd was consequently the first military writer to move beyond what Hamilton regarded as the dogmatic systems of tactics that preoccupied earlier military thinkers such as Guibert.[27] Lloyd adopts an 'enlarged view' of war because he concentrated on the question of how to use or manoeuvre an entire army, thereby superseding earlier questions of how to arrange or form the components of an army.[28] His history is almost entirely composed as a detailed description of the contending armies' manoeuvres on campaign with little concern for extraneous matters such as the political objectives surrounding the war. He explains the routes armies took to traverse the country, the locations of their encampments and defensive positions, and the manner in which the armies approached one another in the lead up to their battles. He also, however, combines his descriptions with his analysis of these military manoeuvres to derive insights into how best to wage a military campaign. It is in this sense that Hamilton considers Lloyd a philosopher, because Lloyd attempts to elucidate the 'incontestable principles' of war and was the first to offer serious thought on 'lines of operations and strategical movements'.[29]

Because he is concerned with elucidating underlying principles, Lloyd has been commonly understood as extending the work of earlier thinkers of the military enlightenment who sought to establish 'rules and principles of universal validity' for understanding the art of war.[30] For Gat, the military enlightenment was based in earlier neo-classical military thought that had been concerned principally with the spatial arrangement and ordering of

---

[26] *The History of the Seven Years' War in Germany, by Generals Lloyd and Tempelhoff; with Observations and Maxims Extracted from the Treatise of Great Military Operations of General Jomini. Translated from the German and French by C H Smith* (London: [1808]), I.vi–vii.

[27] *The History of the Seven Years' War in Germany*, I.vi.

[28] Gat, *A History of Military Thought*, 75; 80.

[29] *The History of the Seven Years' War in Germany*, I.vi.

[30] Gat, *A History of Military Thought*, 68.

troop formations. Neo-classical military thought drew on the precepts of geometry that assumed space was isotropic, homogeneous in all directions, and so uniformly determined by mathematical laws.[31] A disembodied and abstract view of war governed neo-classicism, which imagined the army as a kind of Newtonian machine reducible to homologous arrangements of soldiers and their carefully calculated movements.[32] The military enlightenment of the mid-eighteenth century continued this geometrical analysis, but it extended its application beyond the arrangement of battlefield formations.[33] This was first seen with the influence of geometry on gunnery and fortifications in Sébastien le Prestre de Vauban's *De l'Attaque et de la Defenses des Places* (1737). By conceptualising fortresses in relation to a series of geometrical figures, Vauban had in effect reduced siege warfare to a science that could be undertaken with an almost clockwork precision.[34] The clear success of Vauban's methods of fortification in turn led to efforts to apply the certainty, order and underlying spatiality of his geometrical approach to understanding the arts of war more generally.[35] While Jacques François de Chastenet de Puységur was the first to attempt this expansion of Vauban's geometrical approach to war more generally, Count Turpin de Crissé developed this much further by conceptualising an entire military campaign as a regularised sequence of events that proceeded much like the conduct of a siege.[36] The geometric approach to the arts of the general reached its apogee, however, with Adam Heinrich Dietrich, Baron von Bülow, for whom strategic thought could be entirely explained through geometrical precepts.[37]

With the first volume of Lloyd's *History* appearing more or less contemporaneously with the work of Turpin de Crissé, military historians have traditionally regarded Lloyd as an exemplary figure of the neo-classical military enlightenment and the effort to apply the geometric certainties of a siege to the waging of an entire campaign. Turpin de Crissé's descriptions of military operations conforms with the shifting use of the term 'campaign', which had lost its earlier association with the seasonality of war to simply mean taking

[31] Mary Poovey, *Making a Social Body: British Cultural Formation, 1830–1864* (Chicago: University of Chicago Press, 1995), 28–30.

[32] Christophe Wasinski, 'On Making War Possible: Soldiers, Strategy, and Military Grand Narrative', *Security Dialogue*, 42, no. 1 (2011): 57–76, 61.

[33] Gat, *A History of Military Thought*, 37.

[34] Gat, *A History of Military Thought*, 37.

[35] Janis Langins, *Conserving the Enlightenment: French Military Engineering from Vauban to the Revolution* (Cambridge, MA: MIT Press, 2004), 203.

[36] Armstrong Starkey, *War in the Age of Enlightenment, 1700–1789* (London: Greenwood Publishing Group, 2003), 38; Gat, *A History of Military Thought*, 39.

[37] Hew Strachan, 'The Lost Meaning of Strategy' *Survival*, 47, no. 3 (2005), 33–54, 35.

the field in the summer, to be almost exclusively used to refer to a military operation as a coherent whole, 'an expedition or continuous series of operations bearing upon a distinct object'.[38] In his reflections on the line of operations, Lloyd was one of the first writers to utilise this conception of the campaign as a united series of events under the strategic control of the general. But he also moves beyond earlier approaches that modelled the campaign on the certainties and regularity of the siege. While it is true that the line of operations still suggests an affiliation with the geometrical or mechanical controlling schema of the early modern era, Lloyd believed that only siege warfare was 'purely geometrical' (vol. I.ii. xxi).[39] Gat concedes, albeit in passing, that Lloyd is more properly considered a spatial rather than a strictly geometrical military thinker, a point underlined by the inclusion of numerous maps in Lloyd's history or what the editor of his history's second volume termed 'Topographical Illustrations' (vol. II. vii).[40] Engberg-Pedersen notes that the military term 'terrain' underwent a radical transformation in the second half of the eighteenth century, from describing the area surrounding a fortress to mean the entirety of the 'topographical space' in which war is fought. The space of a campaign was no longer simply conceptualised as geometrical and homogeneous but was becoming vectoral, premised on temporality, resistance and specificity.[41] In his emphasis on topographical illustration, Lloyd played a key role in these developments. He dispensed with the framework of a siege to introduce a new kind of understanding of military campaigns as a series of movements within specific terrains.

In addition, Armstrong Starkey observes that Lloyd's thought exhibits a range of concerns with human passions that extend beyond an earlier mechanical understanding of the human.[42] In part reflecting the influence of de Saxe on Lloyd, Patrick Speelman further emphasises this aspect of Lloyd's

---

[38] 'campaign, n.', *OED Online*, June 2021 (Oxford: Oxford University Press, 2019), www.oed.com/view/Entry/26752?rskey=xpncgO&result=1&isAdvanced=false, accessed 18 August 2021.

[39] Bousquet, *The Scientific Way of Warfare*, 37; and Gros, *States of Violence*, 54–56.

[40] Gat, *A History of Military Thought*, 130–31. Jomini quite pointedly rejects the assumption that war might be reduced to geometry, adding that Napoleon's campaigns appeared to 'belong more to the domain of poetry than to that of the exact sciences', Henri-Antoine Jomini, *Summary of the Art of War, or a New Analytical Compend of the Principal Combinations of Strategy, of Grand Tactics and of Military Policy*, trans. O. F. Winship, and E. E. McLean (New York: Published for the Proprietors, by G. P. Putnam & Co., 10 Park Place, 1854), 134.

[41] Engberg-Pedersen, *Empire of Chance*, 43–44. The first use of 'terrain' in English in the modern sense is dated to 1766 in the *Oxford English Dictionary*, the same year as the first volume of Lloyd's history, 'terrain, n. and adj.', *OED Online*, June 2021 (Oxford: Oxford University Press, 2019), www.oed.com/view/Entry/199501?redirectedFrom=terrain, accessed 18 August 2021.

[42] Starkey, *War in the Age of Enlightenment*, 59–60.

work by tracing the roots of what he terms Lloyd's 'military sociology' into his adaptation of Montesquieu's political thought. He thereby aligns Lloyd with the similar development of Montesquieu by mid-eighteenth-century Scottish Enlightenment thinkers such as Adam Smith and Adam Ferguson, who elaborated an embryonic human sciences through their reflections on political economy and civil society.[43] Although Lloyd was not directly involved with the Scottish Enlightenment, he had fought alongside Charles Stuart in the unsuccessful Jacobite rebellion, the defeat of which may have been foundational to the way Scottish Enlightenment thought theorised the historical development of societies and their relation to war.[44] So too, far from neo-classicism entirely dominating arts of the era, new aesthetic models appeared in mid-century Britain with Edmund Burke's theorisation of the sublime and Alexander Gerard's reflections on genius that were of enormous influence upon the early development of aesthetic thought and which leave traces in Lloyd's concerns with sublimity and genius.[45] Lloyd's thought is as much oriented towards a late Enlightenment moment that rejected the mechanical in a turn to the historical and naturalistic, the formation even of a new poetics of knowledge altogether surrounding military thought.

A Critical History of War

In combining history with philosophical reflections on the art of war, Lloyd was elaborating a new generic mode for the development of military thought. Lloyd's history, it must be admitted, provided a far from complete account of the Seven Years War. The first volume only covered Frederick's campaigns in 1756 and 1757, the second his campaigns in 1758–59. Lloyd had intended to expand his history beyond the war in Germany to cover campaigns in Portugal and elsewhere, but he died before completing the second volume, which was prepared for publication by his editor, Lord Fielding.[46]

---

[43] Speelman, *Henry Lloyd and the Military Enlightenment*, 66–67; and Speelman, *War, Society and Enlightenment*, 380. On the Scottish Enlightenment thought and the formation of human sciences, see Johan Heilbron, Lars Magnusson and Björn Wittrock, eds, *The Rise of the Social Sciences and the Formation of Modernity* (Dordrecht: Kluwer Academic Publishers, 1998), 10–12.

[44] Reinhart Koselleck, *The Practice of Conceptual History: Timing History, Spacing Concepts*, trans. by Todd Samuel Presner et al. (Stanford: Stanford University Press, 2002), 80.

[45] For an overview of aesthetic thought in Britain during these years, see Paul Guyer, *A History of Modern Aesthetics. Volume 1: The Eighteenth Century* (Cambridge: Cambridge University Press, 2014), 95–243.

[46] On Fielding's involvement, see Henry Lloyd, *A Political and Military Rhapsody, on the Invasion and Defence of Great Britain and Ireland. Illustrated with three copper-plates. By the Late General Lloyd. To Which is Annexed, a Short Account of the Author, and a Supplement by the Editor* (London: Sold by Debret, Piccadilly; Sewell, Cornhill; Clark, Lincoln's Inn; and Mayler, Bath, 1792), v.

Lloyd's was far from being the only history of the Seven Years War to appear in the wake of the conflict, Hamish Scott observing that this was the first war with its own historiography.[47] Although the majority of these histories were published in the victor nations of Britain and Prussia, the conflict attracted considerable attention from French authors, such as Guibert, who saw Frederick's new tactical innovations 'as the most remarkable in the science of war'.[48] Reinhart Koselleck has proposed that it was in attempts to grapple with the unprecedented nature of the Seven Years War that a modern form of historical consciousness first appeared.[49] He argues that the vast scale of the wars, widely regarded today as the first global or world war, meant that historians were unable to rely on individual witnesses to make sense of the conflict and so were forced to turn to abstractions to deduce deeper, underlying causes.[50] Summarising developments within historiography of the latter half of the eighteenth century, he states:

> This is especially clear in the case of the Seven Years' War. The only problem was that the motivating factors underlying events escaped the direct experience of those individually affected. The overall concatenation of events could no longer be dealt with in an annalistic manner; a higher degree of abstraction was demanded of historians to compensate for the disappearance of direct experience.[51]

Koselleck argues that the long-standing classical articulation of a division between history and poetry collapsed in the aftermath of the war. As defined by Aristotle, and by extension neo-classical thinkers of the seventeenth and eighteenth centuries, history related the disorderly narrative of empirical facts, while poetry elucidated the causal logic governing historical facts.[52] The two forms reflected an elementary distinction between the accidental and the universal, with the accidents of history traditionally relegated to a secondary status beneath the generalisations and coherence of poetry. The

---

[47] Hamish Scott, 'The Seven Years' War and Europe's Ancien Régime', *War in History* 18, no. 4 (November 2011): 419–55, 428.

[48] *A General Essay on Tactics. With an Introductory Discourse upon the Present State of Politics and the Military Science in Europe. To which is Prefixed a Plan of a Work, Entitled, The Political and Military System of France. Translated from the French of M. Guibert. By an Officer* (London: Printed for J. Millan, opposite the Admiralty, Whitehall, 1781), l.

[49] Reinhart Koselleck, *Futures Past: On the Semantics of Historical Time*, trans. and intro. Keith Tribe (New York: Columbia University Press, 2004, 244.

[50] On the vast scale and impact of the Seven Years War, see Scott, 'The Seven Years' War and Europe's Ancien Régime', in Mark Danley and Patrick Speelman, eds, *The Seven Years' War: Global Views* (Leiden: Brill, 2012).

[51] Koselleck, *Futures Past*, 244.

[52] Rancière, *The Politics of Aesthetics*, trans. and intro. Gabriel Rockhill (London: Continuum, 2004), 36–38.

reconceptualisation of history that Koselleck detects with the Seven Years War was typified by a merging of the two forms. Novelists turned to realism while historians absorbed elements of poetry into their writing as they elaborated a conception of historical meaning, order and form:

> One of the properties of the eighteenth-century experiential shift, in which history was formulated in terms of a new reflexive concept, was that the line dividing the camps of historians and creative writers became osmotically porous. It was demanded of the writer, especially the writer of novels, that he articulate historical reality if he wished to be convincing and have influence. On the contrary, the historian was asked to render plausible the possibility of his history through the use of theories, hypothesis, and reasoning. Like the writer, he was to distil from his history its meaningful unity.[53]

Koselleck proposes that one way this change can be seen is in the downgrading of annalistic histories. It was no coincidence, he insists, that modern journalism progressed so markedly during the latter half of the eighteenth century as it filled the role left by the disappearance of the annalistic record of history.[54] What is more, writing itself became increasingly crucial to the formation of history as the failure of direct experience also meant that poetic theorisation of historical causality was dependent upon the interpretation and analysis of other historical writing.[55]

This shift in how history was written in response to the scale of the Seven Years War is most clearly visible in Lloyd's generic experimentation that interlaced a history of the war with analysis of the underlying principles of waging war. Lloyd explains in the preface to his *History* that he aims to draw together the best methodological elements from both historical and what he terms didactic approaches to writing on war. He provides what he considered a far more detailed and exact history than any former accounts of war, while simultaneously insisting that only in this detailed historical account can the 'rules and precepts' of war be elucidated (vol. I.ii. ii). He describes his work as following a 'new plan', in which:

> He proposes to give a clear and exact account of the most essential transactions which have occurred during the course of this important war. These will serve as a basis and foundation upon which he will write a commentary, wherein the various principles of war will be occasionally explained. (vol. I.ii. iii)

---

[53] Koselleck, *Futures Past*, 206.
[54] Koselleck, *Futures Past*, 245.
[55] On the emergence of this network of military texts, see Wasinski, 'On Making War Possible', 65.

Lloyd explains that he has written his history 'so that the reader may be able to form a proper judgment' of the military operations and battles of the contending generals in the war (vol. I. 47). This means that he eschews much of the nationalist bias and lengthy accounts of political or legal frameworks apparent in his contemporaries' writing, accounts that often sought to explain and defend the essential justice of the war and which left the narrative embedded within what Foucault terms a juridical model of history.[56] Lloyd still provides extensive background information on the political ambitions of each of the states involved in the war, but he nonetheless clearly strives to remove his analysis of war from politics and into a specifically military sphere, adopting, as Catherine Gallagher has noted, a synoptical overview of the events of the war.[57]

As such, Lloyd seeks to systematically assess the relative significance of different decisions made by generals on campaign. Although his primary contribution to the history of strategic thought was his attempt to evaluate the actions of generals via the concept of line of operations, he only defined the concept in his ancillary writing on invasion. Nonetheless, the concept is exemplified in his history as he focusses on the movement, supply and arrangements of the contending armies, armies existing for Lloyd like travellers who move between points within a country.[58] For example, he observes of the closing movements of the campaigns in 1756:

> Having neglected to occupy the defiles leading to Pirna, it became impossible to relieve the Saxons, at least on the left of the Elbe; because twelve or fifteen battalions, which the king posted any where between Lowositz and Pirna, could not be forced by an attack on their front; and, if you attempted to turn their right-wing, by sending a corps over the mountains at Altenberg, it is so far off that the enemy might, either from his troops in Bohemia, or from those in Saxony, anticipate you. We cannot, therefore, conceive why marshal Brown did not occupy some of these defiles, as, in our opinion, the success of this campaign, and perhaps of the war, depended on this step. (vol. I. 22)

---

[56] See, for example, Oliver Goldsmith, *The Martial Review; Or, a General History of the Late Wars; Together with the Definitive Treaty, and Some Reflections on the Probable Consequences of the Peace* (London: printed for J. Newbery, in St. Paul's Church-Yard, 1763). On the juridicial model of history, see Michel Foucault, *Society Must be Defended: Lectures at the Collège de France, 1975–1976*, trans. David Macey (London: Penguin Books, 2004), 79–80; 168–69.

[57] Catherine Gallagher, 'The Formalism of Military History', *Representations* 104 (fall 2008): 23–33, 26.

[58] Henry Lloyd, *A Political and Military Rhapsody, on the Invasion and Defence of Great Britain and Ireland. Illustrated with Three Copper-plates. By the late General Lloyd. To Which is Annexed, a Short Account of the Author, and a Supplement by the Editor. The Second Edition. With Additions and Improvements* (London: 1792), 35.

Obviously, histories of war had always described the movements of the contending armies. But Lloyd saw the army's movements as virtually the sole factor determining the outcomes of a war.[59] In his account of movements around Pirna, Marshal Brown's decision on the placement of his troops, the covering of a defile that would limit the movements of the Prussians, Lloyd reveals what he takes to be the key to the success of the campaign, even the success of the whole war. The outcome of the war, from Lloyd's perspective, can be almost entirely explained through analysis of the manoeuvres of the contending armies. Contemporary histories to that of Lloyd continued to focus as much on political as strictly military concerns, meaning that their descriptions of campaigns and battles lacked this consistent analytical focus on the movements of the armies. Often little more than chronologies of events, they could at times ascribe equal analytical importance to the army's movements, morale, fortitude, politics and even treasonous behaviour. Asking why General Braddock's attack on the fort du Quesne in 1755 was unsuccessful, the author of *An Impartial History of the Late War* (1763), John Almon, simply concluded that there had been 'much inquiry and animated debate', while the officers involved charged their soldiers with cowardice.[60] At one point the author of *An Impartial History of the Late Glorious War* (1764) breaks his narrative of the contending armies' operations to describe a Native American fighter vaulting over a barricade to kill a French soldier and take his musket, using the narrative to exemplify the fighting style and spirit of Native Americans.[61] Lloyd deliberately excludes such reasoning and material from his discussions. While observing that there were many skirmishes of light troops during the winter of 1756–57, for example, he pointedly declines to analyse these engagements because from his perspective they 'have little or no influence on the success of war' (vol. I. 27).[62]

---

[59]   Gat, *A History of Military Thought*, 75.

[60]   John Almon, *An Impartial History of the Late War. Deduced from the Committing of Hostilities in 1749, to the Signing of the Definitive Treaty of Peace in 1763* (London: printed for J. Johnson, opposite the Monument; and J. Curtis, in Fleet-Street, 1763), 77.

[61]   *An Impartial History of the Late Glorious War, from it's Commencement to it's Conclusion [sic]; Containing an Exact Account of the Battles and Sea Engagements; Together with Other Remarkable Transactions, in Europe, Asia, Africa, and America: with the Characters of those Wise and Upright Statesmen, who Plann'd, and the Illustrious Heroes, by Whose Courage and Conduct, Together with the Unparallell'd Bravery of our Land and Sea Forces, Great-Britain Obtained a Series of Victories, Scarcely Equalled in the Annals of this, or any other Nation. With Remarks on the Peace, the State of Parties when it was Concluded, and An Account of the Inhabitants, Extent, Product, Trade and Importance, of the Places Ceded to Great-Britain* (Manchester: Printed by R. Whitworth, 1764), 16.

[62]   Although, as Hamilton points out, he is not always consistent; for example, see vol. 2, p. 18 where he states that the Austrians gained 'considerable advantage' from the number of their light troops.

Focussing on operational movements, Lloyd also develops a vastly more detailed account of the events and location of the various campaigns. As he states of his writing:

> Those historians, both ancient and modern, who have given us an account of different wars, though in many respects extremely valuable, are not as accurate as they might, and ought to be.
>
> They do not describe, with sufficient precision and exactness, the countries wherein the wars were carried on, nor the particular spots upon which some great transaction happened; the number, species, and quality of the troops which composes the respective armies are generally omitted. (vol. I. ii. ii)

Lloyd not only consistently provides official figures for the relative strengths of the contending armies, but he also makes precise assessments of how many soldiers might be required to defend or be supplied by a province. He finely tunes numbers to his analysis of events and explanations of the rationales behind commanders' decisions. He can judge the propriety of Marshal Brown's efforts to defend Prague by comparing the failure of his 50,000 Austrian defenders with Marshal Belleisle's successful defence of the city some years earlier with only 15,000 (vol. I. 59). Alternatively, Rosbach is a decisive battle because of the vast discrepancy in casualties, 300 Prussian killed and wounded against 800 French killed and 6,000 taken prisoner (vol. I. 97). Aligning with a broader concern for statistics that underpinned late Enlightenment thought on the social, the individual soldier operates for Lloyd as something like a unit of analysis in calculating the effectiveness of strategic decisions.

So too, far more precise geographical descriptions appear in Lloyd than in his contemporaries' histories, his accounts functioning as highly detailed topographical figurations of war. Partly this is conveyed through Lloyd's use of maps that were not only extremely detailed, but which also showed the sequential movements of forces during battles and to which he makes frequent references within his history. For example, Lloyd takes painstaking care in his descriptions of how the armies were situated within their environments in his account of the Battle of Kolin:

> the right of the infantry, was posted on a high hill, quite close to an open wood occupied by the light troops. At a small distance before the front was the village of Krzeczor, in which some battalions were placed very properly, as they could with ease be sustained by the line. The hill, on which this village stands, presents, towards the right, very high and steep precipices, which cannot be passed by any species of troops. At the bottom of this hill is another village, which was likewise occupied by some infantry. Out of the hill, a little behind this last village, runs a rivulet almost perpendicular

to the enemy's line; the banks of it are very high and craggy. Behind this
rivulet Nadasti's corps was at first placed, and then in [map reference] F. F.
so that the enemy could not advance to attack the line, without presenting
his flank to this corps. (vol. I. 62–63)

References to geographical features are obviously not absent from his contemporaries' histories of the war, but they are not documented with the
detail or close relation to operations that characterise Lloyd's history. John
Entick provides an account of the Battle of Kolin, in his *General History of
the Late War* (1763), that describes the Austrian position by simply stating
that the ground was almost inaccessible owing to 'difficult defiles at the foot
of the hills', a comment that leads to his broader speculation on the moral
qualities of the Prussian soldiers.[63] In Lloyd's history there is a thickening
and proliferation of such geographic details, which no longer function as
generalisations because they demonstrate a continuous, precise and carefully assessed series of effects upon events. Hence, the reader is invited to
consider Lloyd's narrative in relation to the map reference at F.F., which
reveals the precise movement of forces across the ground. The effect is to
build a picture in which events and actions are unable to be understood
except in relation to the specific terrain within which they occur.

While building a detailed account of history and focussing on the
manoeuvres of the armies, Lloyd also proceeds by constantly referring his
reader to his judgements on what the various generals ought to have done to
achieve success. Lloyd's history stands in relation to an ideal that allows the
reader to form a 'proper judgement' (vol. I. ii). This means, however, that
his painstakingly reproduced empirical details are matched in his history
with what Catherine Gallagher describes as his stock-in-trade of theoretical
reflection and a technique that came to dominate military history written
in this mould: the use of counterfactual speculation around military operations.[64] Counterfactuals work against what we know of history by presenting

---

[63] John Entick, *The General History of the Late War: Containing it's Rise, Progress, and Event, in
Europe, Asia, Africa, and America* [sic]. *And Exhibiting the State of the Belligerent Powers at the
Commencement of the War; Their Interests and Objects in it's Continuation* [sic]; *and Remarks on the
Measures, which Led Great Britain to Victory and Conquest. Interspersed with the Characters of the
Able and Disinterested Statesmen, to Whose Wisdom and Integrity, and of the Heroes, to Whose Courage
and Conduct, We are Indebted for that Naval and Military Success, which is Not to Be Equalled in the
Annals of This, or of Any Other Nation. And with Accurate Descriptions of the Seat of War, the Nature
and Importance of our Conquests, and of the Most Remarkable Battles by Sea and Land. Illustrated with
a Variety of Heads, Plans, Maps, and Charts, Designed and Engraved by the Best Artists.... By the Rev.
John Entick, M.A. and Other Gentlemen.* 5 Vols (London: 1763), II.251.

[64] Gallagher, 'The Formalism of Military History', 26.

alternative historical outcomes on the premise of what might, could or should have happened. Reflecting on the operations in the days leading up the Battle of Leuthen, Lloyd criticises the Austrians for not having taken advantage of the Schweidnitz river as a defence against the Prussians:

> Having passed the Schweidnitz the 4th, they were informed the enemy was advancing towards them; Why not instantly repass that river, and put it before them, rather than behind? Though this river is but small, yet its banks, for the most part, are very marshy; insomuch that an army cannot pass it without the greatest difficulty, and scarce at all if they meet with any opposition. If the Austrians had done this, and have sent a strong corps higher up on their left flank, with their light troops on the same side as the enemy, on the road that leads to Striegau, we do not think his majesty would have attempted to pass the river; and, if he did, the corps above mentioned would have been on his flank during the passage and the action; and, as they were much stronger than he was, having their army covered by the Schweidnitz, they could have posted 20,000 men on their flank; which would have made it impossible for the enemy to pass the river. He would, therefore, in all probability, have marched to Striegau, in order to bring the Austrians from their advantageous situation, by endeavouring to cut off their communication with Bohemia. In this case, the corps, posted, as we suppose, on their left, would have been at Striegau before the enemy; and the whole army must have marched behind Schweidnitz with the right at Hohen Giersdorff, and the left towards Friberg; which would have secured the road by Landshut to Bohemia, and their communication with that country. (vol. I. 137)

Here he runs to several orders of counterfactual distance from the historical events – the redeployed Austrians would have rendered it impossible for the Prussians to cross the Schweidnitz river and so instead, 'in all probability', they would have marched to Striegau to cut off the Austrians' communication. The counterfactual allows Lloyd to isolate and highlight the key elements that determined outcomes, namely the importance of the armies' operational movements and the line of operations linking the armies to their communications and supply. The counterfactual enables him to construct a viewpoint that moves his history into a far greater abstraction or distillation of meaning.

Niall Ferguson has proposed that the counterfactual mediates between contingency and determination in understanding historical causality. Although counterfactuals do not assume an underlying or overarching law of history, they do allow speculation on causation and so avoid seeing history as a merely random accretion of events. As Ferguson states, 'if we want to say anything about causation in the past without invoking covering laws, we really have to use counterfactuals, if only to test our causal hypotheses'.[65] Ferguson's assertions have been questioned, in part because it is arguably possible to use counterfactuals to shore up a deterministic understanding of history. Nonetheless, the counterfactual encourages probabilistic thinking by highlighting significant details and demonstrating where random deviations occur from expected norms.[66] Gallagher assumes a similar position when she situates the counterfactual against deterministic understandings of history.[67] While she associates such determinism with Koselleck, it was in relation to war that Koselleck himself had adopted a more qualified view of historical determinism. He proposes that history can be divided between accounts of the victors and the vanquished, with the former supporting a view of history in terms of the unique and decisive actions that led to victory and the latter framing an understanding of the long term structural undercurrents that had inexorably led to defeat.[68] Koselleck points to the Battle of Leuthen as exemplary of the aporetic tensions that exist between events and structures as historical explanations – Frederick's victory could not be entirely explained with recourse to underlying structural elements, but neither was it entirely unrelated to the surrounding military or political contexts.[69] Lloyd's account of the battle demonstrates how the counterfactual operates as a third term between structure and event that attempts to make sense of this aporia by examining the underlying conditions that establish victory and defeat. For Lloyd, counterfactual speculation is always underpinned by questions of what is probable or most likely in the manoeuvres and success of the armies that enable his history to reveal and interrogate underlying principles as much as it explicitly deploys those principles to make sense of events. Lloyd deduces what Jomini saw as his most significant principle from his account of the Battle of Leuthen: that a good general will bring more numbers to bear at the critical point (vol. I. 139). If, as Engberg-Pedersen has argued, Clausewitz's thought on war culminates with his systematisation of military campaigns around mathematical probability, a probabilistic approach has some basis in the underlying generic framework by which Lloyd drew together history and theory.[70]

[65] Niall Ferguson, 'Virtual History: Towards a "Chaotic" Theory of the Past', in *Virtual History: Alternatives and Counterfactuals*, ed. Niall Ferguson (New York: Basic Books, 1999), 1–90, 81.

[66] Paul Schuurman, 'What-If at Waterloo. Carl von Clausewitz's Use of Historical Counterfactuals in his History of the Campaign of 1815', *Journal of Strategic Studies* 40, no. 7 (2017): 1–23, 11–12.

[67] Gallagher, *Telling It Like It Wasn't*, 26.

[68] Koselleck, *The Practice of Conceptual History*, 76–83.

[69] Koselleck, *The Practice of Conceptual History*, 125; Koselleck, *Futures Past*, 110.

[70] Engberg-Pedersen, *Empire of Chance*, 56–61.

The Age of History and the Principles of War

Although Lloyd's didactic, or critical, military history provided a strikingly new generic approach, his writing has nonetheless more commonly been viewed as adhering to an earlier set of neo-classical artistic principles concerned with identifying universal rules or principles of war.[71] This neo-classical approach, Gat argues, would not be reconfigured until the Romantic theories of Georg Heinrich von Berenhorst and, more importantly, Clausewitz, who drew upon Kantian aesthetics to argue that military genius does not follow rules but creates rules and thereby produces unexpected results. However, to delimit Lloyd's work as neo-classical, and so as overtly geometrical in its conception, does not account for the significance of his generic experimentation that profoundly influenced subsequent military thinkers. Of critical importance is that Lloyd reorders an established hierarchy of genres surrounding the history of war and so rescinds any simple notion that history teaches by example. Despite his writing still retaining neo-classical elements, it also puts into question this classical inheritance, which continued to teach military command by maxim and example rather than the interpretation of history. While Lloyd's work does not completely break with a neo-classical aesthetic, therefore, it can be understood in terms of Koselleck's argument that the historiography of the Seven Years War marks a rupture in historical consciousness that aligns with an emerging conception of aesthetics. Lloyd's theorisation of war operates within a new aesthetic that finds its roots less in the geometrical and mechanical than in naturalised modes of thought concerned with the empirical and the organic.

Echoing Koselleck's thought on historiographical change in the latter half of the eighteenth century, Rancière has also drawn attention to the collapse of the Aristotelian distinction between the poetic and the historical.[72] Unlike Koselleck, Rancière does not explain this with explicit reference to the Seven Years War. He does, however, offer a similar conception to Koselleck of how a new kind of relationship between representation and history originated in the political and military spheres during the eighteenth century.[73] For Rancière, modes of representation are bound by distinct regimes of the arts that determine the way in which a given era conceptualises the nature

[71] See Gat, *A History of Military Thought*, 72.
[72] Jacques Rancière, *The Politics of Aesthetics: The Distribution of the Sensible*, trans. with an intro. by Gabriel Rockhill and an afterword by Slavoj Žižek (London: Continuum, 2004), 35–41.
[73] Jacques Rancière, 'Aesthetics and Politics Revisited: An Interview with Jacques Rancière', interviewed Gavin Arnall, Laura Gandolfi and Enea Zaramella, *Critical Inquiry* 38 (Winter 2012): 289–97.

and practice of art and writing.[74] Such regimes are not simply composed of a set of rules by which art is produced, but represent the ways in which art is embedded within social worlds. Regimes of art account for the norms, assumptions and practices of composition; they determine the specific forms by which speakers address different audiences and the ways in which language and meaning are understood to relate to the world. In sum, regimes of art are characterised by distinct regimes of political visibility and social decorum that structure questions of what we might say about the world, how we might say it and to whom we might speak. The neo-classical representative regime of the arts of the seventeenth and eighteenth centuries is grounded in a history of the great deeds of men of action that are recounted in narratives designed to pass the lessons of history on to other great men.[75] Of critical importance is what Aristotle terms the '*inventio*', the intellectual or rational dimension of art, over the '*dispositio*' and the '*elocutio*', or material and formal elements, and hence the central significance of the story itself over how it is told.[76] All representational form is exemplified, in this regime, by the importance of narratives that operate within a community of great men and their decisive, commanding and exemplary actions.

Any given regime of the arts is not without contradictions, however, because the effort to ensure the appropriate visibility of certain subjects equally requires that a vast amount of the social world be ignored or rendered invisible.[77] In the hierarchical ordering of the representative regime much must be excised from any account of great actions to make them appear intelligible, whether characters cast into minor genres or ordinary details of life simply omitted. A crucial element of Rancière's thought is that art regimes do not simply replace one another, but always overlap and are themselves divided by contradictions, albeit one or another regime rises to dominance at any given time in history, in part by resolving the contradictions of an earlier regime. This can be seen in the way the representative regime lost ground to what Rancière terms the aesthetic regime that assumed dominance at the end of the eighteenth century and, in various ways, continues today. Although Rancière regards Friedrich Schiller's *Letters on Aesthetic Education* (1794) as a defining document of this new regime, he associates the regime's appearance with a long 'silent revolution' that stretched across the latter half of the eighteenth century and accordingly includes,

---

[74] Rancière, *The Politics of Aesthetics*, 20.
[75] Rancière, *Mute Speech*, 47.
[76] Rancière, *Mute Speech*, 49.
[77] Rancière, *Mute Speech*, 51.

for example, Johann Joachim Winckelman's review of the Belvedere torso from 1764.[78] Art and literature in their modern forms relinquish mimetic representation and a genre system preoccupied with the correct ordering and decorum of the world, to offer instead a revelation of the world's underlying equality and expressivity.[79] Genres collapse and intermingle as anything and everything becomes capable of expressing meaning, a development that fundamentally displaces the centrality of heroic action and oratory. Rather than represent the decorum of a community of great actors and their speech, writing assumes an anonymous and democratic equality in which anyone or anything is privileged to 'speak'.

This aesthetic shift does not simply concern fine arts, however, but is as much embedded in new approaches to history.[80] The modern era of the aesthetic regime equally figures as what Rancière terms an 'age of history' because modern historical writing is itself governed by 'Romantic poetics'.[81] Here Rancière echoes similar accounts by Koselleck and Foucault on the role of historicism in the formation of knowledge at the end of the eighteenth century. Modern forms of disciplinary knowledge coalesced around the loquacious hidden inner forces of objects of study rather than conform to a taxonomic arrangement of order that shaped neo-classical knowledge. Rancière describes this change as the merging together of two approaches to history based on what he terms documents and monuments. Documents represent those forms of writing by which the archivists, ambassadors and secretaries of the illustrious compile sources about the actions of the great men of history. The documents are, in other words, 'text on paper written intentionally to make a memory official'.[82] In the age of history, however, documents are intermingled with what Rancière terms historical monuments, unofficial documents and ephemera, 'that which preserves memory through its very being ... The monument is the thing that talks without words, that instructs us without intending to instruct us'.[83] Historical monuments represent the vast, anonymous records of history that reveal

---

[78] Jacques Rancière, *Aisthesis: Scenes from the Aesthetic Regime of Art*, trans. Zakir Paul (London: Verso, 2013), 2; Jacques Rancière, *The Aesthetic Unconscious*, trans. Debra Keates and James Swenson (Cambridge: Polity, 2009), 31. On Rancière's understanding of how the aesthetic regime developed through a silent revolution, see Gabriel Rockhill, 'The Silent Revolution', *SubStance*, 33, no. 1 (2004): 54–76.

[79] Jacques Rancière, 'The Politics of Literature', *SubStance*, 33, no. 1 (2004): 10–24, 14–18.

[80] Paul Guyer counters traditional views of the aesthetic as an autonomous realm by revealing that, since the concept was first discussed in the eighteenth century, there has been little consensus as to whether aesthetics is separate from other aspects of human life, Guyer, *A History of Modern Aesthetics*, 28–29.

[81] Rancière, *Figures of History*, 21–24.

[82] Rancière, *Figures of History*, 22.

[83] Rancière, *Figures of History*, 22.

the truth of ordinary life and 'speak' without any deliberate or intentional effort to instruct. They also, therefore, privilege the role of the historian who compiles and makes sense of what they reveal.[84] As Koselleck also proposes, traces of poetry infiltrate into history, or as Rancière suggests of new modes of understanding in the age of history, '[t]here is no science … but that of the hidden. And the production of this hidden is a poetic operation essential to the constitution of knowledge in historical study'.[85]

Admittedly, Rancière diverges from Koselleck's conception of historical writing when he intimates that the age of history is not fully formed until later in the nineteenth century.[86] So too, Rancière at times appears to view Romantic poetics as a specific break with any form of military or strategic thought that could call into question whether his concerns with history have relevance for understanding Lloyd. Although Rancière recognises a fundamental unity between military strategy and ideas of art, military strategy is based on 'fictions', accounts of 'fictive battle', that produce an 'official fiction' based on the writing of the great men of history and their claims to mastery.[87] Strategic history represents a 'tautology of power', in which history repeatedly recounts the myth that the actions and decisions of the great generals really did lead to victory.[88] Rancière implies that strategic thought is associated with a representative regime because it is lodged in a belletristic past of speech and action, a regime exemplified by the scene of the great general haranguing his soldiers.[89] Yet although reading military thought into the aesthetic regime runs somewhat counter to Rancière's own concerns, he has also described relations between military strategy and the aesthetic regime by pointing to the existence of what he terms a 'military semiology' that he locates in Clausewitz's efforts to interpret the hidden depths of war.[90] Such a military semiology had already informed Lloyd's efforts to find significance in the silent 'arrangements of bodies' and 'plots of land' that constitute military campaigns.[91]

Lloyd's generic experimentation brings together these two elements of the documents and monuments to fundamentally disrupt the belle-letteristic history of his neo-classical inheritance. His history is, of course,

---

[84] Rancière, *Figures of History*, 23.
[85] Rancière, *Names of History*, 52.
[86] Rancière, *Figures of History*, 23.
[87] Jacques Rancière, *The Politics of Literature* trans. Julie Rose (Cambridge: Polity, 2011), 74; See also Jacques Rancière, 'The Reality Effect and the Politics of Fiction', Public Lecture at ICI Berlin, www.ici-berlin.org/events/jacques-ranciere/, accessed 15 April 2022.
[88] Rancière, *The Politics of Literature*, 74.
[89] Rancière, *Mute Speech*, 48.
[90] Rancière, *The Flesh of Words*, 115.
[91] Rancière, *The Flesh of Words*, 115.

tightly linked to documents supplied by officers in the contending armies who act as the secretaries and archivists of their commanders. Typically, Lloyd advances his history by briefly describing the key events of military actions and then quoting official military accounts from both sides of the conflict before concluding with this own reflections and analysis of the events. After giving his own account of the Battle of Rosbach, for example, Lloyd includes accounts from both Prussian and French sources, observing:

> Many relations of this battle were published by authority: that of Vienna is too general, and gives a very imperfect idea of it; we shall, therefore, omit it, and give that of Berlin, and another wrote by an officer in the combined army; which, with what we have said on the subject, will enable the reader to form a proper judgment of this extraordinary transaction. (vol. I. 97–98)

Lloyd follows with a series of analytical reflections in which he critiques the French forces for their failure to prevent the juncture of the Prussian army, which he determines from 'inspection of the map' (vol. I. 103). As he turns to analysis, however, so he equally treats these documents as though they were historical monuments, texts that he must decipher, compare and evaluate. Through Lloyd's analysis, these texts instruct us of the underlying rationale and analysis of what happened – a rationale of which the authors themselves were unaware. In other words, these documents are not able to 'speak', or reveal their full meaning, until reframed through Lloyd's analysis. The documents of power, for Lloyd, now bear traces of a history that was silent to its actors, and it is Lloyd, as historian, who assumes the highest position of authority and knowledge.

Although Lloyd is still constructing a version of what Rancière would term an official fiction that sees significance in the great actions of the generals and their strategies, Lloyd's 'fiction' no longer represents a simple tautology of power because it takes as its very task the decipherment of those strategic actions of the powerful. Lloyd's generic experimentation departs from earlier official discussion of strategic knowledge that remained embedded in the genre that underpinned the analysis of war – the memoirs of the great men themselves. Resembling classical sources, such as Caesar's commentaries, the memoirs of Maurice de Saxe, Marquis Feuquière, Raimondo, Count of Montecuccoli and Frederick the Great were amongst the most commonly read military books in eighteenth century Britain and undoubtedly influenced the conduct of warfare.[92] The military memoir represents

---

[92] Mark Danley, *Military Writings and the Theory and Practice of Strategy in the Eighteenth-Century British Army* (PhD diss., Kansas State University, 2001), 74.

the most official of documents that these great men chose to leave, bypass-
ing even the intermediaries of the archivists and secretaries. Presented as a
set of maxims for waging campaigns, military memoirs were hardly concerned with accounting for every detail of the great man's life. They were,
however, reflecting the assumption that the great commander's life is worth
representing because the stories of great men have unparalleled capacity
for instruction. Henri de La Tour d'Auvergne, Vicomte de Turenne published his *Military Memoirs and Maxims of Marshal Turenne* (1740) because
memoirs and maxims were, in effect, the same thing.[93] Interspersing his
own maxims with those of other illustrious leaders, Turenne's book, moreover, contributed to a lineage of historical examples formed from the
speech and action of great men. Turpin de Crissé sums up such belief when
he observes that instruction in war comes from 'The Alexands of Parma,
the Spinolas, the Gustavuses, the Weimars, the Condés, the Turennes, the
Montécucullis, the Vendomes, the Marlboroughs, the Eugenes, and all
the great men who have gone before us'.[94] These military memoirs and
maxims show great men instructing other great men, using an ongoing
series of maxims that could guide future action and drew liberally upon a
long classical inheritance. Feuquières expressly states in his memoirs that he
has written his experiences for his son, but he ranges freely from his own
experiences to examples from Hannibal, Turenne and other generals, locat-
ing his own genealogy within this classical lineage. In this sense, the experiences recorded are wholly exemplary of universal maxims of behaviour.
Feuquières even concludes in his chapter on battles that 'I have collected all
the general Rules which can be given, with Regard to this grand Operation
of War'.[95] Maïzeroy may have been the first modern thinker to adopt the
term strategy, but he similarly supposes that one can only teach the sublime
principles of strategy through examples.[96] Examples, of course, might fail
and there is considerable room for chance, the always surprising role of

---

[93] Henri de La Tour d'Auvergne, Vicomte de Turenne, *Military Memoirs and Maxims of Marshal Turenne. Interspersed with Others, Taken from the Best Authors and Observations, with Remarks. By A. Williamson, Brigadier-General* (Dublin: Reprinted by and for George Faulkner, in Essex Street, 1740).

[94] Turpin de Crissé, *An Essay on the Art of War. Translated from the French of Count Turpin, By Captain Joseph Otway. In Two Volumes* (London: Printed by A. Hamilton, for W. Johnston in Ludgate-Street. 1761), I.iii.

[95] Antoine de Pas, Marquis de Feuquières, *Memoirs of the Late Marquis de Feuquieres, Lieutenant-General of the French Army. Written for the Instruction of his Son. Being an Account of all the Wars in Europe, from the Year 1672, to the Year 1710.* 2 Vols (London: 1737), I.2.

[96] Paul-Gédéon Joly de Maïzeroy, *Théorie de la Guerre, Où l'on Expose las Constitution et de la Cavalerie, leurs Manoeuvres Élémentaires, avec l'Application des Principes à la Grande Tactique, Suivie de Démonstrations sur la Stratégique* (Lausanne: Aux Dépens de La Société, 1777), 301.

'*fortuna*' itself being a crucial lesson of history for Frederick the Great.[97] There is even at times a degree of cynicism about the role of the past, de Saxe, for example, complaining that earlier military thinkers were entirely deficient in crafting a military science.[98] De Saxe attempts to improve upon this earlier military thought, however, by writing his own memoirs.[99] Even de Saxe, therefore, continued to operate within the same 'experiential space' of classical military thought, a space shaped by an underlying historical continuity embedded in the pedagogical role of the 'memoir-literature'.[100]

Lloyd's generic experimentation breaks open this neo-classical obsession with the 'great men' and their exemplary actions and maxims as the key to military command. In Lloyd's account, war appears to necessarily escape the full grasp of those who are waging and writing about their experiences, as history no longer appears as a storehouse of examples or a living teacher, but becomes itself an object of critical attention and an artefact to be studied.[101] Modern history no longer takes instruction from historical examples and experience because events are necessarily singular and incapable of repetition – the lessons of history must be grasped in relation to historical structures, as only these are iterative across time.[102] Lloyd conforms to this modern discovery that history is always 'more' than any account that is made of it and that historians can no longer rely on received wisdom.[103] He writes a dense history of precise movements, statistics and topographical geographical features that are no longer wholly exemplary but always lodged in a specific empirical reality. Reflecting on Marshal Brown's dispositions at the Battle of Lowositz in 1756, Lloyd observes that:

> From the description we have given of the ground, it appears evident, that the marshal could not possibly obtain any other advantage, than perhaps to repulse the enemy; which, from the bad choice of his camp, was very improbable. But; even supposing he had beat him back as far as the Vineyards on the Loboschberg, he certainly could never have forced him from

---

[97] Koselleck, *Futures Past*, 118.

[98] Maurice de Saxe, *Reveries, or Memoirs Upon the Art of War by Field-Marshal Count Saxe. Illustrated with Copper-plates. To Which are Added Some Original Letters, Upon Various Military Subjects, Wrote by the Count to the late King of Poland, and M. de Folard, Which Were Never Before Made publick: Together with His Reflections Upon the Propagation of the Human Species. Translated from the* French (London: Printed for J. Nourse, at the Lamb, opposite Katherine-street, in the Strand, 1757), iii.

[99] Koselleck, *Futures Past*, 133.

[100] Koselleck, *Futures Past*, 31.

[101] Amy J. Elias, 'Past / Future', in *Time: A Vocabulary of the* Present, ed. Joel Burgess and Amy J. Elias (New York: New York University Press, 2016), 35–50, 38.

[102] Koselleck, *Futures Past*, 255; 112–14.

[103] Koselleck, *Futures Past*, 32–33.

thence, and from the Homolka mountain; because, to form these two attacks, he must have filed through the villages of Lowositz and Sulowitz, and have formed between those villages and the mountains upon which the Prussian army, with above 100 pieces of cannon, was posted, and in many places within musket-shot of the ground where the Austrians must have formed. I appeal therefore to all military gentlemen, whether in these circumstances such a manoeuvre was possible. (vol. I. 24)

The importance of Marshal Brown's actions only come to light through Lloyd's meticulous concerns with the details of this piece of ground and the precise strength and positioning of the armies in respect to vineyards, villages and mountains. While earlier military writers such as Turenne, Turpin de Crissé, de Saxe and Feuquières had all explicitly stated that a general must know the country, they appear unconcerned with such precise circumstances that could never be abstracted into exemplarity.[104] When Turpin de Crissé concludes his discussion of geographical detail, it is to turn attention to an overarching maxim, the virtue of precaution.[105] What Lloyd offers is, instead, a version of a military semiology that reads the grounds and events of war for meaning while acknowledging that it is impossible to account for all circumstances, even as he strives to make sense of specific circumstances. The most important elements are precisely those that remain beneath the surface of any classical example.

By uniting empirical details with counterfactuals, Lloyd's writing undermines the very identity of the great men of history. His writing represents an inversion of the qualities that made the classical memoir so central because he subordinates the speech of great men to the mute speech of historical detail and monuments, the imaginative capacity to read the silent speech of the world. Gallagher has proposed that the counterfactual orientation of military history as developed from Lloyd preshadows a postmodern aesthetic that is bound up with the collapse of referentiality and character altogether. As she explains of the counterfactual forms of military history derived from his writing:

> 1) They need a stable substratum of uncontroversial facts, but the counter-facts described in the narrative exceed the facts; 2) they tend to privilege the role of individuals in history, but they also de-realize those individuals by fracturing them onto multiple versions; and 3) they are oriented toward

---

[104] Turenne, *Military Memoirs and Maxims of Marshal Turenne*, 2; Turpin de Crissé, *An Essay on the Art of War*, iii; De Saxe, *Reveries, or Memoirs Upon the Art of War*, 122–23; Feuquières, *Memoirs of the Late Marquis de Feuquieres*, 236–37.

[105] Turenne, *Military Memoirs and Maxims of Marshal Turenne*, 10.

future action, but they repeatedly slide sideways across a menu of simultaneous options. Therefore, on the levels of plot, character, and temporality, counterfactual history produces narrative features that we sometimes call 'post-modern': indeterminacy, multiplicity, and non-linearity.[106]

But rather than regard Lloyd as tentatively foreshadowing the postmodern, his historical writing can be more readily seen to lie on the cusp of the new kind of poetics associated with the long and silent revolution of the aesthetic regime. Lloyd's generic experimentation is itself a way of engaging with the contradictions of an earlier regime and its inability to systematise empirical detail or to analyse historical details that fall outside the wisdom and examples supplied by great men. In Lloyd's history, the exemplarity of action is far less important than the analysis of action – what is striking about strategic thought is even that it is an analysis of command and leadership that displaces the traditional centrality of the man of action altogether, breaking action into indeterminacy and multiplicity.

Clausewitz described this new approach to military historical analysis when he noted that '[t]heory need not be a positive doctrine, a sort of manual for action ... It is an analytical investigation leading to a close acquaintance with the subject'.[107] This is a new art of war founded not in the theatrical living speech that is aware of its community, military thought as a 'manual for action', but in the orphaned letter and the judgement of writing and reading, in Lloyd's phrase, the judgement now of 'all military men' (vol. I. xxxix). Rancière argues that it is in his *Wallenstein* trilogy (1800) that Schiller, the first thinker of the 'aesthetic state', was also the first to reveal the 'failure of strategy' because he recast the general, Wallenstein, as impotent and so no longer a figure who epitomised action. This sense of strategic failure was already apparent, however, in Sterne's earlier *Tristram Shandy* (1759–67), in which the veteran officer, Uncle Toby, is incapable of knowing where exactly he was wounded at the siege of Namur. First started during the Seven Years War, the novel posits that the certainties of geometry have given way, as Engberg-Pedersen shows, to a new conception of war as the 'topographical order' of movement and terrain that render war inherently imbued with chance encounters and uncertainty.[108] Uncle Toby may be impotent and incapable of certainty, but his efforts to reconstruct an account of the siege

---

[106] Catherine Gallagher, 'Telling It Like It Wasn't', *Pacific Coast Philology*, 45 (2010): 12–25, 15.

[107] Carl von Clausewitz, *Historical and Political Writings*, ed. and trans. Peter Paret and Daniel Moran (Princeton: Princeton University Press, 1992), 207–08.

[108] Anders Engberg-Pedersen, 'The Refraction of Geometry: Tristram Shandy and the Poetics of War, 1700–1800', *Representations* 123, no. 1 (2013): 23–52, 43.

nonetheless reveal a new kind of aleatory war knowledge. This 'failure' of the general as a man of action is exemplified by Lloyd's reconceptualisation of military leadership.[109] It was with the clearing of the historical weight of exemplarity that a new understanding of the arts of military leadership could emerge that built upon the basic approach of 'the age of history' to read the empirical and historical in a systematic manner.

The Living Forces of War

If Lloyd's history can be read in relation to a new aesthetic regime that collapses the centrality of the general as a man of action, there is a curiously supplementary reappearance of such men when he records their deaths in battle in his footnotes (vol. I, 12–13). These generals appear wholly divorced from action because Lloyd inscribes their biographies, instead, into the mere state of living and dying. For Rancière, the movement away from the representation of action is, in turn, intrinsically linked to the emergence of an aesthetic concern with the 'empirical nature of life', the mundane, mass, unconscious, repetitive and biological existence of the living mass of people.[110] He identifies this new aesthetic sensibility with the era's revolutionary politics, which had demonstrated the enormous military potential possessed by the masses.[111] Indeed, the military literature that emerged in the wake of the Seven Years War was critical to the establishment of the military infrastructure, administration and organisational capacities that enabled the latter wars of the French Revolution to assume their truly mass and revolutionary character. With Frederick the Great's disciplinary regime the army was widely considered to have been perfected as a 'military machine'. Yet the unprecedented success of his armies also led to far reaching debates in the aftermath of the Seven Years War was also bound up in far reaching debates about the effect, significance and use of his new kind of army.[112] Lloyd proposes that nothing in either ancient or modern warfare had been as significant as Frederick's campaigns in 1757 (vol. I. 147). Such concerns are reflected in Deleuze and Guattari's understanding of the 'war-machine', which expands Foucault's description of disciplinary power by drawing on Paul Virilio's analysis of modern war and speed as it has evolved

---

[109] Rancière, 'The Reality Effect and the Politics of Fiction'.
[110] Rancière, *The Politics of Literature*, 9–10.
[111] Rancière, *Mute Speech*, 24.
[112] Michel Foucault, *Discipline and Punish: The Birth of the Prison*, trans. Alan Sheridan (New York: Vintage, 1991), 165.

since Frederick the Great.[113] Following Virilio, they propose that the war-machine is distinct from the machine more generally because it functions as a weapon rather than a tool, and is consequently concerned with projection and motion rather than equilibrium and interiority.[114] The war-machine, in other words, is possessed of its own qualities, passions, desires and vectoral movements. As Frederick's military machine revealed its full capacities, therefore, so attention turned to the nature of the war-machine and reflection on the power and capabilities of the military collective. The army began to be seen less as a mechanical entity to be arranged and used than as a vital living force to be harnessed, directed and managed.[115]

As a collective, the army can, at one level, be contrasted with the collective existence or life of the national population. Deliberately composed within an imposed hierarchy, the army does not exist as a naturally occurring biological entity like the population, but as a culmination of an artificial, machinic set of disciplinary mechanisms that find their ultimate expression in the precise geometrical arrangements of the military camp.[116] The army appears at first sight, therefore, as a multiplicity of disciplinary individuals rather than a natural population or global mass shaped by an overall set of natural processes surrounding birth, sickness, procreation and death.[117] Viewed as a work of grand tactics, Lloyd's history can be seen in continuity with disciplinary regimes that, as Foucault shows, culminate with tactical arrangements that allow the co-ordination and control over masses of disciplined bodies.[118] The modern army reflects the artificiality that governed the thought of rule in an era of *raison d'état*.[119]

---

[113] Gilles Deleuze and Félix Guattari, *A Thousand Plateaus: Capitalism and Schizophrenia*, trans. and foreword Brian Massumi (London: Continuum, 2004), 435–45; Éric Alliez and Maurizio Lazzarato, Clausewitz and *la Pensée 68*, trans. Ames Hodges and Katharine Wallerstein, *Critical Times* I, no. 1 (2018): 49–59, 53–54; Paul Virilio, *Speed and Politics*, trans. Marc Polizzotti, intro. Benjamin H. Bratton (Los Angeles: Semiotext(e), 2006), 78.

[114] Deleuze and Guattari, *A Thousand Plateaus*, 436–37.

[115] A related concern with the vitalism of strategic writing is apparent in Elaine Scarry's much-cited critique of how official languages of war mask or elide injury by reimagining armies as living entities via the 'fiction' of strategic writing. See Elaine Scarry, *The Body in Pain: The Making and Unmaking of the World* (Oxford: Oxford University Press, 1985), 136.

[116] Foucault, *Discipline and Punish*, 171.

[117] Michel Foucault, *Society Must Be Defended: Lectures at the Collège de France, 1975–1976*, ed. Mauro Bertani and Alessandro Fontana, trans. David Macey (London: Penguin Books, 2004), 242–43.

[118] Foucault, *Discipline and Punish*, 162–64, 170. On the contemporary distinction between tactics, grand tactics and the French 'strategique', see John MacDonald, *Instructions for the Conduct of Infantry on Actual Service* (London: Printed for T. Egerton, Military Library, Whitehall, 1807), xlvii; and xcviii.

[119] Foucault, *Security, Territory, Population*, 349.

Yet Foucault also suggests an alternative way of conceptualising the army as a collective when he notes, although very much in passing, that the military represented, along with doctors, the first 'managers of collective space'.[120] He postulates that medical concerns with habitation and military concerns with 'campaigns' were even more important than the writing of thinkers such as Montesquieu in the historical development of sociological knowledge of space, circulation and even the 'population'.[121] Deleuze has expanded upon Foucault's brief insights by insisting that his work cannot be limited to questions of disciplinary confinement, but must be read in relation to Virilio's expansive thought on war, speed and movement in the control of space.[122]

While Foucault closely follows the military authors Guibert and Maïzeroy in marking tactics as the culmination of discipline, he fails to fully consider how both thinkers introduce critical qualifications into their thought as to how tactics operated in real situations. As Guibert describes the importance of tactics to military science, he proposes:

> they are this science itself, because they teach how to constitute troops, order them, move them, get them to fight; because tactics alone may make up for numbers, and handle the multitude; lastly, it will include knowledge of men, weapons, tensions, circumstances, because it is all these kinds of knowledge brought together that must determine those movements.[123]

Discipline enables the composition and management of a mass of soldiers, but Guibert also recognises the need for new kinds of 'science' or 'knowledge' that can fully comprehend the 'tensions' and 'circumstances' surrounding the uses of this formed mass of soldiers. A similar point is raised by Maïzeroy when he completes his work on discipline and tactics by noting the necessity of the sublime science or dialectic of strategy in conducting the army's overall manoeuvres.[124] Indeed, as Gat observes, the concept of tactics only held a primary place in military thought of the 1760s and 1770s, when it was quickly subordinated to new conceptions of strategy.[125] Foucault did eventually elaborate on the relation between

---

[120] Michel Foucault, *Power/Knowledge: Selected Interviews and Other Writings, 1972–1977*, ed. Colin Gordon, trans. Colin Gordon, Leo Marshall, John Mepham and Kate Soper (New York: Pantheon Books, 1980), 150–51.
[121] Foucault, *Power/Knowledge*, 150–51.
[122] Gilles Deleuze, *Foucault*, trans. and ed. Seán Hand (London: Continuum, 1999), 36.
[123] Quoted in Foucault, *Discipline and Punish*, 168.
[124] Maïzeroy, *Théorie de la Guerre*, 300–01.
[125] Gat, *A History of Military Thought*, 34.

tactics and strategy, but only in his subsequent work on sexuality and without any specific inquiry into military thought.[126] Strategy, however, comes into existence as a military concept at the moment that discipline was first fully conceptualised and elaborated into a universalised system of tactics. Moving beyond concerns with the tactical composition of forces, strategy supplanted the earlier focus on discipline and tactics because it is concerned with a set of questions about the circumstances surrounding the use of armies on campaign within the vast realms of 'collective space'. The culmination of disciplinary techniques in the late eighteenth century also marks a threshold for new kinds of understanding of the army as a collective entity or even a quasi-organic population.

Although Lloyd still draws on earlier thought about discipline and tactics, he crosses this threshold much further than Guibert and Maïzeroy. When Lloyd supplements his history with a second volume that expounds his theories of war, he qualifies the idea that the army can be understood as a 'pure machine' because he recognises that the army must also be applied to circumstances in ways that complicate its status as a 'multitude' (vol. I.ii. 69). It is true that Lloyd's second volume offers maxims that could be read as broadly neo-classical in orientation; indeed it even went under the title of memoirs in France. But in this supplementary work we see the effects of his newly naturalised approach to history and rejection of earlier exemplary wisdom and the dictates of geometry. He equally introduces a naturalised quality into these questions of the application and conduct of the collective:

> In the preceding part, we have considered an army as a machine, with which the different operations of war, are to be performed; and endeavoured to point out the method which appears to us most adapted for the construction of it, so that it may have the properties required to render it perfect. An army, however, differs essentially from a pure machine: this is formed in such a manner, that when applied, it must necessarily produce a given effect, in proportion to its strength. It can have but one principle of motion, whereas in an army, each individual part has, within itself, the spring and source of action, which it may exert or not at pleasure. It follows, therefore, that however advantageously the parts, that is, the men are ranged, the whole will remain motionless, if the leader, who has the direction of their forces, cannot offer such motives as will induce them to act, and in the manner he prescribes. He cannot create action in individuals, he cannot

---

[126] For an account of the relation between strategy and tactics, see Michel Foucault, *The History of Sexuality; Volume One: An Introduction*, trans. Robert Hurley (London: Penguin Books, 1981), 100.

force them to act, he can only persuade and direct ... This is what I call the philosophy of war, which, in my opinion, is the most difficult and sublime part of this or any other profession. It supposes a perfect knowledge of the passions, because it is from that source, a general must draw his arguments to persuade or dissuade, as circumstances may require. (vol. I.ii. 69–70)

Lloyd's depiction of the general in terms of oratory and personal character admittedly suggests his ongoing affiliation with an earlier, neo-classical ideal of war epitomised by the general addressing his troops.[127] Even Lloyd's conception of sublimity here, that the knowledge of how to direct an army represents the most 'sublime part' of war, appears derived from the classical rhetoric of Longinus and his eighteenth-century inheritors. Nonetheless, although Lloyd in part remains aligned with a neo-classical conception of the army, his insistence that the commander cannot simply force his troops into action also implies that he sees the army as possessing a quasi-natural status as a collective. The army appears as an entity that is more than a collection of individuals but which always remains a 'multitude', which must, he therefore implies, be understood and managed at a collective level (vol. I.ii. 71). He puts forth a newly naturalised or vitalised conception of the army, where '[a]n army [is] like the sea, is sometimes calm and slothful, at others furious and outrageous, wholly ungovernable; both extremes are to be equally avoided' (vol. I.ii. 70). As a multitude, the army is never definitely or finally under the general's control.

As he develops what he regards as the philosophy of war, Lloyd reconfigures a traditional rhetorical conception of sublimity into a 'naturalised' form of sublimity linked to grandeur and its correlative inner mental states and perceptions.[128] Peter De Bolla has proposed that the development in Britain of a new conception of sublimity was related to the fear of infinitely increasing public debt to pay for the Seven Years War.[129] This fear, in turn, shaped the development of the autonomous subject who tries to control the excess of both debt and sublimity, while rendering the public itself into a unified body. Something analogous can be seen with Lloyd's understanding of the army as a multitude that exceeds taxonomic order, the army acquiring the natural grandeur associated with the sea, but which simultaneously invites the general to the exercise of conducting

[127] Rancière, *Mute Speech*, 48.
[128] Philip Shaw, *The Sublime* (London: Routledge, 2006), 5.
[129] Peter de Bolla, *The Discourse of the Sublime: Readings in History, Aesthetics and the Subject* (Oxford: Basil Blackwell, 1989), 6.

and leading that excess.[130] The multitude, of course, is a loaded term in political philosophy with a long history initiated by Hobbes' reflections on the transformation of the multitude from a state of war or nature to a state of civilisation under the sovereign rule. The multitude, for Hobbes, represents an undifferentiated mass that lies beyond the order imposed by rights and justice and which can only be ordered in so far as it concedes all rights to the sovereign. For any order to operate, the multitude must come together under one will as a multiplicity or a people.[131] This was approximately the sense in which the term multitude had earlier been utilised in military thought. Guibert believed the general could only command by breaking the multitude apart through disciplinary practices and tactics, because the general is always 'blinded by the immensity, dazed by the multitude'.[132] De Saxe and Turpin de Crissé, likewise, used the term multitude to describe the army, but only to refer to an army of barbarians or an army that had fallen into a state of indiscipline and that would, Turpin de Crissé observed, be slaughtered if it were to engage an opposing army.[133]

Lloyd complicates these earlier concerns with order and discipline because in his thought the army remains a multitude and so inherently occupies a quasi-natural state. If discipline and tactics establish control through regimes of training and ordering that constitute a multiplicity out of individuals, then strategy, by its very nature, functions as a science concerned with the use of a given order of multiplicity and thus always relies upon the prior operation of discipline and tactics. Understood as an entity to be applied, used and developed through a nascent concern with 'strategical movements', the army assumes in Lloyd's writing a set of naturalistic characteristics that disrupt the mechanistic approach of neo-classical thought. Julian Reid observes that this is effectively how Foucault understands strategy: as the organisation of the tactical forces derived from disciplined individuals into an overarching command of populations.[134] Command is both raised to sublime qualities in Lloyd's thought, but it is equally complicated

---

[130] Shaw, *The Sublime*, 38.
[131] For a discussion of the origins of the idea in Hobbes, see Paolo Virno, *A Grammar of the Multitude: For an Analysis of Contemporary Forms of Life*, trans. Isabella Bertoletti, James Cascaito and Andrea Casson, foreword Sylvère Lotringer (Los Angeles: Semiotext(e), 2004), 22.
[132] Quoted in Foucault, *Discipline and Punish*, 148.
[133] De Saxe, *Reveries, or Memoirs Upon the Art of War*, 272; Turpin de Crissé, *An Essay on the Art of War*, vol. II. 58.
[134] Julian Reid, 'Life Struggles: War, Discipline and Biopolitics in the Thought of Michel Foucault', in *Foucault on Politics, Security and War*, ed. Michael Dillon and Andrew W. Neal (Basingstoke: Palgrave, 2011), 65–92, 78.

by its concern with the knowledge and autonomy required to master and shape the grand, excessive passions of the army's fears, desires and forces. It is precisely the understanding of these collective passions that lifts strategy into the realm of sublimity and genius. If Lloyd's history is infused with philosophical speculation on the nature of war, conversely, the empiricism or naturalism of his historical narrative of war carries over to shape his philosophy of war, moving his account beyond mechanical Prussian drill routines and reflections on tactical order because, he insists, '[n]ature must be improved, not annihilated' (vol. I.ii. xxxvi).

Lloyd's naturalised form of military thought opens in two related directions, inaugurating a militarised sociology concerned with the nature of the army as a collective and reconceptualising the general as a figure of sublimity and genius. As Rancière observes, sociological analysis and reflections on genius emerged simultaneously in the aesthetic regime because they are entangled around twinned concerns with, on the one hand, the artistic will and, on the other hand, the involuntary or natural processes that circulate through life. The aesthetic regime, he insists, is bound by its relation to the world of the sensible and so it is shaped by contradictions or tension between the intentional and the unintentional, the active and passive, the world of action and that of physical life.[135] Where Aristotle's classical poetics had sought to keep logos and pathos entirely separate, asserting only the importance of the logos or reason and will and its manifestation in action, a new poetics disrupts this division so that the logos cannot be thought apart from the pathos, or transient, emotional living realm of life necessity.[136] Kantian aesthetics raised the significance of genius by proposing that genius does not follow rules but creates the rules of art, yet in Kant's conception the rules that genius 'creates' must themselves be understood as a manifestation of nature through genius in ways that genius itself cannot fully comprehend.[137] For Rancière, however, genius emerges in conjunction with complementary historical and sociological modes for understanding the realm of sensibility. The commonplace citing of Shakespeare's genius as an artistic model emerged at the same moment that a proto-sociological analysis developed as a way of reading the ordinary details of life as an expression of the spirit of an age.[138] If war, in other

---

[135] Rancière, *The Politics of Aesthetics*, 23.
[136] Jacques Rancière, *The Aesthetic Unconscious* trans. Debra Keates and James Swenson (Cambridge: Polity Press, 2009), 18, 28.
[137] Rancière, *The Aesthetic Unconscious*, 24.
[138] Rancière, *Mute Speech*, 147–48.

words, begins to be oriented around the sublime genius of the general, his genius is only recognisable in relation to an emergent idea of the natural life of the army, through the intersection of conscious and unconscious elements, the interplay between meaning and the meaningless.[139] If the Seven Years War inaugurated a new aesthetic that ruptured neo-classical thought, as suggested by Koselleck and De Bolla, it also brought into being a new aesthetic conception of military strategy that is reflected in Turpin de Crissé, Maïzeroy, Lloyd, Jomini and Clausewitz's insistence upon the poetry, sublimity and genius of the general. Lloyd's conception of the general addressing his troops as a figure confronting the uncontrollable, ever-changing moods of the sea is to reorient the epitome of neo-classical action or 'logos', by reconceptualising the general as though an artist raging with the 'pathos' of unconscious, living, sensible forces.

In part, Lloyd demonstrates a proto-sociological concern with understanding the underlying nature of the army. He was criticised for questioning the correct costume and hats for soldiers to wear, but such concerns suggest a way of thinking about the soldier as a living body that must be correctly clothed to maximise its capacities and potential.[140] At the level of the army's collective movements, he acknowledges that war could only be reduced to geometrical precision if one had perfect knowledge of the country (vol. I.ii. xxxi). While Lloyd was far from the first thinker to recognise that geography affected the nature of military operations, for Lloyd, geography not only renders geometrical precision impossible, but it also creates a distinctly military set of concerns that must be understood by the commander:[141]

> Next to this local geography of a country, the natural history, and political constitution of it is an object that deserves the utmost attention; the quantity and quality of its productions, soil, climate, food, and form of government; because on these the physical and moral qualities of the inhabitants entirely

---

[139] On aesthetics, war and the general, see Nick Mansfield, 'Destroyer and Bearer of Worlds: The Aesthetic Doubleness of War', in *Tracing War in British Enlightenment and Romantic Culture*, ed. Neil Ramsey and Gillian Russell (Basingstoke: Palgrave Macmillan, 2015), 188–203; and Nick Mansfield, *Theorizing War: From Hobbes to Badiou* (New York: Palgrave Macmillan, 2008), 33.

[140] Colin Lindsay, *Extracts from Colonel Tempelhoffe's History of the Seven Years War: His Remarks on General Lloyd: On the Subsistence of Armies; and on the March of Convoys. Also a Treatise on Winter Posts. To Which is Added a Narrative of Events at St. Lucie and Gibralter, and of John Duke of Marlborough's March to the Danube, with the Causes and Consequences of that Measure. By the Honourable Colin Lindsay, Lieutenant Colonel of the 46th Regiment. In Two Volumes* (London: Printed for T. Cadell, in the Strand, 1793), vol. I, xiii.

[141] For an earlier account of the importance of geography, see, for example, Turpin de Crissé, *An Essay on the Art of War*, vol. I. ii–iv.

depend. Those who inhabit the plains, and rich countries, are generally effeminate and bad soldiers, impatient under the least fatigue, are soon sick, require too much food, and are less active than those of the mountains, and in every respect inferior to them. What did not the poor Highlanders do? What did they not suffer? They will live when an Englishman, though animated with equal courage, and love of glory, will perish. (vol. I.ii. xxxi–xxxii)

Lloyd's concerns extend across a range of 'physical and moral' elements that constitute the nature of a country and the collective life of soldiers. He pioneers awareness of the natural properties of the army as he elaborates the necessity for a systematic, knowledge of the passions, music, sex and political systems in commanding the army. When a commander addresses the army as a multitude, he must, Lloyd argues, make recourse to these fields of knowledge because they enable the commander to see how the multitude functions in its unconscious or naturalised elements. Lloyd's thought here remains rudimentary: his analysis of the political systems is largely lifted from Montesquieu, his underlying sense of passions has an overly formalist concern with pleasure and pain, and the effects of music on the passions consists of one short paragraph. But, critically, when he assess the effects of music he adds:

> It were to be wished some able musician and philosopher would make experiments, by executing different pieces, to a promiscuous audience of men and women of different ages, soldiers in particular; the result would shew what species of harmony was most adapted to raise courage in the troops. (vol. I.ii. 96)

Insisting upon the importance of experimentation and analysis, Lloyd pushes towards a new kind of military thought that resembles the human sciences in its efforts to study, systematise and apply the natural propensities of the human. His writing, in this sense, not only reflects a turn to a naturalised version of sublimity first fully described in Edmund Burke's *Philosophical Enquiry on the Sublime* (1757), but it also follows Burke in the way it merged a traditional rhetorical approach to war with an understanding of vital human powers, an approach that Clifford Siskin argues was central to the emergent Humean science of man.[142] Believing himself that '[n]o author has treated this subject so far', Lloyd was the first military thinker to imagine war through the formation of something approaching a 'military sociology' (vol. I.ii. 70).[143]

---

[142] Clifford Siskin, *The Work of Writing: Literature and Social Change in Britain, 1700–1830* (Baltimore: Johns Hopkins University Press, 1998), 66.
[143] Speelman, *Henry Lloyd and the Military Enlightenment*, 66.

Yet Lloyd also repeatedly considers the conduct of operations in relation to the involuntary, unconscious, empirical qualities that constitute the army's relationship to the natural milieu. Taken in their entirety, a knowledge of qualities that manifest within the army are united with the 'most sublime art of conducting mankind' (vol. I.ii. xxxiii). Such a concern with conduct was, Foucault points out, essential to the rise of governmental forms of power and rule. He proposes that in the modern era there was a fundamental relation between control and knowledge, in which one always governs or conducts the behaviour of others in relation to knowledge and analysis of those others.[144] Modern government, in other words, operates according to knowledge of a population.[145] Hence Lloyd's belief that any rules for waging war must take account of the nature and circumstances of the army:

> They then recall their rules, and want to make every thing, the rivers, woods, ravines, mountains, &c. &c. subservient to them; whereas their precepts should, on the contrary, be subject to these, who are the only rules, the only guide we ought to follow; whatever maneuver is not formed on these, is absurd and ridiculous. (vol. I.ii. vii–viii)

The sublimity and genius of the general is intimately related to an understanding of the natural elements that infuse and surround the army, such as knowing how to position the army or a military camp within a specific ground (vol. I, 54), while Lloyd conversely observes that the greatest folly for a general is to move an army where it cannot subsist (vol. II. 165). Lloyd's conception of the line of operations was widely criticised in subsequent thought as being overly geometrical, yet it also reveals how strategic thought originates in naturalised concerns with feeding an army. The line of operations is represented by the fixed points set by stores and logistical arrangements and between which all of an army's manoeuvres must proceed. To simply live off the ground would transform the army into a horde of Tartars and lay waste to all of Europe (vol. I.ii. 70). If Lloyd's conception of lines of operation underpinned emergent theorisations of strategy, it does so by grounding strategy in the assumption that the army is a living organism.

Military thought thus resonates with the same set of questions about how to feed the population that were equally crucial to the biopolitical

---

[144] Michel Foucault, *On the Government of the Living: Lectures at the Collège de France, 1979–1980*, ed. Michael Senellart, trans. Graham Burchell (Basingstoke: Palgrave Macmillan, 2014), 12.

[145] Foucault, *Security, Territory, Population*, 76.

thought of political economy.[146] Political economy will take such questions in an entirely different direction by conceptualising the economy in ways that suppose the free circulation and actions of economic activity within the population rather than consider the movement and circulation of armies.[147] Nonetheless, as Foucault implied in his reflections on the management of collective space, military concerns with manoeuvres are not entirely disconnected from the formation of thought on the circulation of populations. Lloyd raises the logistics of feeding of the army from a wholly secondary to a primary concern in military thought, placing this naturalism of the army at the origins of his new conception of strategy. It is in terms of the army's collective life that it must be organised and manoeuvred. Even when his strategic thought is at its most abstract, his writing on Frederick's concentration of his forces at the Battle of Leuthen, Lloyd remains concerned with how the commander uses his army in relation to the specific ground and the facility of the soldiers in marching (vol. I. 139). War might be a rational or even in large part a geometrical application of the general's will, but the traces of the pathos, of the army itself as a quasi-natural, living entity remain apparent in these naturalised origins for the concept of strategy. The army appears as though a living organism, a pseudo-population that is not simply under the will of the general, but an organism or multitude with its own, independent properties that must be correctly managed and understood using genius and military science.

In his analysis of generic transformation in the eighteenth century, Siskin observes that the genres of history and system were increasingly aligned towards the end of the eighteenth century, as disciplinary bodies of knowledge, systems, began to develop their own history.[148] Enlightenment efforts to build master systems that might account for all knowledge were giving way to alternative approaches and genres that elaborated upon the narrow but deep historical realms of proto-disciplinary knowledge. Lloyd's greatest contribution to the history of military thought can be understood in this sense – his creation of a new genre that established a historical approach to military thought. He did not simply introduce the concept of line of operations, but fundamentally altered the generic boundaries of military thought in ways that facilitated its emergence as a discrete and modern science. This is apparent in the debate over Lloyd's history

---

[146] Foucault, *Security, Territory, Population*, 341–54.
[147] Foucault, *Security, Territory, Population*, 349.
[148] Clifford Siskin, *System: The Shaping of Modern Knowledge* (Cambridge, MA: MIT Press, 2016), 56.

launched by Tempelhoff and Jomini, who both drew upon, even as they critiqued, Lloyd's approach. Hamilton went so far as to publish a new edition of Lloyd by interspersing his account of Frederick's campaigns with those of Templehoffe and Jomini, noting:

> From the method which General Tempelhoff had adopted in the composition of his first volume, it was impossible to separate his labours from those of Lloyd ... and in order to elucidate the conflicting arguments of the two historians, extracts from Jomini's *Traite des Grandes Operations Militaires*, under the denomination of reviews, have been subjoined.[149]

The new genre of critical military history, in which critical analysis is interwoven with historical explication, began to be more productive of military thought than the personal maxims or experience of generals. Jomini saw Lloyd's history as a new beginning for military thought, arguing that Lloyd's account of a campaign revealed far more than 'all the dogmatic works put together', while announcing that his own work was built on Lloyd's historical analysis of military operations.[150] Jomini even believed that the best results of all military thought derived from this didactic-critical history, including the work of Clausewitz whom he nonetheless criticises for having copied much of his own analysis of campaigns.[151] However much Clausewitz rejected the systematic or scientific approach of Jomini and adopted a counter-Enlightenment position, his work followed the generic form of critical military history that Jomini believes originated with Lloyd. Clausewitz's contemporary editor, Peter Paret, observes of Clausewitz that 'his method consisted in a permanent discourse between observation, historical interpretation, and speculative reasoning'.[152] Foucault insists that debate can only proceed along such clearly opposing lines, in which opponents find themselves in 'mutually adversarial positions', if the debate happens in relation to a tightly woven historical field.[153] The tactical reversals possible in modern military thought, that Clausewitz so directly appears as an oppositional, Romantic or counter-Enlightenment thinker to the Enlightenment positivism of Jomini, is directly related to the homogeneity

---

[149] *The History of the Seven Years' War in Germany*, I.x–xi.
[150] Jomini, *Summary of the Art of War*, 13. On the direct influence that Jomini took from Lloyd, see Speelman, *War, Society and Enlightenment*, 6–7. Von Bülow would take a distinct view when he established Tempelhoff as the key to the line of operations, but was as equally building on this historical work.
[151] Jomini, *Summary of the Art of War*, 21.
[152] Paret, 'The Genesis of On War', 16.
[153] Foucault, *Society Must Be Defended*, 208.

of the historical field in which both were working. What stabilised this historical field surrounding war was the new kind of military historical knowledge and analysis pioneered by Lloyd's military history.

It is significant, therefore, that Clausewitz describes the 'military machine' in strikingly similar terms to those earlier used by Lloyd to portray the army as something other than a 'pure' machine:

> The military machine – the army and everything related to it – is basically very simple and therefore seems easy to manage. But we should bear in mind that none of its components is of one piece: each part is composed of individuals, every one of whom retains his potential of friction.[154]

If Clausewitz's innovation was to see that war is fought in a resistant medium, and hence that it always poses problems that defy the commander's will, he also recognises that this resistance is intrinsically related to the 'factors inherent in the war-machine itself'.[155] Clausewitz's emphasis on the general's motivation and emotion went hand in hand with an effort to account for the moral and living forces that animate the army. While Gat observes that the roots of such thought lie in Lloyd's historical writing, he dismisses this association in favour of highlighting Clausewitz's Romanticism as an interest in the forces that defied earlier, Enlightenment approaches.[156] Military thought cannot, however, be wholly divided between an Enlightenment ideal of control and an anti-rationalist Romantic concern with vitalism, because both forms of thought emerged out of new conceptions about managing the mass as a living collective.[157] Both approaches assume a naturalistic conception of the army that advances beyond the mechanical.[158] Even Jomini, who considered strategy a positive science, was still compelled to deduce his theory of strategy by acknowledging that the army was not a singular entity under the commander's will:

> If every army were a solid mass, capable of motion as a unit under the influence of one man's will and as rapidly as thought, the art of winning battles would be reduced to choosing the most favorable order of battle, and a general could reckon with certainty upon the success of manoeuvres arranged beforehand. But the facts are altogether different; for the great difficulty of

---

[154] Clausewitz, *On War*, 119.
[155] Clausewitz, *On War*, 579.
[156] Gat, *A History of Military Thought*, 184.
[157] Gat, *A History of Military Thought*, 184.
[158] For a brief summary of the similarities between Enlightenment and Romantic military thought, particularly around their shared engagement with questions of 'collective identity', see Pichichero, *The Military Enlightenment*, 230–33.

the tactics of battles will always be to render certain the simultaneous entering into action of the numerous fractions whose efforts must combine to make such an attack as will give good ground to hope for victory: in other words, the chief difficulty is to cause these fractions to unite in the execution of the decisive manoeuvre which, in accordance with the original plan of the battle, is to result in victory.[159]

Strategy only comes into existence through the recognition that the army is not a simple mass, but is also a multitude that possesses, however notionally, its own forms of motion and resistance.

It is of course the case that Clausewitz would go far beyond Lloyd and Jomini in his analysis of the factors inherent to the war machine, even proposing that war is distinct from other arts because it is defined by the application of the commander's will to 'an animate object' and so is defined by the 'conflict of living forces' as armies react to and clash with one another.[160] But Clausewitz notes that the resistance in the war machine is not about disobedience, it is not a matter of discipline, but a concern with the 'physical and moral' elements that compose the army. But these, he concludes, must come down in the final instance to the basic matter of 'living forces':

> The machine's resistance need not consist of disobedience and argument, though this occurs often enough in individual soldiers. It is the impact of the ebbing of moral and physical strength, of the heart-rending spectacle of the dead and wounded, that the commander has to withstand – first in himself, and then in all those who, directly or indirectly, have entrusted him with their thoughts and feelings, hopes and fears. As each man's strength gives out, as it no longer responds to his will, the inertia of the whole gradually comes to rest on the commander's will alone.[161]

The commander's will, his logos, is here synonymous with the elementary foundation of the modern pathos of war, lodged finally in the brute fact of life and death. Strategy is, above all, a capacity to maintain will in the face of the 'heart-rending spectacle of the dead and wounded'.

[159] Jomini, *Summary of the Art of War*, 126.
[160] Clausewitz, *On War*, 149.
[161] Clausewitz, *On War*, 104.

CHAPTER 3

Robert Jackson's Medicalisation of Military Discipline

Warfare was profoundly transformed by the evolution of military disciplinary practices in early modern Europe. First instituted in its modern form by the recovery and adaptation of disciplinary schemas from classical writing on war, military discipline reached its zenith with the mid-eighteenth-century armies of Frederick the Great (King Frederick II) of Prussia. Following his successes in the Seven Years War (1756–63), Frederick's disciplinary practices were introduced into armies across Europe. They were adapted for use in Britain via Sir David Dundas' *Principles of Military Movement* (1788), which formed the basis of the government's standardised tactical drill routines during the French Revolutionary and Napoleonic Wars.[1] Yet even as Frederick's approach spread, numerous military authors also reacted against what they saw as the overly mechanical emphasis of his methods. Drill routines that conformed with those of Frederick sought total control over the soldier's body by offering precise regulations for the way the soldier stood and moved. Critiques of this approach instead emphasised the importance of soldiers' natural aptitudes, morality, conduct and even intelligence.[2] As discussed in Chapter 2, for example, the military strategist Henry Lloyd supposed that the soldier must be treated as something much more than a simple machine; his natural qualities must be 'improved' rather than 'annihilated' by disciplinary regimes.[3]

Michel Foucault's account of the formation of the disciplinary society drew heavily on his analysis of military drill practices of the late eighteenth

---

[1] On Dundas's development of Frederick's drill routines, see *A Treatise on the Duty of Infantry Officers, and the Present System of British Military Discipline. With an Appendix* (London: Printed for T. Egerton, at the Military Library, Near Whitehall, 1795), 1.

[2] See Christy Pichichero, *The Military Enlightenment: War and Culture in the French Empire from Louis XIV to Napoleon* (Ithaca: Cornell University Press, 2017), 67 and 113; Ilya Berkovich, *Motivation in War: The Experience of Common Soldiers in Old-Regime Europe* (Cambridge: Cambridge University Press, 2017), 169; and Arnaud Guinier, *L'Honneur du Soldat: Éthique Martiale et Discipline Guerrière dans la France des Lumières* (Ceyzérieu: Champ Vallon, 2014).

[3] Henry Lloyd, *The History of the Late War in Germany; Between the King of Prussia, and the Empress of Germany and Her Allies*, vol. I (London: 1766), I, xxxvi.

century, but his work concentrated on the mechanical forms of corporeal drill without fully examining the subsequent critiques that advanced 'naturalised' conceptions of military discipline.[4] This has resulted in a distorted view of disciplinary practices that unduly emphasises their mechanical, orderly, physical and hierarchical dimensions. Theorists of modern military disciplinary practices have, accordingly, dismissed Foucault's account because it appears to have little to say about the ongoing evolution of modern military forces.[5] Far from mechanical automatons, modern soldiers have been required to exercise enormous levels of initiative, while esprit-de-corps and personal bonds, or 'subjective motivations', appear far more important than the bodily drill and disciplinary obedience of the eighteenth century.[6] Yet Foucault was aware that modern discipline developed through reactions against mechanical forms of discipline, and his late work sought to correct his earlier thoughts on discipline by focussing on governmental forms of conduct. The 'mechanical body' was only a first step in the complete development of the disciplined subject, which was dependent upon a view of the evolutionary growth and internal capacities of the organic, living or natural body.[7] Conceived as a body possessed of interiority and motivation, a body that could command itself and which possessed a psyche or 'soul', the natural body played a crucial role in the transformation of disciplinary procedures at the start of the nineteenth century into biopower.[8] Yet Foucault never incorporated his more expansive views on discipline into his account of military discipline and hence into a full account of the training, conduct and subjectivity of the natural body.[9]

---

[4] See Michel Foucault, *Discipline and Punish: The Birth of the Prison*, trans. Alan Sheridan (New York: Vintage, 1991); and Michel Foucault, 'The Meshes of Power', trans. Gerald Moore, in *Space, Knowledge and Power: Foucault and Geography*, ed. Jeremy W. Crampton and Stuart Elden (Aldershot: Ashgate, 2007), 153–62.

[5] For critiques of Foucault's account of military discipline, see Brieg Powel, 'The Soldier's Tale: Problematising Foucault's Military Foundations', *Review of International Studies* 43, no. 5 (2017): 833–54; Philip Smith, 'Meaning and Military Power: Moving on From Foucault', *Journal of Power* 1, no. 3 (2008): 275–93. John Levi Martin, 'The Objective and Subjective Rationalization of War', *Theory and Society* 34 (2005): 229–75; Richard F. Hamilton, *The Social Misconstruction of Reality* (New Haven: Yale, 1996), 181–84.

[6] Martin, 'The Objective and Subjective Rationalization of War', 264.

[7] Foucault, *Discipline and Punish*, 155.

[8] On biopower, see in particular Michel Foucault, *The History of Sexuality. Volume One: An Introduction*, trans. Robert Hurley (Harmondsworth: Penguin Books, 1981), 135–45.

[9] In an interview in the early 1980s Foucault reflected on the emotional experiences of soldiers at war since the nineteenth century, but only in passing and without reference to his writing on discipline; see Michel Foucault, 'Friendship as a Way of Life', in *Ethics: Subjectivity and Truth. The Essential Works of Michel Foucault, 1954–1984*, ed. Paul Rabinow, trans. Robert Hurley et al., vol. 1 (New York: The New Press, 1997), 135–40, 139.

This chapter reassesses this question of the military discipline of the natural body by focussing on one of the leading works to reconceptualise Frederick's disciplinary regime, Robert Jackson's *A Systematic View of the Formation, Discipline and Economy of Armies* (1804).[10] A military doctor who played a significant role in the reformation of Britain's military medical services, Jackson also sought to radically revise British military disciplinary practices. He dismissed what he viewed as the overly mechanical approaches to drilling soldiers that had been adopted from Frederick, to offer instead an analysis of underlying motivations and performance of the soldier (209). Writing in the aftermath of the First World War, J. F. C. Fuller described Jackson's book as not only one of the most significant analyses of military discipline but also one of the first truly scientific treatments of war.[11] Jackson's proposal to move beyond the mechanical approach to military discipline by instead cultivating the soldier's personal initiative does not simply represent an expression of a more refined sensibility or ethics.[12] Rather, his ideas can be understood in relation to Foucault's analysis of governmental forms of discipline and the concomitant rise of biopower. Biopower concerns corporeal discipline and the training of the natural body, but it also extends past the disciplinary institution to encompass a life conceived in its totality, to thus encourage forms of self-direction and unite individual drives and behaviours with social and biological norms.[13] Conceptualising military discipline in relation to such concerns, Jackson's work conforms with Rancière's 'new regime of writing' that reorients discipline from the imposition of commands to the training of conduct, judgement and perception.[14] Concerned with the expressive, free mind capable of independent judgement, Jackson's book even demonstrates a striking alignment with an emergent Romantic poetics. While, as Christoph Menke argues, aesthetics and discipline would develop in distinct fashion, the aesthetic cannot be understood solely as the counterweight to discipline, but rather the two forms represent twinned modes

---

[10] Robert Jackson, *A Systematic View of the Formation, Discipline and Economy of Armies* (London: Printed for John Stockdale, Piccadilly, 1804). All further references are in the body of the text.

[11] John Frederick Charles Fuller, *The Foundations of the Science of War* (London: Hutchinson and Co. (Publishers) Ltd, Paternoster Row, EC, 1926), 18.

[12] On the relationship between military thought and the humanism of the Enlightenment, see in particular Pichichero, *The Military Enlightenment*.

[13] Jeffrey T. Nealon, 'The Archaeology of Biopower: From Plant to Animal Life in *The Order of Things*', in *Biopower: Foucault and Beyond*, ed. Vernon W. Cisney and Nicolae Morar (Chicago: The University of Chicago Press, 2016), 138–57, 139.

[14] See Jacques Rancière, 'The Politics of Literature', *SubStance* 33, no. 1 (2004): 10–24, 18.

for the practical development of the natural body that is bounded by the senses.[15] Demonstrating its own concerns with life, writing and embodied cognition, the military disciplinary regime first given rational form by Jackson reveals striking affinities with, even as it inverts and redirects, the organicism of Romantic aesthetic thought.

Jackson's Systematic View of the Disciplined Soldier

Born in Stonebyres, Scotland in 1750, Jackson had an inauspicious upbringing as the son of a small landholding farmer and apprentice to a surgeon in the town of Biggar in southern Scotland. However, he went on to become inspector general of military hospitals and one of the strongest advocates for medical reform in the British army. His earliest military service was as a doctor's assistant and surgeon's mate with the 60th regiment in Jamaica in the 1770s, and subsequently the 71st regiment during the American Revolutionary War in Georgia, the Carolinas and Virginia.[16] Although he did not complete his medical degree until 1785, after his return to Europe, he gained considerable medical experience during the war in America and witnessed first hand the devastating effects of colonial disease. He wrote extensively on fevers in the 1790s with *A Treatise on the Fevers of Jamaica with Observations on the Intermittent Fever of America* (1791) and *An Outline of the History and Cure of Fever, Epidemic and Contagious* (1798).[17] Disease was by far the leading cause of death of soldiers stationed in the West Indies and southern colonies of the Americas. In the campaigns in the West Indies between 1793 and 1798 nearly 12,000 soldiers died each year from fevers.[18] Yet, as Alan Bewell has noted, there was an almost complete

---

[15] Christoph Menke, 'Aesthetic Nature: Against Biology', *The Yearbook of Comparative Literature* 58 (2012): 193–95; Christoph Menke, 'Two Kinds of Practice: On the Relation between Social Discipline and the Aesthetics of Existence', *Constellations* 10. No. 2 (2003): 199–210, 200–01.

[16] Norris D. Saakwa-Mante, 'Jackson, Robert (bap. 1750, d. 1827), Military Surgeon and Medical Writer', *Oxford Dictionary of National Biography*. 23 September 2004, https://doi.org/10.1093/ref:odnb/14547, accessed 5 August 2021.

[17] Robert Jackson, *A Treatise on the Fevers of Jamaica with Observations on the Intermittent Fever of America; and an Appendix Containing Some Hints on the Means of Preserving the Health of Soldiers in Hot Climates* (London: Printed for J. Murray, No. 32, Fleet-Street, 1791); Robert Jackson, *An Outline of the History and Cure of Fever, Epidemic and Contagious; More Especially of Jails, Ships, and Hospital: The Concentrated Endemic, Vulgarly the Yellow Fever of the West Indies. To Which is Added an Explanation of the Principles of Military Discipline and Economy; With a Scheme of Medical Arrangement for Armies* (Edinburgh: Printed for Mundell & Son; – and for T. N. Longman, and Murray & Highley, London, 1798).

[18] Alan Bewell, *Romanticism and Colonial Disease* (Baltimore: Johns Hopkins University Press, 1999), 76.

silence surrounding colonial disease in the eighteenth century. It was only by the 1770s that records were maintained of the numbers of sailors dying from disease in the British navy, while the military only began to demonstrate significant concern with ameliorating sickness of soldiers by the 1780s. Jackson was not alone in addressing concerns with disease in the army, but he was one of the first and most ardent to argue that death rates could be reduced.[19] He believed that disease was brought on by a bad arrangement of soldiers' living conditions and hygiene, and was not, therefore, simply the result of the overall hardships of the soldier's life.[20] Returning to service as a military surgeon with the outbreak of the French Revolutionary War, he was rapidly promoted to the British inspector of hospitals. His promotion, however, was against advice from the army medical board, which resisted his approach to revitalising military medical arrangements.[21]

Jackson's interest in military discipline evolved out of his experiences as a military doctor. His second book on the history and cure of fever concludes with a second part that outlines a range of observations on the nature of military discipline, which he believed had been poorly managed in the British military despite its enormous importance.[22] He insists that health acts as the hinge upon which effective discipline depends, as it is through the techniques of the physician that one can improve the 'health, vigour and virtue of the man'.[23] Jackson had observed that military hospitals exhibited higher mortality rates than general hospitals, and he had deduced the simple reason that military hospitals were placed under military rather than medical care.[24] Reversing this dichotomy between the medical and the military, Jackson asserts that military discipline must take into account the functionality and health of the body if the soldier is to be correctly and completely trained for war. As he explains in his *Sketch of the History and Cure of Febrile Diseases* (1817), 'intimate knowledge of the animal structure with a correct estimate of the laws of its movement is a

---

[19] Robert Jackson, *A Sketch of the History and Cure of Febrile Diseases; More Particularly as they Appear in the West-Indies Among the Soldiers of the British Army* (Stockton: Printed and Sold by T. and H. Eeles; Sold Also by R. Fenner, Paternoster Row, London, 1817), 599–600; Bewell, *Romanticism and Colonial Disease*, 78.

[20] Jackson, *A Sketch of the History and Cure of Febrile Diseases*, 599–600.

[21] For an overview of Jackson's career, see Catherine Kelly, *War and the Militarization of British Army Medicine, 1793–1830* (London: Pickering and Chatto, 2011), 24–29 and 34–42.

[22] Jackson, *An Outline of the History and Cure of Fever*, 343.

[23] Jackson, *An Outline of the History and Cure of Fever*, 344.

[24] Jackson, *A Sketch of the History and Cure of Febrile Diseases*, 604.

necessary knowledge for those who assume the task of arranging materials into a military fabric, for whatever purpose that fabric be intended'.[25]

Jackson's *Systematic View* offers a complex account of military discipline because it analyses the underlying foundations of military drill and disciplinarity. As he explains in his preface, he was far freer to elaborate his own views on military discipline than other authors because he was not a military officer and so had not already been indoctrinated into a school of thought on the subject (xi). His resulting treatise offers a 'general' and 'philosophical' account of a 'system of discipline', because it seeks to expound foundational principles governing human movement and physiology, in so far as these are relevant to the military. He opens with a general overview of the human as an 'organic mechanism' possessed of an internal, governing intelligence that is shared by all organic forms (xvi). The experience of revolutionary war and the rise of volunteering in Britain in the 1790s undoubtedly provides a context for Jackson's conception of the soldier as a self-motivated individual. Yet writing as a doctor, Jackson retains a fundamentally embodied view of the soldier as he advances an organic or even vitalist conception of the soldier's internal drives. Explicating what he sees as the organic mechanisms that inform and govern the soldier's conduct, Jackson proceeds to elaborate in a series of chapters how best to discipline this organic body. He considers the natural and cultural origins of soldiers, as determined by nationality, geography and climate, elaborates upon his principles of bodily movement and considers how to organise tactics upon his principles. The book concludes with a wide-ranging discussion of how to maintain the soldier through dietary regimes, dress and exercise.

By approaching the soldier, therefore, from a primarily medical rather than military perspective, Jackson was drawing attention to the importance in military disciplinary practices of what Foucault conceptualised as the 'natural body', a body conceived not as mechanical but as organic and living because it contains its own functional constraints and motivations.[26] Discipline, for Foucault, refers to the specific forms of training and related punitive measures that were employed with increasing frequency within early modern institutions such as the workshop, hospital and barracks. Concerned with maximising the productivity of an individual, disciplines in effect treated an individual's body as though it were a machine that could be precisely manipulated to perform actions. Foucault identifies

---

[25] Jackson, *A Sketch of the History and Cure of Febrile Diseases*, 602.
[26] Foucault, *Discipline and Punish*, 155.

four sets of techniques that facilitated this development of the regulation and instruction of the body. The most elementary mechanism concerned the distribution of individuals in space to enable their individual super-vision.[27] Exemplified through the distribution of bodies into beds, cells or dormitories in military hospitals, prisons and barracks, this mode of distribution developed into an array of techniques for partitioning indi-viduals according to their rank, class or function.[28] Secondly, discipline involved the prescription of regulated and specific movements to control the bodily actions of individuals. Military drill routines were exemplary of this approach as they functioned through precisely coded require-ments for cadenced marching, correct posture and routines for loading and firing muskets.[29] Foucault observes that these techniques revealed new forms of understanding about the body that in turn allowed the imposi-tion of graduated exercises that could increase the body's power over time through increasingly complex movements. Finally, discipline refers to the composition of forces in which every individual takes an assigned place within a group or collective so that their powers could be combined in co-ordinated actions or, as described in the military realm, into co-ordinated tactics.[30] These forms of training not only shaped bodily behaviours, how-ever, but through the process of supervision and testing also ultimately led individuals to internalise disciplinary regimes to efficiently conduct their own behaviour. Bodily disciplinary practices ultimately have the effect of producing an individualised psyche or subjectivity, as an individual not only learns how to conduct his or her own behaviour in line with norms but also equally comes to see him or herself as individuated on the basis of their relationship to those norms. Developed as a set of codified practices around the body, therefore, discipline led to what Foucault terms docile bodies that are simultaneously obedient and yet capable of performing precisely calibrated actions useful for those who command.

A key point that Foucault advances, however, is that the intensifica-tion of disciplinary power's hold over the body, the prescription of ever more precise and detailed regulations of bodily actions, also led to a grow-ing awareness of the body's resistance to disciplinary techniques. As Gilles Deleuze observed, Foucauldian conceptions of power always operate in relation to resistance, in which a modern conception of life is premised

---

[27] Foucault, *Discipline and Punish*, 141–49.
[28] Foucault, *Discipline and Punish*, 143.
[29] Foucault, *Discipline and Punish*, 149–56.
[30] Foucault, *Discipline and Punish*, 162–68.

on the body's capacity to resist the imposition of force.[31] The second set of disciplinary techniques described by Foucault, the prescription of bodily movements, gave rise over time to a perception that the body possessed its own functional requirements and organic constraints. To perfect the disciplinary practices around soldiers' drill, for example, the disciplinarian had to take account of the resistance offered to military movements by the natural position of the hips or the way that soldiers' legs are hinged. Disciplinary techniques must be adjusted to the physical properties of the body, a process that gave rise to an understanding of the naturalness or normality of a body.[32] Foucault does not suppose that a natural body simply exists independently of disciplinary techniques. Rather, it is discipline itself that begins to shape what is to be considered natural or normal about a body, as a body's 'naturalness' only becomes apparent through its resistance to mechanical impositions of disciplinary techniques.

The French military theorist Jacques Antoine-Hippolyte, Comte de Guibert was the first to critique the artificial military drill advocated by Frederick. Cognisant of how the natural body resisted mechanistic approaches to drill, Guibert argued in his *General Essay on Tactics* that the body's natural proclivities, 'intention of nature and the construction of the human body', must be incorporated into drill routines.[33] Jackson's conception of military discipline builds on Guibert's critique, but because Jackson holds a medical view of the soldier he is able to elucidate a far more complex understanding of how the natural body functions. Jackson repeatedly attacks the mechanical principles of discipline that had developed out of Frederick's military drill, because these are concerned, Jackson believes, merely with the outer appearance and apparent forms of the body's movements (65–66). The mechanical nature of British discipline can be seen in the government's *Rules and Regulations for the Formations, Field-Exercise, and Movements, of His Majesty's Forces* (1793), which provided specific instruction on the stance and movements of soldiers. The basic position of the soldier is established as a geometrically precise positioning of the body:

> The equal squareness of the shoulders and body to the front is the first and great principle of the position of a soldier. – The heels must be in a line, and

---

[31] Gilles Deleuze, *Foucault*, ed. and trans. Seán Hand (London: Continuum, 1999), 77.

[32] John S. Ransom, *Foucault's Discipline: The Politics of Subjectivity* (Durham: Duke University Press, 1997), 48.

[33] Foucault, *Discipline and Punish*, 155.

closed. – The knees straight, without stiffness, – The toes a little turned out, so that the feet may form an angle of about 60 degrees.[34]

Similar regulations were provided for marching, the soldier's instruction being that the 'length of each pace, from heel to heel, is 30 inches, and the recruit must be taught to take 75 of these steps in a minute'.[35] Here, the soldier is first expected to perform the 'ordinary step' before progressing to the more complex 'oblique step', 'quick step' and finally the 'quickest step'. The soldier must perform precisely regulated and graduated movements that ensure his body becomes increasingly more capable and effective, while simultaneously under the perfect control of his commander.

For Jackson, such instruction is far too mechanical and has little to do with the actual functions, gait, stance or, notably, judgements of the body. Although he retains a sense that the body is a mechanical entity, he believes that it is simultaneously an 'animated instrument' (147; 3–4). He insists that discipline must be arranged according to 'the powers of exertion rather than the semblance of external figure', to encompass, therefore, the internal principles that animate the 'animal structure' of the soldier (xii). Without such principles, he argues, any apparently uniform behaviour lacks reliable foundations and will simply 'break to pieces under the shock of rude accidents' (3). The soldier is conceptualised, therefore, not as a body that can be mechanically formed into any stance or set of actions, his feet and heels set at 60 degrees or the length of his stride at 30 inches, but is conceived as a living organism that operates through its own drives, internal regularities and structured temporal progressions as it develops habits over time. Jackson thus insists that for the military officer to command, it is crucial that he understand how the body functions, he must possess 'a knowledge of the general laws which animal structure obeys' (4). The officer must be informed by a medical understanding of the body, Jackson concluding that 'some acquaintance with anatomy and the laws of physiology is indispensable for the tactician; for, from these sources it can only be known, correctly, how an animal body acts, and what it is capable of enduring' (4). He offers as an elementary example the importance of correctly regulating a soldier's movements:

---

[34] *By His Majesty's Command. Adjutant General's Office, June 1, 1792. Rules and Regulations for the Formations, Field-Exercise, and Movements, of His Majesty's Forces* (London: War-Office Printed; and sold by J. Walter, at Homer's Head, Charing-Cross, 1793), 3.
[35] *Rules and Regulations for the Formations, Field-Exercise, and Movements, of His Majesty's Forces*, 6.

The human figure is erect naturally. When erect, it has dignity in its movement and majesty in its aspect: when well poised, it has the power of sustaining itself longer than in any other position; for it supports movement with facility, in proportion as it is correctly placed upon a just balance. As this is demonstrable, it is important that soldiers be well set up, according to the military phrase, that is, well placed upon the haunches; so that all the joints and joining of the different parts be brought to bear equally, and be practised in bearing fairly upon each other. That part of training young soldiers, allotted to setting up, is not therefore intended to effect a matter of appearance, which is merely pleasing to the eye. It has a positive use; for if the positions be erect and just, the movement is graceful and easy; and, where graceful and easy, it is supported with comparatively little exertion. (147–48)

No longer concerned with length, angles and appearance, Jackson emphasises that it is the ease and grace of the body that follows from this correct arrangement of movement. The body is understood as a living organism with its own proportions and bearing that result from its underlying anatomy. The graceful movements that can result from following these natural proclivities of the body, moreover, require the least amount of exertion, thereby ensuring a more efficient maximisation of the force of the body. Considered 'as a mechanical, but animated instrument', training of the soldier's body must not be directed at appearance, but at a more complete vision of 'the ability of movement and the power of action' (147).

Jackson proposes that the soldier can only be adequately trained, therefore, by regarding his outer appearance as a series of signs that reveal these inner capacities. The officer must, accordingly, subject the soldier to a far more intensive supervisory regime. Earlier guides for officers demonstrated little concern that the officer should understand the specific capacities of individual soldiers or manage the well-being of soldiers under his care. An *Essay on the Art of War* (1707) had recommended that officers watch their soldiers to ensure that they clean their firearms to prevent them from rusting and that they made sure that cavalry did not sell the oats intended for their horses.[36] But Jackson concerns himself with the complete health of the soldier, pushing far beyond questions of discipline to consider the

[36] *The Art of War. In Four Parts. Containing, I. The Duties of Officers of Horse. II. Of Officers of Foot. III. Of a Soldier in General, with Variety of Examples of Such as Have Been Disgrac'd for Being Ignorant of Them. IV. The Rules and Practice of War by All Great Generals; The Order of Marching, Incamping, Fighting, Attacking and Defending Strong Places, and the Method of Surprizing Garrisons, or Armies, and of Bearing up of Quarters. Written in French by Four Able Officers of Long Service and Experience, and Translated into English by an English Officer. Illustrated with Several Copper Cuts* (London: Printed, and sold by J. Morphew, near Stationers-Hall, 1707), 132–33.

regulation of his diet, clothing, sleeping arrangements, cleanliness, exercise and mental states. Jackson believes, for example, that it is crucial for the officer to know

> that the feet of the soldier are actually free from blisters; that the toes are not beset with corns, which, independently of pain, impair the power of the limbs; that the nails do not grow into the flesh; and that the shoes, while they are sufficiently strong to endure the march, are also sufficiently easy, so as not to confine the necessary play of the foot or injure parts by their pressure. (305)

There is a proliferation of details that must fall under the officer's observation, whether of the soldier's feet, toes or toenails, details that demand considerable knowledge on the part of the officer himself about the inner workings of the human body. Moreover, many of these details only reveal themselves over time and in relation to 'bodily exertion', for example, when soldiers reach their limits of exhaustion during the army's march (3).[37] Jackson extrapolates that tall soldiers so favoured by traditional military disciplinarians because of their parade ground appearance are not as effective on campaign as soldiers who possess hardy and well-proportioned limbs. Understood as a living organism, it also follows that the soldier's body evolves over time and so requires a far more extended period of training than the mechanical forms of discipline suppose. Discipline must target the underlying habits that give grace to a body's motion before moving on to a concern with teaching the specifics of cadenced military steps (173–74). The disciplinarian must not only understand how the interiority of the body operates, but must encourage the soldiers' full exertions and 'organic growth' (12).

As such, Jackson also focusses on the need to train the soldiers' mind because the soldier, like any organism, is possessed of 'sensibility' that is the source of its animation and exertion (xix, 3). In his analysis of the soldiers' mental faculties, Jackson develops ideas associated with an eighteenth-century view of human sensibility and embodied cognition. Such views had principally stemmed from David Hartley's associationist theories of the nervous system, which had established the nerves as a physical basis for mental states.[38] Hartley's theories served, in effect, as Britain's response to the materialism of Julien Offray de La Mettrie, whose ideas were profoundly important for

---

[37] Jackson, *An Outline of the History and Cure of Fever*, 352.
[38] For an overview of Hartley's ideas and his reception by subsequent thinkers, see Lisa Ann Robertson, *The Embodied Imagination: British Romantic Cognitive Science* (PhD diss., University of Alberta, 2013), 31–81.

the development of military thought as it came to encapsulate concerns with the initiative or self-direction of the soldier.[39] While to some extent continuing an earlier mechanical view of the human body, these ideas also opened up a way of thinking that could orient physicality around emergent concepts of vitality. In his earlier work on fevers, Jackson had offered a corporeal account of mental states when he argued that a fever must be understood as a corruption of the physical nerves and brain.[40] Further developing this corporeality, Jackson imagines the mind as integral to the body's interiority, or, as he states, all organic bodies contain within them 'a certain instinctive, though unconscious intelligence or faculty, directing to what is useful, even regulating in some manner the measure of what is necessary' (xviii). It is thus as important to understand how the mind animates the human body as it is to focus on the physical properties of such animation. He observes:

> in higher class of animals, possessed of locomotive power and faculties of mind, the law of organic action, though hinging upon a common basis, assumes a wider range. It possesses a great variety of form … Human action, for instance, does not spring solely from direct corporeal impression. It originates from objects which are remote. It is called up by memory or recollection of past impression: and, as it sometimes arises originally in this manner, so it is capable of being modified in its progress by similar causes, – causes not corporeal, or not apparent to the eye. (xvii)

Jackson's understanding of how the body takes up impression recalls Hartley's similarly corporeal understanding of memory.[41] In line with a broader body of British thought, from Humphry Davy to Samuel Taylor Coleridge, Jackson nonetheless pushes beyond Hartley's more mechanical emphasis as he draws closer to a view of 'organic action' that takes a wider range and variety because of the actions and impressions of the mind.[42] The mind does not passively receive instruction or impressions from its

---

[39] On the similarity between La Mettrie and Hartley, see G. J. Barker-Benfield, *The Culture of Sensibility: Sex and Society in Eighteenth-Century Britain* (Chicago: University of Chicago Press, 1996), 7. On the importance of La Mettrie as a liminal figure between mechanical and vitalist ideas of the body, see Minsoo Kang, *Sublime Dreams of Living Machines: The Automaton in the European Imagination* (Cambridge, MA: Harvard University Press, 2011), 131. For his importance within the military context, see Yuval Noah Harari, *The Ultimate Experience: Battlefield Revelations and the Making of Modern War Culture, 1450–2000* (Basingstoke: Palgrave Macmillan, 2008), 133–34.

[40] Jackson, *A Treatise on the Fevers of Jamaica* 148–49.

[41] Joseph Priestly, *Hartley's Theory of the Human Mind on the Principles of the Association of Ideas; with Essay Relating to the Subject of It* (London: Printed for J. Johnson, No. 72, St. Paul's Church-Yard, 1775), 208.

[42] Robertson, *The Embodied Imagination*, 8.

surrounding environment, but is itself an active agent informed by the remote objects of memory. Just as the body exhibits organic growth, so the mind develops over time as it too acquires new habits and powers of perception (187). While Jackson is deeply embedded in a materialist reading of the body, he nonetheless directs attention as much to the necessity of cultivating the moral habits of soldiers as the habits of his body; the greatest soldiers are those who possess 'bodily and mental organs, trained, by habit, to move in the proper channel' (17). Viewing the body in terms of interiority, therefore, Jackson conceives the individual as a composite of embodiment and psychology, or as he clarifies in the third edition of *A Systematic View* (1845), '[t]o produce united action of bodily power and sympathy of mental affections is the legitimate object of the tactician. It constitutes military education; and it is important to success in war'.[43]

Dismissing, therefore, the carefully choreographed movements of the well-drilled soldier as too rigid and mechanical to be effective on a battlefield, he offers instead his own idealised vision of the soldier's body: 'sunburnt complexion, a hardy and weather-beaten visage, with a penetrating eye and firm expression of countenance, sinewy and elastic limbs, traces of muscle strongly imprinted, indicating capacity of action, and marking experience of service' (89).

What Jackson foregrounds as 'the attractive beauties of a soldier' are elements that suggest a meaningful interiority and temporality and that constitute marks of 'experience of service' (89). Jackson's view of the ideal soldier contrasts markedly with the example of the perfectly disciplined soldier that Foucault locates in a French *ordonnance* of 1766, 'holding their heads high and erect; to standing upright, without bending the back, to sticking out the belly, throwing out the chest and throwing back the shoulders'.[44] For Jackson, the ideal soldier's body is not perfectly upright, rigid and taut, but is instead a body that exhibits signs of inner processes and experience, inner qualities that are evidenced by its visage, complexion and expression. Limbs and countenance do not conform to a pre-established ideal of martial order but indicate the latent capacities of the soldier, its elasticity, judgement and perception. Jackson's ideal of the soldier is manifested as a figure who develops over time, whose

---

[43] Robert Jackson, *A Systematic View of the Formation, Discipline and Economy of Armies. By the Late Robert Jackson, M.D., Inspector General of Army-Hospital. The Third Edition, Revised, with a Memoir of His Life and Services, Drawn up From His Own Papers, and the Communication of His Survivors* (London: Parker, Furnivall, and Parker, Military Library, Whitehall, 1845), 241.

[44] Foucault, *Discipline and Punish*, 135.

physical appearance bears the traces less of correct discipline than experience, habit and performance. Critically, therefore, the natural body that Jackson outlines is living and animated, capable of guiding or orienting itself through its own, internal actions. It is obviously not possible to take Jackson's work as entirely definitive of the era's disciplinary practices, but he does offer an exemplary rationale and account of discipline. In his vision of the ideal soldier he supplies a paradigmatic figure of the natural body as 'the bearer of forces and the seat of duration'.[45]

Composition of the Tactical Realm

When the *Systematic View* was published in a third edition in 1845, its editors announced that the new edition was needed because the book had been comparatively 'unknown' prior to that time (iii). Yet, if Jackson's ideas remained subordinate to Dundas' 'mechanical' approach, Jackson nonetheless was patronised by the British commander in chief, the Duke of York, and his ideas may well have influenced Sir John Moore's experimental training of light infantry at his Shorncliffe encampments in the early 1800s.[46] Moore was heralded as the leading general in Britain prior to his death at the Battle of Corunna in 1809, having had extensive service during the French Revolutionary Wars and eventually rising to command the British army during its early campaigns in Portugal and Spain in 1808–09. He was also heavily involved with the defence of Britain, and the encampment at Shorncliffe was in part born out of Moore's belief that a French invasion would have to be met on the beaches by a highly trained and determined force.[47] Moore's training regime dispensed with the harsh punishments employed by the rest of the British army and instead sought to cultivate a professional pride in the soldiers.[48] He ensured soldiers exercised frequently and rose early, and that minor infringements were resolved amongst the soldiers themselves. He also required officers to understand and practise everything that they demanded of their soldiers,

[45] Foucault, *Discipline and Punish*, 155. On Foucault's use of paradigms, see Giorgio Agamben, *The Signature of All Things: On Method*, trans. Luca D'isanto with Kevin Attell (New York: Zone Books, 2009), 9–32.

[46] John Frederick Charles Fuller, *Sir John Moore's System of Training* (London: Hutchinson and Co, Paternoster Row, 1924), 85 and 216. The influence may have been through Jackson's first iteration of these ideas in *An Outline of the History and Cure of Fever* in 1798.

[47] Fuller, *Sir John Moore's System of Training*, 66–67.

[48] David William Davies, *Sir John Moore's Peninsular Campaign, 1808–1809* (The Hague: Martinus Nijhoff, 1974), 13–14.

while he organised games and races that both raised morale and encouraged mutual respect between the officers and men. Moore would never face French invasion in Britain, but the light soldiers he trained would go on to play a decisive role under the Duke of Wellington's generalship during the Peninsular War as the light brigade. Epitomised by the elite 95th Rifle Regiment, the regiments forming the brigade not only undertook the traditional role of light troops in performing ancillary military operations such as reconnaissance and covering retreats, but increasingly supplemented the grand operations and battles of armies.[49] Among the first universal soldiers, able to perform any and all military roles, they are today recognised as lying at the origins of the modern soldier.[50] Moore's interest in Jackson's views were also reflected by the then adjutant general, Harry Calvert, who likewise demonstrated an interest in the training techniques of light infantry that would eventually influence the drill routines derived from Dundas and so bring these changes to the army more generally.[51]

The leading criticism of Foucault's work on military discipline is that he understands military tactics in a manner that is too corporeal and mechanical to account for such new modes of individual motivation and initiative that were born from revolutionary war.[52] One of Foucault's most egregious historical errors is his assertion that the replacement of the smoothbore musket by the rifle was critical to the development of Frederick's military drill routines in the mid-eighteenth century. Foucault believes that the rifle compelled disciplinary training to concentrate on the individual soldier rather than simply treating him as part of a mass, because:

> more accurate, more rapid than the musket, it gave greater value to the soldier's skill; more capable of reaching a particular target, it made it possible to exploit fire-power at an individual level; and, conversely, it turned every soldier into a possible target, requiring by the same token greater mobility.[53]

However, Frederick's armies made hardly any use of rifles, which were only introduced into European armies to any extent in the mid-nineteenth century. Because of the complexities of using a rifled musket, nearly all

---

[49] Mark Urban, *Rifles: Six Years with Wellington's Legendary Sharpshooters* (London: Faber and Faber, 2003).

[50] Davies, *Sir John Moore's Peninsular Campaign, 1808–1809*, 15.

[51] Edward J. Coss, 'The British Army', in *European Armies of the French Revolution, 1789–1802*, ed. Frederick C. Schneid (Norman: University of Oklahoma Press, 2015), 107–47, 124; Fuller, *Sir John Moore's System of Training*, 216.

[52] Powel, 'The Soldier's Tale'; Smith, 'Meaning and Military Power'; Martin, 'The Objective and Subjective Rationalization of War'; Hamilton, *The Social Misconstruction of Reality*, 181–84.

[53] Foucault, *Discipline and Punish*, 163.

soldiers prior to this point used smoothbore muskets that were notoriously inaccurate, meaning that, as Gunther E. Rothenberg argues of the Napoleonic Wars, 'tactical doctrines still called for the highest volume of fire in a short time and not for individually aimed fire'.[54] Foucault went on to qualify his remarks in a lecture he presented at the University of Bahia, Brazil, where he asserts that what was critical in the development of military discipline was the introduction of the 'relatively quick-fire rifle', or, in the original French, 'fusil au tir relativement rapide'.[55] Foucault's point here only becomes historically accurate if 'fusil' is translated, as appears more appropriate in this context, as musket – muskets being much faster to load than the period's rifles. This subtle change nonetheless leaves open a conceptual space in Foucault's understanding of military discipline between the massed rapid fire of the earlier musket and, alternatively, the individually aimed fire of the subsequent rifle. Only with the drill routines theorised by Jackson and developed by Moore via the formation of specialist regiments such as the 95th Rifles were large numbers of soldiers trained in individually aimed rifle fire. Moore's light troops were exemplary of a new approach to war fought at the individual level, in which soldiers were trained to fight in relatively flexible or open lines and so depended, at least at some level, upon their own initiative, motivation, skill and mobility. To understand the evolution of disciplinary practices, therefore, it is crucial to recognise that Frederick's drill routines only represented a first step in the longer development of military disciplinary practices. Only with the rifle was discipline able to fully progress beyond its earlier and formative 'technique of masses' to operate at an 'individual level'.[56] Fuller even proposed at the start of the twentieth century that prior to the mechanisation of war there had been two distinct modern military disciplinary systems, that of Frederick and that of Moore.[57] It is Moore's system that has come to underpin modern disciplinary regimes of soldiering.

Associated with a new disciplinary regime of the natural body, the rise of light infantry reflects the shifting demographics of the late eighteenth

[54] Gunther E. Rothenberg, *The Art of Warfare in the Age of Napoleon* (Bloomington: Indiana University Press, 1980), 66.

[55] Michel Foucault, 'The Meshes of Power', trans. Gerald Moore, in *Space, Knowledge and Power: Foucault and Geography*, ed. Jeremy W. Crampton and Stuart Elden (Aldershot: Ashgate, 2007), 153–62, 159; Michel Foucault, 'Les Mailles du Pouvoir', in *Dits et Ecrits. 4: 1980–1988*, ed. Daniel Defert and François Ewald (Paris: Gallimard, 1994), 182–201, 191.

[56] Foucault, *Discipline and Punish*, 163.

[57] John Frederick Charles Fuller, 'British Light Infantry in the Eighteenth Century', Introduction to *Sir John Moore's System of Training*, 242.

century, in which the growth of the population was met with concomitant changes in environments and expansion into the colonies. It was noted by contemporaries such as General Francis Wimpfeen that light infantry represented a solution to the massive increase in the number of soldiers fielded by the French Revolutionary armies, which lacked sufficient time or resources to adequately drill new recruits in the earlier, mechanical techniques, meaning that their soldiers were forced to fight with personal 'activity, spirit, energy, and vigour'.[58] Similar problems were encountered by American revolutionary armies, particularly before Washington's reforms. But Richard Glover also speculates that light infantry were crucial in the regions where French and American revolutionary armies fought because of the broken and dense nature of the terrain: the forests of America resembled the countryside of the Low Countries, which was subject to a range of enclosure movements over the course of the eighteenth century that broke up the country and greatly limited the capacity of armies to manoeuvre or reconnoitre their opponents.[59] The questions of how best to train light infantry was, for this reason, central to Britain's response to the threat of French invasion between 1797 and 1805 because south-east England was a quintessentially enclosed environment. Such environmental changes, however, are intimately linked to the growth of population in these same years. The enclosure movements and colonialism were both fuelled by increasing populations and an associated agricultural revolution. Underpinning the development of the new tactical field associated with the flexibility and vigour of light infantry, in other words, were critical strategic urgencies thrown up by demographic changes. As William McNeill argues, the revolutionary changes in warfare of this era derived from the pressing demands of managing rapidly growing populations.[60] There was a concomitant need to master and control populations, to let the mass or multitude at some level command itself within increasingly

[58] Francis Wimpffen, *The Experienced Officer; or Instructions by the General of Division, Francis Wimpffen to his Sons, and to All Young Men Intended for the Military Profession: Being a Series of Rules Laid Down by General Wimpffen, to Enable Officers of every Rank, to Carry on War, in All Its Branches and Descriptions, Form the Least Important Enterprises and Expeditions, to the Decisive Battles, which Involve the Fate of Empires. The Corrected and Revised Edition of the Latest Date, Illustrated by Notes. With an Introduction, by Lieutenant Colonel Macdonald, of the First Battalion of Cinque Port Volunteers; the Translator of the French Tactics, F.R.S. &c.* (London: Printed for T. Egerton, Military Library, Whitehall, by C. Roworth, Bell Yard, Fleet Street, 1804), x–xi.

[59] Richard Glover, *Peninsular Preparation: The Reform of the British Army, 1795–1809* (Cambridge: Cambridge University Press, 1963), 124.

[60] William H. McNeill, *The Pursuit of Power: Technology, Armed Force, and Society since A.D. 1000* (Chicago: University of Chicago Press, 1982), 185–87.

complex and foreign environments. This was a task reliant on military power's capacity to harness and cultivate the soldier's own initiative and vigour.

From the start of the nineteenth century, in other words, military discipline moved away from its mechanical roots and closer to what Foucault defines as biopower. Biopower can be understood as an intensification of earlier forms of disciplinary power over the body that lifted discipline from its institutional housing and into a surrounding socius.[61] No longer was discipline concerned with bodily docility and usefulness, with predetermining bodily movements, so much as it worked on the formation of a subjectivity capable of administering itself. Admittedly, Foucault developed his related idea of biopolitics in distinction to discipline, because the former refers to techniques used to administer the population rather than the disciplinary focus on training the individual body. Nonetheless, as argued in Chapter 1, the two forms were not 'mutually exclusive', but rather took a variety of forms by which they could be 'articulated with each other' so that strengthening an individual's capacities would support the overall health of the population and vice versa.[62] This combination lies at the heart of biopower, the simultaneous growth and co-ordination of both individuals and populations.[63] As Jeffrey Nealon argues, where only part of an individual's identity is associated with the disciplinary institution, whether a student, prisoner or worker, biopolitical categories such as sexuality or health shape the entirety of an individual's subjectivity, while simultaneously linking an individual with an encompassing social domain.[64]

Biopower is not so much a distinct form of control, therefore, but, at least in part, the result of the increasing intensity and totality in the operation of disciplinary power. It occurs, as Thomas Lemke observes, at the intersection of biological regulation with liberal freedoms and social norms.[65] Nealon similarly proposes that biopower intensifies the forms of

[61] Jeffrey T. Nealon, *Foucault Beyond Foucault: Power and Its Intensifications Since 1984* (Stanford: Stanford University Press, 2008), 47.

[62] Michel Foucault, *Society Must Be Defended: Lectures at the Collège de France, 1975–1976*, ed. Mauro Bertani and Alessandro Fontana, trans. David Macey (London: Penguin Books, 2004), 250.

[63] Foucault, *The History of Sexuality*, 140. As noted in the introduction, however, Foucault does not use the term entirely consistently. For a discussion, see Thomas Lemke, *Biopolitics: An Advanced Introduction*, trans. Eric Frederick Trump (New York: New York University Press, 2011), 34.

[64] Nealon, 'The Archaeology of Biopower', 139.

[65] Thomas Lemke, *Foucault, Governmentality, and Critique* (London: Routledge, 2012), 44.

disciplinary control associated with correct bodily movements to incorporate pastoral care and techniques by which individuals work on their own conduct.[66] Thus, while Foucault intimates that the psyche or soul first emerges out of the imposition of bodily discipline, which individuates a subject in relation to norms of behaviour, this individualised psyche in turn opens itself to further development through internal and symbolic mechanisms.[67] Alan Milchman and Alan Rosenberg distinguish two forms of subject formation in Foucault's work, '*assujettissement*' by which discipline fashions the individual out of its norms of behaviour, and 'subjectivation' by which individuals continue to cultivate their own subjectivity in relation to the truth.[68] In the modern era, the disciplined subject ceases to be a clockwork automaton directed by command from outside, merely through the powers of '*assujettissement*', because life comes to be understood as something that orients itself, that is capable of its own 'subjectivation'. Nealon reads Foucault's more directly biopolitical thoughts back into his broader concerns with the idea of populations and living species:

> This new technique does not simply do away with the disciplinary technique, because it exists at a different level, on a different scale, and because it has a different bearing area, and makes use of very different instruments. Unlike discipline, which is addressed to bodies, the new non-disciplinary power is applied not to man-as-body but to the living man.[69]

Biopower extends discipline into ever more meticulous, complete and individualised forms as it circulates through the living human. Discipline begins in the institutions and the supervisory gaze, but it migrates out into the world and so into governmental forms that integrate corporeal and symbolic processes of control to enable 'government at a distance'.[70] Taking a more expansive view of this history, Lemke suggests that the concept of governmentality works as a 'missing link' in Foucault's oeuvre because it draws together his work on the government of populations and individuals, while also uniting work on domination and techniques for forming the self.[71]

---

[66] Nealon, *Foucault Beyond Foucault*, 41–44.

[67] Lemke, *Foucault, Governmentality, and Critique*, 29–31.

[68] Alan Milchman and Alan Rosenberg, 'The Aesthetic and Ascetic Dimensions of an Ethics of Self-Fashioning: Nietzsche and Foucault', *Parrhesia* 2 (2007): 44–65, 55.

[69] Foucault, *Society Must Be Defended*, 242.

[70] Rose, *Powers of Freedom*, 49.

[71] Thomas Lemke, 'Foucault, Governmentality, and Critique', paper presented at *Rethinking Marxism Conference*, University of Amherst (MA), 21–24 September 2000, 1–2. See also Lemke, *Foucault, Governmentality, and Critique*, 29–31.

It is possible to overstate the novelty of Jackson and Moore's concerns with soldierly conduct, as forms of pastoral care had long accompanied earlier, mechanical disciplinary training. Ilya Berkovich, for example, has shown at length that armies of the eighteenth century were often as concerned to ensure the correct conduct of soldiers as they were to impose rigorous bodily exercises.[72] Arnaud Guinier similarly notes that the idea of the soldier as an unthinking automaton fails to account for the more complex forms of military training appearing in the eighteenth century that were increasingly drawing on ideals of citizenship and motivation.[73] The long-standing antipathy in Britain towards the standing army and the common soldier meant that such views took time to penetrate into British military disciplinary practices, which, for example, still maintained order through the relatively crude corporeal punishment of flogging. But flogging was widely abhorred in Britain because of its association with slavery, including by army officers such as Moore, and there was a growing belief that the overall effect of flogging was to simply degrade the spirit of the soldier.[74] As Secretary of State for War and the Colonies from 1806–07, William Windham introduced various army reforms to ensure that military service would be more acceptable to the common soldier, reducing the length of service and introducing pensions that reflected growing concerns with the soldiers' entire subjective experience rather than simply his bodily discipline.[75] Writing in response to Windham, the author of the *Observations on the Character and Present State of the Military Force of Great Britain* (1806) proposed that 'it is not so much on mechanical dexterity, as on the acquisition of peculiar moral habitudes, that the distinctive superiority of disciplined troops incontestably depends'.[76] Although discipline was never entirely somatic, it was becoming increasingly total and internalised as disciplinary practices targeted the natural rather than the merely

---

[72] Berkovich, *Motivation in War*, 95–127.

[73] Guinier, *L'Honneur du Soldat*.

[74] Daniel Ussishkin, *Morale: A Modern British History* (New York: Oxford University Press, 2017), 36–38.

[75] William Windham, *New Military Plan. The Speech of the Rt. Hon. Wm. Windham, Secretary of State, &c. Relating to the Regular Army, Militia, and Volunteers. Delivered in the House of Commons, on Thursday, April 3, 1806* (Norwich: Printed and Sold by Stevenson and Matchett, and May be Had of All Other Booksellers, 1806). On the introduction of pensions into the British army, see Caroline Nielson, 'Disability, Fraud and Medical Experience', in *Britain's Soldiers: Rethinking War and Society, 1715–1815*, ed. Kevin Linch and Matthew McCormack (Liverpool: Liverpool University Press, 2014), 183–201. On discipline and pensions, see Foucault, *Psychiatric Power*, 47.

[76] *Observations on the Character and Present State of the Military Force of Great Britain* (London: Published by J. Hatchard, Piccadilly; and by A. Constable & Co. Edinburgh, 1806), 8.

mechanical body. Discipline was coming to take as its object a living or organic body that grows, that has its own drives, that unites the individual with a surrounding socius, that is no longer directly shaped by authority and obedience but by its own drives and actions.[77]

This shifting set of cultural assumptions is evinced by the proliferation of Romantic era war poetry that idealised the common soldier as a defender of the nation. Betty Bennett even detects some of the roots of Romanticism in the shifting poetic identity of the ordinary soldier, who was for the first time appearing as a figure of national importance treated with the respect that had formerly been reserved solely for the nation's officers.[78] William Wordsworth elaborates something of this perspective in the 'Discharged Soldier' passage of *The Prelude*, in which he encounters a soldier on the road who relates his history to the poet, '[h]e told in few plain words a soldier's tale'.[79] Meagre and with long arms, Wordsworth's discharged soldier resembles Jackson's idealised soldier's 'weather-beaten visage' and 'sinewy limbs', the poem depicting the soldier as a 'veteran' possessed of latency and experience, a figure of individualised 'solitude' with his own tale and vision of the world. Wordsworth's figuration of the soldier even seems to be subtly responsive to ideas of demographic change as the vagrant soldier is untethered from community, having returned recently from the 'Tropic islands' and now lingering 'in the public ways'. In obvious and striking contrast to Jackson, Wordsworth's soldier is conceptualised in terms of fear and trauma, the soldier appearing to Wordsworth as a 'ghostly figure' who mumbles in pain before meeting the poet and even speaks with a spectral quality, 'in all he said | There was a strange half-absence'. Wordsworth produces what McLoughlin views as an early version of a veteran's poetic concerned with the inexpressible physical suffering of war. But as in other war poetry of the period, Wordsworth more commonly conjoined this new conception of a free soldier to themes of national defence, such as his call to the 'Men of Kent' to 'prove your hardiment' by repelling French invasion.[80] The common soldier may have come to be recognised as a free individual, but almost exclusively this was

---

[77] Lemke, *Foucault, Governmentality, and Critique*, 44. On the modern conception of life as internally motivated and linked with autonomy, see Davide Tarizzo, *Life: A Modern Invention*, trans. Mark William Epstein (Minneapolis: University of Minnesota Press, 2017), 1–13.

[78] Betty T. Bennett, 'Introduction', to *British War Poetry in the Age of Romanticism: 1793–1815*, ed. Betty T. Bennett (New York and London: Garland, 1976), 66.

[79] William Wordsworth, *The Prelude: A Parallel Text*, ed. James C. Maxwell (Harmondsworth: Penguin, 1971), 160–67.

[80] William Wordsworth, 'XXIII. To the Men of Kent. October, 1803', in *The Poetical Works of William Wordsworth ... in Six Volumes ... A New Edition* (London, 1849), 64. Literature Online.

only in so far as he could be associated with the common cause of national defence as the 'vanguard of liberty'.

As military discipline formed around the natural or organic body, then, so it was also incorporating this freedom or liberty of the masses into a vision of military power. In effect, just as disciplinarians were learning how to incorporate the 'resistance' offered to mechanical forms of discipline by the organic body, so they were also learning how to incorporate forms of 'resistance' to political authority. Notably, Moore and Jackson had both first gained experiences of war while fighting in British colonial territories in America, the West Indies and Ireland. In part, this meant that they were elaborating new regimes of discipline and health that overlapped with emergent pressures of demographic expansion, colonialism, social transformation and revolution. They were keenly aware of the health of soldiers under their care, and Moore's training regime incorporated a far greater attention to correct medical care.[81] Yet these were conflicts against American revolutionaries, rebellious slaves in the West Indies or Irish rebels in which both men had witnessed the defeat of mechanically trained disciplined soldiers by soldiers who lacked military discipline. Jackson had observed such events in the American Revolutionary War when a group of sixty new recruits to the 71st regiments had been able to hold off a column of 2,000 Americans despite having 'no skill in the tactic of the king of Prussia' (196). Henri Bouquet had earlier sought to develop lessons from the light infantry fighting in America by concentrating on the skills that could be learnt from the Native Americans, for whom, he believed, 'love of liberty is innate in the savage, and seems the ruling passion in the state of nature'.[82] In his reflections, however, Bouquet turned to classical sources to grasp the importance of liberty. Jackson, conversely, turned to a medicalised understanding of the body that recognises this 'state of nature' in the very structures and composition of the body and its psyche. He establishes an ideal of the soldier that draws on an idea of freedom or resistance that is both political

[81] Fuller, *Sir John Moore's System of Training*, 22–23.
[82] William Smith, *An Historical Account of the Expedition Against the Ohio Indians, in the Year 1764. Under the Command of Henry Bouquet, Esq: Colonel of Foot, and Now Brigadier General in America. Including his Transactions with the Indians, Relative to the Delivery of their Prisoners, and the Preliminaries of Peace. With an Introductory Account of the Preceeding Campaign, and Battle at Bushy-Run. To Which are Annexed Military Papers, Containing Reflections on the War with the Savages; a Method of Forming Frontier Settlements; Some Account of the Indian Country, with a List of Nations, Fighting Men, Towns, Distances and Different Routs. The Whole Illustrated with a Map and Copperplates. Published from Authentic Documents, by a Lover of His Country* (Philadelphia: Printed and Sold by William Bradford, at the London Coffee-House, the corner of Market and Front Streets, 1765), 38.

and natural. What we see with Jackson and Moore's reflections on their colonial experience is the simultaneous reinterpretation of drill through the 'resistance' of the medicalised or natural body and the incorporation of a degree of political autonomy of the rebellious slave, revolutionary citizen or even the free 'savage' into the field of military discipline. Reflecting Wimpfeen's observation that light troops required 'activity, spirit, energy and vigour', Jackson insists that the soldier in the field must ultimately be expected to regulate himself (304). A dimension of regulated freedom came to inform military practice, in particular for the light infantry of the British army who exemplified the use of flexible tactical arrangements.

Essential to the completion of a totalising disciplinary power, however, was the proliferation of tasks for managers, supervisors and subaltern officers, as supervision grew to 'became ever more necessary and more difficult'.[83] Similarly to the forms of conduct associated with sexuality, a greater part of the impact of biopower was initially felt in the development of a nascent professional or middle class that, over the course of the revolutionary era, was coming to find itself united with the nation's wars.[84] Newly heightened concerns were raised about how to command in the field and, even more notably, how to command oneself. These were concerns that went far beyond the traditional emphasis on ensuring the officer's loyalty and obedience.[85] The Royal Military College was established in Britain in 1801 to formalise the instruction of officers, its originator, John Gaspard Le Marchant, believing that it would be the 'single greatest thing ever done for the army'.[86] Thomas Reide noted in the *Staff Officer's Manual* (1806) that there was uncertainty about how exactly to educate the officer, but concluded that it must require the most expansive education:

> Various are the disputes, how and where officers are to be educated, and what they ought to know? In our opinion there can be little doubt upon the matter; give them the best possible education, and teach them every thing which is necessary to be known by an accomplished gentleman in a free country.[87]

---

[83] Foucault, *Discipline and Punish*, 174.

[84] Foucault, *The History of Sexuality*, 120–22. On the importance of the wars in defining a nascent middle class identity, see John E. Cookson, 'The English Volunteer Movement of the French Wars, 1793–1815: Some Contexts', *The Historical Journal* 32, no. 4 (1989):867–91, 868.

[85] Greg Dening, *Mr Bligh's Bad Language: Passion, Power and Theatre on the Bounty* (Cambridge: Cambridge University Press, 1992), 148–49.

[86] Hugh Thomas, *The Story of Sandhurst* (London: Hutchinson, 1961), 15–16.

[87] Thomas Reide, *The Staff Officer's Manual; in Which is Detailed the Duty of Brigade Majors and Aides de Camp, in Camp, Garrison, Cantonments, on the March, and in the Field; with a Preliminary Essay on the Education of Young Gentlemen intended for the Military Profession. By Brigade Major*

Echoing Burke's insistence upon the traditions of the spirit of the gentleman as a 'free' nation's greatest defence, Reide nonetheless supposes that the gentleman does not simply inherit nobility because gentlemanly accomplishments must be constituted through an expansive education.

The first book associated with the Royal Military College was Francis Jarry's *Instructions Concerning the Duties of Light Infantry in the Field* (1803), in which Jarry opined that with a French invasion looming, light infantry would be crucial to the defence of the nation. The light infantry officer operated independently and so had to realise that 'everything that he wants he must find in himself'.[88] Further reflecting on the ideal officer, Reide quoted the Duke of York to the effect that education was crucial for the British officer because he, more than the officer of any other nation, operated at a distance from government or his senior commanders and consequently required a level of intelligence, knowledge and independence that rivalled other armies' generals.[89] Likewise, the underlying premise of the *Essays on the Theory and Practice of the Art of War* (1809) is that the general cannot have an eye to all the 'infinite multitude of details' that constitute war, which must therefore be looked after by junior officers.[90] Frederick had earlier offered some prescriptions for such detail with his 'maxims and instructions for the light troops and all officers commanding in detachment', clearly conscious that light troops escaped the full scrutiny of the general's attention.[91] But his commentary remains at the level of maxims that prescribe a series of actions, his instructions to hussars, for example, insisting that 'he must not, by any means, alight from his horse,

Thomas Reide, *On the Staff of the London and Home District; Author of a Treatise on the Duty of Infantry Officers, Military Finance, &c. &c.* (London: Printed for T. Egerton, Military Library, near Whitehall, 1806), 9.

[88] Francis Jarry, *Instructions Concerning the Duties of Light Infantry in the Field. By General Jarry, Commandant of the Royal Military College at High Wycombe. By Command of His Royal Highness, Field-Marshal, The Duke of York, Commander in Chief* (London: Printed by Cox, Son, and Baylis, No. 75, Great Queen Street, Lincoln's-Inn-Fields. For A. Dulau and Co., Soho-Square, 1803), iv.

[89] Reide, *The Staff Officer's Manual*, 7.

[90] *Essays on the Theory and Practice of the Art of War; Including the Duties of Officers on Actual Service, and the Principles of Modern Tactics. Chiefly Translated from the Best French and German Writers. By the Editor of the Military Mentor. In 3 Volumes* (London: Printed for Richard Phillips, Bridge-Street, Blackfriars. By T. Gillet, Crown-court, Fleet-street, 1809), I. 23.

[91] Frederick II, King of Prussia, *Military Instructions, Written by the King of Prussia, for the Generals of his Army: Being His Majesty's own Commentaries On his former Campaigns. Together with Short Instructions for the Use of his Light Troops. Light Troops. Illustrated with Copper-Plates. Translated by an Officer* (London: Printed for T. Becket and P. A. de Hondt, in the Strand, 1762), 1–8.

or stop at an alehouse to drink'.[92] In contrast to Frederick's instructions for the light troops, where instruction is framed as an interdiction on soldiers' behaviour, the *Essays* recognise that there cannot be precise prescriptions for such regulation.[93] Arguing therefore that 'it is impossible to lay down specific rules for every case', the *Essays* seeks to enable the officer to 'guide himself'.[94] It repeatedly claims that theory cannot supply a want of practice; the individual officer's judgement is crucial.[95]

These books were expressing the same set of concerns raised by Jackson, that the correct orientation of a free mind is crucial in war. Jackson insists that the soldier who has been trained to operate in open order, in flexible, mobile lines, is a soldier possessed of an 'intelligence'; or, as Jackson states, he has an 'idea in the mind' when he operates and so is a figure who must make decisions or act upon his own judgement when at war. This capacity for judgement above all turns on the soldier's correct use of his eye, because the mind must have its own object of attention, whereas the mechanical soldier has no object of attention. The soldier must possess 'an eye' that is 'penetrating and discerning; it is exercised in conveying intelligence for the information of the judgement' and is reflected in a countenance 'expressive of a free mind'.[96] Such views were anathema to eighteenth-century disciplinary practices that could still only conceptualise freedom negatively – to issue maxims for the hussar not to stop at an ale house. But soldiers are far more valuable, according to Jackson, in so far as they can freely use their 'eye' and so exercise intelligence, discernment, judgement and freedom. He presents a view echoed by Clausewitz, who similarly saw judgement in war as identical to correct perception; the key problem in war was the 'difficulty of accurate recognition'.[97] Clausewitz sums up the entire experience of the soldier by equating the soldier with the eye:

> In war the experienced soldier reacts rather in the same way as the human eye does in the dark: the pupil expands to admit what little light there is, discerning objects by degrees, and finally seeing them distinctly. By contrast, the novice is plunged into the deepest night.[98]

[92] Frederick II, King of Prussia, *Military Instructions*, 188.
[93] *Essays on the Theory and Practice of the Art of War*, I. 244 and 139.
[94] *Essays on the Theory and Practice of the Art of War*, I. 270 and 6.
[95] *Essays on the Theory and Practice of the Art of War*, I. 5.
[96] *Carl* Von Clausewitz, *On War*, ed. and trans. Michael Howard and Peter Paret (Princeton: Princeton University Press, 1984), 143; 146.
[97] Clausewitz, *On War*, 117.
[98] Clausewitz, *On War*, 122.

Capacity in war is defined by the '*coup d'oeil*', a term derived from landscape painting meaning to take in a whole scene at a glance or glimpse that came to refer in military parlance to the ability to instantly recognise the tactical or strategic advantages of any given terrain.[99] As the author of *The Military Cabinet* (1809) claimed, what was important in the training of the officer was that 'it is necessary that every military reader should have as many points as possible presented to his imagination, in order to make him what a good officer ought to be, All Eye – Caution – Decision – and Rapidity'.[100]

Discipline originally relies on the disciplinary gaze that places the disciplined subject under constant supervision; the perfect disciplinary regime would be constituted by an eye that saw everything.[101] To effect discipline, therefore, the subaltern officer must ensure that the disciplinary gaze reaches down into the very depths of each soldier's life. But as revolutionary war moved to the level of the population, so the tactical situations of war were diversifying and proliferating to become just as opaque to the officer on service as Jackson had supposed the soldier's body had become to the disciplinarian. Where military discipline originally concentrated soldiers into barracks and camps to ensure they were fully subjected to a supervisory military gaze, the forms of governmental discipline that developed in tandem with the rise of light infantry required the military gaze to be turned outwards into the field. The gaze that had been directed inwards at the soldier in order to supervise must now be internalised and directed out into the tactical realms of an external world to enable individual conduct, judgement and command at a distance.[102] Jonathan Crary has argued that the surveillance techniques of discipline began to overlap with the cultivation of forms of attention in the nineteenth century, so that 'panoptic and attention techniques now operate reciprocally'.[103] It was

---

[99] Clausewitz, *On War*, 578.

[100] *The Military Cabinet; Being a Collection of Extracts from the Best Authors, both Ancient and Modern; Interspersed with occasional remarks, and arranged under different heads. The whole calculated to convey instruction in the most agreeable manner, and to give to young officers correct notions in regard to many subjects belonging to or connected with the military profession. In three volumes. By Capt. T.H. Cooper, half pay 56th Regt. Infantry, Author of a practical guide for the Light Infantry Officer* (London: Printed by R. Wilks, Chancery Lane, for T. Egerton, Military Library, Whitehall; Sherwood, Neely, & Jones, Paternoster-Row; and B. Crosby & Co. Stationer's Court, 1809), 4.

[101] Foucault, *Discipline and Punish*, 171–73.

[102] On the relationship between the external and internal in Foucault's thought, see Deleuze, *Foucault*, 36.

[103] Jonathan Crary, *Suspensions of Perception: Attention, Spectacle, and Modern Culture* (Cambridge, MA: MIT Press, 1999), 76. For a longer survey of forms of military attention in the Romantic era, see Lily Gurton-Wachter, *Watchwords: Romanticism and the Poetics of Attention* (Stanford: Stanford University Press, 2016).

now critical to regulate this freedom of judgement that defined the officer in the field. Nowhere, of course, was this more keenly felt than with light troops, who were commonly understood, Clausewitz remarked, as the eyes of the army.[104] In his study of light infantry, Colonel Coote Manningham insisted that light troops were precisely that, a light that must shine on war to enable it to be comprehended.[105] Indeed, Clausewitz even insisted that the officer must acquire the skills of the light soldier, the 'hussar and jäeger'.[106] Jackson's work was linked to generic developments at the end of the eighteenth century that saw the emergence of a wealth of materials concerned with instructing the officer's powers of perception.

Writing and the Poetics of Military Discipline

The theorist of military information technologies Paul Virilio contends that perception has always been critical to the historical development of warfare. Historical modes of vision are simultaneously the forms by which weapons operate, so that the enemy who is to be killed or captured must equally be observed and understood, even captivated by one's own spectacle of military power.[107] Believing that 'the history of battle is primarily the history of radically changing fields of perception', Virilio argues that war in the twentieth century came to be dominated by the technical media of cinema that accelerated the rate at which information could flow, approaching the absolute speed of light and hence the effective erasure of all spatial distance.[108] Concerned with the relationship between warfare and contemporary forms of visual media, Virilio only sketches a very brief history of earlier forms of military perception.[109] However, this longer history of media and war was, to some extent, developed by Friedrich Kittler, who described his work on media as an attempt to catch up with Virilio's insights on the relationship between war and technologies of perception.[110] Extending Virilio's claims, Kittler argues that modern, technical media are

---

[104] Clausewitz, *On War*, 302.
[105] Fuller, *Sir John Moore's System of Training*, 136.
[106] Philipp Von Hilgers, *War Games: A History of War on Paper*, trans. Ross Benjamin (Cambridge, MA: MIT Press, 2012), 42.
[107] Paul Virilio, *War and Cinema: The Logistics of Perception*, trans. Patrick Camiller (London: Verso, 1989), 8.
[108] Virilio, *War and Cinema*, 10.
[109] Virilio, *War and Cinema*, 3–4.
[110] Friedrich A. Kittler, *Optical Media: Berlin Lectures 1999*, trans. Anthony Enns (Cambridge: Polity Press, 2010), 42.

always related to war, indeed, he postulates that war constitutes the historical a priori of modern media.[111] He identifies the first critical development of technical media in the optical telegraph networks that were introduced during the French Revolutionary wars and which, he claims, transformed warfare because they allowed divisions to operate independently of a central command.[112] These were not the first use of telegraphic systems in war, which, Kittler notes, go back to antiquity. Yet with the telegraph systems developed for the command of French Revolutionary armies, and adopted by the British navy in 1795, the telegraph ceased to send simple prearranged signals that could issue or trigger commands. Instead, the telegraph began to operate as a systematic dissemination of military information that could issue commands and receive intelligence at a vastly accelerated rate.

The French Revolutionary and Napoleonic Wars represented the first stage in what Kittler understands as the development of the modern 'innovation factor' in war.[113] Here, Kittler critiques Marshal McLuhan's argument that media emerge from the need to supplement the body by suggesting instead that media emerge from the need for warring armies to defeat their opponents by continually developing better military technologies. As he states:

> The media don't emerge from the human body, rather you have, for example, the book, and the military generals in considering how they can subvert the book or the written word, come up with the telegraph, namely, the telegraph wire; and then to offset the military telegraph, they come up with the wireless radio, which Hitler builds into his tanks. In England Alan Turing or Churchill ponder a way to beat Germany's radio war, and they arrive at the computer to crack the radio signals – and the German goose is cooked, that's the end of the war.[114]

While Kittler is concerned with the wartime development of technical media in distinction to the far older media form of writing, he nonetheless also insists that technical media primarily evolved from a military concern to progress beyond the intrinsic limitations of writing, to defeat or

---

[111] Geoffrey Winthrop-Young, *Kittler and the Media* (Cambridge: Polity Press, 2011), 134.

[112] Friedrich Kittler, 'The History of Communication Media', *CTheory* (July 1996), www.ctheory.net/articles.aspx?id=45, accessed 24 June 2019.

[113] On the 'innovation factor' in war, the ways in which military technologies always emerge in an effort to defeat earlier military technologies, see Gilles Deleuze and Félix Guattari, *A Thousand Plateaus: Capitalism and Scizophrenia*, trans. and foreword Brian Massumi (London: Continuum, 2004), 626, n. 76.

[114] Friedrich A. Kittler, 'Technologies of Writing: Interview with Friedrich A. Kittler', interviewed by Matthew Griffin and Susanne Herrmann, *New Literary History* 27, no. 4 (1996): 731–42, 738.

'subvert' books through new technologies of observation and command at a distance. This implies, therefore, that the book was also involved in the innovation factors of war in so far as it too sought to condense and transmit information. He does not explicitly adduce a wartime dimension for the Romantic book, but he does recognise proto-cinematic qualities in Romantic poetics that suggests a lineal relation with twentieth-century technologies of military perception.[115] The Romantic era book originates within a media revolution that bears traces of these military developments, as writing was seized by the state as a mechanism for promulgating and intensifying disciplinary practices.[116] As much as the telegraph, Romantic era writing and reading allowed the operation of command at a distance as they instigated new, governmental forms of discipline.

The new media form of Romantic writing might not therefore serve as an extension of the body as McLuhan argues, but nonetheless military books correlate with specific bodily disciplinary practices that informed early modern and, subsequently, modern warfare. Earlier changes associated with the early modern military revolution were impossible without print culture and the dissemination of drill books. McLuhan observes that early modern print had been a 'militant transformer' because it revolutionised the modes of perception governing the era's military strategy and weapons.[117] But a new, modern, writing culture was also taking shape in relation to a new politics of revolutionary war. Rancière views this as a 'new regime of writing' that superseded the earlier associations of writing with speech and command by placing emphasis on perspective and the decipherment of signs.[118] The drill books that flourished in the early modern era had been akin to theatrical scripts that provided the commands an officer must use to correctly control the soldiers' mechanical bodily movements. The rise of light infantry and the imperatives of command at a distance were similarly met with an outpouring of military disciplinary

---

[115] Kittler, *Optical Media*, 112.

[116] Friedrich A. Kittler, *Discourse Networks 1800/1900* (Stanford: Stanford University Press, 1990), 18; Miranda Burgess, 'Nation, Book, Medium: New Technologies and Their Genres', in *Genres in the Internet: Issues in the Theory of Genre*, ed. Janet Giltrow and Dieter Stein (Amsterdam: John Benjamins Publishing Company, 2009), 193–219, 215; on the media revolution of Romanticism, see Celeste Langan and Maureen N. McLane, 'The Medium of Romantic Poetry', in *The Cambridge Companion to British Romantic Poetry*, ed. James Chandler and Maureen N. McLane (Cambridge: Cambridge University Press, 2008).

[117] Michael MacDonald, 'Martial McLuhan I: Framing Information Warfare', *Enculturation* (December 2011), http://enculturation.net/martial-mcluhan, accessed 24 June 2019.

[118] Rancière, 'The Politics of Literature', 18.

writing, but this writing offered a more sophisticated system of command than that which governed mechanical forms of discipline. Foucault does not give sufficient emphasis to this when he suggests that tactics operate through a 'precise system of command', where

> [f]rom the master of discipline to him who is subjected to it the relation is one of signalization: it is a question not of understanding the injunction but of perceiving the signal and reacting to it immediately, according to a more or less artificial, prearranged code. Place the bodies in a little world of signals to each of which is attached a single, obligatory response.[119]

In this account, discipline appears to operate much like early modern tele-graph systems, built around 'artificial, prearranged code' and automatic obedience. In contrast to this idea of discipline as the mere 'signal of com-mand' (144), Jackson's system of discipline sought to cultivate the soldier's personal judgment, to allow him to direct himself using his 'penetrating and discerning' eye (143). The soldier is exemplified by 'light infantry' fighting in America who repeatedly managed to 'humble the pride of the disciples of the mechanical school' (144–45). McLuhan had pointed to such a shift in his similar remarks on light infantry of the American Revolutionary War, who were successful not because they habitually hunted with the rifle but because they were literate: '[m]arksmanship is not the gift of the native or the woodsman, but of the literate colonist. So runs this argument that links gunfire itself with the rise of perspective, and with the extension of the visual power in literacy'.[120] New forms of military writing can be equated with this politics of writing because they elaborate new ways of making and disseminating meaning in an era of literature and the human sciences, which utilised the 'visual powers' of perception in ways that went beyond the traditional imposition of commands.[121]

Following Rancière's understanding of a new regime of writing in the Romantic era, this change can be understood in terms of the subject's self-formation by 'reading' and decoding the network of signs that compose the world.[122] The tactical knowledge derived from discipline is not wholly formed from drill and the coordination of bodies, the carceral interiorisa-tion of the disciplinary gaze. It is also dependent upon the regulation of the subject's own gaze. A new regime of writing not only structures disci-plinary practices but also regulates a subjective orientation of the soldier

[119] Foucault, *Discipline and Punish*, 166.
[120] Marshall McLuhan, *Understanding Media: The Extensions of Man* (London: Routledge, 2001), 372.
[121] Rancière, 'The Politics of Literature', 18.
[122] Rancière, *The Politics of Literature*, 13.

and his perception, understanding and judgement. The expansion of discipline into tactics and the resulting movement out of the carceral space of the barracks or camp and into the field meant that the soldier had to learn to orient himself in relation to the truth of any given tactical situation. The writing that helps shape the individual through disciplinary mechanisms that 'besiege' the individual in turn enables the subject to orientate itself as it moves out from the 'closed fortresses' of disciplinary institutions and into the 'free' world beyond the institution.[123] The officer or light soldier who reports on this 'free' world must also learn to read and interpret signs, and so is bounded by networks of writing and reading that govern this new mode of disciplinary authority.

He must, in other words, learn how to see and understand the inner depths of both the body and environments, to see and judge correctly, to read hidden forces and to rapidly distil information to its essence. The realm of military reconnaissance and information, the small wars of light infantry, was also, therefore, the realm of writing and hermeneutic reading. War is no longer primarily governed by its spectacular theatricality, but all nature now carries the potential of conflict and so throws the military officer back onto the powers of his reason and interpretation. The enemy must now be understood as a force dispersed into nature who can only be detected through practices of reading and interpreting signs.[124] Kittler suggests that since the First World War, technical media from wristwatches to music have functioned as 'boot camps for perceptions', because they train the eye how to understand the rapidly accelerating speeds at which information travels and so prepare the population for new kinds of wars.[125] But the aesthetics of the Romantic era book had earlier served as a boot camp for perceptions as it mapped disciplinary structures into the subjective realms revealed by the expansion of discipline into biopower. A new hermeneutic of reading oriented the subject towards a regime of signs, enabling the soldier to achieve the *coup d'oeil*, the tactical glimpse, that could elucidate the inner meanings of war's obscurity. A new regime of writing enabled the junior officer to extend vision, command and the rapid dissemination of information into tactical spaces that resisted the general's gaze or control. The junior officer allowed war to transcend the limitations of distance because he was translating command into a more complex system of reason.

---

[123] Foucault, *Psychiatric Power*, 48–50; Foucault, *Discipline and Punish*, 211.
[124] Hilgers, *War Games*, 41–42.
[125] Geoffrey Winthrop-Young, *Kittler and the Media* (Cambridge: Polity Press, 2011), 133.

Rancière does not simply document the rise of a new regime of writing, but is concerned, above all, with the instability of this writing and its conjunction with the politics of emancipation that typified the democratic age. In his assessment, Romanticism operates as a 'literarity' that can break with and move beyond the 'symptomatology' or hermeneutics of human sciences because of its capacity to reorder common assumptions about the perceptible world.[126] An age of writing, therefore, develops in two distinct directions: breaking with all former generic constraints on meaning or, alternatively, establishing a human scientific approach that attempts to pin down the truths of the world. Or, as Gabriel Rockhill proposes, '[w]riting is consequently caught in a continual conflict between democratic literarity and the desire to establish a true writing of the word made flesh'.[127] But the 'democratic literarity' of Romanticism is not wholly distinct from circuits of military writing and their symptomatic readings of nature. Romantic cultural poetics were themselves deeply embedded in a wartime culture, a culture governed by the mediation of distant war and the circulation of what Mary Favret identifies as a 'structural trauma' produced by the apprehensive experience of waiting for war news.[128] Kevis Goodman similarly explores the wartime roots of Romanticism by tracing its new poetics to an emergent discourse of nostalgia that had emerged as a way of making sense of the forced movements, dislocations and traumas of a world ravaged by revolution and war.[129] If Romanticism has roots in a medicalised discourse of nostalgia, nostalgia itself can be understood as a military disease associated with the displacements and uncertainties of military command and management that demanded new modes of militarised attention and perception.[130] As Aris Sarafinos observes in his reflections on Burke's sublime, biopolitical thought emerges out of a

---

126 Samuel A. Chambers, *The Lessons of Rancière* (Oxford: Oxford University Press, 2013), 115; Jacques Rancière, *The Politics of Aesthetics: The Distribution of the Sensible*, trans. and intro. Gabriel Rockhill, with an afterword by Slavoj Žižek (London: Continuum, 2004), 33.

127 Gabriel Rockhill, 'Appendix I. Glossary of Technical Terms', in Jacques Rancière, *The Politics of Aesthetics: The Distribution of the Sensible*, intro. and trans. Gabriel Rockhill (New York: Continuum, 2004), 93.

128 Mary A Favret, *War at a Distance: Romanticism and the Making of Modern Wartime* (Princeton: Princeton University Press, 2009), 161.

129 Kevis Goodman, 'Romantic Poetry and the Science of Nostalgia', in *The Cambridge Companion to British Romantic Poetry*, ed. James Chandler and Maureen N. Mclane (Cambridge: Cambridge University Press, 2008), 195–216, 201.

130 Thomas Dodman, *What Nostalgia Was: War, Empire, and the Time of a Deadly Emotion* (Chicago: University of Chicago Press, 2018), 73; on Romanticism and military forms of perception, see Gurton-Wachter, *Watchwords*; and Jeffrey N. Cox, *Romanticism in the Shadow of War: Literary Culture in the Napoleonic War Years* (Cambridge: Cambridge University Press, 2014), 49–55.

'series of interdiscursive realignments' that unite medical knowledge with the insights of aesthetics.[131] Christoph Menke likewise argues that aesthetic training is critical to the completion of discipline because it enables the individual to independently read signs and make judgements, and so allows an individual to comport him or herself towards the truth.[132] Reflecting on Schiller's concerns with aesthetic education, which he regards as the 'first manifesto' of the modern aesthetic regime of art, Rancière similarly proposes that aesthetic cultivation is necessarily linked to the management and creation of new modes of communal life.[133]

The intensification of discipline into biopower occurred within this medicalised-military cultural milieu. Indeed, it is perhaps more than simply a coincidence that both Jackson and Schiller served as military doctors. Linda Marilyn Austin has traced how Schiller's thoughts on naive and sentimental poetry were based on his treatment of the nostalgic military patient 'Grammont' at the Stuttgart Military Academy.[134] Schiller's cure was based on the belief that time spent strolling in the countryside could stand in for the lost, native country that Grammont had left behind when he embarked upon military service. Romantic poetry might thus serve as a cure for the nostalgia caused by the forced movements or pathologies of motion engendered by war. But Jackson's 'manifesto' for a new kind of disciplinary regime could also be read, in its own way, as a cure for the pathologies of motion associated with war.[135] In his attention to the bodily resistance offered by mechanical or forced military movements, Jackson was similarly attacking compulsory motion, but doing so by proposing that motion must be organised to allow internalised, organic and self-directed movement. Where Schiller found a cure for military nostalgia in the poetry of the countryside, Jackson regards sublime nature as a training for war:

---

[131] Aris Sarafianos, 'Pain, Labor, and the Sublime: Medical Gymnastics and Burke's Aesthetics', *Representations* 91, no. 1 (2005): 58–83, 77.

[132] Christoph Menke, 'A Different Taste: Neither Autonomy nor Mass Consumption', in *Cultural Transformations of the Public Sphere: Contemporary and Historical Perspectives*, ed. Bernd Fischer and May Mergenthaler (Oxford: Peter Lang, 2015), 183–202.

[133] Jacques Rancière, 'The Aesthetic Revolution and Its Outcomes', *New Left Review* 14 (2002): 133–51, 133.

[134] Linda Marilyn Austin, *Nostalgia in Transition, 1780–1917* (Charlottesville: The University of Virginia Press, 2007), 4–15.

[135] Jackson eventually went on to extrapolate an even more far-reaching politics of life based on his understanding of the physical nature of the human: *An Outline for the Political Organization and Moral Training of the Human Race* (Stockton, CA: Printed for the Author, by W. Robinson, 1823).

Cataracts and precipices, the fury of the elements, in storms of wind and rain and thunder, as they strike the imagination forcibly and awfully at the time, so they leave an impression of something sublime, which grows and expands with reflexion, in the calm which succeeds. A new channel is opened for the course of grand ideas: experience is gained of things which are common, and often formidable in war: the judgment is ripened; and the mind acquires confidence, because it has gained knowledge. But, while the mind gains knowledge of useful things, its ideas are elevated to higher regions of conception. Its powers expand in the act of ascending lofty mountains; and its conceptions acquire a magnitude, which corresponds with the command of the eye. (15)

The sublime experiences of nature, awful mountains and storms will elevate and expand an individual's mind in a manner peculiarly suited to war and the exercise of judgement, conception and the 'command of the eye'. Jackson elaborates a basic function of the sublime as a concern with training the senses and preparing the individual for the encounter with terror and pain.[136] To cure the sickness or failure of motion, for the soldier to move freely beyond the mechanics of the strict disciplinarian in accord with the natural proclivities of the organic body, the soldier must be adept at the reading practices developed within Romantic poetics.

The aesthetic regime can be seen in both a new poetry and a new politics of sense, a new way of being in the world that locates the individual not in relation to rhetoric, speech and the hierarchy of genre, but to a new kind of experience of the natural world and its interpretation.[137] Where, formerly, a rhetoric of action determined who could see and say what mattered, now any wanderer sees the same thing because the individual's perceptions are just as valuable and valid as those of the king or general. Possessed of a radical democratic potential for emancipation, the poem resembles the march of revolutionaries into battle, Rancière even labelling the lyric poem's encounter with nature a 'reconnaissance trip'.[138] Clausewitz was conscious that the importance of imagination in war might leave the poet 'shocked', but similarly held that imagination was critical for the soldier in the field.[139] *Essays on the Theory and Practice of the Art of War* models the reconnaissance officer on the poet or painter, who must cultivate 'a quick

[136] Simon Strick, *American Dolorologies: Pain, Sentimentalism, Biopolitics* (Albany: State University of New York Press, 2014), 26.

[137] Jacques Rancière, *The Flesh of Words: The Politics of Writing*, trans. Charlotte Mandell (Stanford: Stanford University Press, 2004), 9.

[138] Rancière, *The Flesh of Words*, 13–14.

[139] Clausewitz, *On War*, 109.

and sure eye', an eye that penetrates and discerns the tactical importance of war to perform the 'power of judgement' that Clausewitz argued was crucial for the officer.[140] Reconnaissance was, for the officer, just like taste for the 'professor of fine arts', because it is an art in which the informed eye must be trained to make its own judgements in practice but which can never be a mechanical application of rules.[141] Of course the introduction of transcendental philosophy into Romantic poetics would stand in tension with the embodied sensory ideas developed from Hartley. So too, there was little settled opinion in the era on the relationship of mind and body. Rancière is adamant that the poem is distinguished from the era's politics, that there is, on the one hand, a 'natural life' that sees the world just like the biopolitical state, and on the other, a 'historical life' that renders life into something political by suspending the teleology of biological and historical determination.[142] The wartime poetry of Romanticism, in effect, assumes something like a counter-strategic relation to military writing. But as Jonathan Culler points out, in this account, lyric subjectivity is constituted in the same manner as the militarised citizen.[143] At their heart lies a new kind of vitalist approach to the natural body and its training.

[140] *Essays on the Theory and Practice of the Art of War*, I. 138; Clausewitz, *On War*, 112.
[141] *Essays on the Theory and Practice of the Art of War*, I. 5.
[142] Rancière, *The Politics of Literature*, 181.
[143] Jonathan Culler, *Theory of the Lyric* (Cambridge, MA: Harvard University Press, 2015), 322–25.

CHAPTER 4

More a Poet than a Statesman
The Epic Vigour of Charles Pasley's Military Policy

While Henry Lloyd's *History* decisively influenced the evolution of military thought, it did so in a manner redolent of Edmund Burke's foundational writing on the sublime.[1] Its importance primarily lay in its generic innovation and the ways in which its somatic approach to war engendered a new set of historical, philosophical and proto-sociological developments in military thought. Lloyd himself helped pioneer one such further field of military knowledge through his widely read *A Political and Military Rhapsody, on the Invasion and Defence of Great Britain and Ireland* (1779).[2] Composed during the American Revolutionary War and initially suppressed by the British government because it contained sensitive information about the security of Britain, Lloyd's *Reflections* nonetheless achieved a posthumous fame during the era of the French Revolutionary Wars. The book was republished seven times between 1790 and 1803, while a French and German translation appeared in 1801 and 1804 respectively.[3] Offering a detailed plan for the defence of Britain from French invasion, the book was clearly of relevance to Britain's precarious situation during the 1790s and early 1800s. But the book was also innovative in its considerations of how the nation could be organised as an effective military force, even sketching themes and ideas that would reappear in the second part of Lloyd's history as he questioned how best to calculate the military effectiveness of population and the industry and spirit with which different

---

[1] Clifford Siskin, *The Work of Writing: Literature and Social Change in Britain, 1700–1830* (Baltimore and London: John Hopkins University Press, 1998), 70.
[2] Henry Lloyd, *A Political and Military Rhapsody, on the Invasion and Defence of Great Britain and Ireland. Illustrated with three copper-plates. By the Late General Lloyd. To Which is Annexed, a Short Account of the Author, and a Supplement by the Editor. The Second Edition. With Additions and Improvements* (London: Sold by Debret, Piccadilly; Sewell, Cornhill; Clark, Lincoln's Inn; and Mayler, Bath, 1792).
[3] Patrick Speelman, *War, Society and Enlightenment: The Works of General Lloyd* (Leiden: Brill, 2005), 328–29.

forms of government wage war.[4] Henri-Antoine Jomini believed he was the first to formulate a 'military policy' that accounted for such matters, but he added that the roots of this concept lay with Lloyd's elaboration of a 'philosophy of war'.[5] Moreover, Jomini was careful to distinguish his understanding of strategy from this philosophy of war by proposing that strategy constituted a positive science against what always shaded into the 'poetry and metaphysics of war' involved with commanding the people's passions and spirit.[6] Carl von Clausewitz similarly offered a philosophical analysis of policy, by suggesting that policy might encapsulate the entirety of war because it brought together all other elements: 'It can be taken as agreed that the aim of policy is to unify and reconcile all aspects of internal administration as well as of spiritual values, and whatever else the moral philosopher may care to add'.[7] In his expansive view of policy, Clausewitz argued that while war had its own laws, in its totality it was 'policy' itself, policy thus 'takes up the sword in place of the pen' and provides the 'guiding intellect'.[8]

The ongoing republication of Lloyd's work on invasion also points to a more extensive philosophical debate in Britain during these years about how the nation was to be administered for war. Despite being overshadowed in studies of Romanticism by the debates surrounding Burke's writing on revolution, inheritance and natural rights, an alternative and in many ways equally significant debate was also taking place in Britain around questions of war.[9] Driven by the political economics of latter Scottish Enlightenment thinkers, this debate was primarily concerned, as Anna Plassart shows, with the relationship between modern, commercial societies and what these thinkers held to be the archaic institution of war. Related to such discussions, a distinctly militarised view of political economical thought emerged in the work of such writers as Robert Walsh, Francis Gould Leckie and, significantly, Charles Pasley. One of the first books to conceptualise military policy, Pasley's *Essay on the Military Policy*

---

[4] Lloyd, *A Political and Military Rhapsody*, 18.

[5] Henri-Antoine Jomini, *Summary of the Art of War, or a New Analytical Compend of the Principal Combinations of Strategy, of Grand Tactics and of Military Policy*, trans. O. F. Winship and E. E. McLean (New York: Published for the Proprietors, by G. P. Putnam & Co., 10 Park Place, 1854), 26; 52.

[6] Jomini, *Summary of the Art of War*, 325.

[7] Carl Von Clausewitz, *On War*, ed. and trans. Michael Howard and Peter Paret (Princeton: Princeton University Press, 1984), 606.

[8] Clausewitz, *On War*, 610; 607.

[9] Anna Plassart, *The Scottish Enlightenment and the French Revolution* (Cambridge: Cambridge University Press, 2015), 99.

and Institutions of the British Empire (1810) was the most prominent piece of military writing at this time to ask how Britain should organise itself for war. The editor of *The Times* went so far as to assert that Pasley's *Essay* was as politically important as Burke's reflection on the French Revolution.[10] A military engineer who had fought in the Peninsular War and Walcheren Campaigns, Pasley believed that Britain desperately needed to become a 'military nation' if it were to prevail in its war with France.[11] Written to encourage Britain's continuing intervention into the Peninsular War, the *Essay* was also responding to Leckie's earlier call for Britain to aggressively build an insular empire. Pasley, however, took inspiration from the geopolitical writings of the seventeenth-century philosopher James Harrington to propose that Britain needed to conquer not just an insular but a universal empire across Europe. Scottish Enlightenment thought on war is characterised by tensions between its embrace of civic republican idealisation of military virtue, ideas introduced into Britain by Harrington, and its economic views on the commercial and hence primarily peaceful progress of modern societies.[12] Pasley draws on Harrington, but does so in an effort to expand modern political economic thought by demonstrating how military aptitudes were entirely compatible with the economic progress of a modern nation.

Pasley argues that Britain must pursue an aggressive war of conquest and found a universal empire because a new era of warfare had dawned in which a nation must either expand or else be overwhelmed and die. Pasley's assertions, this chapter argues, can be understood in relation to Carl Schmitt's conception of the birth of a modern, liberal nomos in world affairs, which he saw as a new kind of relationship between territory, law and war.[13] It is a striking coincidence that Schmitt saw Britain's intervention into the Peninsular War as an elementary moment in the formation of this new nomos because it unleashed the absolute enmity of the guerrilla or partisan into European warfare.[14] However, this chapter also examines Pasley's writing in relation to Agamben's reworking

[10] *The Times*, 11 February 1811, Issue 8217, 2.

[11] Charles Pasley, *Essay on the Military Policy and Instructions of the British Empire*, part 1 (London: Printed by D. N. Shury, Berwick Street, Soho; For Edmund Lloyd, Harley Street, 1810), 458. All further references to this edition of Pasley's *Essay* are featured in the body of the text.

[12] Matthew McCormack, *Embodying the Militia in Georgian England* (Oxford: Oxford University Press, 2015), 20.

[13] Giorgio Agamben, *Homo Sacer: Sovereign Power and Bare Life*, trans. D. Heller-Roazen (Stanford: Stanford University Press, 1998),12.

[14] Giorgio Agamben, *Stasis: Civil War as a Political Paradigm*, trans. Nicholas Heron (Stanford: Stanford University Press, 2015), 2.

of the nomos around the concept of biopolitics. Much as does Lloyd in formulating his 'philosophy of war', Pasley develops his ideas of military policy in terms of the sublime task of managing the passions, vigour and health of a population and so addresses concerns that lie at the heart of modern biopolitics. In doing so, however, the *Essay* also furthers our understanding of the aesthetic construction of the nation because it posits a new kind of sublime epic of national survival. Indeed, Pasley not only attracted enormous attention from key British political figures, including the then Foreign Secretary, Marquess Wellesley, but equally from an array of Romantic authors, including William Wordsworth, Samuel Taylor Coleridge, Sir Walter Scott, Robert Southey, Jane Austen and Maria Edgeworth, who, while wary of his calls for conquest, were deeply impressed by the underlying aesthetics of this thought.[15] Marx proposed that the conditions of epic had become impossible in the age of 'powder and lead' and the transformation of 'song and saga' into print.[16] In his reflection on the unity of art with the management of life, however, Rancière sees a new form of epic emerging in the era of print, an epic that was 'written' on the living materiality of the nation by new kinds of engineers.[17] The literary bard who arises from within the nation to lead it in war is replaced with the military engineer who oversees the administration of the nation's martial vigour. War had become the literary province of the military author.

The Military Science of Population

The modern state form and its attendant legal system of international relations were consolidated with the peace of Westphalia (1648), which not only concluded the Thirty Years War (1618–48) but also gave rise to an international politics grounded in reason of state.[18] While war was obviously not abolished, the Westphalian system nonetheless established a

[15] Arnold D. Harvey, *Collision of Empires: Britain in Three World Wars, 1793–1945* (London: Hambledon Press, 1992), 135. On Romantic authors' response to Pasley, see Neil Ramsey, '"A Question of Literature": The Romantic Writer and Modern Wars of Empire', in *Stories of Empire: Narrative Strategies for the Legitimation of an Imperial World Order*, ed. Christa Knellwolf and Margarete Rubik (Trier: Wissenschaftlicher Verlag Trier, 2009), 49–68.

[16] Quoted in Marcello Musto, ed., *Karl Marx's Grundrisse: Foundations of the Critique of Political Economy 150 Years Later*, foreword Eric Hobsbawm (Abingdon: Routledge, 2008), 24.

[17] Jacques Rancière, *The Flesh of Words: The Politics of Writing*, trans. Charlotte Mandell (Stanford: Stanford University Press, 2004), 106–07.

[18] For an overview of the significance of the peace, see Derek Croxton, *Westphalia: The Last Christian Peace* (New York: Palgrave Macmillan, 2013).

more regulated and peaceful Europe because it allowed states freedom to govern themselves while placing a range of civilised restraint on wars between states. It gave rise to a European balance of power that displaced an earlier view that European states existed in accord with an eschatological realisation of universal empire, millennial kingdom of Christ or new Rome.[19] The foundations were consequently laid for the possibility of liberal or cosmopolitan end to war with the interlocking of discrete states into a European political system. However, critiques of liberalism offered by Foucault and Schmitt have analysed these developments less in terms of the progress of civilised reason than in terms of the birth of new forms of state power and rule, or what Schmitt views as the historically contingent *jus publicum Europaeum*.[20] Foucault and Schmitt also add, however, that the formation of the modern state system involved the formation of distinct procedures for both internal and external forms of state control.[21] Corresponding with a new international system, therefore, the early modern era witnessed the creation of forms of policing designed to ensure that the internal government of the state would lead to the state's aggrandisement within the system of states. In distinction to contemporary policing practices, early modern policing was concerned with a diverse array of practices and laws that regulated matters ranging from marriages to public health regimes, and which could penetrate into the most intimate of social behaviours. It operated through what Foucault describes as a pastoral power, where the task of government was conceptualised as akin to the running of the royal household, the people who were governed being required to be brought under strict care and administration through police practices.[22] And while external politics always ran up against the limits imposed by wars and other hostile states, internal policing had no natural limits. Because the state perpetually sought to strengthen its position

---

[19] Mitchell Dean, *The Signature of Power: Sovereignty, Governmentality and Biopolitics* (London: Sage, 2013), 135.

[20] Mark Neocleous, 'Perpetual War, or "War and War Again": Schmitt, Foucault, Fascism': *Philosophy Social Criticism* 22, no. 2 (1996): 47–66; Louiza Odysseos and Fabio Petito, 'Introduction: The International Political Thought of Carl Schmitt', in *The International Political Thought of Carl Schmitt: Terror, Liberal War and the Crisis of Global Order*, ed. Louiza Odysseos and Fabio Petito (Abingdon: Routledge, 2007), 1–17, 3–4. For a re-evaluation of the overall importance of the Westphalian peace, see Benno Teschke, *The Myth of 1648: Class, Geopolitics, and the Making of Modern International Relations* (London: Verso, 2009).

[21] Dean, *The Signature of Power*, 106 and 135. See also Mitchell Dean, *Governmentality: Power and Rule in Modern Society* (London: Sage, 2010), 107.

[22] Michel Foucault, *Security, Territory, Population: Lectures at the Collège de France, 1977–1978*, ed. Michel Senellart and trans. Graham Burchell (Basingstoke: Palgrave Macmillan, 2007), 104–05.

within the international system, it required a constant vigilance on the behaviours of its subjects.

This police dimension of the state was not well developed in Britain because political thought in the seventeenth century had primarily been focussed on civil war and the exercise of sovereign authority rather than on the demands of international war.[23] A British tradition of natural law resistance to the authority of the state served to limit the circulation of the state's police procedures.[24] Policies associated with the police were not entirely absent from Britain. William Blackstone drew attention to such policies in his *Commentaries on the Laws of England* (1769), in which he described the police as the 'due regulation and domestic order of the kingdom', a form of 'public health' that regulated issues ranging from clandestine marriage to idle soldiers and the vagrancy of gypsies.[25] But policing in Britain was always focussed more on crime than the regulation and optimisation of public health. In his commentary on police in England, Pierre Jean Grosley noted the lack of regulation, supposing that 'here justice prosecutes offences without attempting to prevent them, through respect for the freedom of the nation'.[26] Foucault even asserts that a new and heterogeneous conception of freedom emerged in British political thought of the eighteenth century.[27] Diverting from Hobbes and Locke's earlier arguments that social cohesion was based upon contractual relations between a sovereign and his or her subjects, Scottish Enlightenment thinkers such as David Hume, Adam Ferguson, John Millar and Adam Smith proposed that civil society evolved historically as a separate domain from the sovereign, with its own independent history, virtues, hierarchies and aptitudes. Freedom was conceived not as a juridical right but as an inherent or natural quality of the society over which a sovereign ruled. Rather than organise society through the police regulation of behaviour, therefore, British political thought posited that good government consisted in the capacity to understand and govern according to the naturally,

[23] Ed Cohen, *A Body Worth Defending: Immunity, Biopolitics, and the Apotheosis of the Modern Body* (Durham: Duke University Press, 2009), 16.

[24] Leonard J. Hume, *Bentham and Bureaucracy* (Cambridge: Cambridge University Press, 2004), 32.

[25] William Blackstone, *Commentaries on the Laws of England. Book the Fourth. By William Blackstone, Esq. Vinerian Professor of Law, and Solicitor General to Her Majesty*, 4 vols (Oxford: Printed at the Clarendon Press, 1769), IV, 162.

[26] Pierre Jean Grosley, *A Tour to London, or, New Observations on England and its Inhabitants*, 2 vols (London: Printed for Lockyer Davis, in Holborn, Printer to the Royal Society, 1772), I.48.

[27] Michel Foucault, *Birth of Biopolitics: Lectures at the Collège de France, 1978–1979*, ed. Michel Senellart and trans. Graham Burchell (Basingstoke: Palgrave Macmillan, 2008), 42.

or independently, occurring properties of society. A new form of governmental reason emerged in which the subjects ruled over by the state had to be understood as members of a population; a collective, living entity that was far more than a collection of subjects.[28]

Conceived in such a manner, however, society's naturalness can be viewed as a contradictory or what Bruno Latour terms a 'hybridized' concept, because while the population operates through naturally occurring regularities and processes, these processes were themselves supported and even at times established by government regulation and administration.[29] Following Mary Poovey's related understanding of how human nature was conceived in the early modern era as the meeting point between nature and human institutions, Ed Cohen proposes that modern conceptions of human life entwine biology and administration in ways that cannot be untangled.[30] This can be seen, for example, in the 'political arithmetic' that was pioneered by William Petty in the late seventeenth century by utilising statistics to calibrate the aleatory events that occurred within populations in an effort to develop more effective government.[31] This statistical analysis revealed hidden regularities within the population, sets of natural processes or phenomena such as rates of birth and death, prevalence of disease or the incidence of particular crimes, which governed collective social and biological life and in turn became the target of government interventions to improve and regulate the overall health and well-being of the population.[32] Knowledge and government of the population came to intersect and promote one another as they together established a modern idea of the population as a collective, living entity, a 'species' or 'race', or, as Foucault summarises, '[a] constant interplay between techniques of power and their object gradually carves out in reality, as a field of reality, population and

---

[28] Foucault, *Birth of Biopolitics*, 291–313.

[29] Cohen, *A Body Worth Defending*, 15. On the paradox of security, that society is a natural given and a cultural artifact, see Mitchell Dean and Kaspar Villadsen, *State Phobia and Civil Society: The Political Legacy of Michel Foucault* (Stanford: Stanford University Press, 2015), 112.

[30] Cohen, *A Body Worth Defending*, 10. See also Roberto Esposito, 'Totalitarianism or Biopolitics? Concerning a Philosophical Interpretation of the Twentieth Century', trans. Timothy Campbell, in *Biopower: Foucault and Beyond*, ed. Vernon W. Cisney and Nicole Morar (Chicago: University of Chicago Press, 2016), 348–60, 357–58.

[31] Andrea Rusnock, 'Biopolitics: Political Arithmetic in the Enlightenment', in *The Sciences in Enlightened Europe*, ed. William Clark, Jan Golinski and Simon Schaffer (Chicago: University of Chicago Press, 1999), 49–68, 49.

[32] Foucault, *Security, Territory, Population*, 74; Michel Foucault, 'The Meshes of Power', trans. Gerald Moore, in *Space, Knowledge and Power: Foucault and Geography*, ed. Jeremy W. Crampton and Stuart Elden (Aldershot: Ashgate, 2007), 153–62, 160–61.

its specific phenomena'.[33] No longer was the strength of a population best developed and directed through obedience to sovereign laws and the distribution of resources, imagined via police regulation. Rather, an effective sovereign was one who possessed knowledge of the natural properties inherent to population, whether these were located at the surface level of the public, its opinions and habits, or the deeper economic and ultimately biological processes that regulated the natural growth and stability of the population.[34] To rule meant to govern with recourse to the human or economic sciences that could facilitate and maximise the effectiveness of these naturally occurring attributes.[35]

Such thought rested on the belief that civil society, or, in Smith's terms, the nation, constituted the underlying motor of history. Civil society develops in accord with its own internal processes, which are composed of the sum of all the activity of its members as they follow their interests and ceaselessly strive to improve their personal conditions. The effect of this activity is to drive the overall progress of society to more civilised, economically developed and socially integrated forms.[36] The history that is constituted by this blind, collective evolution of society is, then, able to be understood as something quite distinct from the idea of history as a lineage of sovereign rule. Critically, it meant that civil society possessed its own relationship to the sovereign's war. Where traditional celebration of a monarch's victories and prowess in war meant that the nation's history could be understood as little more than a sequence of wars, now war appears as little more than a temporary disruption of the underlying development of social and economic forces. While this meant that Scottish Enlightenment thought prioritised questions of economic development and the progress of society towards peace, it also meant that these thinkers introduced new conceptions of war as they sought to make sense of its negative or distant relationship to the nation.[37] Reinhart Koselleck even proposes that

---

[33] Foucault, *Security, Territory, Population*, 79. Michel Foucault, *Society Must Be Defended: Lectures at the Collège de France, 1975–1976*, ed. Mauro Bertani and Alessandro Fontana, trans. David Macey (London: Penguin Books, 2004), 242–47.

[34] Foucault, *Security, Territory, Population*, 71.

[35] For qualifications of Foucault's approach, which tends to flatten some of the distinctiveness of the emergence of the population in the eighteenth century, see Luca Paltrinieri, 'L'Emergence de la Population comme Objet de Gouvernement au XVIIIeme Siècle, en France', *Colloque International Jeunes Chercheurs en Démographie*, University of Paris X, 17–18 November 2010.

[36] Foucault, *Birth of Biopolitics*, 307.

[37] Hans Joas and Wolfgang Knöbl. *War in Social Thought: Hobbes to the Present* (Princeton: Princeton University Press, 2012), 27. On the Scottish Enlightenment and war, see also Mark Neocleous, '"O Effeminacy! Effeminacy!": War, Masculinity and the Myth of Liberal Peace', *European Journal of International Relations* 19, no. 1 (2013): 93–113.

the historical frameworks used by the Scottish Enlightenment to explain societal progress were derived from the Scottish experience of defeat in war against England, which had impelled recognition of historical forces outside a sovereign's own political control.[38] Adam Ferguson believed, for example, that war gave rise to civil society because it provided a rationale for the original constitution of social groups, insisting that 'without the rivalship of nations, and the practice of war, civil society itself could scarcely have found an object, or a form'.[39] In such ways, Scottish Enlightenment thought examined how the social acquired its own distinct relation to war, asking questions about how war is mediated by social institutions, modes of knowledge and national characteristics[40]

Seeking to understand the relationship of a modern commercial nation to war, Scottish Enlightenment thought was also intervening into existing debates in Britain about the relative merits of the militia and the standing army. The English Civil War (1642–51) had stimulated perceptions of the standing army as a source of tyranny over the nation's liberties. Such views gained renewed prominence in the aftermath of the Glorious Revolution at the end of the seventeenth century, as the Bill of Rights prohibited the maintenance of a standing army during peacetime and forced Parliament to enact the Mutiny Act each year to renew the army. Such thought also overlapped with the civic republican ideals first introduced into Britain by Harrington that championed the military value of a militia force in opposition to the standing army. Inheriting this view, many Scottish Enlightenment thinkers were deeply concerned with how to combine a civic republican discourse with emergent ideas of political economy.[41] Placed into a question of historical progress that views society as moving away from its warlike origins, militia service allowed a society to retain the forms of virtue that were otherwise depleted by commercial progress and the attendant growth of idleness and luxury.[42] The standing army is not simply an institution open to arbitrary authority and abuse; it also corrupts the virtues of society because its very existence will lead to a neglect of military virtue amongst

---

[38] Reinhart Koselleck, *The Practice of Conceptual History: Timing History, Spacing Concepts*, trans. Samuel Presner et al.; foreword Hayden White (Stanford: Stanford University Press, 2002), 76–80.

[39] Adam Ferguson, *An Essay on the History of Civil Society. By Adam Ferguson, LL. D. Professor of Moral Philosophy in the University of Edinburgh* (Dublin: Printed by Boulter Grierson, Printer to the King's most Excellent Majesty, 1767), 35.

[40] Jason Edwards, 'Foucault and the Continuation of War', in *The Metamorphoses of War*, ed. A. Plaw (Amsterdam: Rodopi, 2012), 21–40, 27–28.

[41] Joas and Knöbl, *War in Social Thought*, 27–28.

[42] John Robertson, *The Scottish Enlightenment and the Militia Issue* (Edinburgh: Donald, 1985), 8.

the population. As Matthew McCormack observes, 'The militia was a key component of a neoclassical worldview, which pitted the virtuous against the forces of corruption'.[43] The displacement of war from society rendered military issues central to Scottish Enlightenment concerns with understanding the effects of the progress of society.

To some extent, anxiety about the corrupting effects and potential for tyranny of a standing army relaxed over the course of the eighteenth century, as new ideas emerged about the relationship between war and military service.[44] The very phrase standing army acquired its modern meaning during the century, no longer referring to a permanent force hired by a magistrate or tyrant, but to a body of 'professional officers and long-service soldiers' funded by the state.[45] In a countervailing view to earlier thinkers on society and war, Smith reversed the civic republican position that placed luxury and wealth in opposition to a population's military capacities by arguing that the kinds of technological and scientific developments brought about by modern commerce were crucial to an effective military. Because of the modern division of labour, the professional soldier was more effectively trained and habituated to war than the part-time soldiers of a militia, meaning that the standing army could achieve unparalleled ascendancy in waging war against armies composed of militia forces.[46] But although the standing army was coming to be an accepted institution within Britain, this did not wholly end the need for a relationship between society and war. It was precisely because society was seen to be distant from war that modern militarism assumed its importance in preparing a nation for war.[47] Smith recognised that even if it was no longer feasible or effective for the vast bulk of the population to participate in war, nonetheless military education and the cultivation of military spirit were still essential for the security of the nation:

[43] McCormack, *Embodying the Militia in Georgian England*, 193.
[44] Paul Langford, *A Polite and Commercial People: England 1727–1783* (Oxford: Clarendon Press, 1989), 688–89.
[45] J. G. A. Pocock, *The Machiavellian Moment Florentine Political Thought and the Atlantic Republican Tradition.* 2nd ed. (Princeton: Princeton University Press, 2003), 410–11.
[46] Adam Smith, *An Inquiry into the Nature and Causes of the Wealth of Nations. By Adam Smith, LL.D and F.R.S. Formerly Professor of Moral Philosophy in the University of Glasgow.* 3 vols (Dublin: Printed for Messrs. Whitestone, Chamberlaine, W. Watson, Potts, S. Watson, Holy, Williams, W. Colles, Wilson, Armitage, Walker, Moncrieffe, Jenkin, Gilbert, Cross, Mills, Hallhead, Faulkner, Hillary and J. Colles, 1776), III. 52.
[47] David A. Bell, *The First Total War: Napoleon's Europe and the Birth of Modern Warfare* (London: Bloomsbury, 2007), 11–12. See also Julian Reid, 'Foucault on Clausewitz: Conceptualizing the Relationship between War and Power', *Alternatives* 28, no. 1 (2003): 1–28, 16.

That in the progress of improvement the practice of military exercises, unless government takes proper pains to support it, goes gradually to decay, and, together with it, the martial spirit of the great body of the people, the example of modern Europe sufficiently demonstrates. But the security of every society must always depend, more or less, upon the martial spirit of the great body of the people.[48]

While Smith was not advocating a thoroughgoing social discipline, he was insisting that no matter how much war was waged by professional armies, the government must still address the progress or decay of the population's military aptitudes and feelings. Smith even imagines military spirit in strikingly biological terms, observing that the government's failure to cultivate military spirit would allow cowardice to spread through the nation like 'a leprosy or any other loathsome and offensive disease'.[49] However much the modern division of labour meant that war was distant from the nation, the nation could not be separated from its wars.

This conception of a military science that would administer the population for war was first fully elaborated by Jacques Antoine-Hippolyte, Comte de Guibert. As had Scottish Enlightenment thinkers, Guibert developed much of his thought on war in relation to civic republicanism and its valorisation of war as a counter to the enervating effects of luxury and commerce.[50] But his conception of a military science goes far beyond calls for national militia service. Foucault suggests that Guibert's belief that '[d]iscipline must be made national' came into effect at the time of Napoleon as disciplinary power crossed a threshold from the enclosed space of institutions to become an 'indefinitely generalizable mechanism of "panopticism"' operating across modern society.[51] Coupled with Guibert's discovery of what Foucault terms 'the natural body', Guibert might be seen as the first to offer a conceptual basis for modern biopower.[52] But Guibert was not simply concerned with military drill or exercises so much as with a more far-reaching military science that would develop the necessary national habits for war. As Guibert claims of modern governments:

---

[48] Smith, *An Inquiry into the Nature and Causes of the Wealth of Nations*, III, 143.
[49] Smith, *An Inquiry into the Nature and Causes of the Wealth of Nations*, III, 144.
[50] Beatrice Heuser, *Evolution of Strategy: Thinking War from Antiquity to the Present* (Cambridge: Cambridge University Press, 2010), 153–54.
[51] Michel Foucault, *Discipline and Punish: The Birth of the Prison*, trans. Alan Sheridan (New York: Vintage, 1991), 169; 217.
[52] Foucault, *Discipline and Punish*, 155.

> There is not one which has made a calculation on the number and constitution of its troops, on the populations of its territories, on the system of its politics, on the national genius of the subject. There is not one to be found, where the profession of a soldier is respected and held in esteem: where its youth receives a military education: where the laws inspire courage, and are foes to effeminacy: where, in a word, the nation is prepared by its customs and its prejudices, to form a vigorous and well disciplined soldiery.[53]

Indeed, Guibert is more commonly remembered not for his tactical innovations but for predicting, prior to the French Revolution, the rise of a nation in arms that would conquer Europe.[54] Going far beyond a concern with how militia service might foster virtue, he insists that a nation's military strength is dependent upon the wide-ranging cultivation of its virtues, customs, vigour and habits. In a striking departure from the equation of national virtues with military service, Guibert declares that military science represents for a nation a form of 'conquests on itself, by carrying, to the highest point of perfection, every branch of their administration'.[55] Far from being something that the government can achieve through decree or law, this required a military science that could guide and encourage the development of national habits and mores.

Later Scottish Enlightenment thinkers were deeply concerned about the nation's military capacities as they grappled with the implications for Britain of the French Revolution.[56] For these thinkers, the primary significance of the Revolution was what it revealed about how war affected social attitudes and behaviours. As the war grew in scale, so there was a need to reassess prevailing assumptions about how societies matured and whether their evolution was invariably towards commerce, prosperity and peace. James Maitland, Earl of Lauderdale, had been one of the first to argue that the war was no longer against French armies, but against France as an 'armed nation', meaning that the only way to combat France was for Britain to similarly become an armed nation.[57] It was a point subsequently echoed by Robert Walsh, who insisted that the nations of Europe must match the military systems of France, which he believed had unleashed a

---

[53] Jacques Guibert, *A General Essay on Tactics. With an Introductory Discourse upon the Present State of Politics and the Military Science in Europe. To which is Prefixed a Plan of a Work, Entitled, The Political and Military System of France. Translated from the French of M. Guibert. By an Officer* (London: Printed for J. Millan, opposite the Admiralty, Whitehall, 1781), lix.

[54] Beatrice Heuser, *Strategy Before Clausewitz: Linking Warfare and Statecraft, 1400–1830* (Abingdon: Routledge, 2018), 180.

[55] Guibert, *A General Essay on Tactics*, xii.

[56] Plassart, *The Scottish Enlightenment and the French Revolution*, 109.

[57] Plassart, *The Scottish Enlightenment and the French Revolution*, 111.

new kind of military power into Europe exactly as Guibert had predicted.[58] A pessimistic view was emerging as to whether historical progress would actually bring peace, leading late Scottish Enlightenment thought away from its civic republican roots to instead address questions first posited by Smith about how best to manage a modern nation through education, print and public opinion.[59] Alongside and in tandem with this political economic thought on war and the population, however, there also arose a body of writing directly concerned with military science and its calls for national vigour. This writing was less concerned with analysis of societal developments than with understanding how this newly emergent military science could work upon the population in ways that echoed Guibert's pronouncements of a nation in arms.

Pasley and the Organic Growth of the Nation

The government's mobilisation of Britain during the French Revolutionary and Napoleonic Wars was matched with a rapid expansion in the publication of military books. Around one in six British men served in some form of military capacity at the height of the wars, a massive increase in soldiering that was augmented by an expanding military literature of drill books, dictionaries and military journals.[60] An unprecedented number of books were also published on the military defences and potential of the nation, particularly following the series of further army reforms introduced by William Windham in his tenure as Secretary for War and the Colonies in 1806. Deemed a veritable 'military revolution', the reforms abolished the defence measures and ad hoc volunteer units first established by Pitt at the start of the French Revolutionary War to instead base Britain's defence entirely upon its regular military forces.[61] With his reforms, the belief that Britain could be defended by either an 'armed peasantry' or a volunteer 'nation in

---

[58] Robert Walsh, *A Letter on the Genius and Dispositions of the French Government, including a View of the Taxation of the French Empire. Addressed to a Friend, by an American Recently Returned from Europe* (Baltimore: Published by P. H. Nicklin and Co.; also by Hopkins and Earle, Philadelphia; Farrand, Mallory and Co. Boston; E. F. Backus, Albany; Williams and Whiting, New York; J. Parker, Pittsburgh; and E. Monford, Wellington and Co., Charleston, South Carolina, 1810), 18.

[59] Plassart, *The Scottish Enlightenment and the French Revolution*, 186.

[60] Linda Colley, 'Whose Nation? Class and National Consciousness in Britain 1750–1830', *Past and Present*, 113 (1986): 97–117, 101; Clive Emsley, 'The Social Impact of the French Wars', in *Britain and the French Revolution, 1789–1815*, ed. H. T. Dickinson (London: Macmillan Education, 1989), 211–27.

[61] Richard Gaunt, 'Ministry of all the Talents (act. 1806–1807)', *Oxford Dictionary of National Biography*. 24 May 2008, https://doi.org/10.1093/ref:odnb/95330, accessed 14 July 2021.

arms' was dissolved in favour of strict military control over all forms of military service.[62] Reflecting this shift away from volunteer forces and towards a professional military were a series of publications that approached the matter of national defence from an almost exclusively military rather than broadly political perspective, including *Thoughts on the National Defence* (1804), *A Dispassionate Inquiry into the Best Means of National Safety* (1806) and *Arcanum of National Defence* (1808).[63] Writing on the state of the nation was central to Romantic historicist thought, as was the desire by authors to intervene into the course of national development.[64] But a definitively military state of the nation was also starting to be elaborated. One way in which a Romantic conception of the spirit of the age was expressed was through the habitual recourse to the nation's martial spirit.

Along with Walsh, the most significant and widely read military authors in Britain during these years included Francis Gould Leckie and Charles Pasley. Robert Walsh was an American author and diplomat who gained fame in Britain for his favourable comparisons of the country to revolutionary France. Leckie was an author and wealthy landowner who had settled in Sicily in 1800. He played a leading role in British intelligence in the country, helping to align the nation's economy with British interests until he was forced to return to England after his identity was discovered.[65] Far less well known than either man when he first began writing, Pasley served as a Royal Engineer and saw military action in multiple campaigns in the Mediterranean, Iberian Peninsula and the Netherlands, including service on Sir John Moore's staff during Moore's ill-fated campaign in Spain. A childhood prodigy, Pasley went on to compose multiple volumes on military engineering and siege warfare during his career in the army, eventually being promoted to head the School of Military Engineering at Woolwich in 1812.[66] Britain's leading expert on the conduct of sieges, his writing and technological innovations were hugely consequential for military engineering, above all his emphasis on the use of the spade that undoubtedly influenced the course

---

[62] McCormack, *Embodying the Militia in Georgian England*, 194.

[63] Plassart, *The Scottish Enlightenment and the French Revolution*, 114–16.

[64] See James Chandler, *England in 1819: The Politics of Literary Culture and the Case of Romantic Historicism* (Chicago: University of Chicago Press, 1998).

[65] Simon Fabrizio, 'The Economist and the Secret Agent. Strategies to Introduce the British Model of Society into Sicily of 1812'. *The European Journal of the History of Economic Thought* 28 (2021): 1–36, 5.

[66] Robert Hamilton Vetch, and John Sweetman, 'Pasley, Sir Charles William (1780–1861), Army Officer'. *Oxford Dictionary of National Biography*. 23 September 2004, https://doi-org.rp.nla.gov .au/10.1093/ref:odnb/21500, accessed 25 May 2021.

of twentieth-century warfare. But his fame as an author rested on his *Essay*, which formed a definitive statement of imperial British ambitions. Written in part from his own experiences fighting in Spain, he offered a remarkably aggressive approach to the question of national defence.

Like Walsh and Leckie, Pasley has been received as a geopolitical thinker. Geopolitics is obviously central to his writing, at the heart of which is his call to Britain to engage in an expansionist course of empire building in its conflict with Napoleonic France. Yet it is also necessary to follow Foucault and Schmitt's emphasis on the relationship between the national and international dimensions of government to draw out more expansive questions of security raised in Pasley's work alongside its geopolitical implications. In various ways, Pasley's writing reflects Guibert's similar concerns with how the government, relying upon military science, could enable the formation of a 'military nation'. Like Guibert, Pasley's work also appeared prophetic as his vision of the future course of the war seemed to be borne out in the years following the publication of his essay. Pasley's insights were even compared at the time with Burke's prophecy of French Revolutionary terrors, although as Michael Sonenscher observes there had been numerous such predictions prior to Burke that were based on a fear of the expansive power of standing armies and war finance.[67] When his *Essay* was republished in a fifth edition at the start of the First World War (1914–18), Pasley was heralded as Britain's response to Clausewitz, having written the 'first really serious attempt to systematise the principles of War as illustrated by Napoleonic methods'.[68]

Pasley composed his essay as a direct response to Leckie's *An Historical Survey of the Foreign Affairs of Great Britain* (1808) (153). Leckie's *Historical Survey* was itself influenced by his time living in Sicily where he had been well connected with British officials in the Mediterranean, including Coleridge and Pasley, along with British generals such as John Moore and Henry Fox, the younger brother of Charles Fox.[69] After he was forced to

---

[67] Michael Sonenscher, *Before the Deluge: Public Debt, Inequality, and the Intellectual Origins of the French Revolution* (Princeton: Princeton University Press, 2009), 23–26.

[68] C. W. Pasley, *The Military Policy and Institutions of the British Empire: An Essay by C. W. Pasley, Captain in the Corps of Royal Engineers*, ed. B. R. Ward, 5th ed. (London: Printed for the Organisation Society by William Clowes and Sons, Limited, 31, Haymarket, London, S.W., 1914), 24. A. D. Harvey suggests Pasley was the equivalent of John Frederick Charles Fuller for the Napoleonic Wars, or in other words, that he was the closest figure Britain had to a Carl von Clausewitz; Harvey, *Collision of Empires*, 307.

[69] Diletta D'Andrea, 'Great Britain and the Mediterranean Islands in the Napoleonic Wars: The "Insular Strategy" of Gould Francis Leckie', *Journal of Mediterranean Studies* 16, nos 1–2 (2006): 79–90, 81.

return to Britain in 1807, Leckie wrote of his concerns about the continued security of Britain's Mediterranean interests, but he also expanded his
thought to consider how the country should employ its navy to defend and
expand its many island possessions and so build what he describes as an
insular empire.[70] His views on the importance of the navy clearly resonated
with other British thinkers who saw the British navy as the best safeguard
of the nation's defence, its redoubtable wooden walls.[71] Britain has even
been dubbed the fiscal–naval state, suggesting that while war, taxation
and state formation were as intrinsically linked in Britain as elsewhere in
Europe, Britain's distinct national character emerged out of its greater reliance on the navy.[72] Yet Leckie advocated a much more aggressive policy of
empire building than other promoters of the navy. His work inaugurated
a shift towards a mid-nineteenth-century conception of Britain as leading
a peaceful free trade empire in which a European balance of power was
no longer maintained through perpetual war but through the civilising
effects of commerce.[73] Leckie lamented that the nation's efforts to maintain a balance of power through piecemeal measures had merely brought
forth the energies of France while limiting that of other nations.[74] The
prevailing balance of power had, in effect, collapsed and could never be
revived in its former establishment.[75] Leckie proposes that a more durable
balance can only be formed if Britain adopts a 'new plan' of aggressively
building an empire united by the sea – an empire of islands and coastal
possessions that could be defended by the British navy and which would
promote Britain's merchant interests, so that 'the scheme of an insular
empire presents itself as the most obvious method to maintain our independence and power'.[76] Unlike the French empire, which was united by

---

[70] Gould Francis Leckie, *An Historical Survey of the Foreign Affairs of Great Britain for the Years 1808, 1809, 1810: With a View to Explain the Causes of the Disasters of the Late and Present Wars* (London: Printed by D. M. Shury, Berwick Street, Soho; and Sold by E. Lloyd, Harley Street, Cavendish Square, 1810), 194–201.

[71] Admiral Philip Patton even echoed Leckie in describing his plans for the safety of the nation as a defence of Britain's insular empire; Philip Patton, *The Natural Defence of an Insular Empire, Earnestly Recommended; with a Sketch of a Plan, to Attach Real Seamen to the Service of Their Country* (Southampton: Printed by T. Nealon, 22, High-Street; Sold by J. Hatchard, Bookseller to Her Majesty, Piccadilly; and by Mottley, Harrison, and Miller, Portsmouth, 1810). All further references are in the body of the text.

[72] Anthony Page, 'The Seventy Years War, 1744–1815, and Britain's Fiscal-Naval State', *War and Society* 34, no. 3 (2015): 162–86.

[73] See Jonathan Haslam, *No Virtue Like Necessity: Realist Thought in International Relations Since Machiavelli* (New Haven: Yale University Press, 2002), 114.

[74] Leckie, *An Historical Survey*, 182.

[75] Leckie, *An Historical Survey*, xv.

[76] Leckie, *An Historical Survey* 195.

war, it would be an empire united by commerce, free trade and mutual enrichment.[77] Britain must conquer, but it would be wholly beneficial to those nations conquered, Leckie concluding that 'if we professed ourselves to be conquerors, any seeming injustice attached to that character would be certainly compensated by the substantial blessings we should confer on humanity'.[78]

Pasley supported Leckie's advice for Britain to adopt an aggressive approach to empire building. The *Essay* offers a series of rationales for this imperial expansion, while elaborating on steps the government could take to establish a vigorous and aggressive foreign policy. The key point that Pasley takes from Leckie is the necessity of growing as a power if England is to avoid defeat at the hands of France, because 'a stationary power cannot possibly resist an increasing one; and that it is therefore right for a nation in our present situation to conquer from a principle of self-preservation' (153).

Where Pasley differs from Leckie is his reformulation of the insular approach to empire building. Leckie presses for the importance of the navy in the defence of Britain, but Pasley argues that Britain must become a 'military nation', defended by an aggressive use of its army. Britain must, Pasley believes, compete militarily with France over the formation of a what he terms, in part echoing Walsh, a universal empire.[79] Although common in Britain during the eighteenth century, the phrase 'universal empire' was normally used to disparage supposed French ambitions to dominate Europe.[80] Pasley, however, draws on Harrington's earlier conception of universal empire as a reference to how a government must at all times either preserve or increase its strength. Harrington had concluded that England's security could only be guaranteed by continually increasing its strength and so forging a universal empire of total European domination. Pasley argues that France under Napoleon is at last about to realise such an ambition to form a universal empire in Europe, and so their designs must be met by Britain's rival construction of a universal empire (29). He therefore urges Britain to adopt an aggressive military policy by launching conquests of other nations, much as it had already done in its

---

77 Leckie, *An Historical Survey*, 18.
78 Leckie, *An Historical Survey* 28.
79 Walsh believed that France was building 'universal domination', Walsh, *A Letter on the Genius and Dispositions of the French Government*, 3.
80 Peter Fibiger Bang and Dariusz Kolodziejczyk, eds, *Universal Empire: A Comparative Approach to Imperial Culture and Representation in Eurasian History* (Cambridge: Cambridge University Press, 2012), 7.

imperial spheres. War must be taken to the continent so that Britain can directly challenge Napoleon by usurping his conquests with its own.

Despite such advocacy of geopolitical expansion, however, Pasley's *Essay* also undertook a thoroughgoing analysis of the inner workings of the nation. Pasley takes Adam Smith's *Wealth of Nations* (1776) as his starting point for his views on national growth, quoting from Smith that 'in every country, the progressive state is the cheerful and hearty state to all the different orders of society; but that the stationary is dull; and the declining, melancholy' (446). While, like Smith, he equates national growth with public health, he argues that Smith has only discussed growth in relation to the country's acquisition of material wealth, not its prosecution of war and efforts to acquire 'national power and glory' (446). Pasley even seems uncertain as to whether the public 'wealth' may be constituted by this national power itself. Asserting that 'the wealth of a state consists in, or at least can only be preserved by its strength and courage', Pasley appears ambivalent as to whether the nation is constituted by the very practices of security that are meant to protect the constitution (508). Catherine Gallagher has shown that a concern with growth was not only crucial to political economics in the Romantic period, but also that as growth became an imperative so it brought with it an attendant awareness of the possibility and fear of decline, so that, '[f]ar from seeming a machine with a fixed input and output, the national capitalist economy was imagined to be a creature facing the distinctly lifelike alternatives of either growing or dying'.[81] Pasley expresses just such a concern with the potential of national failure or even death should it fail to grow. In his *Views on Military Reform* (1811), Edward Sterling proposed that Pasley was the writer who had most dramatically revealed '[t]hat a stationary kingdom must finally be subdued by one which is progressive'.[82]

For Pasley, a recovery of Harrington is vital because contemporary thinkers, Smith, Hume and even Lloyd, could not account for the unprecedented scale of the current war. They saw war as something that was fundamentally distant from Britain, something that had become, in Smith's words, merely the morning 'entertainment' for readers of the daily newspapers (133). So too, by concerning themselves with wealth, they failed

---

[81] Catherine Gallagher, *The Body Economic: Life, Death, and Sensation in Political Economy and the Victorian Novel* (Princeton: Princeton University Press, 2009), 22–23.

[82] Edward Sterling, *Views of Military Reform. By Edward Sterling, Esq. Formerly Captain in the 16th Regiment of Foot*, 2nd ed. (London: Printed by C. Roworth, Bell Yard, Temple Bar. For T. Egerton, Military Library, Whitehall, 1811), xii.

to develop a view of the true strength of a nation (132). The wealth and economic growth of the nation, Pasley argues, cannot be set against its power as a military nation. While using the basic approach of political economic thought, he nonetheless maps out his own understanding of how Britain is placed in its war against France (15–16). For Pasley, there are five 'grand and leading points' in determining the strength of a nation at war, namely 'their population – their revenue – their means of rearing seamen – the energy of their executive government – and the spirit and patriotism of their people' (16–17). Using this framework, Pasley proposes that Britain will eventually be defeated in its conflict with France because on each point France is not only larger than but will also eventually out-grow Britain (15–16). France has a greater population, its taxation system is flawed but can generate more revenue, they only need time to raise more seamen, the executive dimension of their government acts with energy and their people have been inspired by revolutionary sentiments. Neglecting its military, Britain is left as though a defenceless child, or, following Burke, an oak that has been planted in a flowerpot and therefore cannot mature to its full size (53; 130). Britain's current conflict is, for Pasley, far larger than a war against Napoleon because it is governed by a set of underlying economic, political and geographic processes that will determine how the contending nations continue to grow into the future

As such, Pasley regards the nation's resources as essential to its success in the war. Although he believes that governing the nation for war is distinct from governing for wealth, waging war nonetheless equally requires recourse to the human or economic sciences as a means to understand and maximise the effectiveness of the nation's capacities. He treats these capacities as natural or biological conditions, which extend from the depths of the nation's organic roots, its rates of marriage and procreation, right through to the 'surface' elements of public opinion and habit.[83] Pasley takes into account how the economic milieu determines the size of the population and its wealth, taxation, agriculture and industry, and links these underlying economic processes with questions of the public's customs and habits, from the history of their naval experiences to their spirit and energy. Reflecting similar sentiments as expressed as Jean-Baptiste Moheau on the role of population in war, identified by Foucault as one of the first thinkers of biopolitics, Pasley presupposes that victory in war cannot be based on wealth alone, but must be based upon biological foundations,

---

[83] Foucault, *Security, Territory, Population*, 75.

the strength and vitality of a national population.[84] Population was, admittedly, of interest to earlier military thinkers. Maurice de Saxe had appended 'Reflections on the Propagation of the Human Species' to his memoirs, in which he set forth proposals for how to reverse the trend for a population to decline over time.[85] His recommendation included pensions for women who produced ten children and laws limiting marriages to five-year terms to ensure that women are free to remarry if a marriage proved sterile.[86] Lloyd had similarly noted the military importance of ensuring a nation maintain a large population.[87] Pasley nonetheless advances his thought further than earlier calls for growing the population. Notably, he draws on Thomas Malthus to argue that a population cannot simply grow indefinitely, because '[t]he population of every country has a natural tendency, at all times, to increase beyond, and is only limited by, the means of subsistence, which its agriculture and other arts afford to its natives' (503). Pasley draws the conclusion that defensive war is a poor strategy because any loss of territory will rob part of the people of their livelihoods and so will have the effect of driving down the population. Conversely, even if an offensive conflict generates more casualties, any such losses will simply stimulate their replacements by natural processes. The government cannot, in other words, simply legislate to increase the population, as de Saxe supposes, because it must respect and work with the organic processes that naturally regulate population growth. The population cannot be seen as a mere aggregate of individuals to be increased or decreased at will, but must be understood and approached as being itself akin to a living entity.

Pasley retains some sympathy with civic republicanism in his consideration of the relative virtues of alternative forms of governments. Lloyd had adapted Montesquieu's analysis of how forms of government influence their subjects, to consider the influence of different types of governments on how nations waged war.[88] Monarchies and republics, Lloyd proposes,

---

[84] Moheau, *Recherches et Considérations sur la Population de la France 1778. Publié Avec Introduction et Table Analytique Par René Gonnard* (Paris: Librairie Paul Geuthner, 13, Rue Jacob, 13, 1912). On Moheau, see Foucault, *Security, Territory, Population*, 22–23.

[85] Maurice de Saxe, *Reveries, or Memoirs Upon the Art of War by Field-Marshal Count Saxe. Illustrated with Copper-plates. To Which are Added Some Original Letters, Upon Various Military Subjects, Wrote by the Count to the Late King of Poland, and M. de Folard, Which Were Never Before Made publick: Together with His Reflections Upon the Propagation of the Human Species. Translated from the French* (London: Printed for J. Nourse, at the Lamb, opposite Katherine-street, in the Strand, 1757), 261–69.

[86] De Saxe, *Reveries, or Memoirs Upon the Art of War*, 265–66.

[87] Lloyd, *A Political and Military Rhapsody*, 18.

[88] Patrick Speelman, *Henry Lloyd and the Military Enlightenment of Eighteenth-Century Europe* (Westport: Greenwood Press, 2002), 66–67.

each waged war in a distinct manner: the desire for honour and recognition within monarchies was met with the even stronger desire for liberty found in republics. The victories of revolutionary armies had offered strong evidence for just such an association, as the republican American and French revolutionary armies appeared to sweep everything before them in the cause of liberty. Pasley is prepared to admit that liberty offers strength to the political and military capacities of the nation, and that it can be recognised as a natural resource of the nation. Yet he also sees himself offering a corrective to those of his contemporaries who have over-emphasised the military strength of 'the spirit of liberty', insisting (46):

> Patriotism and all other sentiments, partaking of enthusiasm, however deep and lasting their seeds may be sown in the mind, cannot be kept in a perpetual state of exaltation. They are apt to lose their force, unless strongly excited and kept alive, by some urgent necessity, by some striking impulse, that comes home, not only to the head, but to the heart, and, as it were, to the eyes of men. (39)

Related to the ephemeral emotions of enthusiasm, patriotism constitutes at best a weak and unreliable military aptitude.[89] It would therefore be erroneous and mere vanity to believe that a nation's military security was determined by its underlying political character. Even the apparent upwelling of liberty in Spain is of little ultimate effect: spurred on simply by enthusiasm, a 'war of the people', Pasley contends, will simply degenerate into a 'war of the populace' (211).

The only reliable defence of the nation, therefore, is to have 'more numerous, braver, better organised, and better commanded armies' (43). For Pasley, the nation's military strength can neither be identified with political liberties nor personal virtues, as they had been for earlier thinkers who continued the civic republican tradition. Rather, Pasley echoes later developments of Scottish Enlightenment thought, typified by writers of the *Edinburgh Review* such as James Mackintosh and James Mill, who saw the horrors of the French Revolution as stemming from the failure of France's institutions to adapt themselves to the realities of progress.[90] A people's democratic impulses, the natural revolutionary enthusiasm acquired by national progress, needed to be matched with the ongoing reform of institutions, legislature and public opinion that could direct

---

[89] On the problems with unregulated enthusiasm in the Romantic era, see Jon Mee, *Romanticism, Enthusiasm, and Regulation: Poetics and the Policing of Culture in the Romantic Period* (Oxford: Oxford University Press, 2003).

[90] Plassart, *The Scottish Enlightenment and the French Revolution*, 224.

and channel that enthusiasm. Working with a similar perspective, Pasley proposes that the military nation must be formed as a composite of, on the one hand, a naturally occurring set of forces and energies, and, on the other hand, a thoroughgoing military administration that can forge the enthusiastic populace into a unified and vigorous military nation. The nation's military spirit, in other words, must be mediated by the nation's military policy and institutions, and it is these that must take responsibility for national wartime vigour:

> What then is wanting to make us a military people, according to the only true definition of the word. Nothing, but a more daring and vigorous system of martial policy, such as has been traced in the preceding chapters of this work; which requires no change in our political constitution, no sacrifice of our commercial pursuits as a nation, nor of our personal comforts as individuals, – and which, so far from involving us in any imitation of French principles or practices, is as contrary to them as light is to darkness. (482)

So although Pasley looks back to Harrington, who advocated the civic republican virtues of the militia, Pasley insists that the question of personally cultivating virtue and avoiding the corruptions of luxury and commerce is no longer necessary for the nation to become militarily effective. The individual need not abandon personal comforts nor partake of the 'French principles' of revolutionary enthusiasm. Rather, the emphasis falls on the population imagined in the mass; it constitutes a populace or rabble that can be forged into a collective military people through a vigorous national military policy. His thought resembles that of Windham, who insisted on the necessity of reforming the volunteers into a regular military force because:

> In a military point of view, the people are no better than the rough ore, or metal in a mine, which can be converted to no useful purpose, nor made of any value, until it is manufactured. So it is with the people, until a sufficient proportion of them is trained and discipline into an army.[91]

While Pasley retains a belief that the populace and its martial spirit is of critical importance for the nation's military defence, Britain's success ultimately resting upon 'fifteen millions of brave, active and ingenious people',

---

[91] William Windham, *New Military Plan. The Speech of the Rt. Hon. Wm. Windham, Secretary of State, & c. Relating to the Regular Army, Militia, and Volunteers. Delivered in the House of Commons, on Thursday, April 3, 1806* (Norwich: Printed and Sold by Stevenson and Matchett, and May be Had of All Other Booksellers, 1806), 5.

the nation's military policy must progress by harnessing this power into armies and aggressive military policies (481).

Although Pasley wants Britain to become a military nation, this neither means simply unleashing the enthusiasm of the populace nor merely enlisting them into the army. Rather, it is a process that must be governed by a form of military science that can understand the naturally occurring aptitudes, habits and processes of the population and work upon these to raise the overall vigour and health of the nation for war. Pasley aligns with Windham's assertion that '[a]rmies are the channels through which a nation acts, and in which its vigor, energy, and power, are collected'.[92] Pasley assumes a logistical view of the nation; he is concerned with how the government acts, but he sees action as always in relation to the life of the population, which appears as a storehouse of force, an object of administration and logistical control.[93] In this sense, his thought reflects Foucault's biopolitical analysis of how the nation has come to appear as a form of living potential:

> One no longer aspired toward the coming of the emperor of the poor, or the kingdom of the latter days, or even the restoration of our imagined ancestral rights; what was demanded and what served as an objective was life, understood as the basic needs, man's concrete essence, the realization of his potential, a plenitude of the possible.[94]

The population was conceived as a fundamentally living organism but one that must be administered and secured in an effort to perpetually increase its overall capacities and potential: 'A different project was also involved: that of the indefinite extension of strength, vigor, health, and life'.[95] Foucault concentrates on how sexuality was conceived 'in the nature of a public potential', but he recognises that such developments were equally linked to broader concerns with medicalisation and health of the nation that encompassed war and security.[96] As Foucault observes, what has been at stake in wars since the French Revolution is the fostering and

---

[92] Windham, *New Military Plan*, 4.

[93] Cohen, *A Body Worth Defending*, 21. For an overview of the nation as a logistical resource for the military, see Julian Reid, *The Biopolitics of the War on Terror: Life Struggles, Liberal Modernity and the Defence of Logistical Societies* (Manchester: Manchester University Press, 2013).

[94] Michel Foucault, *The History of Sexuality: Volume One: An Introduction*, trans. Robert Hurley (London: Penguin Books, 1981), 145.

[95] Foucault, *The History of Sexuality*, 125.

[96] Foucault, *The History of Sexuality*, 24; 137; Michel Foucault, 'The Birth of Social Medicine', in Michel Foucault, *Power: The Essential Works of Michel Foucault, 1954–1984*, ed. James D. Faubian, trans. Robert Hurley et al., vol. 3 (London and New York: Penguin Books, 1994), 134–56, 135.

development of life.[97] Pasley was writing at this same moment in which war began to be understood from a medicalised viewpoint concerned with the vigour and health of the nation. When Edmund Burke turned to the problem of war with France, he offered a medicalised account of the contagion of French revolution that led him to advocate aggressive war as a means for expelling this contagion, where only 'measures of vigor' could save Britain from sickness and death.[98] Pasley similarly argues for aggressive military vigour as the only hope for staving off the 'disease' of national despondency that must otherwise befall the nation and inexorably lead to its defeat (532).

War and the Nomos of Universal Empire

It is still necessary to recognise the residual neo-classical element in Pasley's analysis of Britain's war with France. As did many writers, including Leckie, Pasley frequently draws an historical analogy between the current conflict and the wars of ancient Rome and Carthage.[99] The problem for British writers, however, was that Britain appeared much more like the seafaring, commercial and ultimately defeated Carthage, with France a resurgent and aggressive imperial Rome. While Pasley follows this equation of Britain with Carthage, he nonetheless advocates Britain to engage in aggressive territorial conquests that resemble the campaigns of Rome. Yet Pasley also recognises the need to draw on a classical analogy because Britain's own modern history has no precedent for the forms of war they are fighting. As he argues:

> In times when the British nation is placed in a situation of danger, to which its past history affords no parallel – menaced with destruction by a much superior force, which is directed by the energy of one of the greatest warriors that has appeared; every man in this country must think with anxiety upon the result: every man must feel, that nothing but the greatest unanimity and firmness on the part of the nation, nothing but the wisest measures on the part of the government, can save us, and with us the rest of the civilized world, from swelling the triumph of the haughty conqueror. (1)

His recourse to the classical conflict between Rome and Carthage does not, in other words, serve as a source of reassuring familiarity for Pasley.

[97] Michel Foucault, 'The Political Technology of Individuals', in *Power*, 403–17, 405.
[98] Quoted in Richard A. Barney, 'Burke, Biomedicine, and Biobelligerence', *The Eighteenth Century* 54, no. 2 (2013): 231–43, 240–41.
[99] Leckie, *An Historical Survey*, 11.

Rather, it provides a way of addressing the absolute violence of the wars, in which not merely the survival of the nation but the future of civilisation itself is at stake. It is this concern with the future of humanity that drives Pasley's turn to universal empire.

In his study of British imperialism during the Romantic era, Saree Makdisi employs the phrase 'universal empire' to associate the development of British imperialism with Gilles Deleuze and Felix Guattari's analysis of the 'universal history' of global capitalism.[100] Makdisi views universal empire as a form of prophecy similar to earlier ideas of a renewed Christian empire, yet reframed as a prophecy of the historical progress of global liberalism.[101] Makdisi's primary task is to examine how Romantic poets resisted universal empire through the recovery of historical difference, meaning that he does not discuss the history of the phrase 'universal empire' in any detail. Nonetheless, his thoughts have a striking parallel with Pasley's conception of universal empire, which represented the most prominent and enduring effort during the Romantic era to prophesy the global order in the explicit terms proposed by Makdisi. Notably, Pasley was overturning a long-established tradition of associating France with universal empire and despotism, while claiming the term for his own distinctive usage. His writing can be understood in relation to developments during the Napoleonic Wars that saw Britain begin to move beyond the traditional balance of power into a universalist idea of progress. If the balance of power remained official British policy, nonetheless this was coming to be reframed in terms of the balance of trade, a realm of globalised free trade and liberalism under the hegemonic power of a benevolent Britain.[102] Pasley updates Harrington's conception of universal empire by uniting Harrington's emphasis on aggression and domination with a prophetic vision of economic liberalism and peace. Britain's territorial expansion would represent a 'blessing to mankind' (529) by rescuing the world from a 'state of slavery' and 'a renewal of the history of the dark ages' if French ambitions for universal empire were to prevail (447–48).

Pasley's view of universal empire can, in this sense, be aligned with Carl Schmitt's sustained analysis of what he termed the global nomos,

[100] Saree Makdisi, *Romantic Imperialism: Universal Empire and the Culture of Modernity* (Cambridge: Cambridge University Press, 1998), 180 and 186, n. 3.

[101] Makdisi, *Romantic Imperialism*, 3; Mitchell Dean, 'Power as *Sumbolon*: Sovereignty, Governmentality and the International', in *Foucault and the Modern International: Silences and Legacies for the Study of World Politics*, ed. Philippe Bonditti, Didier Bigo and Frédéric Gros (New York: Palgrave Macmillan, 2017), 97–114, 106–07.

[102] Paul Hirst, *Space and Power: Politics, War and Architecture* (Cambridge: Polity, 2005), 38–39.

a concept that, as Samuel Baker proposes, has a striking affinity with Romantic conceptions of culture.[103] Baker follows Makdisi's theorisation of Romantic Imperialism, but shifts his focus to propose the vital significance of oceanic thought in Romantic responses to empire.[104] British theorists of culture, Baker argues, modelled their idea of culture on the imperial reaches of the sea, at once attesting to the insularity of oceanic nations and yet also pointing to the networks of circulation and global expanse within which the nation exists. Coleridge and Wordsworth developed their thought in relation to Leckie's geopolitical analysis of insular empire, as they wove a modern idea of culture into Britain's dominant, maritime position in world affairs. While Baker concedes that to link Schmitt's views to such a broadly conceived Romantic conception of culture represents a totalising tendency, he notes that Romantic authors themselves shared Schmitt's 'zeal for totalization'.[105] But focussing on Leckie, Baker does not continue his study past the point at which this earlier naval emphasis was being transmuted into Britain's concerns with its terrestrial second empire and Pasley's militarised conceptions of the nation.[106] Schmitt had even suggested such a continuum of development in his *Sea and Land*, in which he argues that the success of the seafaring Britain gave rise to strategic thought 'in terms of bases and lines of communication', those key concepts of strategy first deployed by Lloyd.[107] Schmitt, moreover, is not concerned with the sea per se, but with the ways in which distinct orders of knowledge associated with the sea and land respectively can be seen to cross, infuse and collapse one another. Baker links British conceptions of the sea to liberal culture, but Schmitt implies that liberal conceptions of the sea equally point to a different set of developments that founded the security mechanisms of the liberal state.

Schmitt's conception of the nomos represents a fundamentally spatial understanding of geopolitics, whereby the *jus publicum Europaeum*, the system of the European balance of power, was premised on a fundamental separation of Europe from its overseas, imperial territories. Within Europe, international laws clearly regulated violence because violence had to be matched with occupation and hence the legal government and

[103] Samuel Baker, *Written on the Water: British Romanticism and the Maritime Empire of Culture* (Charlottesville: University of Virginia Press, 2010), 54–55.
[104] Baker, *Written on the Water*, 258.
[105] Baker, *Written on the Water*, 55.
[106] Baker, *Written on the Water*, 189–209.
[107] Carl Schmitt, *Land and Sea*, trans. and Foreword Simona Draghici (Washington DC: Plutarch Press, 1997), 51.

administration of conquered territories.[108] However, within Europe's imperial territories across the sea, war's violence was waged without this same
legal restraint because warfare here was simply based on conquest rather
than the political incorporation of territories.[109] War waged on the land
and sea accordingly developed two distinct conceptual frames for understanding violence. While the land-based laws of war were concerned with
the correct government of occupied territory, the areas beyond the sea were
effectively lawless, and so warfare here was conducted as little more than
state sanctioned piracy and enthralment.[110] Schmitt believes that the *jus
publicum Europaeum* collapsed after the First World War to form a new,
liberal nomos, but he argues that this was not because of the victory of
liberal freedom. Rather, it was because the laws of the land and sea could
no longer be held apart, meaning that the unlimited nature of violence
beyond Europe had returned to haunt European war. War could no longer be waged within legal constraints but had become increasingly total,
fuelled by forms of absolute enmity and so waged without any regard to the
restraints on wars required for the legal occupation of territory. Liberalism
in Schmitt's view is not defined by its lack of concern with war so much
as it is bounded by new ways of waging war that collapse distinctions
between law and violence.[111]

Despite his focus on the twentieth century, Schmitt was also aware of the
impact of the Napoleonic Wars on the formation of a new nomos and
the shifting boundaries between the forms of warfare he associated with
the land and sea. Napoleonic Europe had, in effect, suspended the operation of the *jus publicum Europaeum* entirely, which was only restored upon
Napoleon's defeat. While Britain was not necessarily the decisive factor in
victory over Napoleon, British sea power had played a critical role and had
thus become integral to the course of European history. Schmitt proposes
that during the Congress of Vienna that concluded the Napoleonic Wars
far less attention was given to the restoration of European dynasties than
to what was seen as the even more pressing task of restraining British sea
power.[112] So too, the nature of war itself had shifted decisively during the

---

[108] Carl Schmitt, *The Nomos of the Earth in the International Law of the Jus Publicum Europaeum*, trans
and annotated G. L. Ulmen (New York: Telos Press Publishing, 2006), 320.

[109] Claudio Minca and Rory Rowan, *On Schmitt and Space* (Abingdon: Routledge, 2015), 223–24.

[110] Schmitt, *The Nomos of the Earth*, 203.

[111] Schmitt, *The Nomos of the Earth*, 354.

[112] Schmitt, *The Nomos of the Earth*, 203. Foucault makes a similar point in his study of the origins of
liberalism, that the Treaty of Vienna concluding the Napoleonic Wars was a compromise between
British claims to command the sea and remodel Europe into a common area with the world as its

wars, no longer regarded as an ordinary element of politics but as something exceptional that posed a crisis for humanity.[113] One of the greatest revolutionary developments related to the wars may have been the transformation of the traditional European balance of power to a generally more peaceful international system based on congresses of the major powers.[114] Schmitt returned to the centrality of this era in his final work on the partisan, wherein he portrayed the partisan, who first emerged with the Spanish guerrillas of the Peninsular War, as a key figure driving the collapse of the *jus publicum Europaeum*.[115] Schmitt believes that we must acknowledge the role of the partisan if we are to shift focus from the history of philosophy and onto the 'reality' of revolution and 'military science'.[116] Although he is adamant that the partisan cannot be likened to the pirates and corsairs of the sea because the partisan is telluric in character, rooted in the living soil of the homeland, modern partisans nonetheless came to be entangled with new and more intense forms of warfare. Their appeals to codes of justice that transcended the legal structures of the state not only led to the failure of legal restraints on war's brutality but also ultimately allowed war to expand into a global conflict of absolute enmity.[117] As the partisan breaks with the telluric nature of warfare, so the partisan is associated with a universalising vision of total military aggression that culminated with Lenin and the Russian Revolution, which first unlocked the full potential of the partisan as a revolutionary force for a new, global nomos.[118]

While Schmitt recognises that the modern partisan who fights with absolute enmity originated in Spain during the Peninsular War, he believes that the Spanish war merely 'lit a spark' that was subsequently contained with the Prussian edict of 1813. While the edict was modelled

market, and Austrian efforts to reinstall the traditional balance of power. The Napoleonic Wars in this view were less another round in European warfare, than a moment of profound debate in the very nature of warfare in which Britain was defining a new liberal idea of war, see Foucault, *Birth of Biopolitics*, 58–60.

[113] Schmitt, *The Nomos of the Earth*, 353–54; For a general history of Britain's role in defeating Napoleon, see Rory Muir, *Britain and the Defeat of Napoleon, 1807–1815* (New Haven: Yale University Press, 1996). On how war came to be regarded as exceptional, see Bell, *The First Total War*, 5–6.

[114] Paul Schroeder, *The Transformation of European Politics, 1763–1848* (New York: Clarendon Press, 1994).

[115] Schmitt observed in his subsequent writing on the partisan that 'In my book *Der Nomos der Erdeim jus publicum Europaeum* the interruption of this principle by the wars of the French revolution and of the Napoleonic era is not treated extensively enough', Carl Schmitt, *The Theory of the Partisan: A Commentary/Remark on the Concept of the Political*, trans. Alfred C. Goodson (Berlin: Duncker & Humblot, 1963 [2004]), 69, n.7.

[116] Schmitt, *The Theory of the Partisan*, 34.

[117] Schmitt, *The Theory of the Partisan*, 65–66.

[118] Schmitt, *The Theory of the Partisan*, 34.

on the Spanish example and unleashed the German people into war as an irregular military force, it also rendered the partisan philosophically and politically respectable.[119] When theorised by Clausewitz and other Prussian military reformers, the partisan represented a new and profound 'potential' in war, who could nonetheless still be safely conceptualised in relation to a telluric people's war that conformed with the traditional laws of European land-based warfare. But Schmitt observes that the partisan, as Napoleon intimated, was first united with international conflict by the ongoing British intervention into the Peninsular War, which reoriented Spanish rebellion into Britain's non-telluric or oceanic form of warfare.[120] Pasley was responding to this British intervention in his philosophical articulation of universal empire, indeed Britain's intervention into the war was itself in no small part a result of Pasley's influence on Britain's Foreign Secretary, the Marquess Wellesley, who adopted policies advocated by Pasley in his prosecution of the war in Spain and Portugal.[121] Leckie had envisioned Britain as a seagoing empire that must build its colonial island territories. Pasley developed Leckie's thought by theorising how warfare associated with the sea, the aggressive imperial expansion that stood beyond the *jus publicum Europaeum*, could be employed within the territories of Europe. Britain, Pasley concludes, must turn to the example of its imperial wars, the wars of the East India Company in India, and apply the same aggressive ideas of conquest to Europe (353). But in his analysis of the conflict with France, Pasley was, just like Clausewitz, primarily concerned with how the military could heighten and control the popular forces that the partisan represented. The Peninsular War and the Spanish rising are significant for Pasley in so far as they help him conceptualise how Britain itself can be formed as a military nation. In a related manner to how Clausewitz reorients the Spanish partisan into a Prussian people's war, Pasley addresses the question of how the military potential of Britain's own populace can be forged into a unified force. From his imperial, oceanic perspective, however, Pasley regards the military potential of the population as something untethered from locality and reoriented around a new kind of strategic aggression. Pasley was not simply equating the general idea of the partisan to regular forms of war, like Clausewitz, but to a new conception of universal empire and absolute enmity that could reimagine Europe as though it were a British imperial

---

[119] Schmitt, *The Theory of the Partisan*, 33.
[120] Schmitt, *The Theory of the Partisan*, 53.
[121] Harvey, *Collision of Empires*, 135.

territory. If Pasley is a key voice heralding a new, liberal nomos, if he looks past the immediate war with Napoleon to a new conception of global conflict charged with absolute enmity as a war for all humanity, this is because he was heralding new ways of administering populations and harnessing their potential for the military institution.

There has been a long tradition of regarding modern society as entangled with the security that guarantees its freedoms and which sees liberalism, in an echo of Schmitt, as at some level an indefinite continuation of war.[122] Seen through the lens of security, liberalism is, for Foucault, a naturalism that is concerned primarily with the government and vigour of the 'biological properties of the human species'.[123] A great deal has been written on Foucault's reversal of Clausewitz's dictum that war is politics by other means, Foucault himself consistently revising this reversal in ways that suggest he did not entirely conflate liberalism and security as identical.[124] Nonetheless, he concluded that war and politics represent two, interchangeable, strategies for dealing with the life of the population, that this entanglement of security or war into politics could at least be seen as the nation adopting a 'military model'.[125] What emerges is a new framework of security concerned with administering the nation's health and potential, and which can turn as readily from administration of sexuality and health to a thanatopolitical violence, a state-based racism that must allow those forces to die that would impinge upon the health or vigour of the nation.[126] Foucault was not alone in recognising the violence of modern liberal politics. Paul Virilio, along with Deleuze and Guattari, built on Foucault's work to develop their analysis of these intersections of politics and war, Virilio establishing the related concept of endocolonisation that sees the state turn on its own people to ensure its security and Deleuze and Guattari assessing how the war machine of the army can come to take over the state through the unlimited goals of total or absolute war.[127]

---

[122] For a brief overview, see Patricia Owens, *Between War and Politics: International Relations and the Thought of Hannah Arendt* (Oxford: Oxford University Press, 2007), 28–29.

[123] Foucault, *Birth of Biopolitics*, 62. Michael Dillon and Julian Reid, *The Liberal Way of War: Killing to Make Life Live* (Abingdon: Routledge, 2009), 9.

[124] Éric Alliez and Maurizio Lazzarato, Clausewitz and *la Pensée 68*, trans. Ames Hodges and Katharine Wallerstein, *Critical Times* 1, no. 1 (2018): 49–59, 52.

[125] On Foucault's reflections on this inversion of Clausewitz's phrase, see Foucault, *History of Sexuality*, 93; Foucault, *Discipline and Punish*, 168. See also Foucault, *Society Must Be Defended*.

[126] Foucault, 'The Political Technology of Individuals', 415–16.

[127] Mark Lacy, *Security, Technology and Global Politics: Thinking with Virilio* (New York: Routledge, 2014), 19–20; Gilles Deleuze and Félix Guattari, *A Thousand Plateaus: Capitalism and Scizophrenia*, trans. and foreword Brian Massumi (London: Continuum, 2004), 464–65.

Hannah Arendt had also reversed Clausewitz's dictum sometime earlier than Foucault to suggest that modern liberalism had come to see politics as a matter of brute force applied to the defence of the state and the security of the natural necessities of life.[128] What is at stake for Arendt is the bureaucratic nature of political violence, violence that cannot be politically questioned and which becomes increasingly attractive as a solution when it is no longer tied to political action but is simply associated with the administration of life.[129] This administrative approach ultimately devolves into organic forms of violence that Arendt believes are the most dangerous feature of modern politics because they are fuelled by the compunction to restore the health of a society and so treat violence as an unquestioned and absolute necessity.[130]

Giorgio Agamben has developed his theories of biopolitics by drawing together the distinct strands of thought articulated by Schmitt, Foucault and Arendt on the relations of security, life and liberalism. Agamben's understanding of biopolitics is complex and is concerned with the long historical lineage by which bare life is created when ever *zoe*, or biological life, is divided off from *bios*, or political life, in ways that have led to the administration of that bare life beyond the dictates of law. Although Agamben traces biopolitics across the long history of Western sovereignty and its relationship to the life of its subjects, he nonetheless agrees with Foucault that in the modern era, natural life becomes the central object or target of political power. While natural life, or *zoe*, has always been distinguished from the *bios* of a good or politically nuanced life, with modernity politics takes as its central, and increasingly only, task the management of *zoe* and accordingly the production of a politicised *zoe* or what Agamben terms 'bare life'. Agamben thus reads the new nomos identified by Schmitt in terms of the modern manifestation of biopolitics, seeing 'a new, bloody, planetary order' in the global civil war inaugurated by capitalism and its permanent state of exception that conflates law, violence and biological life.[131] A liberal way of war is apparent, therefore, in efforts to secure the biological or natural properties of life, to logistically administer life in an effort to increase its capacities and productivity, to ensure that life fully lives. As Agamben proposes, we can see a convergence of liberalism and

---

[128] Hannah Arendt, *The Promise of Politics*, ed. and intro. Jerome Kohn (New York: Schocken Books, 2005), 150–51. On Arendt's reversal of Clausewitz, 199–200.
[129] Hannah Arendt, *On Violence* (San Diego: Harcourt Brace & Co., 1970), 81.
[130] Arendt, *On Violence*, 75.
[131] Giorgio Agamben, *Homo Sacer: Sovereign Power and Bare Life*, trans. Daniel Heller-Roazen (Stanford: Stanford University Press, 1998), 14 and 37–38.

totalitarian forms of state power in their shared interest in the constitution, management and administration of bare life, or life in which law and violence are blurred.[132]

As had Schmitt, therefore, Agamben understands a shift to the liberal nomos and its wars of humanity as intensifying wars, because the relationship to a just enemy is now broken, and war devolves into the management of humanity. What replaces the war that, in Schmitt's phrasing, simply chases an enemy back inside her borders is, instead, the genocidal wars that now see life itself at stake. In his work on the nomos, Schmitt argued that liberal modernity did not transcend the political to eradicate war, but displaced war into the economic to frame new forms of the political friend-and-enemy distinctions:

> A war waged to protect or expand economic power must, with the aid of propaganda, turn into a crusade and into the last war of humanity. This is implicit in the polarity of ethics and economics, a polarity astonishingly systematic and consistent. But this allegedly non-political and apparently even antipolitical system serves existing or newly emerging friend-and-enemy groupings and cannot escape the logic of the political.[133]

But Agamben offers a distinct reading of Schmitt's nomos by proposing that the political logic that cannot be escaped in modernity is not the friend-and-enemy distinction, but the relation of the political to natural life, the *zoe* to its *bios*, the politicisation of the natural state of the living population. If Europe represents the domain of law, the zone of exclusion is where life is not simply abandoned to the law, but subject to a law of force, violence and necessity, where politics is reduced to merely the policing of life. As Agamben notes, therefore, the *jus publicum Europaeum* had traditionally been established by its inclusive exclusion of a zone beyond European legal jurisdiction, where the only law is the violence of force and brute necessity. The process by which the *jus publicum Europaeum* breaks down, whereby the destructive war of the ocean and empire is imposed upon Europe, has its roots, Agamben proposes, in the way that a permanent state of exception grows from within the state to produce a new 'paradigm of security' concerned simply with the administration of life.[134] In effect, we see a universalising of the zone of exclusion and its realm

---

[132] Agamben, *Homo Sacer*, 9–11.

[133] Carl Schmitt, *The Concept of the Political. Expanded Edition*, trans and with intro. George Schwab, foreword Tracey B. Strong and notes Leo Strauss (Chicago: University of Chicago Press, 2007), 79.

[134] Giorgio Agamben, *State of Exception*, trans. Kevin Attell (Chicago: University of Chicago Press, 2005), 14.

of organic, administrative, destructive violence onto European territory through the elevation of bare life into the most elementary and central political concern.[135]

Agamben still follows Schmitt in linking this break with the First World War, in part also drawing on Arendt's concerns with the stateless refugees who emerged from the conflict as people outside all political community. The war, therefore, called into question the status of human rights and the nature of the human, enabling the creation of refugee camps that could administer lives severed from all political community. But as Éric Alliez and Maurizio Lazzarato suggest, Agamben's concerns with law and rights downplays the far more extensive framework of militarised power associated with total war and the 'military model of organisation' that was critical to the formation of modern disciplinary society.[136] As Pasley's work demonstrates, these were models first widely developed and deployed during the French Revolutionary and Napoleonic Wars, while the wars themselves were among the first to be understood through themes of national organicism, life and infection that laid the seeds of modern racial thought.[137] To suggest that European war is reoriented in terms set by unlimited imperial violence, a war of universal empire, can also be linked to the development of these military models of organisation that find their clearest expression in Pasley's enunciation of military policy and universal empire. In Pasley's combination of conquest and growth, of inner vigour and limitless expansion, of national life and death, we might see an early stirring of a new biopolitical nomos in world affairs. Pasley will no longer conceptualise the national population as telluric volunteers but as a living resource, a 'rough ore, or metal in a mine' that can be treated as a potential or storehouse of force.[138] It is the proliferation of these military models and their politicisation of life that remodels Europe into a new 'paradigm of security' that functions akin to the state of nature. Baker's account of the maritime conception of Romantic culture as an 'oceanic fable of culture' can be paired with this conception of a new global nomos as an aggressive idea of militarism that reoriented the state in relation to the pure administrative violence of war as it had traditionally been waged upon and beyond the oceans.

[135] Agamben, *Homo Sacer*, 37–38.
[136] Éric Alliez and Maurizio Lazzarato, *Wars and Capital*, trans. Ames Hodges (South Pasadena: Semiotext(e), 2016), 293–94.
[137] Hannah Arendt, *The Origins of Totalitarianism* (San Diego: Harcourt Brace, 1976), 175.
[138] Windham, *New Military Plan*, 5.

Vitalising the Living Nation

While war has come to form a core historical context for understanding British Romantic culture, the effects of war are typically understood as a dissonant noise or trace of foreign violence.[139] Romanticism has been read as a literature of trauma, a riposte or reworking of military modes of attention and history, or even an aesthetic preservation of ancient military traditions in so far as these might serve as a corrective for national decline in a commercial age.[140] Romantic literature is routinely identified, therefore, with the growth of modern liberal commercial entertainments, a nascent mass media and a belief in national progress that can be defined by their shared rejection of war, force and dictatorship.[141] Yet while Romanticism can be associated with the peaceful ambitions of modern liberalism, this liberal culture is itself deeply entangled with forms of security from which it purportedly remains distant. Both Romantic aesthetics and biopolitical security find their core concerns in an understanding of 'life as power'.[142] For Rancière, the aesthetic is deeply interconnected with the political. Aesthetics moves in two different directions in the Romantic era because art is always entangled with efforts to forge new modes of life and community. Echoing Agamben's concerns with the link between totalitarianism and liberalism, Rancière nonetheless shifts this idea to a more clearly articulated proposition on literature and life when he argues that 'the everyday aestheticized life of a liberal society and its commercial entertainment' must be understood as the converse of the 'totalitarian attempts at making the community into a work of art' through their mutual investments in the arts that shape and respond to life.[143] The Romantic state's growing military control over life represents a sombre shadow that formed against and

---

[139] Mary A. Favret, *War at a Distance: Romanticism and the Making of Modern Wartime* (Princeton: Princeton University Press, 2010).

[140] See Favret, *War at a Distance*; Lily Gurton-Wachter, *Watchwords: Romanticism and the Poetics of Attention* (Stanford: Stanford University Press, 2016); Duncan, *Modern Romance and Transformations of the Novel: The Gothic, Scott, Dickens* (Cambridge: Cambridge University Press, 1992), 73.

[141] Ian Duncan, *Modern Romance and Transformations of the Novel*; Saree Makdisi, *Romantic Imperialism: Universal Empire and the Culture of Modernity* (Cambridge, Cambridge University Press, 1998); Jerome Christensen, *Romanticism at the End of History* (Baltimore: The John Hopkins University Press, 2000); Anne Frey, *British State Romanticism: Authorship, Agency, and Bureaucratic Nationalism* (Stanford: Stanford University Press, 2010).

[142] Denise Gigante, *Life: Organic Form and Romanticism* (New Haven: Yale University Press, 2009), 3.

[143] Jacques Rancière, 'The Aesthetic Revolution and Its Outcomes', *New Left Review*, no. 14 (2002): 133–51, 133.

alongside Romantic cultural conceptions of liberal society's commercial entertainments and their aesthetic reconstruction of life, military thought offering its own prescriptions and capacities for the 'arts' of living.

If Pasley foreshadowed a new nomos and its 'paradigm of security', his writing nonetheless remains strikingly discursive because he did not offer a fully developed programme for forging the military nation and its security apparatus. Indeed, Pasley defines what he calls martial policy in curiously aesthetic terms as 'the spirit and views with which war may be conducted' (106), a definition that recalls that of Jomini and Clausewitz that policy represents something like a metaphysics or philosophy of war, Clausewitz even noting that 'policy is nothing in itself'.[144] In effect, Pasley was developing an aesthetics of life that counterpoints even as it replicates the aesthetics of Romanticism's liberal culture and the role of the imagination in defining the nation.[145] The positive reception of Pasley by so many British poets and novelists was in no small part due to their appreciation of these aesthetic qualities, the manly tone and vigour of his writing and what it therefore implied about the shaping of national identity and character. Admittedly his support for aggressive conquest was too much to countenance for many writers: Southey and Wordsworth both voiced their disapproval and even the staunchly pro-war *Anti-Jacobin Review* declined to fully support what it saw as his 'Machiavellian policies' because it did not want to see Britain become a 'conquering nation'.[146] But an enormous appreciation for his writing is visible in Jane Austen's attraction to Pasley's moral purity and concern for the nation, elements that she saw reflected in his manly writing style, healthy tone and heroic stance towards war.[147] Southey praised the *Essay* for the 'ability with which it is written', and Wordsworth even concluded that Pasley had written more as a 'poet' than a 'statesman', producing a 'mighty poetry' that lent a moral purity to questions of military policy.[148]

---

[144] Clausewitz, *On War*, 606.

[145] See Benedict Anderson, *Imagined Communities: Reflections on the Origin and Spread of Nationalism* (London: Verso, 1991).

[146] Robert Southey, 'Review of *Essay on the Military Policy and Institutions of the British Empire*', *The Quarterly Review* 5 (1811): 403–37; William Wordsworth, 'Letter to Captain Pasley, Royal Engineers. March 28, 1811', in Christopher Wordsworth, ed., *Memoirs of William Wordsworth*, (London, Edward Moxon, 1851), vol. 1, 416; *Antijacobin Review* (1811): 135 and 132.

[147] Vivien Jones, 'Reading for England: Austen, Taste and Female Patriotism', *European Romantic Review*, 16 (2005): 221–30.

[148] Southey, 'Review of *Essay on the Military Policy and Institutions of the British Empire*', 403–04; Wordsworth, 'Letter to Captain Pasley, Royal Engineers. March 28, 1811', 419.

The editors of the *Monthly Review* understood his *Essay* as essential reading for a literary journal:

> Under the present political circumstances of our empire, the subject of its defence against a foreign enemy is become very interesting and important. It is to be expected, therefore, that a number of writers will be induced to discuss it; and though, as not being a question of *literature*, it is not strictly within the province of literary critics, it so immediately concerns us as members of the state, that we can neither view it with indifference nor pass over the investigation in a slight manner.[149]

The editors are clear that Pasley's *Essay* is not literature, but they nonetheless read the essay as though it had interrupted and replaced the literary. The *Essay*, they imply, possesses a supplementary existence, wherein, even though it lies outside literature, it nonetheless serves to displace or replace literature by raising awareness that we are 'members of the state', as though mapping a movement between literature and state security. We might even align Pasley's *Essay* with Makdisi's insistence that all Romantic era writing functioned as a form of prophecy concerned with the dawning of the 'universal empire' of global modernity.[150] Pasley was offering one of the most widely read and direct prophecies of universal empire as he crafted a vision of the military nation.[151]

Understood as a new kind of a poet for the military nation, Pasley's writing can nonetheless be distinguished from the bardic nationalism that had, since the mid-eighteenth century, united British poetry with warlike heroism and patriotism while contributing to a renewed poetic concern with the nation and its heritage. Foundational to this bardic poetry was James McPherson's *The Works of Ossian* (1765), which appeared partly in response to the military defeat of the Highlands and a desire to encourage the reformation of a Scottish militia.[152] Bardism was deeply tied to the rise of a national identity marked by war, empire and conquest as it invoked ancestral qualities that could meliorate the morals and character of the modern, commercial nation. Bardism was thus always about an invented tradition, a way of reconnecting to lost martial traditions that were themselves softened for a new reading audience. Yet

---

[149] *Monthly Review, or Literary Journal* 66 (1811): 199.
[150] Makdisi, *Romantic Imperialism*, 3.
[151] Favret, *War at a Distance*, 91–92.
[152] Eric Gidal, *Ossianic Unconformities: Bardic Poetry in the Industrial Age* (Charlottesville: University of Virginia Press, 2015), 1–2.

bardism nonetheless played a role in defining a British national identity that was forged in war against its French Other.[153] Katie Trumpener extends argument about the bard by focussing on Britain's own imperial peripheries, but here too bardic nationalism emerges out of national conflict and ancestral powers.[154] This turn to ancestral military traditions was, moreover, still significant during the French Revolutionary and Napoleonic Wars, especially in the self-proclaimed bardic role adopted by Scott.[155] But poets from Coleridge to Wordsworth, amongst others, also adopted a bardic role that emphasised the importance of volunteers and militia forces.[156] For Robert Gordon, Wordsworth represents the high-water mark of this bardic tradition and its expression of the military energies of the nation.[157] Beyond the end of the wars, however, any such idealisation of military volunteering declined markedly. Writing in 1816 in the immediate aftermath of the wars, Wordsworth effectively rescinded his bardic role when he looked back to Pasley's *Essay* to propose that 'Scientific Military Establishments' had become essential 'in the present state of Europe', even though reliance on military institutions would 'impair our civil energies'.[158] In his post-war turn to novels, Scott likewise relinquished the bardic role that he had played during the wars. He continued to regard military honour as a source of virtue and energy for a commercial society, but even that approach was, as discussed in Chapter 5, coming to be displaced by a different kind of military poetics, a bio-aesthetics focussed on the wounded, suffering body.[159]

[153] Simon Bainbridge, *British Poetry and the Revolutionary and Napoleonic Wars* (Oxford: Oxford University Press, 2003), 51–53.

[154] Katie Trumpener, *Bardic Nationalism: The Romantic Novel and the British Empire* (Princeton: Princeton University Press, 1997).

[155] Bainbridge, *British Poetry and the Revolutionary and Napoleonic* Wars, 53; Robert C. Gordon, *Arms and the Imagination: Essays on War, Politics, and Anglophone Culture* (Lanham: Hamilton Books, 2009), 10. For more general discussions of the centrality of bardic nationalism in Romantic cultural formations, see Jeff Strabone, *Poetry and British Nationalisms in the Bardic Eighteenth Century: Imagined Antiquities* (Cham: Palgrave Macmillan, 2018); and Francesco Crocco, *Literature and the Growth of British Nationalism: The Influence of Romantic Poetry and Bardic Criticism* (Jefferson: McFarland & Company, Publishers, 2014).

[156] John R. Watson, *Romanticism and War: A Study of British Romantic Period Writers and the Napoleonic Wars* (Basingstoke: Palgrave Macmillan, 2003).

[157] Gordon, *Arms and the Imagination*, 250.

[158] William Wordsworth, *Letters of the Wordsworth Family from 1787–1855* (London: Ardent Media, 1969), 84–85; see 'Arts and the Imagination', 249.

[159] Duncan, *Modern Romance and Transformations of the Novel*, 73. This general tendency was echoed in France, where authors such as Stendhal and Alfred Victor, Comte de Vigny, understood their present as a dull shadow of the glorious Romance of the Napoleonic Empire.

While Pasley insisted that it was 'mere poetry' to assume that patriotic enthusiasm rather than disciplined armies could win a war (44), his very need to dismiss poetry suggests how deeply his own philosophy of war arose within a cultural field shaped by concerns with state power and government. What is more, by the early 1800s, as Britain found itself at war with Napoleonic rather than Revolutionary France, poets such as Coleridge and Wordsworth were addressing war less as bards than as themselves resembling scientific military writers, associated with Walsh, Leckie and Pasley. As Anne Frey asserts, Romantic authors turned to the state in the post-war era because they saw state institutions as best placed to govern national cultural habits and feelings.[160] Romantic cultural formations have even been seen as requiring state institutions to ground their pedagogical capacities because it was only through the intercedence of the state that cultural differences within the nation could be resolved. The state, in other words, produces a vision of 'universal humanity', a conception of culture that in some sense is epitomised or even pioneered by the figure of the military author who represent the scientific military establishments that protect that very universality of the state.[161] Wordsworth regarded Pasley as writing more like a great poet than a statesman, a view that parallels Lloyd's earlier emphasis on the general as a figure who leads the multitude like a poet, while, in a curious parallel, Wordsworth elsewhere imagined the poet as though a general leading a campaign.[162] An idea had emerged of a state based or serious poetry, what Henry Crabb Robinson called, in response to Wordsworth's military writing, a 'serious poetry' rather than the 'mere poetry' of patriotism.[163] This serious poetry, the mighty poetry of Pasley's military policy, the construction of a new philosophy or metaphysics of war, an art of the nation and its prophecies, was coming to assume critical significance in the way that war was to be written about and conceptualised for the military nation.

---

[160] Anne Frey, *British State Romanticism: Authorship, Agency, and Bureaucratic Nationalism* (Stanford: Stanford University Press, 2010). See also David Lloyd and Paul Thomas, *Culture and the State* (New York: Routledge, 1998); and Mark Redfield, *The Politics of Aesthetics: Nationalism, Gender, Romanticism* (Stanford: Stanford University Press, 2003). On writing, aesthetics and empire, see Dermot Ryan, *Technologies of Empire: Writing, Imagination, and the Making of Imperial Networks, 1750–1820* (Newark: University of Delaware Press, 2013),

[161] Redfield, *The Politics of Aesthetics*, 46.

[162] Ryan, *Technologies of Empire*, 130.

[163] Henry Crabb Robinson, 'On the Spanish Revolution', *The London Review* 2, no. 4 (1809): 231–75.

Looking back from 1849, Pasley believed that his *Essay* had been vital to Britain's success in the wars. As he argues of his call for 'a more vigorous system of warfare':

> These opinions are admitted to have produced more effect on the public mind than any of the numerous publications on the defence of the country, or on the management of the war, that appeared in those days of national danger and difficulty, and therefore my essay contributed, so far as such a work could possibly do, that is in a comparatively humble degree, to the success of the war.[164]

But if Pasley was the leading prophetic writer of the later Romantic era, he was also redefining the nation's relationship to war. No longer emphasising the nation's warlike ancestry, associated with bardism and militia service, he was instead promulgating a new kind of national identity secured by military institutions. Situated within a 'liberal discourse of politics', war ceased to be central to national history.[165] Once war is waged in service of a universal empire covering the globe, to humanity itself, so there are no longer any territorial enemies, only enemies to humanity. In the terms set by Adam Ferguson, civil society can no longer define its form in relation to other nations. Rather than the nation define itself through war against a hostile other, as Linda Colley shows Britain had done against France during the eighteenth century, a nation began to be defined in relation to its institutional capacities to administer itself and hence to form itself into a state:

> What characterizes 'the' nation is not a horizontal relationship with other groups (such as other nations, hostile or enemy nations, or the nations with which it is juxtaposed). What does characterize the nation is, in contrast, a vertical relationship between a body of individuals who are capable of constituting a State, and the actual State itself ... its ability to administer itself.[166]

Foucault argues that there was accordingly a transcription of a historical discourse on war, in which this foundational national discourse, the nation's relation to a hostile Other race, became internalised to society. Race war reappears through the internal pressures of a normalising society,

---

[164] Quoted in Pasley, *The Military Policy and Institutions of the British Empire*, 5th ed, 6.

[165] Jason Edwards, 'Foucault and the Continuation of War', in *The Metamorphoses of War*, ed. A. Plaw (Amsterdam: Rodopi, 2012), 21–40, 28.

[166] Foucault, *Society Must be Defended*, 223.

the imperatives of the military model and its institutional controls, as the functioning of military institutions morph and shape the nature of historicism and war.[167] This is, Foucault remarks, an 'authoritarian colonization' of the discourse on race war, an effort to realign this war with the nation as a universal agent of history.[168] The nation is no longer inherently a 'partner in barbarous war', but represents the core of the state, its ability to administer, manage and organise the potential of national life.[169] In one sense, then, this is also why the state comes to be so important in transcending cultural divisions to produce the universal human, not because it elevates class divisions to a 'transcendental body', but because it takes as its focus the imminent living body, life itself.[170]

War, of course, does not disappear but continues to exist as an admixture of atavism and technological progress. But rather than play a constitutive role in forming the nation, war became principally an external, ephemeral and instrumental element within a longer, peaceful history of national development.[171] But war is also, therefore, reframed from its role in defining the nation against its belligerent Other, to a more fundamental association with the protection of the nation in a biopolitical mode. A thanatopolitical dimension enters into social discourse in which it is the very question of life itself that comes to be at stake in war, even as wars become ever more violent and bloody. And if we assume that the nation is itself imaginary, as Benedict Anderson argues, we might suggest that the imagination, Pasley's aesthetic form of military policy, now plays a role in defining these contours of life and death. Foucault intimates that the key characteristic of biopolitical or liberal war is the vivifying power of death.[172] Schmitt gives support to this idea when he argues that within the framework of liberalism it is only by imagining its negation, in death and the threat of war, that the nation could assume a form. Although Schmitt regards the aesthetic as the very antithesis of the serious realm of politics, derived as it is from the liberal entertainments of Romanticism, he nonetheless conceptualises the nation's political existence in strikingly aesthetic terms.[173] As

---

[167] Foucault, *Society Must be Defended*, 23; 60–62.
[168] Foucault, *Society Must be Defended*, 58–59; 236–37.
[169] Foucault, *Society Must be Defended*, 223.
[170] Redfield, *The Politics of Aesthetics*, 12.
[171] Foucault, *Society Must be Defended*, 236.
[172] Foucault, *Society Must be Defended*, 257.
[173] For a reading of Schmitt in relation to the aesthetic of war, see Nick Mansfield, 'Destroyer and Bearer of Worlds: The Aesthetic Doubleness of War', in *Tracing War in British Enlightenment and Romantic Culture*, ed. Neil Ramsey and Gillian Russell (Basingstoke: Palgrave Macmillan, 2015), 188–203, 197–200.

Neil Levi explains in his reading of Schmitt via Rancière, 'The form of life becomes visible through the "real possibility" of its negation by the enemy. This negation gives *Gestalt* to the question of who we are'.[174] A new kind of aesthetic of the nation emerges in this sublime operation of war that, to draw on Burke's theorisation of the sublime as a form of bio-aesthetics concerned with pain and danger, gives a form to the nation in relation to its impending death.[175]

Of all the writers on war in Britain at this time, Pasley was noted for having most clearly shifted discourse surrounding national defence towards the fundamental tension of life and death that gave rise to just such a sense of the 'real possibility' of negation in war. For Pasley, the war with France is elevated beyond a national conflict to a conflict for universal empire and the future of humanity. The nation no longer forms itself in war against its French Other, but against otherness itself. It forms in relation to the stark division of life and death. Pasley does not work on the public mind by recalling ancient martial traditions, like the bard who affirms the nation's warlike relation to its French Other. Rather than reproduce what he dismisses as this 'mere poetry', he produces a form of writing that seeks to enable the 'public mind' to become aware of its complete negation in death and so, in consequence, to become aware of itself as a living entity, to grasp how the nation is at heart a living population.[176] When Pasley calls for vigour as the key to success in war, vigour seems to lack content, but nonetheless his call appears to performatively invigorate the nation, enabling it to adopt a serious, political grasp of war. It is as though to succeed in war the nation had to embrace a new *bios* altogether, a *bios* lodged in its *zoe* that could allow the nation to hand itself over to the totality of necessary strategic administration, giving itself over to 'the managers of life and survival'.[177] If Pasley takes over from the bardic role, it is also because the specific or unique qualities of the nation are no longer of foremost importance; the community of feeling that founds the nation is not so much a set of positive values but is the fear engendered by existential threats to life.

---

[174] Neil Levi, 'Carl Schmitt and the Question of the Aesthetic', *New German Critique*, 34, no. 2 (2007): 27–43, 30.

[175] Simon Strick, *American Dolorologies: Pain, Sentimentalism, Biopolitics* (Albany: State University of New York Press, 2014), 26.

[176] On the relationship between the public and the population, see Foucault, *Security, Territory, Population*, 75.

[177] Foucault, *History of Sexuality*, 137.

Pasley might even be seen as heralding the tradition of liberal epic that registers this bloody dimension of liberalism as it supplants the epic poet of war with the writing of the historian.[178] Indeed, while Baker proposes that we read Romantic genres in relation to modes of government, it is a way of reading that has no room for epic because of its relation to conquest.[179] Napoleon's failure to unite Europe had clearly shown that conquest was no longer a legitimate political course of action.[180] There is, of course, a 'pudeur of epic' in the eighteenth century that saw the rise of softened heroes; war becomes Romantic in the sense of a tradition that can be revived to invigorate commercial culture.[181] It is through his appeals to 'conquest', however, that Pasley's *Essay* might be read as a version of the liberal epic. Rancière suggests that the epic indeed 'changed its meaning in the time of Hegel' to encompass both the effort to strive for totality and the manifestation of the living flesh, or, as he notes, following Hegel's own reflections on how spirit manifests in war, 'the epic is the becoming-flesh of the spirit of a people'.[182] A new form of writing emerges that is concerned with the totalitarian construction of this living community:

> '[G]ood' writing can also be writing that is more than what is written, writing that is not written on papyrus, parchment, or paper, but is inscribed in the very texture of things, as an actual modification of the perceptible world … This book is no longer traced with signs on paper, signs that isolate men and build up phantoms of democratic politics. This new book is traced with the ways of a true communication, the ways of iron and water that actually link together men, their actions and their thoughts.[183]

A new form of epic emerges, in other words, from those engineers who operate upon the living world, and where 'the most beautiful poem is the living community'.[184] Pasley represents one such engineer who turns to this constitution of the living community in war, who seeks to render this 'becoming-flesh' of the spirit of the people through his development

---

[178] Edward Adams, *Liberal Epic: The Victorian Practice of History from Gibbon to Churchill* (Charlottesville: University of Virginia Press, 2011), 19.

[179] Baker, *Written on the Water*, 156.

[180] On the end of the legitimacy of conquest, see Arendt, *The Origins of Totalitarianism*, 128.

[181] Claude Rawson, 'War and the Epic Mania in England and France: Milton, Boileau, Prior and English Mock-Heroic', *The Review of English Studies* 64, no. 265 (2013): 433–53, 446.

[182] Jacques Rancière, *The Flesh of Words: The Politics of Writing*, trans. Charlotte Mandell (Stanford: Stanford University Press, 2004), 119.

[183] Rancière, *The Flesh of Words*, 106–07.

[184] Rancière, *The Flesh of Words*, 120.

of military policy and its philosophy of war. At the very least, by encouraging the nation to contemplate its death in war, his writing assumes an epic form because it enabled the public to see itself as a living entity, to imagine itself as the collective life of the population. The *Essay* offers a new aesthetic of the nation that shares a kinship with Romantic prophecy of universal empire because both are entangled with a new poetics lodged in an emergent, global nomos. It represents an epic conquest or totalising of war that is ultimately a nation's conquest of itself.

CHAPTER 5

Thomas Hamilton's Wordsworthian Novel of War
Sexuality, Wounding and the Bare Life of the Soldier

When it first noticed Thomas Hamilton's *The Youth and Manhood of Cyril Thornton* (1827), the *Quarterly Review* was so struck by the novel's resemblance to an eyewitness account of military service that it believed Hamilton had launched an entirely new genre of fiction, the 'military novel'.[1] Hamilton's book, indeed, went on to inspire a generation of military and naval novelists working in the 1830s and 1840s, themselves, like Hamilton, writing in the wake of a burgeoning military literature of reminiscences, memoirs, biographies and tales of war that had achieved widespread commercial success in Britain by the 1830s.[2] Notwithstanding the prominence of military writing in the early nineteenth century, however, critics have directed little substantive attention to military novels, typically relegating the genre to a militaristic and light-hearted version of the historical novel.[3] War has, it is true, long been recognised as the 'prototypical content' of historical novels.[4] But as critics such as Ian Duncan and Jerome Christensen have argued, in the historical novel's paradigmatic form the soldier hero ultimately rejects the archaic romance of military honour in favour of marriage and domestic life.[5] The hero's path to maturity and social integration, they contend, allegorises the nation's own movement away from a past dominated by national conflict and towards a modern, liberal world of commercial prosperity and peace. In this account, war may be central to the historical novel, but war nonetheless only appears as an

---

[1] *The Quarterly Review* 37, no. 73 (1828): 521.
[2] Neil Ramsey, *The Military Memoir and Romantic Literary Culture, 1780–1835* (Farnham: Ashgate, 2011).
[3] Richard Maxwell, 'The Historical Novel', in *The Cambridge Companion to Fiction in the Romantic Period*, ed. Richard Maxwell and Katie Trumpener (Cambridge: Cambridge University Press, 2008), 65–89, 81.
[4] Fredric Jameson, *The Antinomies of Realism* (London: Verso, 2013), 266.
[5] Ian Duncan, *Modern Romance and Transformations of the Novel: The Gothic, Scott, Dickens* (Cambridge: Cambridge University Press, 1992), 51–105; and Jerome Christensen, *Romanticism at the End of History* (Baltimore: Johns Hopkins University Press, 2000), 153–75.

aestheticised romance that can invigorate and yet which stands outside the progress and political control of modern life.

Despite its appellation by the *Quarterly Review* as a military novel, *Cyril Thornton* in fact follows very closely the underlying structure of the historical novel as it traces its eponymous hero's journey from war to the domestic felicity of companionate marriage. Where it does veer away from the prototype of the historical novel, however, is in the way it preserves military honour as a form of aesthetic romance. To understand how exactly it refashions military honour, it is imperative to understand the novel's intersection with the modern, biopolitical nation. A growing body of work in Romantic studies has proposed that it is no coincidence Romantic literature should have arisen at the same historical moment as the modern birth of biopolitics, linked as they are through themes of organic form, vitality and the power of life.[6] The nineteenth-century novel, epitomised by the *Bildungsroman*'s focus on the 'ordinary administration of life' and its culmination with the hero's marriage, appears synonymous with the consolidation of modern regimes of biopower concerned with the vitality and biological functions of the living body.[7] Not only is *Cyril Thornton* bound up with biopolitical questions of sexuality and marriage, however, but it also aligns sexuality with what Foucault saw as the dark underside of biopower, a 'thanatopolitics' concerned with eliminating threats to life and strengthening the nation's military capacities through the vitalising powers of death.[8] Where the historical novel places death and wounding into the distant past, *Cyril Thornton* fails to dismiss suffering so easily. Pointing to the legacy of war's trauma on the everyday, the novel enacts a transformation of the historical novel into the military novel by introducing a new version of military honour for the modern, commercial nation.

---

[6] See Alastair Hunt and Matthias Rudolf, eds, *Romanticism and Biopolitics*, Romantic Circles Praxis Series (December 2012), https://romantic-circles.org/praxis/biopolitics/HTML/praxis.2012.hunt-rudolf.html, accessed 8 June 2018. On the Romantic ideology as a rhetorical reconstruction of the politics of health, in which poetry is viewed as holding a pharmacological role as either cure or disease, see Dino Franco Felluga, *Perversity of Poetry: The Romantic Ideology and the Popular Male Poet of Genius* (Albany: State University of New York Press, 2005), 2.

[7] Franco Moretti, *The Way of the World: The Bildungsroman in European Culture*, trans. Albert Sbragia (London: Verso, 2000), 34–35; on marriage and biology in the nineteenth-century *Bildung* novel, see Heike Hartung, *Ageing, Gender, and Illness in Anglophone Literature: Narrating Age in the Bildungsroman* (New York: Routledge, 2016).

[8] On thanatopolitics, see Michel Foucault, 'The Political Technology of Individuals', in *Power: Essential Works of Foucault 1954–1984*, ed. James D. Faubian, trans. Robert Hurley et al., vol. 3 (London: Penguin, 2000), 403–17, 416; and Agamben, *Homo Sacer*, 72.

This chapter argues that in doing so, *Cyril Thornton* also inaugurated a new form of war literature altogether. For Paul Fussell, modern war literature is characterised by the ways in which it transforms the traditional quest narrative of war romance from its exaltation of the hero into an embodied 'romance' of survival.[9] As the first novel to self-consciously map a personal experience of war onto the tradition of historical romance, *Cyril Thornton* can be seen as lying at the heart of this idea of modern war literature as a transformation of 'literary "romance"'.[10] Aligning the military novel with a subsequent tradition of war novels, however, can also reveal a new dimension to this history of war and literature that asks us to reconsider the pharmacological elements of care and death surrounding war's trauma. Building on Chapter 4's concerns with the way military literature displaced a traditional bardic nationalism, this chapter also considers how the military novel developed in relation to the martial aptitudes of the military nation. It argues that the aesthetic formation or *Bildung* of the officer in the military novel also represents an essential element in the full development of biopower surrounding war. If sexuality aligns individual sexual inclinations with a vigorous procreativity, so discourses on military service and wounding could align individual pain and the risk of death with the demands of a racialised nation. Establishing an aesthetic based on the soldier's suffering body, *Cyril Thornton* recasts war in terms of the vitalising qualities of wounding and death.

Thomas Hamilton and Tales of War

Thomas Hamilton was born into a family that exemplified the economic and social progress of Scotland during the closing decades of the eighteenth century. His father, William Hamilton, was Regius Professor of anatomy and botany at Glasgow University, having taken over this role from his own father, Thomas, in 1781.[11] His mother, Elizabeth, was the daughter of a successful Glaswegian merchant, William Stirling. Despite the loss of their father at a young age, Thomas and his brother William continued their schooling and attended university, Thomas studying at Glasgow, while William began at Edinburgh and concluded his study at

---

[9] Paul Fussell, *The Great War and Modern Memory*, (Oxford: Oxford University Press, 2013), 140–41.
[10] Fussell, *The Great War and Modern Memory*, 141.
[11] Thomas Wilson Bayne and Douglas Brown. 'Hamilton, Thomas (1789–1842), Novelist and Travel Writer', *Oxford Dictionary of National Biography*. 23 September 2004; https://doi.org/10.1093/ref:odnb/12129, accessed 18 April 2017.

Oxford. If his family was associated with the rising prosperity and intellectual culture of Scottish civil society, Hamilton's early life was nonetheless fundamentally shaped by the French Revolutionary and Napoleonic Wars (1792–1815). Born in Glasgow in 1789, he had barely known life outside war by the time he entered the British army in 1810. Taking a commission in the 29th regiment, he served in Canada and the Iberian Peninsula during the Peninsular War (1808–14). He was wounded twice while fighting in Spain, but continued to serve with the army for the duration of the wars with Napoleon. He retired from the army in 1818, settling in Edinburgh and marrying Anne Montgomery in 1820.

Taking up a career as a writer, Hamilton associated himself with the circle around *Blackwood's Edinburgh Magazine* (1817–1980), which had launched the magazine in 1817 as a Tory response to the established, and staunchly Whig, *Edinburgh Review*. While the earliest issues of *Blackwood's* were soundly ignored, the magazine soon achieved notoriety with its scathing reviews of Coleridge and the Cockney School and its antipathy towards the *Edinburgh Review*. Hamilton became a regular contributor to the magazine, even living for a time shortly after his marriage at John Lockhart's cottage Chiefswood (Lockhart was one of the principal writers for the magazine, along with James Hogg, Thomas De Quincey, William Maginn and Felicia Hemans).[12] At Chiefswood, Hamilton was a close neighbour of Sir Walter Scott, and received regular visits from Scott, William Blackwood (*Blackwood's* publisher) and Hemans, with whom he and his wife were on good terms and corresponded frequently. Hamilton's brother William was also a major figure in British literary circles, playing an essential role in the continuation of Scottish Enlightenment thought into a second generation by uniting Kant's philosophy with that of Thomas Reid.[13]

The literary magazines established after the war years, including the *London Magazine* (1732–) and the *New Monthly Magazine* (1814–84) alongside *Blackwood's*, had a considerable impact on British literary culture. The rise of the magazine was integral to the formation of a new, mass readership in these years, as exemplified by its miscellaneous assortment of articles, anonymous authorship, combative style and lack of formal arrangement of materials. Departing from the style of earlier review periodicals, such as the

---

[12] Robert Morrison and Daniel Sanjiv Roberts, "'A Character So Various, and Yet So Indisputably its own': A Passage to *Blackwood's Edinburgh Magazine*', in *Romanticism and Blackwood's Magazine: 'An Unprecedented Phenomenon'*, ed. Robert Morrison and Daniel Sanjiv Roberts (Basingstoke: Palgrave Macmillan, 2013), 1–19, 3.

[13] Thomas Martin Devine and Jenny Wormald, eds, *The Oxford Handbook of Modern Scottish History* (Oxford: Oxford University Press, 2012), 381.

Edinburgh Review, the new magazines were principally concerned with social life rather than with reviewing other books.[14] With their attention focused on an increasingly urbanised and globally aware Britain, the magazines presented the world to their readers as a tumult of ideas, characters and scenes, in which a single Edinburgh or London street could be imagined as teeming with the total experience of the nation. Yet so too, the magazines propounded a view of the aesthetic power of poetry as counter to the very modern life that the magazines themselves portrayed.[15] In doing so, the magazines played a pivotal role in shifting Enlightenment ideas of culture as moral and social improvement towards a Romantic understanding of culture as the sentimental and aesthetic preservation of traditions within the modern nation that could limit or ameliorate the enervation suffered by commercial society.[16]

Blackwood's, however, was also a champion of the military biographical writing that had risen to prominence in Britain by the end of the 1820s. Several of the *Blackwood's* writers besides Hamilton produced tales of military service, including William Maginn and George Gleig. Gleig's *The Subaltern*, by far the most celebrated of this writing, was serialised and subsequently published by *Blackwood's* in 1825, eventually running to multiple editions, while Maginn edited two collections of military tales, the *Military Sketch Book* (1827) and *Tales of Military Life* (1829), both published by Henry Colburn.[17] Hamilton himself published an account of his military experiences in *Blackwood's* in a series of articles from 1826 to 1830 under the pseudonym Captain Spencer Moggridge, entitled 'Letters from the Peninsula'. He also invented the character Sir Morgan Odoherty who featured in a series of satirical vignettes in *Blackwood's* and was otherwise known as Ensign Odoherty because of his brief military career, albeit a career that culminated rather ingloriously with Odoherty missing the British assault at the siege of New Orleans because he was busy searching for his lost snuff-box.[18] Inspired by such writing, dozens of

---

[14] Richard Cronin, *Paper Pellets: British Literary Culture After Waterloo* (Oxford: Oxford University Press, 2010), 162.

[15] In his correspondence with Wordsworth, Hamilton suggested that *Blackwood's* was a not a good vehicle for poetry; see Stephen C. Behrendt, 'William Wordsworth and Women Poets', *European Romantic Review*, 23:6 (2012): 635–50, 643–44.

[16] Ian Duncan, *Scott's Shadow: The Novel in Romantic Edinburgh* (Princeton: Princeton University Press, 2007), 72.

[17] George Gleig, *The Subaltern* (Edinburgh: William Blackwood, 1825); William Maginn, *The Military Sketch-book: Reminiscences of Seventeen Years in the Service Abroad and at Home* (London: Henry Colburn, 1827); William Maginn, *Tales of Military Life. By the Author of 'The Military Sketch Book'*, 3 vols (London: Henry Colburn, 1829).

[18] *Blackwood's Edinburgh Magazine* 2, no. 12 (March 1818): 685. On Hamilton's creation of the fictional Odoherty, see David E. Latané, *William Maginn and the British Press: A Critical Biography* (New York: Routledge, 2016), 30.

military veterans had, by the start of the 1830s, gone on to pen their memoirs of service on campaign, prompting one reviewer to declare that Gleig had invented a 'lively school of writing' with *The Subaltern*.[19]

Hamilton's *Cyril Thornton*, published by William Blackwood in 1827, was one of the first works to appear in this new 'school of writing', composed as it was of Hamilton's fictionalised account of his experiences as a subaltern officer on campaign during the Peninsular War.[20] Hamilton also went on to write *Annals of the Peninsular Campaigns* (1829), a history of the Peninsular War that represents one of the first military histories written solely for a popular audience, 'the great mass of the public', with no regard for professional, military readers.[21] He was, in other words, a key figure in expanding and popularising this new military 'school of writing' because he was also transforming war into a new kind of popular reading for the general, civilian, public. In composing *Cyril Thornton*, Hamilton drew on much from his contemporaries' military memoirs, developing further, as I explain later, the military picturesque of Gleig's *The Subaltern*.[22] Hamilton also, however, decisively transformed the genre of the military memoir because he mapped it onto the three-volume historical novel to thereby integrate the modern military tale with the form of historical romance that had been consolidated by Scott. Scott's historical novels were a decisive influence on British literature during the 1820s, ultimately casting their shadow over almost all European novels written in the first half of the nineteenth century with their alignment of personal *Bildungsroman* and national history. In his novels, Scott celebrated the progress of Scotland into a modern nation fully integrated with the rest of Britain, yet he did so by imaginatively incorporating the romance, naturalism and aesthetic appeal of the Highlands into British national culture. That Hamilton should have drawn on Scott as he novelised the military tale is unsurprising, especially given that Scott's historical novels were at the centre of the *Blackwood's* cultural project to which Hamilton himself had contributed. Hamilton's adaptation of Scott can, in turn, be seen to have been pivotal to the subsequent development not just of military and naval novels, but equally to the establishment of a

[19] *Gentleman's Magazine* 101 (1831): 68.
[20] *The Quarterly Review* 37, no. 73 (1828): 521.
[21] Thomas Hamilton, *Annals of the Peninsular Campaigns: From MDCCCVIII to MDCCCXIV*, 3 vols (Edinburgh: William Blackwood; and London: T. Cadell, 1829), vol. I. ii.
[22] Ramsey, *The Military Memoir and Romantic Literary Culture*, 137–63.

nineteenth-century tradition of militarised imperial adventure.[23] With reviews of *Cyril Thornton* almost unanimously positive, Hamilton was even described by *Blackwood's* in 1833 as greater than 'any living romance writer', having inherited the mantle from the 'father of romance' following Scott's death in 1832.[24]

Displacing the Romance of Love and War

Ian Duncan aligns *Cyril Thornton* with what he terms the Western or Glaswegian version of the Scottish historical novel first pioneered by John Galt.[25] Focussing, therefore, on the short time that Thornton spent at the University of Glasgow, Duncan entirely overlooks the book's status as the originator of the military novel. In one of the very few studies of the genre of the military novel, a PhD thesis from 1956, Jeremiah Allen points out that *Cyril Thornton* shares its narrative structure with Scott's first, and archetypal, historical novel, *Waverley* (1814).[26] Set at the time of the Jacobite Rebellion of 1745, Scott's novel relates the story of Edward Waverley, a lieutenant in a regiment of British dragoons, whose travels in the Highlands of Scotland with clan leader Fergus McIvor leave him captivated by the immense beauty of the region and the romance of the Jacobite cause to restore Charles Stuart to the throne.[27] Falling in love with Fergus' sister Flora, Waverley accompanies the Jacobite army on its invasion of England. The novel, however, charts Waverley's growing realisation that their cause is doomed, that the Highlanders' ambitions represent a mere romance hopelessly fighting against the rising tide of a modernising world. As Duncan has detailed, while traditional military codes of behaviour and emotion, what the novel describes as 'military honour', are paramount to the Jacobites, such honour simply appears as an archaic and violent relic of

---

[23] Michael Paris, *Warrior Nation: Images of War in British Popular Culture, 1850–2000* (London: Reaktion Books, 2000); Patrick Brantlinger, *Rule of Darkness: British Literature and Imperialism, 1830–1914* (Ithaca: Cornell University Press, 1988); Graham Dawson, *Soldier Heroes: British Adventure, Empire and the Imagining of Masculinities* (New York: Routledge, 1994); and Martin Green, *Dreams of Adventure, Deeds of Empire* (New York: Basic Books, Inc., 1979).

[24] *Blackwood's Edinburgh Magazine* 34, no. 210 (September 1833): 288. For reviews of *Cyril Thornton*, see the *Quarterly Review* 37, no. 73 (1828); and the *Edinburgh Review* 52, no. 103 (1830).

[25] Duncan, *Scott's Shadow*, 39.

[26] Jeremiah Mervin Allen, *The British Military Novel: 1825–1850* (PhD diss., University of Colorado, 1956), 112.

[27] Sir Walter Scott, *Waverley; or, 'Tis Sixty Years Since*. 3 vols, 2nd ed. (Edinburgh and London: Printed by James Ballantyne and Co. for Archibald Constable and Co. Edinburgh; and Longman, Hurst, Rees, Orme, and Brown, London, 1814).

former times.[28] Chastened by his experiences and naivety, Waverley abandons the Jacobites and sensibly returns home to England to marry Rose Bradwardine, his personal maturation and marriage standing as a homology for a national history of progress from war and civil strife to Britain's settled modern condition of commerce and national unity.[29] Yet while Waverley's abandonment of romance drives the novel's plot, romance nonetheless remains in the novel's closing chapter, where the scene of domestic harmony at Waverley's estate of Tully-Veolan is accompanied by a portrait of Waverley and Fergus in their Highland costume, the painting itself framed with the weapons Waverley had carried during the war.[30] The painting suggests that military honour glows forth as aesthetic romance at the very moment that it is historically superseded.[31] Lifted into the realm of culture, military honour is available as a romance to invigorate, but not politically control, modern Britain.

The eponymous protagonist of *Cyril Thornton* closely follows Waverley's *Bildung* path to maturity during an equally turbulent and decisive, if more recent, period of Britain's national and military history. Like Waverley, Thornton comes to reject his earlier romantic notions of military honour and passionate love for a companionate marriage and relocation into the social order of a modernising Britain. The plot of *Cyril Thornton* turns on a childhood incident that profoundly shapes Thornton's life, his accidental shooting of his younger brother during a hunting trip his father had forbidden the pair from undertaking. Distraught and outraged at the death of his youngest son, Thornton's father, a wealthy landowner in southeast England, disinherits his only remaining son from the family estate, Thornhill. Forced to turn to a career to support himself, Thornton decides to join the army owing to a boyhood enthusiasm for the romance of the 'military life' (vol. I. 18).[32] The novel tracks Thornton's maturation through his education at the University of Glasgow, his service as an officer in the army on campaign during the Peninsular War and his romantic entanglements while at home in England that eventually lead by the novels'

---

[28] Duncan, *Modern Romance*, 73.
[29] Duncan, *Modern Romance*, 89–90.
[30] Scott, *Waverley*, vol. III. 359.
[31] On the ways in which Scott uses romance as a consolation for the loss of an aristocratic order, see also Ina Ferris, *The Achievement of Literary Authority: Gender, History, and the Waverley Novels* (Ithaca: Cornell University Press, 1991), 79–104; and Miranda J. Burgess, *British Fiction and the Production of Social Order, 1740–1830* (Cambridge: Cambridge University Press, 2000), 186–234.
[32] Thomas Hamilton, *The Youth and Manhood of Cyril Thornton* (Edinburgh: William Blackwood; and London: T. Cadell, 1827). All further references are in the body of the text.

conclusion to his marriage.[33] The novel proceeds as a *Bildungsroman* by thwarting the desires of Thornton's youthful romance as he comes to a melancholy maturity and a settled, domestic life.

Thornton's personal experience of war is fundamental to this process as it sets hardship, injustice, suffering and wounding against his youthful visions of military heroism and romance. In a similar manner to the young Waverley, Thornton's romantic view of war is formed through his reading, particularly of the great generals of the seventeenth and early eighteenth centuries: Eugene, Peterborough, Gustav and Vauban (vol. I. 18). His enthusiasm for war is further inflamed by hearing tales of old generals, and becomes a consuming 'ardour' when he first dons his uniform (vol. II. 19). Yet the novel also contrasts his military zeal with the physical suffering that he endures on campaign. Looking back in later life, he can only reflect with a chastened maturity: 'It is with a smile on my lips, yet with something of melancholy in my heart, that I recall these sallies of strong though boyish enthusiasm. The glow of feeling which produced them soon faded, and is long since gone' (vol. I. 130).

His first experiences of soldiering are of garrison service in Canada, where he is repeatedly exasperated by the demands of the martinet Colonel Grimshawe, eventually being sent to prison for failing to powder his hair (vol. II. 57). Beset by the arbitrary authority of military power, his romantic notions of war are further defeated by the appalling suffering and hardship he encounters on active military service, what he terms the 'fatigues and hazards of a campaign' (vol. III. 82). His military career culminates, however, with his wounding at the Battle of Albuera in 1811, one of the most brutal battles of the Peninsular War. He describes in intimate detail his 'acute bodily suffering' after he is wounded, recording the medical operations that saved his life: 'I gasped convulsively for breath, yet at every respiration, was nearly suffocated by the blood, which gurgled from my throat, and obstructed the action of my lungs' until a doctor removed a small protuberance, 'a mass of coagulated blood', that let him breathe again (vol. III. 171–73).

The novel not only contrasts Thornton's personal experience of war's suffering with his own earlier romantic idealism, but it also sets his military experience against the romantic naivety of aristocrats who are shown

---

[33] The plot also loosely follows Hamilton's own life. In a telling allusion to the novel's indebtedness to *Waverley*, however, we also hear that Thornton's maternal grandfather was 'a captain of dragoons, who served in Scotland somewhere about the middle of last century, [and] married the blooming Miss Rebecca' (vol. I. 41).

to have little experience of war but who nonetheless hold a pompous and ill-founded self-regard for their military sagacity and honour. Thornton describes Lord Amersham, for example, as having been 'bred a soldier' and as a 'hero with the blood of the noblest chivalry in his veins', but Thornton is conscious that Amersham had never encountered 'the hazards of the field, or the vicissitudes of climate', and so holds merely the 'empty honours' of his profession (vol. I. 244). Listening to Amersham and an elderly general descant on the war in Spain, Thornton can only comment on their ignorance: 'the old fable of the Mountain and the Mouse, could not have been more fully illustrated. To me, who, from personal observation, knew something of the facts and circumstances of the war, nothing could appear more puerile and jejune than their remarks (vol. III. 17–18).

In one scene, Thornton attempts to explain war to the Amershams and their friends by describing a battle in terms of an arrangement of dishes on a dinner table:

> This, the English, who are represented by these dishes, wish to take, and the French, who are those dishes opposite, wish to defend. Then the English send this Venison-pasty, which is a brigade of infantry, to attack the Sirloin of beef, which, as I said before, is a hill, with a fort on the top of it. The French seeing this, send up that dish of Maintenon cutlets as a reinforcement. (vol. II. 375)

The novel's humour implies that the aristocracy are incapable of understanding war as anything more than a social occasion. It is a point the novel underscores when the Amersham's friend, Colonel Culpepper, moves the dishes to get at the curry. Representative of the aristocracy's ignorance of real war and its privations, the colonel is merely 'an adept in the science of good living' (vol. II. 372).

This ironic portrayal of aristocratic knowledge of war carries over to the novel's depiction of the British commander in chief (from 1809 to 1811), Sir David Dundas, whom Thornton meets when he attends a levee at the horse guards to make a case for his promotion on the advice of Lord Amersham (vol. III. 75). Dundas had risen to prominence after he produced a version of the Prussian system of manoeuvres for the British army, *Principles of Military Movements, Chiefly Applied to Infantry* (1788), which informed the standard drill procedures for British infantry during the French Revolutionary and Napoleonic Wars. Although Dundas is described as retaining the air of a soldier, his resemblance to a soldier is to the strict disciplinarian Frederick the Great. As depicted in *Cyril Thornton*, Dundas is a relic of the past: 'He was an emaciated old man, apparently in the very last stage of physical debility, and evidently altogether unequal, to the arduous and important duties of the office, to which he had been recently appointed' (vol. III. 78). Far different from the energetic and animated Wellington, whom Thornton encounters in the field, Dundas embodies an older and increasingly outmoded idea of aristocratic patronage, privilege and mechanical ideas of war (vol. III. 94). Thornton had read 'Dundas on the Eighteen Manoeuvres' as he travels to Portsmouth to embark for military service in Newfoundland, but he falls asleep while reading in his carriage and on waking realises that his ship has sailed without him, forcing him to arrange his own passage to join the vessel (vol. II. 25). This central document of British military exercise appears useless for Thornton's real experience of war. At the levee, Thornton also meets a Major O'Shaughnessy, a captain of seventeen years' standing who had only recently received a brevet majority, despite having

> endured all varieties of climate—he had fought in the East, and in the West—had been taken prisoner by Tippoo Saib—and shot through the body, at the capture of Guadaloupe. In his return from India, the ship in which he sailed, had been wrecked, and his wife and two children drowned. With all this series of service and suffering, he still remained a captain. (vol. III. 76–77)

The novel asks us to see war as far more than simply rote learning of mechanical martial drill or a sociable occasion associated with aristocratic prestige. As explained in more detail later, the novel sees the truth of war as being grounded in the soldier's suffering body.

For Henry Crabb Robinson, *Cyril Thornton* read more like an autobiography than any novel he knew, although he also added: 'There is but one incident novel-like, his amours'.[34] If the military scenes resemble those found in contemporary military memoirs, the love story loosely resembles that of Waverley's romance with Flora, as Thornton falls in love with his beautiful and spirited cousin, Lady Melicent de Vere, daughter of Lord and Lady Amersham. A romance forms between Thornton and Melicent when he visits her at Staunton Court, much to Thornton's surprise that she should have any interest in a man whose estate provides only 'two or three thousand a-year' (vol. I. 263). If marriage between the pair appears improbable on financial grounds the suitability of their attachment is further undermined by Thornton's overly romantic disposition. As Lady Melicent herself notes of Thornton's attentions:

[34] Edith J. Morley, ed., *Henry Crabb Robinson on Books and their Writers*, 3 vols (London: Dent, 1938), vol. II. 577.

The love you talk of, is the love not of real life, but of romance. It is the love one reads of in a novel, of some high-born heroine in a cottage among the Welsh mountains, or in the south of France, preceded generally by some thing about the cooing of doves, and followed by a copy of verses, or a serenade from some noble lover in disguise. (vol. III. 54)

Thornton's romance with Lady Melicent comes to an end after he is wounded at the Battle of Albuera, his face being too disfigured, he believes, for someone of her standing. Returning to England, he discovers that she had, in fact, already begun an alternative liaison with Lord Lyndhurst. His only comfort comes from his childhood playmate, the long suffering, humble and angelic Laura Willoughby. Despite his earlier indifference towards her, 'I had ever regarded Laura with strong affection; but she had never been to me the object of vehement and engrossing passion' (vol. III. 231), he comes by novel's end to see her instead as crucial to his future happiness. Disavowing passionate love, Thornton marries Laura, and the story concludes with the pair taking over Thornton's family estate on the death of his father. Thornton declares at the novel's conclusion that he is satisfied to never again venture out into the world because '[t]he full capacity of my affections was filled at home' (vol. III. 369). Far from his marriage serving as a culmination of his romantic adventures, therefore, marriage functions as a turn to the ordinary that replaces his earlier enthusiasm for extraordinary adventure and the romance of military honour and glory.

Like *Waverley*, *Cyril Thornton* is a love story in which the junior military officer leaves behind his youthful romantic ideas of love and a military enthusiasm, ideas formed from tales of romance and heroism, for a quiet domestic life of companionate marriage. In a further analogy between the two novels, *Cyril Thornton* does this in the context of a modernising Scotland, imagined through transformations of Glasgow:

Though in the external aspect of Glasgow, little change was apparent from the lapse of years, which had intervened since my former visit, yet a great change was certainly observable in the manners and mode of life of its inhabitants. Wealth had evidently increased [...] Nothing, in short, could be more striking than the almost total revolution, which a few years had effected in the tastes and habits of the community. The spirit of improvement was evidently abroad. (vol. III. 339–40)

Yet *Cyril Thornton* is not only a Scottish or Glaswegian novel. Fundamentally, it transposes the allure of romance and its accompanying naivety onto the English aristocracy. In this sense it resembles Austen's *Persuasion* (1818), itself partly modelled on *Waverley*, which follows the fortunes of Anne Elliot after her father, the baronet Sir Walter Elliot, succumbs to his debts and is forced to rent out their home, Kellynch Hall, to Admiral Croft and his wife, Sophia.[35] As the aristocrat Elliot loses his ancestral home to a naval officer, so his daughter Anne marries the naval officer Captain Frederick Wentworth, although only after an initially failed courtship in which Wentworth had been rejected by Anne's family for lacking a sufficiently elevated aristocratic heritage. As the novel reveals, however, while aristocrats such as Elliot had been squandering their resources, naval captains such as Wentworth had been saving Britain from French invasion. Through the marriage of Anne and Wentworth, Austen imaginatively unites the aristocracy with the newly won heroism and national service of the navy. In a similar way, the military officer Thornton may be beneath the station of an aristocrat such as Lady Melicent de Vere, but he nonetheless comes to take over the estate of Thornhill and thus bring the hard-fighting military officer into British aristocratic tradition. Like so much fiction of this period, then, *Cyril Thornton* explores and seeks to resolve tensions between the emergent professional or middle classes and the existing aristocratic order as its hegemonic authority began to wane.[36] Like *Persuasion*, though, *Cyril Thornton* explores these ideas in relation to a newly configured institutional identity of the military. Delegitimising the connection that had traditionally existed between the aristocracy and war, it builds instead an association between war, the nation and the heroism of the military that imaginatively realigns aristocratic tradition with the institutional authority, national importance and moral virtues of the professional military officer.

In so doing, however, the two novels also complicate the form of historical romance on which they draw. Both novels still locate military honour in the past as they celebrate a modernity defined through marriage and settled, domestic peace. But so too, both novels suggest that military honour is not simply consigned to the past but still has some role in directing and shaping British society.[37] *Cyril Thornton* can be productively understood, therefore, by examining it in relationship to work on the late-Romantic novel that underscores the shifting political terrain of post-war

[35] On the ways in which Austen's *Persuasion* drew on *Waverley* (along with Scott's other novels, *The Antiquary* and *Guy Mannering*), see Jocelyn Harris, *A Revolution Almost Beyond Expression: Jane Austen's* Persuasion (Newark: University of Delaware Press, 2007), 111–12.

[36] Gary Kelly, *English Fiction of the Romantic Period, 1789–1830* (New York: Longman, 1989), 13.

[37] On broader cultural attitudes to the naval officer as a figure of national leadership in these years, see Timothy Fulford, 'Romanticizing the Empire: The Naval Heroes of Southey, Coleridge, Austen, and Marryat', *Modern Language Quarterly* 60, no. 2 (1999): 161–96.

Britain and emergent ideas of governance, command and power.[38] *Cyril Thornton* embodies the underlying imperative of Scott's novels and *Blackwood's Edinburgh Magazine*, the preservation of romance as a means to ameliorate the enervation of a modern, commercial society. It does so, however, by developing an element that only lies in embryonic form in *Waverley* – the impact of war upon the officer's bodily health and vitality. Waverley is only welcomed home by his relatives after Colonel Talbot relates a tale of Waverley's gallant behaviour in the war, a story confirmed by Waverley's physical appearance, an 'athletic and hardy character' acquired from his military campaigning.[39] Taking further *Waverley's* passing concern with the embodied and vitalising qualities of military service and its marks on the body, *Cyril Thornton* develops a new aesthetic vision of romance that is centred on what *Blackwood's* saw as lying at the heart of the novel, the 'living flesh-and-blood man and gentleman'.[40]

Biopolitics, Marriage and Wounding in the Post-War Novel

For Anne Frey, the post-war novels of Scott and Austen can be conceptualised as part of what she terms a British 'State Romanticism', a broad-based reorientation of Romantic aesthetics in the post-war era onto the power and authority of state institutions.[41] Insisting upon the values of meritocracy, nascent middle-class virtue and a unified nation, so this new aesthetic was equally concerned with questions of governmental reason. In constructing her analysis, Frey draws on Foucault's account of the progression of governmental forms of power and rule during the Romantic era, in particular the complementary yet distinct political rationalities of pastoral care and liberalism.[42] Pastoral care works through the

---

[38] Anne Frey, *British State Romanticism: Authorship, Agency, And Bureaucratic Nationalism* (Stanford: Stanford University Press, 2010). For an account of the Victorian novel that similarly draws on ideas of liberalism, see Lauren M. E. Goodlad, *Victorian Literature and the Victorian State: Character and Governance in a Liberal Society* (Baltimore: Johns Hopkins University Press, 2003).

[39] Scott, *Waverley*, vol. III. 333. In a related manner, Austen draws attention to Admiral Croft's 'weather-beaten' visage as evidence of his robust health and years of service in the navy, Jane Austen, *Persuasion*, ed. Patricia Meyer Spacks (New York: W. W. Norton, 1995), 16.

[40] *Blackwood's Edinburgh Magazine* 22, no. 128 (1827): 83. For a longer genealogy of Romanticism's concerns with the wounded officer, see also Daniel O'Quinn 'Invalid Elegy and Gothic Pageantry: André, Seward and the Loss of the American War', in *Tracing War in British Enlightenment and Romantic Culture*, ed. Neil Ramsey and Gillian Russell (Basingstoke: Palgrave Macmillan, 2015), 37–60.

[41] Frey, *British State Romanticism*, 3.

[42] On Foucault's account of governmentality, see Michel Foucault, *Security, Territory, Population: Lectures at the Collège de France, 1977–1978*, ed. Michel Senellart, trans. Graham Burchell (Basingstoke: Palgrave Macmillan, 2007), 87–114.

cultivation of individual and public habits, feelings, attitudes and actions. In contrast, liberalism is concerned with limiting government, ensuring its non-intervention in order to preserve the free functioning of civil society. But, as Frey explains, liberalism fosters individual freedoms precisely because these freedoms came to be seen as central to the development of habits and feelings necessary for the cultivation of the nation's potential. Liberalism and pastoral care are, in other words, distinct approaches to government that are nonetheless deeply entwined around a mutual concern with the development of the life processes of those who are governed. The novel appears as a means for developing the pastoral care of a living population, able to extend state authority into realms it would not otherwise reach because liberalism imposed limitations on more direct and formal kinds of state intervention.

Frey has not been alone in reading nineteenth-century literature in relation to Foucault's conceptualisation of governmental practices. Lauren Goodlad, for example, has similarly described later Victorian novels in terms of liberal governmentality.[43] However, in their analyses they are primarily concerned with the liberal dimensions of rule in Britain, and do not, therefore, consider governmental processes in terms of the exercise of power upon the vital and natural properties of life that liberal rule seeks to preserve and foster. What can be added to their accounts, in other words, is an understanding of what Foucault analyses in terms of biopolitics, an art of government that he believes emerged upon the foundations of this new regime of governmentality.[44] Studies of biopolitics and Romanticism have contended that it is no coincidence Romanticism should have emerged contemporaneously with the modern biopolitical management of life. This is not to suggest that any kind of settled consensus has yet emerged on the relationship between literature and biopolitics.[45] Nonetheless, what they share in the Romantic era is a fundamental concern with understanding and harnessing an idea of 'life as power'.[46] The reconceptualising of aristocratic values that we see documented in the late Romantic novel was linked to developments in the nature of government, a transition from an earlier sovereign symbolics of

---

[43] Goodlad, *Victorian Literature and the Victorian State*.

[44] Michel Foucault, *Birth of Biopolitics: Lectures at the Collège de France, 1978–1979*, ed. Michel Senellart, trans. Graham Burchell (Basingstoke: Palgrave Macmillan, 2008), 21–22. See also Foucault, *Society Must Be Defended*, 243.

[45] Hunt and Rudolf, *Romanticism and Biopolitics*.

[46] Denise Gigante, *Life: Organic Form and Romanticism* (New Haven: Yale University Press, 2009), 3.

blood to the biopolitical analytics of sexuality.[47] Guido Mazzoni goes so far as to suggest that in the form of the novel launched by Austen, '[n]othing is important but life'.[48] Power exercised through biopolitics was no longer tied to symbolic spectacles of sovereign or aristocratic power, kinship, patrilineage, alliance and war, where power ultimately rested on the sovereign's right to kill and hence a combination of bloody violence and blood relations. Linked, rather, with the growth of capitalism and its concerns with the corporeality of labour, power sought to ensure the proliferation of life and its productivity.

Clearly one way that a vitalist biopolitics operates in the late Romantic novel is through its laudation of companionate marriage.[49] Given that the governmental administration of life began to dominate over the state's concerns with territorial sovereignty, it is hardly surprising that marriage should have emerged as a vital institution of modern government in which the Malthusian couple takes a privileged location in national identity.[50] As Heike Hartung argues in her biopolitical reading of the Romantic era *Bildung* novel, marriage appears as the endpoint of a youth's maturation because it provides a link between the completion of social integration and the hero's full biological development.[51] In a similar vein, Vlasta Vranjes regards Austen's *Persuasion* as pivotal to the centrality of marriage in the modern novel.[52] By concluding with the rekindled courtship and peripatetic marriage of Anne and Wentworth, the novel reimagines marriage not only outside any associations with dynastic lineage and alliance but also equally beyond any settled domestic location. While to some extent offering a cosmopolitan view of gender, the novel also presents an abstracted picture of marriage as an institution lying at the heart of the modern nation. Similarly reflecting on *Persuasion's* peripatetic marriage, Eric Walker notes that marriage is not only central to post-war writing, but also that marriage

---

[47] Foucault, *History of Sexuality*, 148.
[48] Guido Mazzoni, *Theory of the Novel*, trans. Zakiya Hanafi (Cambridge, MA: Harvard University Press, 2017), 376.
[49] On the importance of the Malthusian couple in the early nineteenth century, see, for example, Michael Parrish Lee, *The Food Plot in the Nineteenth-Century British Novel* (London: Palgrave Macmillan, 2016), 12.
[50] Frey, *British State Romanticism*, 7. For a biopolitical reading of the novel that discusses the unity of sexuality with gender, see Nancy Armstrong, 'When Gender Meets Sexuality in the Victorian Novel', in *The Cambridge Companion to the Victorian Novel*, ed. Deirdre David, 2nd ed. (Cambridge: Cambridge University Press, 2012), 170–93.
[51] Hartung, *Ageing, Gender, and Illness in Anglophone Literature*.
[52] Vlasta Vranjes, *English Vows: Marriage and National Identity in Nineteenth-Century Literature and Culture* (PhD diss., University of California, 2009), 24.

emerges in this writing as what he terms the compulsory grounds of identity, so foundational to identity that it almost passes without mention.[53]

Yet Walker also observes that the peripatetic marriage of *Persuasion* is
itself paradoxical. He proposes that by leaving the domestic unsettled,
the novel reveals a deep entanglement between marriage and war in the
post-war period.[54] While war can be described as being waged to make
the world safe for marriage, Walker argues that this safety is never fully
achieved in post-war writing. As Austen observes of Anne's marriage at the
conclusion of *Persuasion*:

> the dread of a future war [was] all that could dim her sunshine. She gloried
> in being a sailor's wife, but she must pay the tax of quick alarm for belong-
> ing to that profession which is, if possible, more distinguished in its domes-
> tic virtues than in its national importance.[55]

Despite the cessation of hostilities and the interlacing of the navy with the
domestic happiness of marriage, the dread and alarm of war remain. One
way of reading this conclusion is that the novel records the invasion into
the home of war's traumatic wounding and death.[56] If, as Ian Baucom
notes, the novelistic template of historical romance set by Scott is one in
which the dead and dying are buried with the past, then *Persuasion*, like
Cyril Thornton, can be seen to refashion the historical novel by revealing
that the dead and dying of history cannot be so easily laid to rest.[57] *Cyril
Thornton* goes so far as to incorporate the wounded and disfigured body of
the military officer into the heart of ancestral Britain. Recounting his suffering after being wounded in battle, Thornton writes of himself as though
his latter life was transfixed by war's trauma: 'These were the feelings of a
suffering body and a diseased mind; but even now, that the circumstances
which occasioned them have passed away, I find evidence of their strength
in the vividness with which they almost, unbidden, present themselves to
my memory' (vol. III. 178).

[53] Eric C. Walker, *Marriage, Writing and Romanticism: Wordsworth and Austen After War* (Stanford: Stanford University Press, 2009), 23.
[54] Walker, *Marriage, Writing and Romanticism*, 90.
[55] Austen, *Persuasion*, 168.
[56] For a reading of how war's trauma penetrates into everyday life and conjugality in the post-war era, see also Mary Favret, *War at a Distance: Romanticism and the Making of Modern Wartime* (Princeton: Princeton University Press, 2010), 170; and Philip Shaw, *Waterloo and the Romantic Imagination* (Basingstoke: Palgrave Macmillan, 2002), 160.
[57] Ian Baucom, *Specters of the Atlantic: Finance Capital, Slavery, and the Philosophy of History* (Durham: Duke University Press, 2005), 282.

But to see suffering only as the return of 'unbidden' feelings, the 'endless impact on a life' of the 'belated experience' of death that Cathy Caruth places at the heart of trauma, is also to downplay the self-conscious role that suffering plays in the novel's reimagining of the soldier.[58] The cultural authority that the novel exercises over the aristocracy is grounded in Thornton's encounter with war's violence. By foregrounding wounding and violence, that is, the novel works to assert the greater moral worth and national importance of the embryonic middle classes and the modern institution of the military.[59]

In his development of Foucault's account of biopolitics, Giorgio Agamben proposes that what is distinctive about the modern world is not so much the simple fact of biopolitical administration of life and bodies as the way that this 'bare life' moves to the centre of political concerns.[60] Defining bare life as 'life exposed to death', bare life can even be related to Caruth's definition of trauma as the collapsing of death into life.[61] Adapting such views to *Cyril Thornton*, reading Thornton himself as a figure of trauma, we might say that the novel operates through its own inclusion of a veritable bare life into the heart of British authority and power. The novel, indeed, resists seeing war's trauma as isolated from Thornton's ordinary life, comparing the suffering of the battlefield with that of the 'humble and inglorious' sick-bed:

> I know by experience, that a sick-bed may afford occasion for the exercise of a higher courage, than is required, under the influence of strong extraneous excitement, to brave death in the field;—that the humble and inglorious sufferer, may display a spirit more truly heroic, than his who perils life, for human honour and applause, in the imminent deadly breach. (vol. III. 174)

Reading from a biopolitical perspective, can we also look at the traumatic residuum of war's unbidden suffering, then, as a remodelling of daily life in terms of a new set of vital imperatives that circulate through the body? In the redefinition of true heroism as the sick bed, might we see a medicalising of bodies and lives, a fundamental concern with both imagining

---

[58] Cathy Caruth, *Unclaimed Experience: Trauma, Narrative, and History* (Baltimore: Johns Hopkins University Press, 1996), 7.

[59] For a broader discussion of how novels united military masculinity with ideas of national improvement, see also Megan A. Woodworth, *Eighteenth-Century Women Writers and the Gentleman's Liberation Movement: Independence, War, Masculinity, and the Novel, 1778–1818* (Farnham: Ashgate, 2011).

[60] Agamben, *Homo Sacer*, 111.

[61] Agamben, *Homo Sacer*, 56.

leadership in terms of vigour, health and disease and with militarising the most intimate of private spaces?

Cyril Thornton may resemble an archetypal *Bildung* of youth and manhood, a story that imagines the officer in relation to the ordinary administration of life, but its conception of life is as much constituted by wounding as it is by marriage. The novel suggests that alongside the biopolitical analytics of sexuality there also emerged something like an analytics of wounding in this era centred on the traumatised body. Indeed, for Foucault a central antinomy in modern political reason is how care of the individual life that informs biopower was matched with a death command and obligation for mass slaughter.[62] The genealogy of the modern subject can be traced through trauma and wounding in addition to sexuality. Ian Hacking explicates the role of trauma in constituting the subject in his conceptualisation of a memoro-politics as a third pole of biopower alongside anatamo-politics of the body and the bio-politics of the population.[63] Drawing out the somatic roots of trauma, with its origins in the violent wound, he proposes that memoro-power not only embodied the 'soul' but enables the soul to be imagined as wounded in the same sense as the body. It thus conceptualised the psyche from an embodied perspective, allowing the soul to be administered or governed as, in effect, a component of the body. Such a conception of trauma can be further elaborated by turning to Mark Seltzer's delineation of modernity as a wound culture. Similarly working with a somatic understanding of trauma, Seltzer adapts Walter Benjamin's reading of the social in terms of the traumatic shocks that modern technologies, media and social forms inflicted upon the modern subject.[64] In defining wound culture, Seltzer observes that the interiority of wounds represents the intimacy of personal experience while simultaneously aligning with social questions of national sacrifice and the embodiment, or vitalising, of national identity. As discussed by Elaine Scarry, pain is undeniable for the one who suffers but because it is a wholly interior experience it cannot be shared by others, leaving pain with a merely imaginary social existence.[65] It is because of this strange structure

[62] Foucault, 'The Political Technology of Individuals', 404–05.
[63] Ian Hacking, 'Memoro-politics, Trauma and the Soul', *History of the Human Sciences* 7, no. 2 (1994): 29–52.
[64] Mark Seltzer, 'Wound Culture: Trauma in the Pathological Public Sphere', *October* 80 (Spring 1997): 3–26.
[65] Elaine Scarry, *The Body in Pain: The Making and Unmaking of the World* (Oxford: Oxford University Press, 1985).

of pain, entirely real to an individual and yet entirely deniable in others, that pain can be lifted out of its source in the wounded body and relocated into culture, ideology or literature as a way of grounding the 'reality' of these abstractions. Such processes, however, demand a widespread recognition of wounding – less a masking or repression of wounding than an exercise of power that perpetually foregrounds, compels, proliferates and identifies discourse on wounding that can enable wounding to be redirected into the life, health and security of the nation.[66] If far less clearly or completely developed than the confessional practices associated with sexuality, there is nonetheless a modern wound culture that is similarly founded on the compulsion to speak of and foreground wounds. As does sexuality, wound culture functions by uniting the interiority of the individual body with the living vitality of the population.

It is in such terms that we can read *Cyril Thornton* and its imaginative integration of trauma into the nation. Arne De Boever has proposed that we can move beyond pastoral readings of the novel, as proffered by Frey and Goodland, to a more fully developed biopolitical reading by adopting a pharmacological approach to biopolitics.[67] He borrows the term from Jacques Derrida and Bernard Steigler, who have analysed writing as a 'pharmakon' that simultaneously serves as both poison and cure. One dimension of the pharmacological reading is an attention to the intertwined elements of life and death that mark biopolitics. Adapting this approach to the study of biopolitics, De Boever suggests that the novel resembles Agamben's conceptualisation of the camp – it is a space in which the life of the characters is entirely under the authority and control of the author, who can make his or her characters live or die on an authorial whim.[68] The novel is, in his reading, a space for the imaginative production of bare life. Drawing on De Boever's insights helps to emphasise the intimate relationship between death and vitality that *Cyril Thornton* establishes. The novel does not simply undercut the traditional romance surrounding war; it equally builds a new kind of romance out of what it views as the redemptive and life-giving figuration of suffering and the exposure to death. The traumatised, disfigured and suffering Thornton can be seen

---

[66] For a detailed discussion of the representation of wounding in British culture during the French Revolutionary and Napoleonic Wars, see Mary Favret, 'Writing, Reading and the Scenes of War', in *The Cambridge History of English Romantic Literature*, ed. James Chandler (Cambridge: Cambridge University Press, 2009), 314–34.

[67] Arne De Boever, *Narrative Care: Biopolitics and the Novel* (London: Bloomsbury, 2013), 34–41.

[68] De Boever, *Narrative Care*, 68.

as this figuration of bare life, a new kind of soldier whose association with the symbolic power of the sword and monarch has been redirected into a concern with his inner self and its embodied entanglements of sexuality and wounding. This chapter concludes, however, by turning to similar concerns with how literature embodies bare life in the work of Jacques Rancière and Christoph Menke. Their work shifts focus away from the concerns with care and freedom that De Boever identifies in biopolitics, to what can be read as a more starkly drawn concern with the controlling mechanisms of biopower. The collapse of the soldier into a traumatic dissipation, his wounding and exposure to death, could simultaneously be read as the revelation of an intensification of discipline into a biopower that assumes a complete hold over life in a movement from the battlefield to the bedroom.[69]

Wounding and Redemption in Cyril Thornton

Cyril Thornton not only undercuts the romance of war by exposing the aristocracy's naïveté and self-regarding indulgences, but it also reorients the symbolics of blood by self-consciously tracing a shift in Thornton himself from the aristocratic killer, gambler and seducer to a figure of companionate marriage and bodily suffering.[70] Having accidentally killed his brother in a hunting accident at the beginning of the novel, Thornton's fratricide is marked, like that of Cain, by a wandering, dissolute and isolated life. Eventually disfigured in war, his wounds leave him with a terrifying visage:

> Such a creature as I gazed on! My face was pale and haggard, my eyes sunk deeply in their sockets, and my features were frightfully distorted by a wound, reaching from the temple to the mouth, by which my upper lip had been divided, and the extent of which was indicated by a long red scar. (vol. III. 185)

Thornton is not only associated with Cain as a killer, however; the association carries over into his illicit encounter with the 'young and beautiful' Mary Brookes, a seamstress whom he comes to know during visits with his sisters to her father's cottage (vol. I. 330). Thornton is haunted

---

[69] For a similar argument in relation to the contemporary soldier, see Greg Goldberg and Craig Willse, 'Losses and Returns: The Soldier in Trauma', in *The Affective Turn: Theorizing the Social*, ed. Patricia Ticineto Clough and Jean Halley (Durham: Duke University Press, 2007), 264–86, 266.

[70] Although the novel is muted about Thornton's predilection for gambling, Thornton does explain that 'I always experienced a degree of pleasing excitement from games of chance', and he loses a considerable sum of money after one evening's play (vol III. 39).

by her beauty and moved by her circumstances, her crushing poverty and a tyrannical, cruel father, and the pair quickly fall in love despite his class position excluding all possibility of marriage. Having thus brought about Mary's 'irretrievable ruin' (she was to be married to a local farmer, Pierce), Thornton describes himself as a 'Vile seducer! unprincipled betrayer of confiding love! Like Cain, shalt thou be branded among men, and go down into the grave with the guilt of perjury on thy soul' (vol. I. 341).

The plot of the novel is resolved, however, through Thornton's confession of his libertine crimes. Identifying himself with his moral failings, Thornton explains to his readers at the end of the novel that 'I have made you the depositary of my confidence. I have laid bare to your view my actions and my motives. You know my errors – I have told you the secrets of my life' (vol. III. 367). The novel, in this sense, conforms to a longer genealogy of confessional accounts of the aristocratic officer that similarly posited the officer as a seducer, gambler and even, if at least indirectly, a murderer. This is seen, for example, in *The Half-Pay Officer; or, Memoirs of Charles Chanceley: A Novel* (1788), a sentimental novel that recounts the dissolute life of the eponymous hero following his sexual indiscretions with a Mrs Walby and subsequent banishment by his enraged father.[71] Turning to a career in the army on the guidance of his father's friend, Major D'Arcy, his experience of military service is associated with gambling rather than fighting and he is eventually forced to sell his commission to pay his debts, having failed to heed D'Arcy's warning: '[s]hun the vices – beware the dissipation – that too generally inhabit a camp' (vol. II. 58). His return to England is marked above all by his fear of poverty, which he views as a far greater trial than his experience of war. This figuration of the licentious aristocratic officer is repeated in *The Talisman: Or, Singular Adventures of an Old Officer; With its Consequences* (1804), which recounts the appalling effects of gambling upon the eponymous officer after his service in Britain's campaigns in Portugal during the Seven Years War. Unable to save his friend from suicide owing to gambling debts, the officer fathers a child out of wedlock and fails to comprehend that the beautiful Lady Caroline T has had acted as his anonymous benefactor and is deeply in love with him.[72] If the hero of the *Half-Pay Officer* is eventually reunited

---

[71] *The Half-Pay Officer; or, Memoirs of Charles Chanceley: A Novel* (London: Printed for the author, by T. Bensley, and Sold by G.G.J. and J. Robinson, Paternoster Row, 1788).

[72] *The Talisman: Or, Singular Adventures of an Old Officer; With its Consequences. Written by Himself* (London: Printed for R. Dutton, No. 45 Gracechurch St; J. Cawthorn, Catherine St.; Chapple, Pall-Mall; and T. Hurst, Paternoster Row; By John Abraham, Clement's Lane, 1804).

with his father because of the softening effects of religion, the *Talisman* concludes with the officer returning to England in lonely despair after realising the full weight of his crimes. Although both novels are keen to proclaim the patriotic valour of the British officer, they nonetheless view military service as deeply linked to forms of vice, and decline to offer anything more than perfunctory and abstract accounts of scenes of war. As the narrator of *The Half-Pay Officer* states, '[i]t is not my intention to write the history of a war' (vol. II. 23).

Although Thornton resembles these licentious aristocratic officers from earlier novels, *Cyril Thornton* also breaks with this earlier confessional tradition because it disentangles war from aristocratic vice in ways that enable his experiences of active military service to serve as a path for his redemption. The novel admittedly reminds us that aristocratic life itself could be decidedly violent. Thornton is shot twice before he even gets to serve in war – first while he is stationed in Canada during a duel when he believes his honour has been impeached by his garrison commander, and secondly in England in more ignominious and remorseful circumstances, when he is shot by an anonymous assailant, presumably Pierce, during his final meeting with Mary. But he is relentlessly self-mocking in these incidents. After being shot in the duel he suffers a tedious recovery, and mocks his own pretension to noble feelings:

> When I remembered the severity of the ordeal through which I had passed, I felt a sensation of pride and self-respect, to which I bad before been unaccustomed.... In my own eyes, I seemed a perfect Bayard, a chevalier *sans peur et sans reproche*. These, at least; were harmless fantasies, and they were happy ones. Why should they be sneered at by the philosopher, or censured by the moralist? (vol. II. 110)

The second time he is shot, his embarrassment compels him to keep the incident secret from his family, leaving him remorseful of his dishonourable lies and another prolonged recovery. His experiences recall his wounding in battle that similarly undercuts any sense of war's romance. The novel treats the concept of honour in a muted, even ironic manner, foregrounding instead the physicality and pain of his wounding. In its review of the novel, *Blackwood's* emphasised its surprise that Thornton was an eminently ordinary individual: there was nothing at all heroic or even particularly skilful in his account of soldiering; he never even killed a Frenchman.[73]

---

[73] *Blackwood's Edinburgh Magazine* 22, no. 128 (1827): 84.

While following a similar narrative trajectory, *Cyril Thornton* nonetheless avoids the grim morality of these earlier novels by establishing Thornton's active military service as a crucial element in his redemption from a seducer and killer to a figure associated with suffering and death. This redemptive element revolves around the novel's references to Cain, which draw an analogy between war and the Gothic.[74] Representative of the solitary wanderer, there are striking resonances between the figure of Cain and a wider Romantic culture of war that was acutely conscious of the dislocations and border crossings engendered by years of conflict – a world of revenants, wanderers and refugees.[75] So too, Cain was central to the Gothic sensibility, appearing as an elementary figure in the literature surrounding the French Revolution and its fears of social dislocation.[76] With the novel set in Spain and Portugal, traditional sites of the Gothic, Thornton's experience of war takes him ever deeper into a realm shrouded by death. Following the retreating French army into Spain, Thornton relates how 'The spectacle of mortality which the roads exhibited, seemed to deepen as we advanced' (vol. III. 123). When the British in turn are forced to retreat, he observes that '[t]he carcases which lay along the road had, since we formerly passed, become putrid, and we breathed an atmosphere, tainted, and redolent of corruption' (vol. III. 218). At one point while marching with the army he wakes to discover he had been sleeping upon a pile of corpses, victims of the ruthless French (vol. III. 114). He is led to conclude that death had become so 'common an occurrence' it was met by himself and his fellow officers with a degree of indifference (vol. III. 87).

Reflecting on the similar prominence of death in Frederick Marryat's naval novels, themselves modelled on the military novel that Hamilton pioneered, Patrick Brantlinger claims that Marryat appears so enamoured with death that his heroes engage in a form of 'altruistic suicide', Brantlinger even likening Marryat's novels to the Gothic and the writing of Marquis de Sade.[77] *Cyril Thornton* is likewise not only shrouded in a

---

[74] On the importance of the Gothic in the development of war literature, see Steffen Hantke and Agnieszka Soltysik Monnet, eds, *War Gothic in Literature and Culture* (New York: Routledge, 2016).

[75] Jeffrey N. Cox, *Romanticism in the Shadow of War: Literary Culture in the Napoleonic Wars Years* (Cambridge: Cambridge University Press, 2014); Simon Parkes, *Home from the Wars: The Romantic Revenant-Veteran of the 1790s* (PhD diss., University of Warwick, 2009); Kevis Goodman, 'Romantic Poetry and the Science of Nostalgia', in *The Cambridge Companion to British Romantic Poetry*, ed. James Chandler and Maureen N. McLane (Cambridge: Cambridge University Press, 2008), 195–216.

[76] Tyler R. Tichelaar, *The Gothic Wanderer: From Transgression to Redemption: Gothic Literature from 1794–Present* (London: Modern History Press, 2012), 46.

[77] Brantlinger, *Rule of Darkness,* 54.

Gothic atmosphere of death, but the novel also equally extends a concern
with death into something like an altruistic suicide. Thornton follows the
basic imperative of biopolitics at the conclusion of the novel, deciding that
he must either marry or return to the battlefield, either make life or else let
himself die. Yet so too, the novel positions death as being, in its own way,
as vital and as life-giving as marriage:

> I could not loiter up and down the world, sick, spiritless, forlorn, seek-
> ing health, yet carrying disease, a wandering stranger in a strange land, to
> become at last the tenant of a foreign grave. Better than this, I thought it
> were to die at home, to mingle my ashes with those of my fathers, to sleep
> in death with those whom I loved in life, to be incorporated with kindred
> earth. But best of all it was, to die as a soldier. If death will not be cheated
> of his victim, rather let me fall in the field, than faulter out my feeble spirit
> in the slow languishing of a sickbed. Who so brave as he for whom life
> retains no charm? Where was the danger from which I would now shrink?
> What peril was there, which my heart would now flutter to encounter? To
> such a termination of my life, I found pleasure in looking forward. My soul
> revolted from the idea of dying in a corner; like Ajax, I would at least perish
> in the light of day. (vol. III. 274–75)

To some extent contradicting himself, where he had earlier elevated the
heroism of the sickbed above that of the battle, falling in battle now
appears to Thornton as more noble than dying at home in bed. The novel
here embodies its traumatic oscillation between surviving and encounter-
ing death, as though it cannot decide where the boundaries between life
and death actually lie, a traumatic oscillation reflected in Hamilton's inde-
cision as to whether he should end the novel with Thornton's marriage
or, in a more 'striking conclusion', his death at the Siege of St Sebastian.[78]
But in this way, the novel also appears sited at a threshold of indistinction
or undecidability between the biological and the political, as the politics
of military conflict are endlessly crossed by concerns with biological life.[79]
Paralleling the battlefield and the sick-bed, the novel, in effect, treats the
soldier's body pharmacologically, exposing it equally to death and life-
giving care in a manner that Arne De Boever sees as lying at the heart of
the novel's biopolitical treatment of life.[80]

But what ultimately marks Thornton's desire for death in war is that
it represents a way of bringing death into the 'light of day', associating

---

[78] Letter from Thomas Hamilton to William Blackwood, 17 November 1826. National Library of
Scotland, MS 4017, fol. 127.
[79] On the biopolitics of military campaigns, see Agamben, *Homo Sacer*, 104.
[80] De Boever, *Narrative Care*, 47.

death, in other words, with health, vigour and freedom. While scenes of war can recall the worst horrors of the Gothic, nonetheless there are also Gothic elements in Thornton's interactions with the British aristocracy at home in England, whether the killing of his brother, banishment by his father or his forlorn liaisons with Lady Melicent. War at one level is also a freedom from Britain's own Gothic ancestry; at war he experiences a peripatetic freedom that entirely contrasts with his status as an outcast or Cain-like revenant from the world of aristocrats. This capacity to see war as a site of freedom is furthered by associating the Gothic elements of war with the 'gratuitous barbarity of the invaders' (vol. III. 120), in which the French, and even the Spanish, appear to wage war with a cruel indifference. The French are, however, far from being depicted simply as Britain's traditional enemy, Thornton even subtly mocking his uncle's servant, Girzy, when she makes such a suggestion (vol. III. 308–09). The difference between Britain and France, rather, appears by contrasting humanity with depravity, the novel thus depicting war in ways that resembles Scott's 'liberal' reading of civil war, in which Scott portrayed war not in terms of competing factions but as a war between the orders of modernity and a traditional barbarity.[81] *Cyril Thornton* re-establishes such a structure within the Napoleonic Wars, to locate Thornton's military service as an opposition to the wanton and barbaric killing, in which Thornton can redeem violence through risking wounding and death.

This association of war with health and restoration is heightened by what Henry Crabb Robinson saw as the Wordsworthianism in the novel. Robinson does not elucidate this point in detail; the association he finds with Wordsworth might simply be observed in the way the novel evinces an appreciation for literature and nature. Thornton even undergoes an aesthetic education of sorts during his walks in Scotland and the Lake District, where he learns to cherish the sublimity of nature and the Wordsworthian consolations of reading, a 'love of literature which has never died within me, and in which I have found a relief and a resource, under circumstances when its place could not have been otherwise supplied' (vol. I. 216). But Thornton does not simply come to see nature as a 'medicament' for life's 'wounds' (vol. I. 237); he also discovers restorative qualities in war and its physical pain. Here, the novel builds on a key element of the military memoir as it was developed by Moyle Sherer and Georg Gleig – the rendering of the soldier into a man of feeling and a tourist of the

---

[81] Duncan, *Modern Romance and Transformations of the Novel*, 52.

military picturesque.[82] As had Gleig, Thornton encounters an aesthetic in
war itself, remarking at one point on his campaigns that 'no sight, I think,
can be more picturesque, than the encampment of a large army by night'
(Vol. III. 127). Developing this beyond a military picturesque to a more
fully realised idea of a Wordsworthian poetics of war's capacity to restore
health, the novel suggests that the confrontation with death and wounding
can lift Thornton altogether out of feelings of forlorn suffering and disease,
wounding seemingly serving as a key to Thornton's final achievement of
manhood as it prompts his rejection of Lady Melicent and marriage to
Laura. As he elsewhere comments of his exposure to death:

> A life of danger and activity is unfavourable to the indulgence of grief. New
> objects and difficulties continually excite our attention, and call for exer-
> tion, and produce at least the fortunate effect, of diverting the mind from
> dwelling too long and unceasingly on hidden sorrows. A soldier cannot
> long abstract his thoughts from the world in which he moves. In him there
> are no slumbering energies, for his duty requires them all, to be in constant
> action. (vol. III. 150)

Exposure to death, danger and suffering are able to excite and vitalise
Thornton's body and mind, placing the individual in a healthy state of
'constant action', war epitomising the 'exertion' that Austen had similarly
viewed as a key spiritual and moral exercise.[83] Like Wordsworth, Thornton
can approach his unbidden memories through a matured love of nature,
the structure of the novel moving him from a 'boyish enthusiasm' surrounding war's glory to a chastened and matured understanding of death
(vol. III. 102).

Most notably, however, this association with death and wounding is
also a means of social connection for Thornton. As he explains when he
meets with his fellow wounded officers at the Estrela Convent in Lisbon,
while he convalesces from his wounds before returning to England:

> It is at a meeting of this sort that one obtains a compendious view of the
> more immediate and direct evils of war. There were men in the very pride
> of youth, whom nature had endowed with constitutions of iron, whose
> bodies were maimed and mangled—whose very looks told of sufferings,
> on which their lips were silent. I could not gaze on them, without a feeling
> of brotherhood and interest. We belonged to the same profession, we had
> been animated by the same hopes, we had fallen martyrs to the same cause.
> How many of the ties which contribute to bind societies together, are less

---

[82] Ramsey, *The Military Memoir and Romantic Literary Culture*, 137–63.
[83] Laura Mooneyham White, *Jane Austen's Anglicanism* (Farnham: Ashgate, 2011), 60.

strong than these! And there was, I thought, a sort of *esprit de corps* among us; the Shibboleth of suffering was common to us all, and though strangers to each other, we naturally spoke in the language of friendship and regard. (vol. III. 189)

Such reflections resemble other works of British State Romanticism, in so far as it envisions bonds of friendship and even brotherhood between strangers as a function of their institutional identity in the military. But *Cyril Thornton* adds to this an idea of the vital importance of wounding and suffering in forging these connections that echoes Scarry's concerns with the ideological work of bodily pain in war, its displacement from the interior to the communal. The novel redefines what is meant by military honour, as it imagines the 'evils of war', war's physical sufferings, as founding a 'language of friendship and regard'. As military honour is associated with physical wounding in war, so the novel redeems the military officer, repositioning him from the aristocratic killer and seducer and into a figure not only of reformed sexuality, but also equally of a renewed vision of national service and collective unity.

The Aesthetic Romance of the Wounded Body

For Georg Lukács it was far from coincidental that the historical novel appeared in the wake of the French Revolutionary and Napoleonic Wars.[84] The wars had transformed Europe through mass propaganda and military mobilisation so that for the first time ordinary individuals began to see themselves as playing a role in the history of the nation. The historical novel did not retell great events but instead offered what Lukács regards as the 'poetic awakening of the people who figured in those events', thereby inverting the belief that history must be understood in relation to the actions of great men.[85] Such figures, or 'world-historical individuals' in Georg Wilhelm Friedrich Hegel's terms, are not absent from the historical novel, but they exist in tension with the idea that the further a hero is from leadership, the more the age itself will be reflected in that individual, embodied in his or her very gestures, emotions and speech.[86] The historical novel focuses on 'managing individuals', ordinary heroes who can be read as a product of the age, a lens through

---

[84] Georg Lukács, *The Historical Novel*, trans. Hannah and Stanley Mitchell (Boston: Beacon Press, 1963), 23–26.
[85] Lukács, *The Historical Novel*, 42.
[86] Lukács, The Historical Novel, 39.

which to understand the collective directions of history. Expanding further such an approach to literature and history, Rancière has even suggested that a modern idea of literature was born from a revolution in the science of history, in which literature emerged in an age of democratic violence as a historical counter-discourse to the strategic reflections of war's great leaders.[87] What marks modern literature in the Romantic era is that it overturned neo-classical genres and rules of order that had established a set of correspondences between bodies and words. The unravelling of this order within a new history of the masses was linked to the capacity for anybody to now become the subject of any kind of writing, allowing ordinary individuals to appear as central characters in the new form of literature defined by the novel.

The memoirs written by subaltern officers in the wake of the French Revolutionary and Napoleonic Wars clearly function in these terms.[88] Such obscure lives had little place within biographical writing, which, as one biographer noted, necessarily excluded those who merely performed the duties of the 'subaltern officers of regiments'.[89] But as Rancière proposes, however, modern literature displaces the biographical focus on the exemplary actions of great men with a new kind of exemplarity: the individual's exemplarity of ordinary historical processes. New forms of biography unite micro- and macro-levels of social existence that render the individual life representative of broader collectives and historical experiences. This new direction established for biographical forms of writing also, therefore, marked a shift from a life of political action to what Aristotle had seen as life lived simply in accord with biological production and reproduction – the obscure life that speaks of the world it embodies, producing what

[87] Jacques Rancière, *The Politics of Literature*, trans. Julie Rose (Cambridge: Polity Press, 2011), 75 and 174–75. Although Rancière follows a traditional view that a modern idea of literature was initially theorised by the German Romantics, he nonetheless regards this theorisation as itself reflecting an earlier and far broader set of developments in forms of writing, Jacques Rancière, *Aesthetics and its Discontents*, trans. Steven Corcoran (Cambridge: Polity Press, 2009), 10.

[88] The term biography is being used here, and later, in the broadest sense of the term, as defined by the *Oxford English Dictionary* as '[a] written account of the life of an individual', and hence referring to all types of life writing, including memoir, autobiography, semi-fictionalised autobiographical novels, and biography.

[89] John Aikin and William Enfield, *General Biography; or, Lives, Critical and Historical, of the Most Eminent Persons of All Ages, Countries, Conditions and Professions, Chiefly Composed by J. Aikin and W. Enfield* (London: Printed for G. G. and J. Robinson, Pater-Noster-Row; G. Kearsley, Fleet-Street; R. H. Evans (Successor to Mr. Edwards), Pall-Mall; and J. Wright, Opposite Bond-Street, Piccadilly. Also at Edinburgh for Bell and Bradfute. 1799), 2; On how modern forms of autobiography emerge out of such breaks with decorum, see James Treadwell, *Autobiographical Writing and British Literature, 1783–1834* (Oxford: Oxford University Press, 2005).

Thomas Carlyle saw as 'the true poetry' of life itself.[90] Unrelated to the great political events and decisions of history, junior officers' experiences simply revealed elements of the ordinary administration and management of life. *Cyril Thornton* was a key work in the formation of this new school of writing or 'true poetry' that formed around junior officers' eyewitness accounts and their experience of the physical hardships of a military campaign. The great commanders of history appear in *Cyril Thornton* as world-historical individuals, but they too are primarily judged in relation to their physicality, vigour and energy rather than their actions, rhetoric and command, whether expressed through Thornton's disdain for Dundas' languor or enthusiasm for Wellington's animated energy. Thornton sees the wars as a time when physicality was paramount, when 'every soldier who had fought in Spain was considered a hero, and a subaltern with a wooden leg attracted as much interest and attention, as Lord Wellington himself' (vol. II. 307).

Cyril Thornton may have allowed the subaltern to speak, yet it only does so by offering the subaltern a fundamentally embodied position from which to speak. Scott's historical novels were crucial to the subsequent formation of the military novel because they enabled the individual to be read as a homology for the nation, thereby allowing the ordinary soldier to be read as other than merely irrelevant or indecorous in speaking of his own exploits at war.[91] *Cyril Thornton* manages this relationship to the nation, however, by casting this homology in strikingly biological terms. Rancière observes that if the break with neo-classicism fundamentally established a rupture with an existing order by which bodies and words were anchored, there is nonetheless a countervailing tendency in modern literary aesthetics that attempted to restore the relationship that emerged from this sense of equality. The nineteenth century was, he claims,

> haunted by the imminent danger that an indifferent equality would come to reign and by the idea that it was necessary to oppose it with a new meaning of the communal body. Literature was a privileged site where this became visible. It was at one and the same time a way of exhibiting the reign of indifferent language and, conversely, a way of remaking bodies with words and even a way of leading words toward their cancellation in material states.[92]

[90] Rancière, *The Politics of Literature*, 176.
[91] See Ramsey, *The Military Memoir and Romantic Literary Culture*, 57–62.
[92] Jacques Rancière, *The Politics of Aesthetics*, trans. and intro. Gabriel Rockhill (London: Continuum, 2009), 57–58.

In his approach to literary analysis, Rancière has eschewed theories of literature that either take a naively empirical approach or that regard words as free-floating signifiers. He advances, instead, a conception of literature as quasi-corporeal or as holding a 'suspensive existence' in which words and bodies are perpetually held in tension. He proposes that literature oscillates between disincorporation and incorporation – literature liberates anyone as a speaking subject yet it also perpetually re-anchors expression back onto bodies and collectivities.[93] Although Rancière does not directly develop his thoughts in relation to biopolitics, his reading of aesthetics and indisciplinarity draws heavily on Foucault's similar concerns with how disciplinary formations establish a specific ethos around a body.[94] Romanticism's own concerns with common life and experience can even be understood, he proposes in a striking if unremarked echo of Agamben, as the appearance of 'bare life' into the field of literature.[95] Stories of the ordinary lives of individuals equally tie those individuals back into historical, social and ultimately biological processes.

Rancière's thought also overlaps with Christoph Menke's concerns with the tensions between the aesthetic and the biological, which Menke, similarly to Rancière, reads in relation to Foucault's thought on the emergent disciplinary exercises surrounding the natural body.[96] While Menke is concerned with how aesthetics can reject the teleological determinism of biology and so work as an expression of freedom, he nonetheless suggests that modernity has always been accompanied by a bio-aesthetics that attempts to resolve these tensions in favour of biology by framing

[93] Rancière, *The Politics of Aesthetics*, 56–57; Jacques Rancière, *Mute Speech*, trans. James Swenson (New York: Columbia University Press, 2011), 62–65; Jacques Rancière, *The Flesh of Words: The Politics of Writing*, trans. Charlotte Mandell (Stanford: Stanford University Press, 2004), 71–93.

[94] Jacques Rancière, 'The Aesthetic Dimension: Aesthetics, Politics, Knowledge', *Critical Inquiry* 36, no. 1 (Autumn 2009): 1–19. See also Jacques Rancière, *Disagreement and Philosophy*, trans. Julie Rose (Minneapolis: University of Minnesota Press, 1999), 27–29.

[95] Jacques Rancière, 'The Reality Effect and the Politics of Fiction', Public Lecture at ICI Berlin, www.ici-berlin.org/videos/jacques-ranciere/part/2/, accessed 29 June 2018. Rancière's understanding of literature also resembles Agamben's passing remarks on literature as an apparatus that shapes 'the gestures, behaviors, opinions, or discourses of living beings': Giorgio Agamben, *What is an Apparatus? and Other Essays*, trans. David Kishik and Stefan Pedatella (Stanford: Stanford University Press, 2009), 14. On Rancière's thought in relation to biopolitics, see Arne De Boever, 'The Politics of Realism in Rancière and Houellebecq', in *Rancière and Literature*, ed. Grace Hellyer and Julian Murphet (Edinburgh: Edinburgh University Press, 2016), 226–48, 230.

[96] For a fuller account of Foucault's account of discipline and the natural body, see Chapter 3. See also Michel Foucault, *Discipline and Punish: The Birth of the Prison*, trans. Alan Sheridan (New York: Vintage, 1991), 155.

aesthetics as a teleology of development.[97] Echoing more general concerns with aesthetics as the ideological formation of modern subjectivity, Menke has posited the acquisition of aesthetic taste as crucial to the formation of the disciplinary self.[98] Taste implies freedom and self-formation but simultaneously aligns subjective experience with objective standards. Taste enables an individual to be self-governing even as it aligns that individual with educational norms and requirements. So too, by acclimatising an individual to the beautiful, the acquisition of taste can assure an individual of his or her natural or organic place in the world. Given that the disciplining of the natural body requires the operation of a teleology, so it finds its expression ultimately in the bio-aesthetics of the *Bildung* that transforms the disciplinary education of the subject into a naturalised, effortless and complete identity.[99]

Admittedly, in its approach to the *Bildung*, *Cyril Thornton* deals with subjects that are far from the realm of taste as he describes piles of rotting corpses and the coagulated blood coughed from his lungs. But the novel also reframes war in ways that render it accessible for a nascent middle-class sensibility by translating war into a form of tasteful, aesthetic romance. *Cyril Thornton* recasts physical, biological suffering through a Wordsworthian lens to imagine war as a realm of natural beauty, community and healing maturity that can render wounding and the threat of death into something life giving and vital. Thornton achieves redemption from his licentious past by embracing his suffering, the novel transforming his experiences of war's discipline and brutality into a version of an aesthetic education. With his experience of war therefore integral to Thornton's path to *Bildung*, the novel also breaks with traditional aristocratic forms of knowledge surrounding warfare by implicitly asserting that war is only knowable through processes of maturity and growth. The novel rejects the notion that an aristocrat such as Lord Amersham might be 'bred for war' simply because of his noble 'blood'. War appears as something that must not only be learned through experience, but also

[97] Christoph Menke, 'Aesthetic Nature: Against Biology', *The Yearbook of Comparative Literature* 58 (2012): 193–95.

[98] Christoph Menke, 'A Different Taste: Neither Autonomy nor Mass Consumption', in *Cultural Transformations of the Public Sphere: Contemporary and Historical Perspectives*, ed. Bernd Fischer and May Mergenthaler (Oxford: Peter Lang, 2015), 183–202, 189.

[99] Denise Gigante observes that the concept of *Bildung* has its roots in the life sciences; see Denise Gigante, *Life: Organic Form and Romanticism* (New Haven: Yale University Press, 2009), 46.

acquired through a growth that is inherently physical. *Cyril Thornton* enables the subaltern to speak of war, but the novel also produces ways of seeing and knowing war that only circulate through embodied circuits of knowledge.

More widely, scholars have begun to challenge the view that the First World War was critical to the emergence of a modern form of war literature by tracing the origins of modern war literature back to the experiences of mass warfare during the Romantic era and the concomitant development at this time of what Kate McLoughlin has dubbed a veteran poetics.[100] This earlier period not only witnessed an outpouring of writing by soldiers on their personal experience of war, but also saw the rise of materialist aesthetics of sympathy and sublimity that underpinned this war writing. Modern war literature is characterised, above all, by its efforts to bear witness to an encounter with the vast and overwhelming traumas of war. If traumatic experiences are, however, too shocking to readily assimilate to consciousness, they nonetheless circulate in war writing as compulsive repetitions and belated, disruptive memories that associate knowledge of war with bodily pain and suffering. Yuval Noah Harari terms this 'flesh-witnessing' – the process by which war takes shape as a *Bildung* framed around the revelatory experience of war's essential physicality.[101] Following Rancière and Menke's understanding of how a materialist aesthetic operates, however, flesh-witnessing could be regarded as implicit to the very idea of modern literature in the aesthetic regime – it is in literature that a mute speech arises, that bodies begin to achieve expression, that words might be cancelled out in material states to become linked to an idea of flesh or a biologisation of identity. In his definition of war literature, Fussell had earlier touched on such insights by suggesting that the war novel is not so much concerned with revealing a physical reality behind war's words as it seeks to reconstruct a new kind of mythic fiction or romance out of bodily experience. War novels, he argues, reorient the traditional quest romance of war, with its exaltation of the hero, into a new kind of 'literary "romance"' of witnessing, physical transformation and survival:

[100] Kate McLoughlin, *Veteran Poetics: British Literature in the Age of Mass Warfare, 1790–2015* (Cambridge: Cambridge University Press, 2018).
[101] Yuval N. Harari, *The Ultimate Experience: Battlefield Revelations and the Making of Modern War Culture, 1450–2000* (Basingstoke: Palgrave Macmillan, 2008), 7.

every total experience of the war is 'romantic' in the strict sense of the term. Every successful memoir of that experience shares something with traditional literary 'romance', and indeed, regardless of its truth or accuracy of documentary fact, in its plot could be said to lean towards that generic category.[102]

In equating the battlefield with the bedroom and so limiting the revelatory significance of bodily pain, *Cyril Thornton* does not decisively set war apart from civilian life, and in this sense might not be viewed as a fully formed version of subsequent war literature and its flesh-witnessing.[103] But by drawing on the romance of the historical novel, *Cyril Thornton* can be regarded as the first novel to attempt such a self-conscious rewriting of romantic tales of war into the literary romance of survival, attuned to a total war of unprecedented Gothic violence, embedded in modern institutions and experienced through the *Bildung* of the 'living flesh-and-blood man and gentleman'.[104]

What can be added, however, is that this new romance of survival equally delimits and controls what can be said and known of war.[105] As much as *Cyril Thornton* liberates the voice of the subaltern officer to speak of his experience of suffering, relating his story as a counter-discourse to neo-classical traditions of the great men of action, it also reorients this experience of war through what Menke has termed a bio-aesthetics, or, to adapt Fussell, a bio-romance, that serves as a necessary complement to the biopower of war and its military literature. The aesthetic is necessary for the subject to embrace its normative identity as freedom and so naturalise discipline as self-governance. The military disciplinary writing that was so essential for the formation of the junior officer can, in this sense, be understood as culminating in the military novel that Hamilton pioneered. Hamilton pointedly portrays Thornton falling asleep reading his copy of 'Dundas on the Eighteen Manoeuvres', modelled as it was on Frederick the Great's mechanical drill routines, but this rejection of the drill manual opens the way for Hamilton to nonetheless recreate, with *Cyril Thornton*, a new kind of manual for the self-governing soldier. To

---

[102] Fussell, *The Great War and Modern Memory*, 140–42.
[103] The first researcher to assess the genre of the military novel treated it in such terms as a failure to articulate the insights found in novels of the First World War; Allen, *The British Military Novel*, 348–50.
[104] *Blackwood's Edinburgh Magazine* 22, no. 128 (1827): 83.
[105] On the relationship between a Romantic era materialist aesthetics and biopolitics, see Simon Strick, *American Dolorologies: Pain, Sentimentalism, Biopolitics* (Albany: State University of New York Press, 2014).

adapt De Boever's Agambenian reading of the general form of the novel, the military novel could be imagined as a version of a military 'camp' that completely exposes the soldier's life to death by collapsing together life and law, force and freedom.[106] *Cyril Thornton* opens an alternative perspective on modern war novels by suggesting an origin in the broader field of military literature and a more expansive idea altogether of a veteran poetics. The school of writing to which the novel contributed, with its embodied stories of war experience would go on to emerge as a central element in subsequent military periodicals of the 1830s and in the development of the vast corpus of militarised Victorian adventure that was to become essential reading across the British empire in the nineteenth century.[107] However much they participated in a literary counter-discourse to military strategy, military novels also represent the culmination of the soldier as a form of bare or politicised life necessary for an emergent Napoleonic strategy built out of Lloyd's philosophy of war and its exercise of force over living beings.[108]

Despite how directly a lineage formed between the military novel and subsequent traditions of the war novel, Hamilton's bio-romance nonetheless clearly played a foundational role in the subsequent formation of militarised Victorian adventure novels. Although this militarisation of adventure in the nineteenth century has traditionally been linked to Scott, this connection downplays the anti-military emphasis of Scott's novels and ignores the ways in which Hamilton adapted Scott or even inherited the mantle of father of romance from Scott. In what has become a dominant reading, Duncan argues that Scott's historical novel can be viewed in relation to post-Waterloo liberalism, as the hero leaves off the romance of historical conflict to return to a unified, commercial, modern Britain, so that, as Duncan suggests, 'the historical novel narrates – and so performs – a dialectical closure of modernity, in which historical conflict yields to

---

[106] Hamilton had earlier used the phrase 'Dundas on the Eighteen Manoeuvres' in a highly critical review of Edward Quillinan's 'Dunluce Castle', in *Blackwood's* in 1819. Mocking Quillinan's poetry as the product of a heavy dragoon, when a soldier's highest literary achievement was at best 'a devlish good letter', Hamilton explained that soldiers only read 'Moore's poems, Tom Jones, and Dundas on the Eighteen Manoeuvres'. That Thornton falls asleep attempting to read Dundas, therefore, also subtly reinforces Hamilton's revision of the soldier in *Cyril Thornton* as a figure associated with literature, reading and taste, *Blackwood's Edinburgh Magazine* 4, no. 23 (1819): 575.

[107] For a brief overview of these subsequent developments, see Ramsey, *The Military Memoir and Romantic Literary Culture*, 68–77.

[108] On the inverse relation between military strategy and war novels, see Yuval Noah Harari, 'Armchairs, Coffee, and Authority: Eye-Witnesses and Flesh-Witnesses Speak about War, 1100–2000', *The Journal of Military History* 74, no. 1 (January 2010): 53–78, 55–57.

civil society'.[109] For Scott, therefore, it is the nation's past that is defined by historical conflict, bound by stories of civil war that pit Britain's races against one another, whether Scots and English or Normans and Saxons, while his novels seek to preserve some memory of those wars through romance, the construction of a symbolic form that translates the remnants of these ancestral, warlike roots into private aesthetics and culture.[110] Here, Duncan extends Frederic Jameson's earlier arguments that nineteenth-century romance reacted against the reification of realism in capitalism through a nostalgia for older forms of social existence and a romanticisation of war.[111] But the historical novel is nonetheless defined by the way it resolves and closes off an historical era of wars, just as the nation's wars against its Catholic, French Other, for Linda Colley, ends with consolidation of a fully formed British national identity at the conclusion of the Napoleonic Wars.[112] The wars may have given rise to the historical novel as the poetic awakening of the people, but the people awakened into a history that, in the modern era, no longer progressed through war. Duncan adds that we need to be concerned with what comes after this closure that coincides with the appearance of the historical novel.

In his reflections on the forms of historicist thought circulating through Scott's new approach to history, Foucault contends that this closure of historical war between the races also inaugurates an embryonic concept of state racism that does not in any way end war. Rather, war shifts from its earlier role of defining the nation against other races, to become lodged in a series of biological, social and national conflicts that circulate within and around the population.[113] War no longer constitutes history; in other words, it becomes biopolitical, defending civil society and moving from a central to a peripheral role in the formation of national identity as war is 'reduced, restricted, colonized, settled, scattered, civilized if you like, and up to a point pacified'.[114] On the one hand, therefore, the nineteenth century saw war move inside the nation, as the military model of discipline, civil pacification and the medicalisation of abnormality. On the

---

[109] Ian Duncan, 'Authenticity Effects: The Work of Fiction in Romantic Scotland', *South Atlantic Quarterly* 102, no. 1 (2003): 93–116, 98.

[110] Duncan, *Modern Romance and the Transformation of the Novel*, 10–11.

[111] Fredric Jameson, *Political Unconscious: Narrative as a Socially Symbolic Act* (London: Routledge, 1983), 91 and 136.

[112] Linda Colley, *Britons: Forging the Nation, 1707–1837* (New Haven: Yale University Press, 1992).

[113] Foucault, *Society Must be Defended*, 216.

[114] Foucault, *Society Must be Defended*, 215.

other hand, war continued through the scattered, reduced and colonising conflicts fought at the frontiers of nineteenth-century imperial expansion. Modern war would consequently come to be intimately bound with a state racism that circulates through the state's new-found imperative to identify caesura's within the realm of life that determine which lives are to be fostered and which lives denied, which thus constantly maps and remaps the borders of social life.[115] War is no longer the ancestral clash of races that can constitute historical formations and political frames, but is simply the constant policing and protection of life at the borders of civilisation and nationhood – both to protect life from threats but equally to ensure the strengthening and vitalisation of life through its exposure to suffering. Foucault's thought draws near to Seltzer's concerns with wound culture when he proposes that what was different and unique about the biopolitical forms of war that appeared in the nineteenth century was the belief that the more the members of a nation are faced with death, the stronger and more vital the nation becomes.[116] What comes after the historical novel, therefore, is also a new kind of national identity. If national identity is no longer defined though war against a racial Other, it is instead aligned with the administration of life, with the relationship that forms between the nation and the institutions of the state that care for the population through making live and letting die.[117]

It is within this biopolitical framing of war that it is possible to understand *Cyril Thornton* as inaugurating a militarised bio-romance for Victorian Britain. The importance of war is central to Franco Moretti's 'distant reading' of Victorian adventure, in which he not only shows that adventure was central to the production of novels in the era, but also that adventure novels are driven by their reverence for war. Yet even though Moretti suggests that war has a stronger hold on the Victorian imagination than merely nostalgic longing, war serving as a controlling presence of aristocratic values for a bourgeois who needs a 'master', he nonetheless still reads war historically and at odds with an emergent middle class.[118] However, rather than portray war in the terms of historical romance, as either the masking operation of nostalgia and ideological illusion or the preservation of history and an archaic aristocratic honour, *Cyril Thornton* can be seen as working with a new conception of war as the biopolitical

---

[115] Foucault, *Society Must be Defended*, 255.
[116] Foucault, *Society Must Be Defended*, 256–58.
[117] Foucault, *Society Must be Defended*, 223.
[118] Franco Moretti, *Distant Reading* (London: Verso, 2013), 177–78.

defence of society. Hamilton still follows the structure of romance he inherits from Scott to recover military honour as aesthetics that can invigorate the nation, but *Cyril Thornton* does not bring military honour back home to Britain as an imaginative recovery of origins and its ancestral lineage, customs, traditions and heritage, figured in ancient weapons and costume. War in *Cyril Thornton* is not portrayed as a historical war of races in which the strength of the nation is defined by domination and conflict, figured as 'its physical vigour, its military aptitudes, or, so to speak, its barbarian intensity'.[119] Pointedly dismissing aristocrats as ignorant of war and its embodied affects, the novel instead aligns war with the development, growth and administration of life. It moves away from a *Bildung* dependent upon the rejection of war's romance to establish a *Bildung* in which growth is achieved through war.

Forging, therefore, a new romance of survival, *Cyril Thornton* brings Thornton's disfigured and traumatised body, his lived experience of war, back into the heart of Britain as an idealisation or naturalisation of disciplinary power. Military honour is transmuted in the novel not simply into a commemorative aesthetics, but into a bio-aesthetics of fleshly scars and amputations. On the one hand, therefore, the return of the soldier to his ancestral home in Britain suggests less a romantic nostalgia than a traumatic haunting that possesses the modern nation and refuses to fully settle war into a distant past. But on the other hand, and equally, the military novel replaces an earlier historical romance based on a nostalgia for ancestral heritage with a militarised bio-romance grounded in the vitalisation of the subject through the encounter with death. The novel reveals the power of wounding to vitalise life, a wounding that suggests the subject's complete inculcation by discipline. The military novel emerges as a distinct form out of the historical novel because it reprises military honour from historical anachronism and into the military's concerns with securing, administering, and managing life; into a concern, in other words, with the military institutional capacities of the nation to govern and administer its living vitality. A militarised Victorian adventure is not simply a nostalgic reflection on war, but a concern with how the living body secures the violent exteriors of capitalist modernity and maps the borders of a new kind of racialised national identity.

---

[119] Foucault, *Society Must be Defended*, 223.

Afterword
Trauma, Security and Romantic Counter-Strategies

This book has argued for a new understanding of modern war writing. Taking an indisciplinary approach concerned with how disciplines acquire authority, it examines how this writing contributed to the formation of a proto-disciplinary field of war knowledge during the Romantic era. Focussed above all on the ways in which this writing sought to marshal the vital powers of the nation and its soldiers, the central argument of this study is that modern war writing established a fundamentally biopolitical perspective on war. This writing materialised as a bio-aesthetics that overlapped with Romantic organic thought to establish something approaching a human science of war concerned with the living forces that constitute military power. Modern war writing took charge of the formation of soldier lives and subjectivity to expand and intensify military power in tandem with the expansion of capitalist power over the worker. This is a view of war writing that, moreover, offers an alternative way of conceptualising the traumatic history of war, because it also highlights the ways in which biopolitical writing on war shapes the subjective experience of trauma. Proposing, therefore, that our understanding of trauma is in danger of remaining entangled with the security apparatus of biopower, this afterword briefly sketches a quite different approach to writing and the violence of history. It does so by considering how war writing could be read in relation to the counter-strategic thought of French theory. With its roots in the military writing of Carl von Clausewitz, and hence the war writing of the Napoleonic era, counter-strategic thought strives to resist the colonisation of war by the modern military and its biopolitical practices.

The long-standing interest in the encounter between literature and political violence in the Romantic age has, in general terms, come to be framed by an understanding of the period's traumatic relation to history. Admittedly, modern conceptions of trauma post-date the Romantic era, as they first appeared in latter nineteenth-century studies of the psychological injuries associated with railway accidents.[1] Trauma represented a new kind of injury, where survivors of accidents who had been physically unscathed would go on to suffer a range of belated symptoms. While signaling a shift from corporeal to psychic wounds, trauma also represented a fundamental disturbance of memory, in which an injury that was not originally experienced would subsequently come to haunt a sufferer through intrusive recollections and corporeal neuroses.[2] Intimately linked to the rise of modern industrial technologies and their profound dislocation of social life, it was only with the First World War, however, that trauma emerged as a mass phenomenon that decisively influenced the field of psychology, especially through Freud's work on the effects of shell shock.[3] Building on the psychoanalytic roots of the study of trauma, literary theorists such as Cathy Caruth and Shoshana Felman have in turn considered the literary implications of such violent historical experiences that are too shocking and overwhelming to be registered as conscious or linguistic experience and which thus pass into the unconscious to replay as nightmares, tremors and flashbacks in later life.[4] Seeing in trauma a confirmation that the violence of history defies language, theorists of trauma emphasise how the repetitive compulsions of the traumatised psyche can nonetheless re-establish an almost literal connection to a history that can itself never be fully known.[5] The symptoms of trauma suggest the visceral return of an originally absent or missed experience, in which the delayed response appears as a manifestation of historical reality.

These conceptualisations of trauma have been enormously influential in literary studies as they extended deconstructive approaches to language into an ethical engagement with historical and political contexts.[6] Understood as a trace or symptom of history's material violence, trauma complicates the tenet that history can never be known outside its textual representation.[7]

[1] Roger Luckhurst, *The Trauma Question* (London: Routledge, 2008), 21.

[2] Karolyn Steffens, 'Modernity as the Cultural Crucible of Trauma', in *Trauma and Literature*, ed. J. Roger Kurtz (Cambridge: Cambridge University Press, 2018), 36–50, 37.

[3] C. Fred Alford, *Trauma, Culture, and PTSD* (New York: Palgrave Macmillan, 2016), 32.

[4] Cathy Caruth, *Unclaimed Experience: Trauma, Narrative and History* (Baltimore: Johns Hopkins University Press, 1996); and Shoshana Felman and Dori Laub, *Testimony: Crises of Witnessing in Literature, Psychoanalysis, and History* (New York: Routledge, 1992). Bessel van de Kolk, one of the key psychologists behind the literary study of trauma, suggests that in times of shock the memory can only function through iconic and sensory forms; see Judith Herman, *Trauma and Recovery* (New York: Basic Books, 1997), 39.

[5] See Ruth Leys, *Trauma: A Genealogy* (Chicago: University of Chicago Press, 2000), 230.

[6] Luckhurst, *The Trauma Question*, 6–8. On deconstruction and trauma, see also Tom Toremans, 'Deconstruction: Trauma Inscribed in Language', in *Trauma and Literature*, ed. J. Roger Kurtz (Cambridge: Cambridge University Press, 2018), 51–65.

[7] Or as Fredric Jameson suggests in his call to always historicise, '[h]istory is what hurts'; Fredric Jameson, *The Political Unconscious: Narrative as Socially Symbolic Act* (London: Routledge, 2002), 88; For a discussion of trauma and new historicist literary studies, see Thomas Pfau, *Romantic Moods: Paranoia, Trauma, and Melancholy, 1790–1840* (Baltimore: Johns Hopkins University Press), 202.

This idea of trauma has, of course, been pivotal in studies of war literature that understand modern war stories a revelation of the unimaginable horror and physical suffering of war.[8] More broadly, though, historicist approaches to Romantic era culture have shared this concern with recovering the traces of a traumatic history in their engagements with industrialisation, patriarchal authority, environmental degradation, imperialism and political conflict.[9] Even in studies that do not directly address trauma, therefore, there are clear concerns with the crises of witnessing and representation that underpinned Romantic responses to the violence of history. Romanticism, in this reading, manifests a traumatic history that cannot otherwise be understood or known. As Caruth observes, if trauma defies representation, then the truth of trauma and hence the 'truth' of history can only become accessible to a listener who shares the intense experience and affects of that trauma in ways that do not resolve history into a coherent narrative.[10] History is revealed in Romantic poetry because it communicates passions that might deny history but which in its very denial of narrative coherence is able to reawaken and even recreate that history.[11] Developing such concerns with the poetic response to trauma and history, Geoffrey Hartman proposes that a Wordsworthian poetics built around the encounter with 'spots of time' can be read as a revelation of the ongoing symbolic presence of this violent, traumatic history.[12]

Yet even as literary studies has incorporated the insights of trauma studies, theorists have voiced concerns about the universalising tendencies of trauma theory and its overemphasis on the uniquely violent and extraordinary episodes of history. Lauren Berlant, for example, has advocated a turn to affect as a way to engage with trauma as a condition of existence rather than as a violent interruption of social normality.[13] Kevis Goodman adopts such an approach in her study of the Romantic sense of history, as she moves from apocalyptic ideas of history's traumatic absence to

---

[8] Kate McLoughlin, *Authoring War: The Literary Representation of War from* The Iliad *to Iraq* (Oxford: Oxford University Press, 2011); and Kate McLoughlin, *Veteran Poetics: British Literature in the Age of Mass Warfare, 1790–2015* (Cambridge: Cambridge University Press, 2018).

[9] Lisa Kasmer, 'Introduction', in *Traumatic Tales: British Nationhood and National Trauma in Nineteenth-Century Literature*, ed. Lisa Kasmer (New York: Routledge, 2018), 1–16.

[10] Alford, *Trauma, Culture, and PTSD*, 37.

[11] Luckhurst, *The Trauma Question*, 11. On Romantic new historicism and trauma, see Kevis Goodman, 'Making Time for History: Wordsworth, the New Historicism', and the Apocalyptic Fallacy, *Studies in Romanticism* 35, no. 4 (1996): 563–77, 572–73.

[12] Geoffrey H. Hartman, 'On Traumatic Knowledge and Literary Studies', *New Literary History* 26, no. 3 (1995): 537–63, 547.

[13] Lauren Berlant, *Cruel Optimism* (North Carolina: Duke University Press, 2011), 9–12.

instead show how a sense of history is mediated by the structures of feeling found in eighteenth-century news and poetry.[14] Mary Favret similarly explores a more diffuse trauma in her engagements with the everydayness or, borrowing a term from Dominick LaCapra, the 'structural trauma' of wartime and its media forms.[15] Romantic culture is distant from war, but war's traumas circulate through alternative temporalities and dissonances associated with belatedness, deferral and obscurity of war news.[16] But as Goodman and Favret intimate in their analyses of how the sense of history is mediated, trauma also has a structure akin to the indexical qualities of modern media itself. This is a point pursued by Allen Meek in his account of the relationship that formed historically between trauma and the modern media – an idea first developed in Walter Benjamin's adaptation of Freudian concepts of trauma that media 'shock' the sensorium of the modern subject.[17] The indexical nature of film, gramophones and photographs, which mediate through the physical traces of sound and light, suggests that it is modern media forms themselves that offer an authentic realisation or experience of history. Applying such ideas to Romantic writing, which exhibits what Goodman identifies an indexical noise of history, a vision emerges of a Romantic 'poetics of modernity' shaped as much by a pervasive wartime trauma as by the spread of the commodity form.[18]

Meek cautions, however, that this relationship between modern media and trauma can leave the experience of trauma open to political manipulation: the felt shock of insight and visceral access to a traumatic history might simply be the effect of the mediated transmission of that history.[19] He thus draws attention to an alternative way of thinking about this nexus of history, violence and mediation by aligning trauma with Foucault's insights into security and biopolitics. Foucault's thought suggests a somewhat different view of how we might conceptualise the relation between the rise of modern technologies and trauma when he

---

[14] Kevis Goodman, *Georgic Modernity and British Romanticism: Poetry and the Mediation of History* (Cambridge: Cambridge University Press, 2004).

[15] Mary A. Favret, *War at a Distance: Romanticism and the Making of Modern Wartime* (Princeton: Princeton University Press, 2009), 160.

[16] Jan Mieszkowski, *Watching War* (Palo Alto: Stanford University Press, 2012), 14.

[17] Allen Meek, *Trauma and Media: Theories, Histories, and Images* (New York: Routledge, 2010), 13.

[18] On these twinned elements of war and the commodity, see David Simpson, *Wordsworth, Commodification, and Social Concern: The Poetics of Modernity* (Cambridge: Cambridge University Press, 2009).

[19] Allen Meek, 'Trauma in the Digital Age', in *Trauma and Literature*, ed. J. Roger Kurtz (Cambridge: Cambridge University Press, 2018), 167–80, 172.

points to the emergence of biology into politics as constituting a society's 'threshold of modernity'.[20] The traumatic encounter between bodies and machines that constitutes modernity could be seen to have originated with the disciplinary practices that sought to refashion the body as though it were a machine. Indeed, it is primarily in relation to the constitution and training of the military body that a nascent trauma has been seen to have developed in late eighteenth-century concerns with the disease of nostalgia.[21] Nostalgia in the eighteenth century was associated as much with the dislocation and travails of military service as the shock of battle's violence, it principally occurred in reaction to the hardships of training regimes, conscription and forced travel, or, in other words, the biopolitical management of military lives.[22] Expanding upon Foucault's concerns with the biopolitical formation of modernity, John Roberts specifically locates the rise of the modern concept of trauma in relation to the new temporality of modernity sketched by Reinhart Koselleck. As the past ceases to guide the future, as the horizon of expectation moves ever further away from the space of experience, there are corresponding demands for ever greater levels of security to bridge that gap between experience and expectation.[23] This temporal shock of the modern lies behind Romantic nostalgia, as the revolutionary birth of the modern dislocates memory and tradition with new and unprecedented experiences that, in turn, trigger a Romantic effort to realign the present with its past.[24] But as theorists of trauma such as Meek and Roberts show, the encounter with a shocking, overwhelming machinic future is connected with a correlative hyper-security that seeks to arrest and manage this unexpected future. So the modern sense of temporal dislocation, the Romantic era nostalgia that emerges out of security and biopower, is met with ever greater efforts to ensure security through the evolution of that same biopower.[25]

[20] Michel Foucault, *The History of Sexuality. Volume One: An Introduction*, trans. Robert Hurley (New York: Penguin Books, 1981), 143.

[21] For an overview of nostalgia in the Romantic era, see Svetlana Boym, *The Future of Nostalgia* (New York: Basic Books, 2001), 3–18.

[22] Thomas Dodman, *What Nostalgia Was: War, Empire, and the Time of a Deadly Emotion* (Chicago: University of Chicago Press, 2018), 73. On nostalgia as a response to the global disruptions of eighteenth-century warfare, see also Kevis Goodman, '"Uncertain Disease": Nostalgia, Pathologies of Motion, Practices of Reading', *Studies in Romanticism* 49, no. 2 (2010): 197–227, 206–07.

[23] John Roberts, *Trauma and the Ontology of the Modern Subject: Historical Studies in Philosophy, Psychology, and Psychoanalysis* (New York: Routledge, 2018), 161–62.

[24] Peter Fritzsche, 'Specters of History: On Nostalgia, Exile, and Modernity', *The American Historical Review* 106, no. 5 (2001): 1587–618.

[25] Roberts, *Trauma and the Ontology of the Modern Subject*, 111. For a related argument on contemporary wars, see Greg Goldberg and Craig Willse, 'Losses and Returns: The Soldier in Trauma', in *The*

Ian Hacking elaborates upon this underlying association between bio-power and trauma in his genealogical history of trauma as the pathologi-sation of memory. He develops a concept of memoro-politics as a third pole of biopower alongside the antamo-politics of the body and the bio-politics of the population.[26] Where the anatomo-politics of discipline and surveillance gives rise to the 'soul', memoro-politics works directly upon the soul by attending to the disturbances of memory associated with trauma.[27] Obviously only one part of the psy-sciences that formed in the nineteenth century to target the deviancies or pathologies of disciplinary subjects, biopower's specific concerns with trauma nonetheless provide, Hacking argues, a mechanism for attaining direct control of the soul via the body because it is a way of imagining the psyche as being 'wounded' in a distinctly embodied manner.[28] In the modern era, therefore, trauma morphs from bodily wounds into psychic wounds that are not experienced consciously, but as an unconscious, somatic disturbance that can threaten to dissolve the developmentally normal individual selfhood or soul that biopower constructs. This is a way of conceptualising the mind, in other words, in line with the biopolitical control of the body and its norms. While memoro-politics in Hacking's account obviously formed much later in the nineteenth century than other elements of biopower, in line with other psy-sciences, the roots of a science of memory nonetheless appear to grow out of Romanticism's simultaneous encounter with the disturbed memory of nostalgia and its rejection of the *ars memoria* of an earlier neo-classical rhetoric.[29] Trauma, in this reading, does not simply emerge out of war's violence, but always appears intimately related to the biopoliticisa-tion of life.

The rise of the memoro-politics of trauma also corresponds with the new temporality of the state that arose once its central political objective devolved to the management and protection of life. Primarily concerned with the control or security of threats to the population, the biopolitical state recon-ceptualised the future as nothing other than the temporality of governmen-tality. The eschatology of an older Christian cosmology was replaced with

---

Affective Turn: Theorizing the Social, ed. Patricia Ticineto Clough and Jean Halley (Durham: Duke University Press, 2007), 264–86, 281–82.

[26] Ian Hacking, 'Memoro-politics, Trauma and the Soul', *History of the Human Sciences* 7, no. 2 (1994): 29–52.

[27] Hacking, 'Memoro-politics, Trauma and the Soul', 33.

[28] Hacking, 'Memoro-politics, Trauma and the Soul', 39–40.

[29] Hacking, 'Memoro-politics, Trauma and the Soul', 47.

the limitless history of the state's empty, homogeneous time.[30] In part, as Foucault argues, the basic structure of this temporality originates with the state's efforts to universally pacify society and so remove wars from within the social body, a process that is essentially completed at the time of the French Revolution and the consolidation of state-based military institutions.[31] Committed to maintaining peace and promoting the well-being of the nation, the state no longer defines its authority as the right to kill but will only engage in violence and killing as a defence and promotion of life. It is notable that war memorials for the war dead not only proliferated across Europe following the French Revolutionary and Napoleonic Wars, but that they also adopted a consistent 'aesthetic' for representing death.[32] While the memorials indelibly united death in war with a national history, they also reduced that history to a homogeneous concern with death with little concern for the specific martial values or glory of each nation. The nation and its history was no longer defined by its warlike virtues forged in war against other nations or races, therefore, but by its internal management of life, by its ability to administer itself and form the institutions of the state.[33] War is biologised and comes to be understood as, above all, a threat to the health and natural development of the population. Transposed into racial relations marked by infection and sickness rather than a conflictual relation between political equals, war is now associated with a racialised evolutionism as a disturbance or pathologisation of national memory and historical progress, a degenerate regression to the warlike past of one's own race.[34] War is understood, therefore, as a traumatic return of violence that compels the state to turn inwards in its effort to restore security via 'a permanent purification' of the nation and its social norms.[35]

By drawing on Foucault's account of biopolitics, therefore, modern trauma appears deeply interconnected with modern security regimes, as both emerge together within the new temporality of the state's government of life. The history revealed by trauma is simultaneously a history

[30] See Michael Dillon, 'Spectres of Biopolitics: Finitude, *Eschaton* and *Katechon*', *South Atlantic Quarterly* 110, no. 3 (2011): 780–92.
[31] Michel Foucault, *Society Must be Defended: Lectures at the Collège de France, 1975–1976*, ed. Mauro Bertani and Alessandro Fontana, trans. David Macey (London: Penguin Books, 2004), 48–49.
[32] Reinhart Koselleck, *The Practice of Conceptual History: Timing History, Spacing Concepts*, trans. Tod Samuel Presner et al., foreword Hayden White (Stanford: Stanford University Press, 2002), 294, 325–36.
[33] Foucault, *Society Must be Defended*, 223.
[34] Foucault, *Society Must be Defended*, 256–57.
[35] Foucault, *Society Must be Defended*, 61.

structured by security and the governmentality of bodies and popula-tions.[36] A politics that seeks emancipation from this management of life must suspend the operation of biopower that, as theorists of biopolitics lament, inexorably turns to killing and death. An entirely uncritical focus on trauma can, however, lead to the acceptance of wound culture and the constitution of a pathological public sphere that can only find unity in spectacles of suffering.[37] One of the most pointed concerns with reading trauma in relation to biopolitics comes out of Roberto Esposito's analysis of immunitary paradigm by which security operates.[38] Following Esposito's biopolitical analysis, trauma can be read as an attempted immunisation of the social that stimulates the ever active productivity of security.[39] Giorgio Agamben, in a similar manner, explores the biopolitical contexts for trauma when he argues that within the nomos of modernity, the collapse of all tradition exposes the essential inoperativity of the human so that nothing retains meaning except life.[40] If modern power now always works by taking control of life and its productivity, our freedom from biopolitical control must be via an inoperativity that leaves open the potential of the body.[41] For Agamben, resisting biopower means rendering life inoperative through forms of 'misuse' of the body that resist biopower's demand that life be productive by instead directing us towards study, profanation or play. However much studies of trauma strive to separate the individual from the demands of strategic calculation, they also suspend this poten-tiality because they relocate the body within what Agamben regards as a sacred space.[42] The inoperative potential of misusing the body is with-drawn behind a glorification of the body's mere appearance, much in the way that the modern war memorial sacralises lives lost in war.

Coming at such questions from a quite different direction than Agamben, Rancière nonetheless similarly reads politics as the capacity to

[36] Allen Meek, *Biopolitical Media: Catastrophe, Immunity and Bare Life* (New York: Routledge, 2015), 20–21.

[37] Mark Seltzer, 'Wound Culture: Trauma in the Pathological Public Sphere', *October* 80 (Spring 1997): 3–26.

[38] Roberto Esposito, *Bios: Biopolitics and Philosophy*, trans. Timothy Campbell (Minneapolis: University of Minnesota Press, 2008), 72.

[39] See Pieter Vermeulen, 'The Biopolitics of Trauma', in *The Future of Trauma Theory: Contemporary Literary and Cultural Criticism*, ed. Gert Buelens (New York: Routledge, 2014), 141–56, 148–51.

[40] Giorgio Agamben, *The Open: Man and Animal*, trans. Kevin Attell (Stanford: Stanford University Press, 2004), 75–77. For an analysis, see Sergei Prozorov, *Agamben and Politics: A Critical Introduction* (Edinburgh: Edinburgh University Press, 2014), 34–35.

[41] Agamben, *The Open*, 92.

[42] Prozorov, *Agamben and Politics*, 35–49.

keep open this potentiality that refuses to determine the 'ethos' of a body.[43] Rancière argues that to think of bodies solely through trauma is to remain indebted to thinking only in terms of what defines or establishes the ethos of the body.[44] To look for the traumatic histories that can be recovered is to assume meaning and essence behind bodies in a manner that duplicates the ongoing disciplinary control of life. It is to reduce speech and meaning to merely the expression or embodied voicing of pain. He also notes that consensus in modern capitalist society is above all maintained by the efforts of military power to generate fear and so assert an ever-growing need for security.[45] Ongoing developments in the psychological study of trauma have themselves revealed how trauma results from the over-arousal of the body's own security mechanisms.[46] Trauma is provoked by overwhelming fear that leaves the body in a heightened state of arousal to danger and hence trapped by its own demands for hyper-security. It follows, therefore, that recovery from trauma cannot be adequately conceived as a disease narrative but must involve an entirely different form of mobilisation of the body that can playfully release it from the hold of fear.

In line with Foucault's analysis of biopolitics, there has been a significant body of French theory concerned with resisting the disciplinary construction of subjectivity within networks of biopolitical security. It is a body of work that specifically formed as a counter-strategic approach to the liberal culture of modern capitalist society, in which contemporary society is seen to have been recoded around the strategic manipulation of populations necessary for capitalist modes of production.[47] Going beyond analysis of a class war, in other words, theorists argued that war and its strategic imperatives permeated the entirety of society. Critically, therefore, counter-strategic thought understands war primarily in relation to its role in the formation of subjectivity. As Julian Reid explains: 'Along with other Counter-strategic thinkers Foucault conceives modern societies forming not out of a resolution of the problem of war nor as a continuation of

---

[43] Jacques Rancière, *Disagreement: Politics and Philosophy*, trans. Julie Rose (Minneapolis: University of Minnesota Press, 2000), 36–37.

[44] Jacques Rancière, *The Future of the Image*, trans. Gregory Elliott (London: Verso, 2007), 109–13.

[45] Jacques Rancière, *Dissensus: On Politics and Aesthetics*, ed. and trans. Steven Corcoran (London: Continuum, 2010), 111.

[46] See, in particular, Bessel van de Kolk, *The Body Keeps the Score: Brain, Mind, and Body in the Healing of Trauma* (New York: Penguin Books, 2015).

[47] Julian Reid, 'Re-appropriating Clausewitz: The Neglected Dimensions of Counter-Strategic Thought', in *Classical Theory in International Relations*, ed. Beate Jahn (Cambridge: Cambridge University Press, 2006), 277–95, 283.

specifically historically defined wars but as a product of a refinement of the role of war in the constitution of relations'.[48]

But counter-strategic thought not only reveals the role of war in shaping subjectivities, it also appropriates war's capacity to shape new forms of subjectivity as it sets out to resist 'the colonisation of war by the state and the military-strategic discourses and institutions on which State power is founded'.[49] A counter-strategic thought that reorients the violent strategic calculations of the military into aesthetic or ludic forms appears in Michel de Certeau's elaboration of tactical resistance to strategies, Gilles Deleuze and Felix Guattaris' hasty weapons or the aesthetic war machine that operates against the state, Jean Baudrillard's fatal strategies, Michael Hardt and Antonio Negri's concerns with the strategies of the multitude, Foucault's analysis of strategic games that resist domination, or even in Derrida's strategies without finality and Rancière's reflections on how art is constituted by strategies that shape the visibility of political grievances in order to resist the 'pacification of the political'.[50] This counter-strategic thought serves as a basic mode for French theory that moves beyond analysis of labour and class to focus on society through the lens of a totalising social conflict and struggle. It is here, in a counter-discourse of war, conflict and strategy, that the body is placed into an aesthetic war machine that could release it from the demands of biopolitical productivity.

Critically, however, counter-strategic thought was not simply utilising war in a metaphorical sense but was based on a recovery of Carl von Clausewitz to propose that modern capitalism is bounded by military power and very real social conflicts.[51] Expanding upon what they term 'the thought of '68', Éric Alliez and Maurizio Lazzarato have proposed a new critique of capitalism in which resistance must be seen in relation to the strategic thought and practices of war because capitalism is above all defined by military conflict and its biopolitical practices.[52] Capitalism, they argue, must be understood as the expansion of a colonial warfare that divides and appropriate populations from their territories through the exercise of state sanctioned force that is now reaching its ecological limits

[48] Reid, 'Re-appropriating Clausewitz', 285.
[49] Reid, 'Re-appropriating Clausewitz', 278.
[50] Jacques Rancière, *On the Shores of Politics*, trans. Liz Heron (London: Verso, 1995), 20.
[51] The recovery of Clausewitz was initiated by Raymond Aron, who represents a key figure in the transition of French thought from Marx to Clausewitz; see Raymond Aron, *Clausewitz: Philosopher of War*, trans. Christine Booker and Norman Stone (London: Routledge & Kegan Paul, 1983).
[52] Éric Alliez and Maurizio Lazzarato, *Wars and Capital*, trans. Ames Hodges (South Pasadena: Semiotext(e), 2016), 291.

in the capitalocene.[53] Similarly drawing on Foucault's work on biopolitics and war, Jacques Bidet argues that social theory must recognise that nations exist within a world system of international conflict, and that war is as essential to our understanding of modernity as capitalism.[54] Agamben draws particular attention to the emancipatory potential of the 'peculiar strategist', Guy Debord, who, along with Alison Becker-Ho, developed *Game of War*, a radical variation of chess that served as a complex simulation of Clausewitz's strategic thought.[55] Debord saw the *Game of War* as his most significant contribution to political theory, its significance lying in its capacity to democratise the strategic leadership of the avant-garde of revolutionary politics by allowing anyone to take the position of the general and so learn to make strategic calculations.[56] Even Fredric Jameson, albeit in a markedly different manner, has proposed that a universal military enlistment could help emancipate society by enabling the military to function in the role of a dual power or counter-government alongside the state.[57] His ideas appear far too militaristic for many commentators, but they nonetheless align with Alliez and Lazzarato's belief that we are waging entirely real wars against capital and even carry echoes of Friedrich Engels' belief that to succeed, the Left would have to 'win over' the nation's professional military forces.[58]

Romantic thought has frequently been read as a precursor to the poetics of post-structuralism because of Romanticism's earlier concerns with questions of language and identity, but it is also possible to draw a connection between Romanticism and the counter-strategic thought of French theory. There was, admittedly, a highly conscious recovery of Clausewitz in French theory of the late 1960s and 1970s, whereas military writing forms a far more generalised and amorphous historical context for Romantic aesthetics. Nonetheless, much as Marxism is informed by its diverse engagements with the Romantic era political economics of David Ricardo, Adam Smith, Thomas Malthus, Jeremy Bentham and others, so French theory's return to Clausewitz can be further expanded

[53] Alliez and Lazzarato, *Wars and Capital*, 30.
[54] Jacques Bidet, *Foucault with Marx*, trans. Steven Corcoran (London: Zed Books, 2016), 176–77.
[55] Giorgio Agamben, *Means Without Ends: Notes on Politics*, trans. Vincenzo Binetti and Cesare Casarino (Minneapolis: Minnesota Press, 2000), 74.
[56] Richard Barbrook, *Class Wargames: Ludic Subversion Against Spectacular Capitalism* (Wivenhoe: Minor Compositions, 2014), 298.
[57] Fredric Jameson, *An American Utopia: Dual Power and the Universal Army*, ed. Slavoj Zizek (New York: Verso Books, 2016).
[58] Barbrook, *Class Wargames*, 284.

by incorporating such military authors as Henry Lloyd, Robert Jackson, Charles Pasley and Thomas Hamilton. While the era is marked by the separation of military and civilian literary worlds, Romanticism none-theless emerged alongside and in tension with the biopolitical exigencies developed in military writing and its response to the period's wars in ways that echo these counter-strategic modes of thought. Romanticism was, as Jerome Christensen and Mary Favret argue, a wartime body of writing. To follow Menke, we can revise Foucault's conception of the Romantic era as the threshold of modernity from merely the biologisa-tion of politics to a more complex tension or conflict between the biologi-cal and aesthetic understanding of the human that both depended upon the disciplinary regime of the natural body.[59] Aesthetics is distinct from discipline, however, because it opens out to a future that is not deter-mined teleologically or in line with an overarching strategic goal. It takes, instead, a counter-strategic relation to the natural body and the dictates of biopower. It is a position broadly shared by Rancière in his similar devel-opments of Foucault, that aesthetics releases the body from the domina-tion that is exercised through the biopolitical arts of making life live. Debord concludes *Comments on the Society of Spectacle* by explicitly draw-ing attention to the profound military significance of the sharpshooters who proliferated during the French Revolutionary and Napoleonic Wars and revolutionised tactics with their 'independent fire', hinting that we must discover our own new tactics for the society of the spectacle.[60] But Romanticism itself can be understood in a counter-strategic relation to these same historical military developments, as it extended its own new 'tactics' of perception, judgement and independent thought out beyond the biopolitical teleology of strategic necessity.

There has, at least, been a long-standing analysis in Romantic studies of authors' reactions to Napoleon, from Byron's complex sense of admi-ration and disappointment to Wordsworth's engagements with a history shaped by Napoleonic conquest.[61] A concern with contesting war might also be seen in the veteran poetics that emerged in the Romantic era, in

---

[59] On the relation between Foucault's early thought on literature and his subsequent work on biopoli-tics, see Azucena G. Blanco, *Literature and Politics in the Later Foucault* (Berlin: Walter de Gruyter, 2020).

[60] Guy Debord, *Comments on the Society of the Spectacle*, trans. Malcolm Imrie (London: Verso, 1990), 87.

[61] For an overview of Romantic poets reactions to Napoleon, see Simon Bainbridge, *Napoleon and English Romanticism* (Cambridge: Cambridge University Press, 1995). On Wordsworth and Napoleon, see Alan Liu, *Wordsworth: The Sense of History* (Stanford: Stanford University Press, 1989).

which the thought and experience of the soldier played a pivotal role in the formation of literature more generally and its rejection of neo-classical art focussed on the exploits of the great general.[62] If we read these traces of a veteran poetics as a counter-strategic thought, Romantic writing can be seen to address, react to, reject and reorient military strategic power as it develops its own aesthetic modes for contesting the military's efforts, in Jacques Antoine-Hippolyte, Comte de Guibert's phrasing, to initiate a nation's 'conquests upon itself'.[63] Jeffrey Cox, for example, examines Romantic writing as an adaptation of the military strategy of border struggles while considering the importance of militarised speed to the evolution of aesthetics.[64] Lily Gurton-Watcher discovers a shared concern with attention in military strategic preparations for invasion and the poetics of Romanticism, arguing that Romantic poetry reorients even as it absorbs the wartime imperatives behind paying attention.[65] Samuel Baker, in a similar manner, proposes that an oceanic conception of culture forms in the Romantic era as a development and redeployment of the geopolitics of Britain's oceanic imperial aggression.[66] Relatedly, reflections on Romanticism and biopolitics have argued for the importance of aesthetics in resisting the operation of biopower in a move that carries forward this counter-strategic potential of Romantic poetry.[67] Undoubtedly far more work remains to be done to develop the underlying question of Romanticism's relation to biopolitics, especially with regard to the deep connection that Foucault and others have drawn between biopolitics and its thanatopolitical shadows. Nonetheless, Romanticism is born of the same era as modern war writing, the two bodies of work sharing a concern with understanding the senses, vitality and power of life that compose the natural body.

[62] McLoughlin, *Veteran Poetics*.

[63] Jacques Antoine Hippolyte, Comte de Guibert, *A General Essay on Tactics. With an Introductory Discourse upon the Present State of Politics and the Military Science in Europe. To which is Prefixed a Plan of a Work, Entitled, The Political and Military System of France. Translated from the French of M. Guibert. By an Officer* (London: Printed for J. Millan, opposite the Admiralty, Whitehall, 1781), xii.

[64] Jeffrey N. Cox, *Romanticism in the Shadow of War: Literary Culture in the Napoleonic War Years* (Cambridge: Cambridge University Press, 2014).

[65] Lily Gurton-Wachter, *Watchwords: Romanticism and the Poetics of Attention* (Stanford: Stanford University Press, 2016).

[66] Samuel Baker, *Written on the Water: British Romanticism and the Maritime Empire of Culture* (Charlottesville: University of Virginia Press, 2010).

[67] For an overview of this work, see Eva Geulen, 'Response and Commentary (Sara Guyer, Marc Redfield and Emily Sun)', *Romanticism and Biopolitics, Romantic Circles Praxis Series*, ed. Alastair Hunt and Matthias Rudolf (December 2012), https://romantic-circles.org/praxis/biopolitics/HTML/praxis.2012.geulen.html. accessed 15 April 2022.

This is not to deny that British Romantic authors have frequently been criticised for their failures to fully condemn war.[68] Favret turns to the concept of structural trauma in part because British Romanticism lacks the more direct refusal of violence that can be seen, for example, in Francisco Goya's 'intolerable' images of the horrors of the Peninsular War, *Disasters of War* (1810–20).[69] Yet if the Romantic era gave rise to militarism, it also revealed the enormous force and power of military thought and its capacity to mobilise the nation. To read Romantic writing in relation to counter-strategies suggests an alternative dimension to this body of wartime writing, to recognise in it a degree of ludic military activity that more broadly dominated Britain in these years through far reaching concerns with national service, volunteering and political participation.[70] Romanticism is a civilian body of work, but Romantic authors were never far from military power, and if a nascent militarism took hold of and redirected volunteering in Britain, as documented in Chapter 4, so, in an inverted manner, did Romantic poetics at times reimagine or even rechannel ideas of military service and mass mobilisation. Of course, there were a diffuse range of relations between Romantic poets and military power, from Coleridge's short enlistment as a dragoon under the pseudonym Silas Tomkyn Comberbache, to Blake's potentially lethal encounter with a drunken soldier accusing him of sedition. But this relation with the military takes on more complexly counter-strategic forms in Byron's involvement with the Greek War of Independence, Shelley's efforts to separate the soldier from the centres of authority to become friends of the people or Austen's role as a historian of the domestic life of the navy.[71] Wordsworth insisted that he would have been best fitted for a soldier had he not been a poet, having 'read books of military history and strategy' and being possessed, he thought, of a 'talent for command'.[72] Kenneth Johnston proposes that Wordsworth's *Lyrical Ballads* (1798) writes back to

[68] Phil Shaw, 'Introduction', in *Romantic Wars: Studies in Culture and Conflict, 1793–1822*, ed. Phil Shaw (Aldershot: Ashgate, 2000), 1–12, 6.

[69] On the intolerable image, see Jacques Rancière, *The Emancipated Spectator*, trans. Gregory Elliott (London: Verso, 2009), 83–105.

[70] On the ludic qualities of volunteering in the 1790s and early 1800s, see Neil Ramsey, '"Making My Self a Soldier": The Role of Soldiering in the Autobiographical Work of John Clare', *Romanticism* 13, no. 2 (2007): 177–88, 178.

[71] See Roderick Beaton, *Byron's War: Romantic Rebellion, Greek Revolution* (Cambridge: Cambridge University Press, 2013); Paul Foot, *Red Shelley* (London: Bookmarks, 1984), 180–81; Brian Southam, *Jane Austen and the Navy* (London: National Maritime Museum Publishing, 2003).

[72] Mary Moorman, *William Wordsworth: A Biography. Vol. 1. The Early Years, 1770–1803* (Oxford: The Clarendon Press, 1957), 152–53.

the *Anti-Jacobin Review's* attacks on contemporary poets and its call for a new kind of poetry, as though Wordsworth were not just part of a culture war, but was intervening in a real 'Minister's War'.[73] If Elizabethan theatre made a 'real, perhaps urgent' use of military writing as playwrights carried war onto the stage, Romanticism could be regarded as having, conversely, a counter-strategic relation to military writing as authors adapted, inverted and countered military knowledge of violent conflict by offering their own elaboration of strategies and command.[74]

Rather than unveil the intolerable horrors behind the spectacle of war, as with the traditions of war writing premised on flesh-witnessing and the revelatory experience of war, counter-strategic forms of writing war can be found in complex, even ludic engagements that develop and revise military thought on war. Such writing could be read as moving away from the position of spectator, with its claims to passivity that must be awakened, to see how the spectator to war can be actively involved with the redistribution of the sensible that constitutes political life and in which, as Rancière proposes, '[a]n emancipated community is a community of narrators and translators'.[75] Romantic counter-strategies can be understood as an effort to resist the colonisation of war by the state and its military institutional apparatus by redeploying strategic knowledge as a resistance to biopolitical control, thereby realigning a knowledge of the strategies and tactics of life with the social matrix that domesticates war. Beyond Romanticism there appears to have been a lineage of ludic encounters with war that in the final instance moves up into key post-modern novels such as Thomas Pynchon's *Gravity's Rainbow* (1973), Kurt Vonnegut's *Slaughterhouse Five* (1969) and Joseph Heller's *Catch 22* (1961).[76] Such writing turns strategic military thought back against itself as it obstructs, problematises and overturns the ideas of ordering and managing life that structure the concepts of strategy and tactics that we have received from the Napoleonic era. Counter- or ludic relations to war suggest a war thought formed out of indisciplinarity and liberation rather than a militarised authority and revelation, while they point to an ongoing relationship between free play and the violence, destitution, suffering and trauma of conflict. It is work that advances more clearly in terms of what Agamben describes as a rendering

---

[73] Kenneth Johnson, 'Romantic Anti-Jacobins or Anti-Jacobin Romantics?' *Romanticism on the Net* 15 (1999), n.p., https://doi.org/10.7202/005862ar, accessed 15 April 2022.

[74] Paul A. Jorgensen, *Shakespeare's Military World* (Berkeley: University of Chicago Press, 1956), viii.

[75] Rancière, *The Emancipated Spectator*, 22.

[76] For an overview of this comic tradition, see McLoughlin, *Authoring War*, 167.

inoperative as it releases bodies into profanation and play. But establishing a relationship back to a tradition of Romantic counter-strategic thought, however, is less to continue the free play associated with the legacy of Romanticism's 'artistic critique', than to engage with the play of contending forces in struggle that operates beyond the divisions of artistic and social critique altogether.[77] It is also a way of thinking that has to take stock of exactly what is meant by struggle, war and resistance, which has to evaluate the potentials and power of alternative strategic or tactical interventions and which, as Debord cautions, has to confront the very real possibility of failure and defeat.

To propose a Romantic counter-strategic thought, to take more literally the concept of an aesthetic war machine, is not in any way to deny the traumas of the Romantic era's violent history. But a turn to counter-strategies can offer a way of understanding the ongoing effects of this traumatic relation to history while recognising that the principal damage of trauma is the fear and hypersecurity it produces in the traumatised body and which, in this sense, links trauma to the operation of biopolitical security. In *Fateful Question of Culture*, Geoffrey Hartman argues that Wordsworth's poetry prevented Britain from succumbing to fascism because it situated the British imagination between abstractions and the concrete reality of bodies.[78] This is a more debatable point if we follow the biopolitical genealogy that Foucault traces from Romantic era biopolitical violence to the Nazi killing machines.[79] Modern biopower appears routed through British imperialism and its elaboration of techniques for the management of life in an era when the whole nation might be rendered into a military camp. But does, at least, Wordsworth's poetry stand outside these processes? David Simpson cautions that Hartman evades history in his turn to Wordsworthian contemplation, and suggests that we must attend to the violence inflicted in history upon 'real lives'.[80] But is Simpson's complaint also to continue, in Agamben's terms, to build our *bios*, our political sense of ourselves, upon our *zoe* or biological existence, to propose that culture must be grounded in the contemplation of the traumatic horror of physical violence? What might be most significant about Hartman's

---

[77] On the artistic critique of capitalism, see Luc Boltanski and Eve Chiapello, *The New Spirit of Capitalism*, trans. Gregory Elliott, new ed. (London: Verso, 2017).

[78] Pieter Vermeulen, *Geoffrey Hartman: Romanticism after the Holocaust* (London: Continuum, 2010), 83; Geoffrey Hartman, *The Fateful Question of Culture* (New York: Columbia University Press, 1997).

[79] See Foucault, *The History of Sexuality*, 149–50.

[80] David Simpson, 'Virtual Culture', review essay of *The Fateful Question of Culture* by Geoffrey Hartman, *Modern Language Quarterly* 60, no. 2 (1999): 251–64, 260.

thought is the extent to which it finds in Wordsworth the power to resist this biopolitical management by moving beyond the oppositions of bodies and abstractions.[81] In this sense, his thought resonates with Georgina Green's biopolitical analysis of Wordsworth's *Convention of Cintra* (1809), a work derided by Coleridge as having 'robbed poetry', but which many saw as conversely raising prose to the level of poetry as Wordsworth took it upon himself to understand the true meaning of the nation's wars.[82] It is in his counter-strategic relation to the nation's military power, his refusal to allow a military control of war that reduced war to 'a petty conflict between soldier and soldier', that Green locates the Romantic era's most compelling effort to reject the biopolitical framing of life by imagining human culture as something other than its biological destiny.[83] The Romantic era gave birth to modern military thought on strategy that is grounded in its control of life and death, but the era also gave birth to a different kind of counter-strategic thought that offers at least some capacity to see how we might emancipate life from strategic necessity.

---

[81] Vermeulen, *Geoffrey Hartman*, 86–90.
[82] Georgina Green, *The Majesty of the People: Popular Sovereignty and the Role of the Writer in the 1790s* (Oxford: Oxford University Press, 2014), 200.
[83] Green, *The Majesty of the People*, 199, 205.

Bibliography

A Treatise on the Duty of Infantry Officers, and the Present System of British Military Discipline. With an Appendix. London: Printed for T. Egerton, at the Military Library, Near Whitehall, 1795.

Adams, Edward. *Liberal Epic: The Victorian Practice of History from Gibbon to Churchill.* Charlottesville: University of Virginia Press, 2011.

Agamben, Giorgio. *Homo Sacer: Sovereign Power and Bare Life.* Translated by Daniel Heller-Roazen. Stanford: Stanford University Press, 1998.

Agamben, Giorgio. *Means without Ends: Notes on Politics.* Translated by Vincenzo Binetti and Cesare Casarino. Minneapolis: University of Minnesota Press, 2000.

Agamben, Giorgio. *The Open: Man and Animal.* Translated by Kevin Attell. Stanford: Stanford University Press, 2004.

Agamben, Giorgio. *The Signature of All Things: On Method.* Translated by Luca D'Isanto with Kevin Attell. New York: Zone Books, 2009.

Agamben, Giorgio. *State of Exception.* Translated by Kevin Attell. Chicago: University of Chicago Press, 2005.

Agamben, Giorgio. *What is an Apparatus? and Other Essays.* Translated by David Kishik and Stefan Pedatella. Stanford: Stanford University Press, 2009.

Aikin, John and William Enfield. *General Biography, or, Lives, Critical and Historical, of the Most Eminent Persons of All Ages, Countries, Conditions and Professions, Chiefly Composed by J. Aikin and W. Enfield.* London: Printed for G. G. and J. Robinson, Pater-Noster-Row; G. Kearsley, Fleet-Street; R. H. Evans. Successor to Mr. Edwards., Pall-Mall; and J. Wright, Opposite Bond-Street, Piccadilly. Also at Edinburgh for Bell and Bradfute, 1799.

Alford, C. Fred. *Trauma, Culture, and PTSD.* New York: Palgrave Macmillan, 2016.

Allen, Jeremiah Mervin. 'The British Military Novel: 1825–1850'. PhD diss., University of Colorado, 1956.

Alliez, Éric and Maurizio Lazzarato. 'Clausewitz and *la Pensée 68*'. Translated by Ames Hodges and Katharine Wallerstein. *Critical Times* 1, no. 1 (2018): 49–59.

Alliez, Éric and Maurizio Lazzarato. *Wars and Capital.* Translated by Ames Hodges. South Pasadena: Semiotext(e), 2016.

Almon, John. *An Impartial History of the Late War. Deduced from the Committing of Hostilities in 1749, to the Signing of the Definitive Treaty of Peace in 1763.* London: printed for J. Johnson, opposite the Monument; and J. Curtis, in Fleet-Street, 1763.

Anderson, Benedict. *Imagined Communities: Reflections on the Origin and Spread of Nationalism.* Revised ed. London: Verso, 2006.

Antijacobin Review, 1811.

Arendt, Hannah. *The Origins of Totalitarianism.* San Diego: Harcourt Brace & Co., 1976.

Arendt, Hannah. *On Revolution.* London: Penguin, 1965.

Arendt, Hannah. *On Violence.* San Diego: Harcourt Brace & Co., 1970.

Arendt, Hannah. *The Promise of Politics,* edited and with an introduction by Jerome Kohn. New York: Schocken Books, 2005.

Armstrong, Nancy. 'When Gender Meets Sexuality in the Victorian Novel', in *The Cambridge Companion to the Victorian Novel,* 2nd ed., edited by Deirdre David, 170–93. Cambridge: Cambridge University Press, 2012.

Aron, Raymond. *Clausewitz: Philosopher of War.* Translated by Christine Booker and Norman Stone. London: Routledge & Kegan Paul, 1983.

Arrighi, Giovanni. *Adam Smith in Beijing: Lineages of the Twenty-First Century.* London: Verso, 2007.

The Art of War. In Four Parts. Containing, I. The Duties of Officers of Horse. II. Of Officers of Foot. III. Of a Soldier in General, with Variety of Examples of Such as Have Been Disgrac'd for Being Ignorant of Them. IV. The Rules and Practice of War by All Great Generals; The Order of Marching, Incamping, Fighting, Attacking and Defending Strong Places, and the Method of Surprizing Garrisons, or Armies, and of Bearing up of Quarters. Written in French by Four Able Officers of Long Service and Experience, and Translated into English by an English Officer. Illustrated with Several Copper Cuts. London: Printed, and sold by J. Morphew, near Stationers-Hall, 1707.

Austen, Jane. *Persuasion,* edited by Patricia Meyer Spacks. New York: W. W. Norton, 1995.

Austin, Linda Marilyn. *Nostalgia in Transition, 1780–1917.* Charlottesville: University of Virginia Press, 2007.

Bainbridge, Simon. *British Poetry and the Revolutionary and Napoleonic Wars.* Oxford: Oxford University Press, 2003.

Bainbridge, Simon. *Napoleon and English Romanticism.* Cambridge: Cambridge University Press, 1995.

Baker, Samuel. *Written on the Water: British Romanticism and the Maritime Empire of Culture.* Charlottesville: University of Virginia Press, 2010.

Bang, Peter Fibiger and Dariusz Kolodziejczyk, eds. *Universal Empire: A Comparative Approach to Imperial Culture and Representation in Eurasian History.* Cambridge: Cambridge University Press, 2012.

Barbrook, Richard. *Class Wargames: Ludic Subversion against Spectacular Capitalism.* Wivenhoe: Minor Compositions, 2014.

Barkawi, Tarak, and Shane Brighton. 'Powers of War: Fighting, Knowledge, and Critique'. *International Political Sociology* 5, no. 2 (2011): 126–43.

Barker, Simon. *War and Nation in the Theatre of Shakespeare and His Contemporaries*. Edinburgh: Edinburgh University Press, 2012.

Barker-Benfield, G. J. *The Culture of Sensibility: Sex and Society in Eighteenth-Century Britain*. Chicago: University of Chicago Press, 1996.

Barney, Richard A. 'Burke, Biomedicine, and Biobelligerence'. *The Eighteenth Century* 54, no. 2 (2013): 231–43.

Baucom, Ian. *Specters of the Atlantic: Finance Capital, Slavery, and the Philosophy of History*. Durham: Duke University Press, 2005.

Bayne, Thomas Wilson, and Douglas Brown. 'Hamilton, Thomas (1789–1842), Novelist and Travel Writer'. *Oxford Dictionary of National Biography*. 23 September 2004. https://doi.org/10.1093/ref:odnb/12129. Accessed 18 April 2017.

Beaton, Roderick. *Byron's War: Romantic Rebellion, Greek Revolution*. Cambridge: Cambridge University Press, 2013.

Behrendt, Stephen C. 'William Wordsworth and Women Poets'. *European Romantic Review* 23, no. 6 (2012): 635–50.

Bell, David A. 'The Birth of Militarism in the Age of Democratic Revolutions', in *War, Demobilization and Memory: The Legacy of War in the Era of Atlantic Revolutions*, edited by Alan Forrest, Karen Hagemann and Michael Rowe, 30–47. Basingstoke: Palgrave Macmillan, 2016.

Bell, David A. *The First Total War: Napoleon's Europe and the Birth of Modern Warfare*. London: Bloomsbury, 2007.

Benjamin, Walter. 'Some Motifs in Baudelaire', in *Illuminations*, edited by Hannah Arendt. Translated by Harry Zohn, 157–202. London: Fontana, 1973.

Benjamin, Walter. 'The Storyteller', in *Illuminations*, edited by Hannah Arendt. Translated by Harry Zorn, 83–109. London: Fontana, 1973.

Bennett, Betty T, ed. *British War Poetry in the Age of Romanticism: 1793–1815*. New York and London: Garland, 1976.

Berkovich, Ilya. *Motivation in War: The Experience of Common Soldiers in Old-Regime Europe*. Cambridge: Cambridge Univesity Press, 2017.

Berlant, Lauren. *Cruel Optimism*. Durham: Duke University Press, 2011.

Bevir, Mark. 'Historicism and the Human Sciences in Victorian Britain', in *Historicism and the Human Sciences in Victorian Britain*, edited by Mark Bevir, 1–20. Cambridge: Cambridge University Press, 2017.

Bewell, Alan. *Romanticism and Colonial Disease*. Baltimore: Johns Hopkins University Press, 1999.

Bidet, Jacques. *Foucault with Marx*. Translated by Steven Corcoran. London: Zed Books, 2016.

Black, Jeremy. *A Military Revolution? Military Change and European Society, 1550–1800*. Atlantic Highlands: Humanities Press International, 1991.

Blackstone, William. *Commentaries on the Laws of England. Book the Fourth. By William Blackstone, Esq. Vinerian Professor of Law, and Solicitor General to Her Majesty*, 4 vols. Oxford: Printed at the Clarendon Press, 1769.

Blackwood's Edinburgh Magazine, 1818–33.

Blakiston, John. *Twelve Years' Military Adventure in Three Quarters of the Globe; or, Memoirs of an Officer Who Served in the Armies of His Majesty and of the*

East India Company Between the Years 1802 and 1814, in which are Contained the Campaigns of the Duke of Wellington in India, and his Last in Spain and the South of France, 2 vols. London: Henry Colburn, 1829.

Blanco, Azucena G. *Literature and Politics in the Later Foucault*. Berlin: Walter de Gruyter, 2020.

Boever, Arne De. *Narrative Care: Biopolitics and the Novel*. London: Bloomsbury, 2013.

Boltanski, Luc and Eve Chiapello. *The New Spirit of Capitalism*. Translated by Gregory Elliott, new ed. London: Verso, 2017.

Bösch, Frank. *Mass Media and Historical Change: Germany in International Perspective, 1400 to the Present*. Translated by Freya Buechter. New York: Berghahn Books, 2015.

Bousquet, Antoine. *The Scientific Way of Warfare: Order and Chaos on the Battlefields of Modernity*. New York: Columbia University Press, 2009.

Boym, Svetlana. *The Future of Nostalgia*. New York: Basic Books, 2001.

Brantlinger, Patrick. *Rule of Darkness: British Literature and Imperialism, 1830–1914*. Ithaca: Cornell University Press, 1988.

Brewer, John. *The Sinews of Power: War, Money, and the English State, 1688–1783*. Cambridge, MA: Harvard University Press, 1990.

British Military Library; or, Journal, 1798–1800.

Broglio, Ron. *Beasts of Burden: Biopolitics, Labor, and Animal Life in British Romanticism*. Albany: State University of New York Press, 2017.

Burgess, Miranda J. *British Fiction and the Production of Social Order, 1740–1830*. Cambridge: Cambridge University Press, 2000.

Burgess, Miranda J. 'Nation, Book, Medium: New Technologies and Their Genres', in *Genres in the Internet: Issues in the Theory of Genre*, edited by Janet Giltrow and Dieter Stein, 193–219. Amsterdam: John Benjamins Publishing Company, 2009.

Butler, Marilyn. 'Culture's Medium: The Role of the Review', in *The Cambridge Companion to British Romanticism*, edited by Stuart Curran, 120–47. Cambridge: Cambridge University Press, 1993.

By His Majesty's Command. Adjutant General's Office, June 1, 1792. Rules and Regulations for the Formations, Field-Exercise, and Movements, of His Majesty's Forces. London: War-Office Printed; and sold by J. Walter, at Homer's Head, Charing-Cross, 1793.

Cahill, Patricia A. *Unto the Breach: Martial Formations, Historical Trauma, and the Early Modern Stage*. Oxford: Oxford University Press, 2008.

Carafano, James Jay. 'Lloyd, Henry Humphrey Evans (c. 1718–1783), Army Officer and Military Writer'. *Oxford Dictionary of National Biography*. 23 September 2004. https://doi-org.rp.nla.gov.au/10.1093/ref:odnb/16836. Accessed 20 June 2021.

Cardwell, M. John. 'The Rake as Military Strategist: Clarissa and Eighteenth-Century Warfare'. *Eighteenth Century Fiction* 19, nos 1 and 2 (2006): 153–180.

Caruth, Cathy. *Unclaimed Experience: Trauma, Narrative and History*. Baltimore: Johns Hopkins University, 1996.

Chambers, Samuel A. *The Lessons of Rancière*. Oxford: Oxford University Press, 2013.

Chandler, James. *England in 1819: The Politics of Literary Culture and the Case of Romantic Historicism*. Chicago: University of Chicago Press, 1998.

Choi, Leon. *Romantic Theory: Forms of Reflexivity in the Revolutionary Era*. Baltimore: Johns Hopkins University Press, 2006.

Christensen, Jerome. 'The Detection of the Romantic Conspiracy in Britain'. *South Atlantic Quarterly* 95 (1996): 603–27.

Christensen, Jerome. *Romanticism at the End of History*. Baltimore: Johns Hopkins University Press, 2000.

Clausewitz, Carl von. *Historical and Political Writings*, edited and translated by Peter Paret and Daniel Moran. Princeton: Princeton University Press, 1992.

Clausewitz, Carl Von. *On War*, edited and translated by Michael Howard and Peter Paret. Princeton: Princeton University Press, 1984.

Cohen, Ed. *A Body Worth Defending: Immunity, Biopolitics, and the Apotheosis of the Modern Body*. Durham: Duke University Press, 2009.

Colley, Linda. 'Whose Nation? Class and National Consciousness in Britain 1750–1830'. *Past and Present* 113 (1986): 97–117.

Colley, Linda. *Britons: Forging the Nation, 1707–1837*. New Haven: Yale University Press, 1992.

Cookson, John E. 'The English Volunteer Movement of the French Wars, 1793–1815: Some Contexts'. *The Historical Journal* 32, no. 4 (1989):867–891.

Coss, Edward J. 'The British Army', in *European Armies of the French Revolution, 1789–1802*, edited by Frederick C. Schneid, 107–47. Norman: University of Oklahoma Press, 2015.

Cox, Jeffrey N. *Romanticism in the Shadow of War: Literary Culture in the Napoleonic War Years*. Cambridge: Cambridge University Press, 2014.

Crary, Jonathan. *Suspensions of Perception: Attention, Spectacle, and Modern Culture*. Cambridge, MA: MIT Press, 1999.

Crocco, Francesco. *Literature and the Growth of British Nationalism: The Influence of Romantic Poetry and Bardic Criticism*. Jefferson: McFarland & Company, Publishers, 2014.

Cronin, Richard. *Paper Pellets: British Literary Culture After Waterloo*. Oxford: Oxford University Press, 2010.

Croxton, Derek. *Westphalia: The Last Christian Peace*. New York: Palgrave Macmillan, 2013.

Csengei, Ildiko. *Sympathy, Sensibility and the Literature of Feeling in the Eighteenth Century*. Basingstoke: Palgrave Macmillan, 2011.

Culler, Jonathan. *Theory of the Lyric*. Cambridge, MA: Harvard University Press, 2015.

Curry, Kenneth. *Southey*. London: Routledge, 2016.

D'Andrea, Diletta. 'Great Britain and the Mediterranean Islands in the Napoleonic Wars: The "Insular Strategy" of Gould Francis Leckie'. *Journal of Mediterranean Studies* 16, nos 1 and 2 (2006): 79–90.

Daly, Gavin. *The British Soldier in the Peninsular War: Encounters with Spain and Portugal, 1808–1814*. Basingstoke: Palgrave Macmillan, 2013.

Danley, Mark. *Military Writings and the Theory and Practice of Strategy in the Eighteenth-Century British Army*. PhD diss., Kansas State University, 2001.

Danley, Mark and Patrick Speelman, eds. *The Seven Years' War: Global Views*. Leiden: Brill, 2012.

Davies, David William. *Sir John Moore's Peninsular Campaign 1808–1809*. The Hague: Martinus Nijhoff, 1974.

Davies, Damian Walford, ed. *Romanticism, History, Historicism: Essays on an Orthodoxy*. New York: Routledge, 2009.

Davies, Huw. 'Networks of Knowledge Mobility within Eighteenth Century British Imperial Militarism'. www.academia.edu/12359005/Networks_of_Knowledge_Mobility_Within_Eighteenth_Century_British_Imperial_Militarism. Accessed 5 August 2021.

Davies, Huw. *Spying for Wellington: British Military Intelligence in the Peninsular War*. Norman: University of Oklahoma Press, 2018.

Dawson, Graham. *Soldier Heroes: British Adventure, Empire and the Imagining of Masculinities*. New York: Routledge, 1994.

De Boever, Arne. 'The Politics of Realism in Rancière and Houellebecq', in *Rancière and Literature*, edited by Grace Hellyer and Julian Murphet, 226–48. Edinburgh: Edinburgh University Press, 2016.

de Bolla, Peter. *The Discourse of the Sublime: Readings in History, Aesthetics and the Subject*. Oxford: Basil Blackwell, 1989.

De Landa, Manuel. *War in the Age of Intelligent Machines*. New York: Zone Books, 1991.

Dean, Mitchell. *Governmentality: Power and Rule in Modern Society*. London: Sage, 2010.

Dean, Mitchell. 'Power as *Sumbolon*: Sovereignty, Governmentality and the International', in *Foucault and the Modern International: Silences and Legacies for the Study of World Politics*, edited by Philippe Bonditti, Didier Bigo and Frédéric Gros, 97–114. New York: Palgrave Macmillan, 2017.

Dean, Mitchell. *The Signature of Power: Sovereignty, Governmentality and Biopolitics*. London: Sage, 2013.

Dean, Mitchell and Kaspar Villadsen. *State Phobia and Civil Society: The Political Legacy of Michel Foucault*. Stanford: Stanford University Press, 2015.

Debord, Guy. *Comments on the Society of the Spectacle*. Translated by Malcolm Imrie. London: Verso, 1990.

Deleuze, Gilles. *Foucault*, edited and translated by Seán Hand. London: Continuum, 1999.

Deleuze, Gilles and Félix Guattari. *A Thousand Plateaus: Capitalism and Schizophrenia*. Translated and foreword by Brian Massumi. London: Continuum, 2004.

Dening, Greg. *Mr Bligh's Bad Language: Passion, Power and Theatre on the Bounty*. Cambridge: Cambridge University Press, 1992.

Der Derian, James. *Virtuous War: Mapping the Military-Industrial-Media-Entertainment Network*. Boulder: Westview Press, 2001.

Derrida, Jacques. *Of Grammatology*. Translated by Gayatri Chakravorty Spivak. Baltimore: Johns Hopkins University Press, 1997.

Devine, Thomas Martin and Jenny Wormald, eds. *The Oxford Handbook of Modern Scottish History*. Oxford: Oxford University Press, 2012.

Dillon, Michael and Julian Reid. *The Liberal Way of War: Killing to Make Life Live*. Abingdon: Routledge, 2009.

Dillon, Michael. 'Spectres of Biopolitics: Finitude, *Eschaton* and *Katechon*'. *South Atlantic Quarterly* 110, no. 3 (2011): 780–92.

Dobie, Madeline. 'The Enlightenment at War'. *PMLA* 124, no. 5 (2009): 1851–54.

Dodman, Thomas. *What Nostalgia Was: War, Empire, and the Time of a Deadly Emotion*. Chicago: University of Chicago Press, 2018.

Doran, Robert. *The Theory of the Sublime from Longinus to Kant*. Cambridge: Cambridge University Press, 2015.

Drake, Michael S. *Problematics of Military Power: Government, Discipline and the Subject of Violence*. London: Frank Cass, 2002.

Dudnik, Stefan and Karen Hagemann. 'Masculinity in Politics and War in the Age of Democratic Revolutions, 1750–1850', in *Masculinities in Politics and War: Gendering Modern History*, edited by Stefan Dudnik, Karen Hagemann and John Tosh, 3–21. Manchester: Manchester University Press, 2004.

Duncan, Ian. 'Authenticity Effects: The Work of Fiction in Romantic Scotland'. *South Atlantic Quarterly* 102, no. 1 (2003): 93–116.

Duncan, Ian. *Modern Romance and Transformations of the Novel: The Gothic, Scott, Dickens*. Cambridge: Cambridge University Press, 1992.

Duncan, Ian. *Scott's Shadow: The Novel in Romantic Edinburgh*. Princeton: Princeton University Press, 2007.

Dupre, Louis. *The Enlightenment and the Intellectual Foundations of Modern Culture*. New Haven: Yale University Press, 2004.

Edinburgh Review, 1803–30.

Edkins, Jenny. *Trauma and the Memory of Politics*. Cambridge: Cambridge University Press, 2003.

Edwards, Jason. 'Foucault and the Continuation of War', in *The Metamorphoses of War*, edited by A. Plaw, 21–40. Amsterdam: Rodopi, 2012.

Eighteenth Century Collections Online.

Elias, Amy J. 'Past / Future', in *Time: A Vocabulary of the Present*, edited by Joel Burgess and Amy J. Elias, 35–50. New York: New York University Press, 2016.

Eltis, David. *The Military Revolution in Sixteenth-Century Europe*. London and New York: Tauris Academic Studies, 1995.

Emsley, Clive. 'The Social Impact of the French Wars', in *Britain and the French Revolution, 1789–1815*, edited by H. T. Dickinson, 211–27. London: Macmillan Education, 1989.

Encyclopaedia Britannica; Or, a Dictionary of Arts, Sciences, and Miscellaneous Literature on a Plan Entirely New. Dublin: printed by James Moore, 1790–98.

Engberg-Pedersen, Anders. *Empire of Chance: The Napoleonic Wars and the Disorder of Things*. Cambridge, MA: Harvard University Press, 2015.

Engberg-Pedersen, Anders. 'The Refraction of Geometry: *Tristram Shandy* and the Poetics of War, 1700–1800'. *Representations* 123, no. 1 (2013): 23–52.

English Short Title Catalogue

Entick, John. *The General History of the Late War: Containing it's Rise, Progress, and Event, in Europe, Asia, Africa, and America [sic]. And Exhibiting the State of the Belligerent Powers at the Commencement of the War; Their Interests and Objects in it's Continuation [sic]; and Remarks on the Measures, which Led Great Britain to Victory and Conquest. Interspersed with the Characters of the Able and Disinterested Statesmen, to Whose Wisdom and Integrity, and of the Heroes, to Whose Courage and Conduct, We are Indebted for that Naval and Military Success, which is Not to Be Equalled in the Annals of This, or of Any Other Nation. And with Accurate Descriptions of the Seat of War, the Nature and Importance of our Conquests, and of the Most Remarkable Battles by Sea and Land. Illustrated with a Variety of Heads, Plans, Maps, and Charts, Designed and Engraved by the Best Artists.... By the Rev. John Entick, M.A. and Other Gentlemen.* 5 vols. London: 1763.

Esposito, Roberto. *Bios: Biopolitics and Philosophy.* Translated by Timothy Campbell. Minneapolis: University of Minnesota Press, 2008.

Esposito, Roberto. 'Totalitarianism or Biopolitics? Concerning a Philosophical Interpretation of the Twentieth Century'. Translated by Timothy Campbell, in *Biopower: Foucault and Beyond*, edited by Vernon W. Cisney and Nicole Morar, 348–60. Chicago: University of Chicago Press, 2016.

Essays on the Theory and Practice of the Art of War; Including the Duties of Officers on Actual Service, and the Principles of Modern Tactics. Chiefly Translated from the Best French and German Writers. By the Editor of the Military Mentor. In 3 Volumes. London, Printed for Richard Phillips, Bridge-Street, Blackfriars. By T. Gillet, Crown-court, Fleet-street, 1809.

Fabrizio, Simon. 'The Economist and the Secret Agent. Strategies to Introduce the British Model of Society into Sicily of 1812'. *The European Journal of the History of Economic Thought* 28 (2021): 1–36.

Favret, Mary A. 'A Feeling for Numbers: Representing the Scale of the War Dead', in *War and Literature*, edited by Laura Ashe and Ian Patterson, 185–204. Cambridge: D.S. Brewer, 2014.

Favret, Mary A. 'Field of History, Field of Battle', *Romantic Circles* (2011). https://romantic-circles.org/praxis/frictions/HTML/praxis.2011.favret.html. Accessed 15 April 2022.

Favret, Mary A. *War at a Distance: Romanticism and the Making of Modern Wartime.* Princeton: Princeton University Press, 2010.

Favret, Mary A. 'Writing, Reading and the Scenes of War', in *The Cambridge History of English Romantic Literature*, edited by James Chandler, 314–34. Cambridge: Cambridge University Press, 2009.

Felluga, Dino Franco. *Perversity of Poetry: The Romantic Ideology and the Popular Male Poet of Genius.* Albany: State University of New York Press, 2005.

Felman, Shoshana and Dori Laub. *Testimony: Crises of Witnessing in Literature, Psychoanalysis, and History.* New York: Routledge, 1992.

Feuquières, Antoine de Pas, Marquis de. *Memoirs of the Late Marquis de Feuquieres, Lieutenant-General of the French Army. Written for the Instruction of his Son. Being an Account of all the Wars in Europe, from the Year 1672, to the Year 1710.* 2 Vols. London: 1737.

Ferguson, Adam. *An Essay on the History of Civil Society. By Adam Ferguson, LL. D. Professor of Moral Philosophy in the University of Edinburgh.* Dublin: Printed by Boulter Grierson, Printer to the King's most Excellent Majesty, 1767.

Ferguson, Harvie. 'The Sublime and the Subliminal: Modern Identities and the Aesthetics of Combat'. *Theory, Culture and Society* 21, no. 3 (2004): 1–33.

Ferguson, Niall. 'Virtual History: Towards a "Chaotic" Theory of the Past', in *Virtual History: Alternatives and Counterfactuals*, edited by Niall Ferguson, 1–90. New York: Basic Books, 1999.

Ferris, Ina. *The Achievement of Literary Authority: Gender, History, and the Waverley Novels.* Ithaca: Cornell University Press, 1991.

Ferris, Ina. 'The Debut of *The Edinburgh Review*, 1802'. *BRANCH: Britain, Representation and Nineteenth-Century History*, edited by Dino Franco Felluga. Extension of *Romanticism and Victorianism on the Net*. https://branchcollective.org/?ps_articles=ina-ferris-the-debut-of-the-edinburgh-review-1802. Accessed 22 August 2019.

Foot, Paul. *Red Shelley*. London: Bookmarks, 1984.

Formisano, Marco. 'Introduction: Stuck in Panduria: Books and War', in *War in Words: Transformations of War from Antiquity to Clausewitz*, edited by Marco Formisano and Hartmut Böhmep, 1–9. Berlin: Walter de Gruyter, 2011.

Forrest, Alan, 'Society, Mass Warfare, and Gender in Europe during and after the Revolutionary and Napoleonic Wars', in *The Oxford Handbook of Gender, War, and the Western World since 1600*, edited by Karen Hagemann, Stefan Dudink and Sonya O. Rose, 159–76. Oxford: Oxford University Press, 2020.

Forrest, Alan, Karen Hagemann and Michael Rowe. 'Introduction: War, Demobilization and Memory in the Era of Atlantic Revolutions', in *War, Demobilization and Memory: The Legacy of War in the Era of Atlantic Revolutions*, edited by Alan Forrest, Karen Hagemann and Michael Rowe, 3–29. Basingstoke: Palgrave Macmillan, 2016.

Foucault, Michel. *Birth of Biopolitics: Lectures at the College de France, 1978–1979*, edited by Michel Senellart. Translated by Graham Burchell. Basingstoke: Palgrave Macmillan, 2008.

Foucault, Michel. *Discipline and Punish: The Birth of the Prison.* Translated by Alan Sheridan. New York: Vintage, 1991.

Foucault, Michel. *Essential Works of Michel Foucault, 1954–1984*. Vol. 1. Edited by Paul Rabinow, translated by Robert Hurley et al., 303–19. New York: The New Press, 1997.

Foucault, Michel. *Foucault Live (Interviews, 1961–1984)*, edited by Sylvère Lotringer. Translated by Lysa Hochroth and John Johnston. New York: Semiotext(e), 1996.

Foucault, Michel. 'Friendship as a Way of Life', in *Ethics: Subjectivity and Truth. The Essential Works of Michel Foucault, 1954–1984*. Volume 1. Edited by Paul Rabinow, translated by Robert Hurley et al., 135–40. New York: The New Press, 1997.

Foucault, Michel. 'Les Mailles du Pouvoir', in *Dits et Ecrits. 4: 1980–1988*. Edited by Daniel Defert and François Ewald, 182–201. Paris: Gallimard, 1994.

Foucault, Michel. 'On the Genealogy of *Ethics: An Overview of Work in Progress*', in *Ethics: Subjectivity and Truth. The Essential Works of Michel Foucault, 1954–1984*. Vol. 1. Edited by Paul Rabinow. Translated by Robert Hurley et al., 253–80. New York: The New Press, 1997.

Foucault, Michel. *On the Government of the Living: Lectures at the College de France, 1979–1980*, edited by Michael Senellart. Translated by Graham Burchell. Basingstoke: Palgrave Macmillan, 2014.

Foucault, Michel. *Power/Knowledge: Selected Interviews and Other Writings, 1972–1977*, edited by Colin Gordon. Translated by Colin Gordon, Leo Marshall, John Mepham and Kate Soper. New York: Pantheon, 1980.

Foucault, Michel. *Psychiatric Power: Lectures at the College de France, 1973–1974*, edited by Jacques Lagrange. Translated by Graham Burchell. Basingstoke: Palgrave Macmillan, 2006.

Foucault, Michel. 'Questions on Geography', interviewed by the editors of the journal *Herodote, in Power/Knowledge: Selected Interviews and Other Writings, 1972–1977*, edited by Colin Gordon. Translated by Colin Gordon, Leo Marshall, John Mepham and Kate Soper, 63–77. New York: Pantheon, 1980.

Foucault, Michel. Security, *Territory, Population: Lectures at the College de France, 1977–1978*. Translated by Graham Burchell. Basingstoke: New York: Palgrave Macmillan, 2007.

Foucault, Michel. *Society Must be Defended: Lectures at the College de France, 1975–1976*, edited by Mauro Bertani and Alessandro Fontana. Translated by David Macey. London: Penguin Books, 2004.

Foucault, Michel. 'Technologies of the Self', in *Ethics: Subjectivity and Truth. The Essential Works of Michel Foucault, 1954–1984*, Volume 1. Edited by Paul Rabinow. Translated by Robert Hurley et al., 223–51. New York: The New Press, 1997.

Foucault, Michel. 'The Birth of Social Medicine', in *Power: The Essential Works of Michel Foucault, 1954–1984*. Volume 3. Edited by James D. Faubian. Translated by Robert Hurley et al., 134–56. London and New York: Penguin Books, 1994.

Foucault, Michel. 'The Confession of the Flesh', interviewed by Alain Grosrichard, Gerard Wajeman, Jaques-Alain Miller, Guy Le Gaufey, Dominique Celas, Gerard Miller, Catherine Millot, Jocelyne Livi and Judith Miller, in *Power/Knowledge: Selected Interviews and Other Writings, 1972–1977*, edited by Colin Gordon. Translated by Colin Gordon, Leo Marshall, John Mepham and Kate Soper, 194–228. New York: Pantheon, 1980.

Foucault, Michel. *The Government of Self and Others: Lectures at the College de France, 1982–1983*, edited by Frédéric Gros. Translated by Graham Burchell. Basingstoke: Palgrave Macmillan, 2010.

Foucault, Michel. *The History of Sexuality. Volume One: An Introduction*. Translated by Robert Hurley. London: Penguin Books, 1981.

Foucault, Michel. 'The Meshes of Power'. Translated by Gerald Moore, in *Space, Knowledge and Power: Foucault and Geography*, edited by Jeremy W. Crampton and Stuart Elden, 153–62. Aldershot: Ashgate, 2007.

Foucault, Michel. *The Order of Things: An Archaeology of the Human Sciences*. New York: Routledge, 1989.

Foucault, Michel. 'The Political Technology of Individuals', in *Power: The Essential Works of Foucault 1954–1984*. Volume 3. Edited by James D. Faubion. Translated by Robert Hurley et al., 403–17. London: Penguin Books, 1994.

Foucault, Michel. 'Titre et Travaux', in *Dits et Ecrits. 1: 1954–1969*. Edited by Daniel Defert and François Ewald, 842–46. Paris: Gallimard, 1994.

Foucault, Michel. 'Truth and Juridical Forms', in *Power: The Essential Works of Michel Foucault, 1954–1984*. Vol. 3. Edited by James D. Faubian. Translated by Robert Hurley et al., 1–89. London and New York: Penguin Books, 1994.

Foucault, Michel. 'What is Enlightenment?', *in Ethics: Subjectivity and Truth. The Essential Works of Michel Foucault, 1954–1984*. Vol. 1. Edited by Paul Rabinow. Translated by Robert Hurley et al., 303–19. New York: The New Press, 1997.

Foucault, Michel. 'What Our Present Is?', interviewed André Berten. Translated by Lysa Hochroth, in *Politics of Truth*, edited by Sylvère Lotringer, 129–43. New York: Semiotext(e), 1997

Fox, Christopher, Roy Porter and Robert Wokler, eds. *Inventing Human Science: Eighteenth-Century Domains*. Berkeley: University of California Press, 1995.

Frederick II, King of Prussia. *Military Instructions, Written by the King of Prussia, for the Generals of his Army: Being His Majesty's own Commentaries On his former Campaigns. Together with Short Instructions for the Use of his Light Troops. Illustrated with Copper-Plates. Translated by an Officer*. London: printed for T. Becket and P. A. de Hondt, in the Strand, 1762.

Freeman, James A. *Milton and the Martial Muse: Paradise Lost and European Traditions of War*. Princeton: Princeton University Press, 1980.

Frey, Anne. *British State Romanticism: Authorship, Agency, and Bureaucratic Nationalism*. Stanford: Stanford University Press, 2010.

Fritzsche, Peter. 'Specters of History: On Nostalgia, Exile, and Modernity'. *The American Historical Review* 106, no. 5 (2001): 1587–618.

Fulford, Timothy. 'Romanticizing the Empire: The Naval Heroes of Southey, Coleridge, Austen, and Marryat'. *Modern Language Quarterly* 60, no. 2 (1999): 161–96.

Fulford, Timothy. 'Sighing for a Soldier: Jane Austen and Military Pride and Prejudice'. *Nineteenth-Century Literature* 57, no. 2 (2002): 153–78.

Fuller, John Frederick Charles. *The Foundations of the Science of War*. Fort Leavenworth: US Army Command and General Staff College Press, 1993.

Fuller, John Frederick Charles. *Sir John Moore's System of Training*. London: Hutchinson and Co, Paternoster Row, 1924.

Fussell, Paul. *The Great War and Modern Memory*. Oxford: Oxford University Press, 2013.

Gallagher, Catherine. 'Telling It Like It Wasn't'. *Pacific Coast Philology* 45 (2010): 12–25.

Gallagher, Catherine. *Telling It Like It Wasn't: The Counterfactual Imagination in History and Fiction*. Chicago: University of Chicago Press, 2018.

Gallagher, Catherine. *The Body Economic: Life, Death, and Sensation in Political Economy and the Victorian Novel.* Princeton: Princeton University Press, 2009.

Gallagher, Catherine. 'The Formalism of Military History'. *Representations* 104 (Fall 2008): 23–33.

Gardner, Kevin J. 'George Farquhar's *The Recruiting Officer*: Warfare, Conscription, and the Disarming of Anxiety'. *Eighteenth-Century Life* 25, no.3 (2001): 43–61.

Gaston, Sean. *Derrida, Literature and War: Absence and the Chance of Meeting.* London: Continuum, 2009.

Gat, Azar. *A History of Military Thought: From the Enlightenment to the Cold War.* Oxford: Oxford University Press, 2001.

Gaukroger, Stephen. *The Collapse of Mechanism and the Rise of Sensibility: Science and the Shaping of Modernity, 1680–1760.* Oxford: Oxford University Press, 2010.

Gaukroger, Stephen. *The Natural and the Human: Science and the Shaping of Modernity, 1739–1841.* Oxford: Oxford University Press, 2016.

Gaunt, Richard. 'Ministry of all the Talents (act. 1806–1807)'. *Oxford Dictionary of National Biography.* 24 May 2008. https://doi.org/10.1093/ref:odnb/95330. Accessed 14 July 2021.

Gentleman's Magazine, 1831.

Geulen, Eva. 'Response and Commentary (Sara Guyer, Marc Redfield and Emily Sun)'. *Romanticism and Biopolitics, Romantic Circles Praxis Series*, edited by Alastair Hunt and Matthias Rudolf (December 2012). https://romantic-circles .org/praxis/biopolitics/HTML/praxis.2012.geulen.html. Accessed 15 April 2022.

Gidal, Eric. *Ossianic Unconformities: Bardic Poetry in the Industrial Age.* Charlottesville: University of Virginia Press, 2015.

Gigante, Denise. *Life: Organic Form and Romanticism.* New Haven: Yale University Press, 2009.

Gilmartin, Kevin, *Print Politics: The Press and Radical Opposition in Early Nineteenth-Century* England. Cambridge: Cambridge University Press, 1996.

Gleig, George. *The Subaltern.* Edinburgh: William Blackwood, 1825.

Glover, Richard. *Peninsular Preparation: The Reform of the British Army, 1795–1809.* Cambridge: Cambridge University Press, 1963.

Goldberg, Greg and Craig Willse. 'Losses and Returns: The Soldier in Trauma', in *The Affective Turn: Theorizing the Social*, edited by Patricia Ticineto Clough and Jean Halley, 264–86. Durham: Duke University Press, 2007.

Goldsmith, Oliver. *The Martial Review; Or, a General History of the Late Wars; Together with the Definitive Treaty, and Some Reflections on the Probable Consequences of the Peace.* London: printed for J. Newbery, in St. Paul's Church-Yard, 1763.

Goldstein, Jan. 'Foucault among the Sociologists: The "Disciplines" and the History of the Professions'. *History and Theory* 23, no. 2 (1984): 170–92.

Goldstein, Jan. 'Foucault's Technologies of the Self and the Cultural History of Identity', in *Cultural History After Foucault*, edited by John Neubauer, 37–54. New York: Aldine de Gruyter, 1999.

Goodlad, Lauren M. E. *Victorian Literature and the Victorian State: Character and Governance in a Liberal Society*. Baltimore: Johns Hopkins University Press, 2003.

Goodman, Kevis. *Georgic Modernity and British Romanticism: Poetry and the Mediation of History*. Cambridge: Cambridge University Press, 2004.

Goodman, Kevis. 'Making Time for History: Wordsworth, the New Historicism, and the Apocalyptic Fallacy'. *Studies in Romanticism* 35, no. 4 (1996): 563–77.

Goodman, Kevis. "Romantic Poetry and the Science of Nostalgia", in *The Cambridge Companion to British Romantic Poetry*, edited by James Chandler and Maureen N. McLane, 195–216. Cambridge: Cambridge University Press, 2008.

Goodman, Kevis. '"Uncertain Disease": Nostalgia, Pathologies of Motion, Practices of Reading'. *Studies in Romanticism* 49, no. 2 (2010): 197–227.

Gordon, Robert C. *Arms and the Imagination: Essays on War, Politics, and Anglophone Culture*. Lanham: Hamilton Books, 2009.

Graves, Donald E. *"Reading Maketh a Full Man": British Military Literature in the Napoleonic Wars: An Annotated Bibliography of the Titles Published by the London Firm of Egerton, 1782–1832*. Godmanchester: Ken Trotman Publishing, 2007.

Green, Georgina. *The Majesty of the People: Popular Sovereignty and the Role of the Writer in the 1790s*. Oxford: Oxford University Press, 2014.

Green, Martin. *Dreams of Adventure, Deeds of Empire*. New York: Basic Books, Inc., 1979.

Gros, Francis. *States of Violence: An Essay on the End of War*. Translated by Krysztof Fijalkowski and Michael Richardson. London: Seagull Books, 2010.

Grosley, Pierre Jean. *A Tour to London, or, New Observations on England and its Inhabitants*, 2 vols. London: Printed for Lockyer Davis, in Holborn, Printer to the Royal Society, 1772.

Gruber, Ira D. *Books and the British Army in the Age of the American Revolution*. Chapel Hill: University of North Caroline Press, 2010.

Guibert, Jacques Antoine Hippolyte, Comte de. *A General Essay on Tactics. With an Introductory Discourse upon the Present State of Politics and the Military Science in Europe. To which is Prefixed a Plan of a Work, Entitled, The Political and Military System of France. Translated from the French of M. Guibert. By an Officer*. London: Printed for J. Millan, opposite the Admiralty, Whitehall, 1781.

Guillory, John. 'The Memo and Modernity'. *Critical Inquiry* 31, no. 1 (2004): 108–32.

Guinier, Arnaud. *L'Honneur du Soldat: Éthique Martiale et Discipline Guerrière dans la France des Lumières*. Ceyzérieu: Champ Vallon, 2014.

Gurton-Wachter, Lily. *Watchwords: Romanticism and the Poetics of Attention*. Stanford: Stanford University Press, 2016.

Gutting, Gary. *Michel Foucault's Archaeology of Scientific Reason*. Cambridge: Cambridge University Press, 1989.

Guyer, Paul. *A History of Modern Aesthetics. Volume 1: The Eighteenth Century*. Cambridge: Cambridge University Press, 2014.

Guyer, Sara. *Reading with John Clare: Biopoetics, Sovereignty, Romanticism*. New York: Fordham University Press, 2015.

Hacking, Ian. 'Memoro-politics, Trauma and the Soul'. *History of the Human Sciences* 7, no. 2 (1994): 29–52.

Hacking, Ian. *The Taming of Chance*. Cambridge: Cambridge University Press, 1990.

Hagemann, Karen, 'The Military and Masculinity: Gendering the History of the Revolutionary and Napoleonic Wars, 1792–1815', in *War in an Age of Revolution, 1775–1815*, edited by Roger Chickering and Stig Förster, 331–52. Cambridge: Cambridge University Press, 2010.

Hagemann, Karen, Gisela Mettele and Jand Rendall, eds, *Gender, War and Politics: Transatlantic Perspectives, 1775–1830*. Basingstoke: Palgrave Macmillan, 2010.

Hale, John R. *Renaissance War Studies*. London: Hambledon Press, 1983.

The Half-Pay Officer; or, Memoirs of Charles Chanceley: A Novel. London: Printed for the author, by T. Bensley, and Sold by G.G.J. and J. Robinson, Paternoster Row, 1788.

Hamilton, Richard F. *The Social Misconstruction of Reality*. New Haven: Yale, 1996.

Hamilton, Thomas. *Annals of the Peninsular Campaigns: from MDCCCVIII to MDCCCXIV*. Edinburgh: W. Blackwood; London: T. Cadell, 1829.

Hamilton, Thomas. Letter from Thomas Hamilton to William Blackwood, 17 Nov 1826. National Library of Scotland, MS 4017, fol. 127.

Hamilton, Thomas. *The Youth and Manhood of Cyril Thornton*. Edinburgh: William Blackwood; and London: T. Cadell, 1827.

Hantke, Steffen and Agnieszka Soltysik Monnet, eds. *War Gothic in Literature and Culture*. New York: Routledge, 2016.

Harari, Yuval N. 'Armchairs, Coffee, and Authority: Eye-Witnesses and Flesh-Witnesses Speak about War, 1100–2000'. *The Journal of Military History* 74, no. 1 (January 2010): 53–78.

Harari, Yuval N. *The Ultimate Experience: Battlefield Revelations and the Making of Modern War Culture, 1450–2000*. Basingstoke: Palgrave Macmillan, 2008.

Hardt, Michael and Antonio Negri. *Multitude: War and Democracy in the Age of Empire*. New York: Penguin Press, 2004.

Harris, Jocelyn. *A Revolution Almost Beyond Expression: Jane Austen's* Persuasion. Newark: University of Delaware Press, 2007.

Hartman, Geoffrey. *The Fateful Question of Culture*. New York: Columbia University Press, 1997.

Hartman, Geoffrey. 'On Traumatic Knowledge and Literary Studies'. *New Literary History* 26, no. 3 (1995): 537–63.

Hartung, Heike. *Ageing, Gender, and Illness in Anglophone Literature: Narrating Age in the Bildungsroman*. New York: Routledge, 2016.

Harvey, Arnold D. *Collision of Empires: Britain in Three World Wars, 1793–1945*. London: Hambledon Press, 1992.

Haslam, Jonathan. *No Virtue Like Necessity: Realist Thought in International Relations Since Machiavelli*. New Haven: Yale University Press, 2002.

Heilbron, Johan. Lars Magnusson, and Björn Wittrock, eds, *The Rise of the Social Sciences and the Formation of Modernity*. Dordrecht: Kluwer Academic Publishers, 1998.

Herman, Judith. *Trauma and Recovery*. New York: Basic Books, 1997.

Heuser, Beatrice. *Evolution of Strategy: Thinking War from Antiquity to the Present*. Cambridge: Cambridge University Press, 2010.

Heuser, Beatrice. *Strategy Before Clausewitz: Linking Warfare and Statecraft, 1400–1830*. Abingdon: Routledge, 2018.

Hilgers, Philipp von. *War Games: A History of War on Paper*. Translated by Ross Benjamin. Cambridge, MA: MIT Press, 2012.

Hirst, Paul. *Space and Power: Politics, War and Architecture*. Cambridge: Polity, 2005.

The History of the Seven Years' War in Germany, by Generals Lloyd and Tempelhoff; with Observations and Maxims Extracted from the Treatise of Great Military Operations of General Jomini. Translated from the German and French by C H Smith. London, 1808.

Holmes, John and Sharon Ruston, eds. *The Routledge Research Companion to Nineteenth-Century British Literature and Science*. New York: Routledge, 2017.

Houlding, John. *Fit for Service: The Training of the British Army, 1715–95*. Oxford: Oxford University Press, 1981.

Hume, Leonard J. *Bentham and Bureaucracy*. Cambridge: Cambridge University Press, 2004.

Hunt, Alastair and Matthias Rudolf, eds. *Romanticism and Biopolitics, Romantic Circles Praxis Series* (December 2012). https://romantic-circles.org/praxis/biopolitics/HTML/praxis.2012.hunt-rudolf.html. Accessed 15 April 2022.

Huntington, Samuel P. *The Soldier and the State: The Theory and Politics of Civil-Military Relations*. Cambridge, MA: Harvard University Press, 1957.

Hynes, Samuel. *On War and Writing*. Chicago: University of Chicago Press, 2018.

An Impartial History of the Late Glorious War, from it's Commencement to it's Conclusion [sic]; Containing an Exact Account of the Battles and Sea Engagements; Together with Other Remarkable Transactions, in Europe, Asia, Africa, and America: with the Characters of those Wise and Upright Statesmen, who Plann'd, and the Illustrious Heroes, by Whose Courage and Conduct, Together with the Unparallell'd Bravery of our Land and Sea Forces, Great-Britain Obtained a Series of Victories, Scarcely Equalled in the Annals of This, or Any Other Nation. With Remarks on the Peace, the State of Parties when it was Concluded, and An Account of the Inhabitants, Extent, Product, Trade and Importance, of the Places Ceded to Great-Britain. Manchester: Printed by R. Whitworth, 1764.

Jackson, Robert. *A Sketch of the History and Cure of Febrile Diseases; More Particularly as they Appear in the West-Indies Among the Soldiers of the British Army*. Stockton: Printed and Sold by T. and H. Eeles; Sold Also by R. Fenner, Paternoster Row, London, 1817.

Jackson, Robert. *A Systematic View of the Formation, Discipline and Economy of Armies. By the Late Robert Jackson, M.D., Inspector General of Army-Hospital. The Third Edition, Revised, with a Memoir of His Life and Services, Drawn up From His Own Papers, and the Communication of His Survivors*. 3rd edition. London: Parker, Furnivall, and Parker, Military Library, Whitehall, 1845.

Jackson, Robert. *A Treatise on the Fevers of Jamaica with Observations on the Intermittent Fever of America; and an Appendix Containing Some Hints on the Means of Preserving the Health of Soldiers in Hot Climates*. London: Printed for J. Murray, No. 32, Fleet-Street, 1791.

Jackson, Robert. *An Outline for the Political Organization and Moral Training of the Human Race*. Stockton, CA: Printed for the Author, by W. Robinson, 1823.

Jackson, Robert. *An Outline of the History and Cure of Fever, Epidemic and Contagious; More Especially of Jails, Ships, and Hospital: The Concentrated Endemic, Vulgarly the Yellow Fever of the West Indies. To Which is Added an Explanation of the Principles of Military Discipline and Economy; With a Scheme of Medical Arrangement for Armies*. Edinburgh: Printed for Mundell & Son; – and for T. N. Longman, and Murray & Highley, London, 1798.

Jackson, Robert. *A Systematic View of the Formation, Discipline, and Economy of Armies*. London: Printed for John Stockdale, 1804.

Jacob, Frank and Gilmar Visoni-Alonzo. *The Military Revolution in Early Modern Europe: A Revision*. London: Palgrave Macmillan, 2016.

Jameson, Fredric. *An American Utopia: Dual Power and the Universal Army*, edited by Slavoj Zizek. New York: Verso Books, 2016.

Jameson, Fredric. *The Antinomies of Realism*. London: Verso, 2013.

Jameson, Fredric. *The Political Unconscious: Narrative as a Socially Symbolic Act*. London: Routledge, 1983.

Jameson, Fredric. 'War and Representation'. *PMLA* 125, no. 5 (2009), 1532–47.

Jarry, Francis. *Instructions Concerning the Duties of Light Infantry in the Field. By General Jarry, Commandant of the Royal Military College at High Wycombe. By Command of His Royal Highness, Field-Marshal, The Duke of York, Commander in Chief*. London: Printed by Cox, Son, and Baylis, No. 75, Great Queen Street, Lincoln's-Inn-Fields. For A. Dulau and Co., Soho-Square, 1803.

Jenks, Timothy. *Naval Engagements: Patriotism, Cultural Politics, and the Royal Navy 1793–1815*. Oxford: Oxford University Press, 2006.

Joas, Hans and Wolfgang Knöbl. *War in Social Thought: Hobbes to the Present*. Princeton: Princeton University Press, 2012.

Johns, Adrian. 'Print and Public Science', in *The Cambridge History of Science: Volume 4: Eighteenth-Century Science*, edited by Roy Porter, 536–60. Cambridge: Cambridge University Press, 2008.

Johns, Adrian. 'The Piratical Enlightenment', in *This Is Enlightenment*, edited by Clifford Siskin and William Warner, 301–20. Chicago: University of Chicago Press, 2010.

Johnson, Kenneth. 'Romantic Anti-Jacobins or Anti-Jacobin Romantics?' *Romanticism on the Net* 15 (1999), https://doi.org/10.7202/005862ar. Accessed 15 April 2022.

Jomini, Henri-Antoine. *Summary of the Art of War, or a New Analytical Compend of the Principal Combinations of Strategy, of Grand Tactics and of Military Policy*. Translated by O. F. Winship and E E. McLean. New York: Published for the Proprietors, by G. P. Putnam & Co., 10 Park Place, 1854.

Jones, Vivien. 'Reading for England: Austen, Taste and Female Patriotism'. *European Romantic Review*, 16 (2005): 221–30.

Jordheim, Helge. 'The Present of Enlightenment: Temporality and Mediation in Kant, Foucault and Jean Paul', in *This Is Enlightenment*, edited by Clifford Siskin and William Warner, 189–208. Chicago: University of Chicago Press, 2010.

Jorgensen, Paul A. *Shakespeare's Military World*. Berkeley: University of Chicago Press, 1956.

Kang, Minsoo. *Sublime Dreams of Living Machines: The Automaton in the European Imagination*. Cambridge, MA: Harvard University Press, 2011.

Kasmer, Lisa, ed. *Traumatic Tales: British Nationhood and National Trauma in Nineteenth-Century Literature*. New York: Routledge, 2017.

Kelly, Catherine. *War and the Militarization of British Army Medicine, 1793–1830*. London: Pickering and Chatto, 2011.

Kelly, Gary. *English Fiction of the Romantic Period, 1789–1830*. New York: Longman, 1989.

King, Ros. '"The Disciplines of War": Elizabethan War Manuals and Shakespeare's Tragicomic Vision', in *Shakespeare and War*, edited by Ros King and Paul J. C. M. Franssen, 15–29. Basingstoke: Palgrave Macmillan, 2008.

King, Ros and Paul J. C. M. Franssen. 'War and Shakespearean Dramaturgy', in *Shakespeare and War*, edited by Ros King and Paul J. C. M. Franssen, 1–11. Basingstoke: Palgrave Macmillan, 2008.

Kittler, Friedrich A. *Discourse Networks 1800/1900*. Stanford: Stanford University Press, 1990.

Kittler, Friedrich A. *Optical Media: Berlin Lectures 1999*. Translated by Anthony Enns. Cambridge: Polity Press, 2010.

Kittler, Friedrich A. 'Technologies of Writing: Interview with Friedrich A. Kittler', interviewed by Matthew Griffin and Susanne Herrmann. *New Literary History* 27, no. 4 (1996): 731–742.

Kittler, Friedrich A. 'The History of Communication Media'. *CTheory* (1996). https://journals.uvic.ca/index.php/ctheory/article/view/14325/5101. Accessed 24 June 2019.

Kittler, Friedrich A. *The Truth of the Technological World: Essays on the Genealogy of Presence*. Translated by Erik Butler. Stanford: Stanford University Press, 2014.

Klancher, Jon P. *The Making of English Reading Audiences, 1790–1832*. Madison: University of Wisconsin Press, 1987.

Kollias, Hector. 'Taking Sides: Jacques Rancière and Agonistic Literature'. *Paragraph* 30, no. 2 (2007): 82–97.

Koselleck, Reinhart. *Futures Past: On the Semantics of Historical Time*, translated and introduction by Keith Tribe. New York: Columbia University Press, 2004.

Koselleck, Reinhart. *The Practice of Conceptual History: Timing History, Spacing Concepts*. Translated by Todd Samuel Presner et al. Stanford: Stanford University Press, 2002.

Kronick, David A. *A History of Scientific and Technical Periodicals: The Origins and Development of the Scientific and Technological Press, 1665–1790*. Metuchen: Scarecrow Press, 1962.

Lacy, Mark. *Security, Technology and Global Politics: Thinking with Virilio*. New York: Routledge, 2014.

Langan, Celeste, and Maureen N. McLane. 'The Medium of Romantic Poetry', in *The Cambridge Companion to British Romantic Poetry*, edited by James Chandler and Maureen N. McLane, 239–62. Cambridge: Cambridge University Press, 2008.

Langford, Paul. *A Polite and Commercial People: England 1727–1783*. Oxford: Clarendon Press, 1989.

Langins, Janis. *Conserving the Enlightenment: French Military Engineering from Vauban to the Revolution*. Cambridge, MA: MIT Press, 2004.

Langsam, Gert Geoffrey. *Martial Books and Tudor Verse*. New York: King's Crown Press, 1951.

Latané, David E. *William Maginn and the British Press: A Critical Biography*. New York: Routledge, 2016.

Lawrence, David R. *The Complete Soldier: Military Books and Military Culture in Early Stuart England, 1603–1645*. Leiden: Brill, 2009.

Lawrence, Philip K. 'Enlightenment, Modernity and War'. *History of the Human Sciences* 12, no. 1 (1999): 3–25.

Leckie, Gould Francis. *An Historical Survey of the Foreign Affairs of Great Britain for the Years 1808, 1809, 1810: With a View to Explain the Causes of the Disasters of the Late and Present Wars*. London: Printed by D. M. Shury, Berwick Street, Soho; and Sold by E. Lloyd, Harley Street, Cavendish Square, 1810.

Lee, Michael Parrish. *The Food Plot in the Nineteenth-Century British Novel*. London: Palgrave Macmillan, 2016.

Lemke, Thomas. 'Beyond Foucault: From Biopolitics to the Government of Life', in *Governmentality: Current Issues and Future Challenges*, edited by Ulrich Bröckling, Susanne Krasmann, and Thomas Lemke, 165–84. New York: Routledge, 2010.

Lemke, Thomas. *Biopolitics: An Advanced Introduction*. Translated by Eric Frederick Trump. New York: New York University Press, 2011.

Lemke, Thomas. *Foucault, Governmentality, and Critique*. London: Routledge, 2012.

Lemke, Thomas. 'Foucault, Governmentality, and Critique', paper presented at *Rethinking Marxism Conference*, University of Amherst (MA), 21–24 September 2000.

Lenoir, Tim and Luke Caldwell. *The Military-Entertainment Complex*. Cambridge, MA: Harvard University Press, 2018.

Levi, Neil. 'Carl Schmitt and the Question of the Aesthetic'. *New German Critique*, 34, no. 2 (2007): 27–43.

Leys, Ruth. *Trauma: A Genealogy*. Chicago: University of Chicago Press, 2000.

Lincoln, Andrew. 'The Culture of War and Civil Society in the Reigns of William III and Anne'. *Eighteenth-Century Studies* 44, no. 4 (2011): 455–74.

Lincoln, Andrew. 'War and the Culture of Politeness: The Case of *The Tatler* and *The Spectator*'. *Eighteenth-Century Life* 36, no. 2 (2012): 60–79.

Lindsay, Colin. *Extracts from Colonel Tempelhoffe's History of the Seven Years War: His Remarks on General Lloyd: On the Subsistence of Armies; and on the March of Convoys. Also a Treatise on Winter Posts. To Which is Added a Narrative of Events at St. Lucie and Gibralter, and of John Duke of Marlborough's March to the Danube, with the Causes and Consequences of that Measure. By the Honourable Colin Lindsay, Lieutenant Colonel of the 46th Regiment. In Two Volumes*. London: Printed for T. Cadell, in the Strand, 1793.

Liu, Alan. 'The New Historicism and the Work of Mourning'. *Studies in Romanticism* 35, no. 4 (1996): 553–62.

Liu, Alan. *Wordsworth: The Sense of History*. Stanford: Stanford University Press, 1989.

Lloyd, David and Paul Thomas. *Culture and the State*. New York: Routledge, 1998.

Lloyd, Henry. *The History of the Late War in Germany; Between the King of Prussia, and the Empress of Germany and Her Allies*, Vol. I. London: printed for the author; and sold by R. Horsfield, in Ludgate Street; L. Hawes and Co. in Pater-Noster Row; J. Dodsley, in Pall Mall; J. Walter, Charing Cross; T. Davies, in Covent Garden; W. Shropshire, New Bond-Street; and E. Easton, at Salisbury, 1766.

Lloyd, Henry. *Continuation of the History of the Late War in Germany, between the King of Prussia, and the Empress of Germany and Her Allies. Illustrated with a Number of Maps and Plans*, Vol. I, Part ii. London: printed for the author, and sold by S. Hooper, the Corner of May's Buildings, St. Martin's Lane, 1781.

Lloyd, Henry. *The History of the Late War in Germany, between the King of Prussia, and the Empress of Germany and Her Allies: Containing the Campaigns of 1758 and 1759*, Vol. II. London: printed for T. and J. Egerton, at the military library, Whitehall 1790.

Lloyd, Henry. *A Political and Military Rhapsody, on the Invasion and Defence of Great Britain and Ireland. Illustrated with Three Copper-plates. By the Late General Lloyd. To Which is Annexed, a Short Account of the Author, and a Supplement by the Editor*. London: Sold by Debret, Piccadilly; Sewell, Cornhill; Clark, Lincoln's Inn; and Mayler, Bath, 1792.

Luckhurst, Roger. *The Trauma Question*. New York: Routledge, 2008.

Lukács, Georg. *The Historical Novel*. Translated by Hannah and Stanley Mitchell. Boston: Beacon Press, 1963.

Lynn, John. *Battle: A History of Combat and Culture from Ancient Greece to Modern America*. New York: Westview Press, 2003.

Lynn, John. 'The Treatment of Military Subjects in Diderot's *Encyclopedie*'. *The Journal of Military History* 65, no. 1 (2001): 131–65.

MacDonald, John. *Instructions for the Conduct of Infantry on Actual Service.* London: Printed for T. Egerton, Military Library, Whitehall, 1807.

MacDonald, Michael. 'Martial McLuhan I: Framing Information Warfare'. *Enculturation* 12 (December 2011). http://enculturation.net/martial-mcluhan. Accessed 24 June 2019.

MacKay, Marina. *Ian Watt: The Novel and the Wartime Critic.* Oxford: Oxford University Press, 2018.

Maginn, William. *The Military Sketch-book: Reminiscences of Seventeen Years in the Service Abroad and at Home.* London: Henry Colburn, 1827.

Maginn, William. *Tales of Military Life. By the Author of 'The Military Sketch Book'*, 3 vols. London: Henry Colburn, 1829.

Magrath, Richard Nicholson. *An Historical Sketch of the Progress of the Art of War.* Dublin: William Curry, Jun. and Company, 9 Upper Sackville-Street, 1838.

Maïzeroy, Paul-Gédéon Joly de. *Théorie de la Guerre, Où l'on Expose las Constitution et de la Cavalerie, leurs Manoeuvres Élémentaires, avec l'Application des Principes à la Grande Tactique, Suivie de Démonstrations sur la Stratégique.* Lausanne: Aux Dépens de La Société, 1777.

Makdisi, Saree. *Romantic Imperialism: Universal Empire and the Culture of Modernity.* Cambridge: Cambridge University Press, 1998.

Mansfield, Nick. 'Destroyer and Bearer of Worlds: The Aesthetic Doubleness of War', in *Tracing War in British Enlightenment and Romantic Culture*, edited by Neil Ramsey and Gillian Russell, 188–203. Basingstoke: Palgrave Macmillan, 2015.

Mansfield, Nick. *Theorizing War: From Hobbes to Badiou.* New York: Palgrave Macmillan, 2008.

Margiotta, Franklin D., ed. *Brassey's Encyclopedia of Military History and Biography.* Washington: Brassey's, 2000.

Martin, John Levi. 'The Objective and Subjective Rationalization of War'. *Theory and Society* 34 (2005): 229–75.

Maxwell, Richard. 'The Historical Novel', in *The Cambridge Companion to Fiction in the Romantic Period*, edited by Richard Maxwell and Katie Trumpener, 65–89. Cambridge: Cambridge University Press, 2008.

McCormack, Matthew. *Embodying the Militia in Georgian England.* Oxford: Oxford University Press, 2015.

McLane, Maureen. *Romanticism and the Human Sciences: Poetry, Population, and the Discourse of the Species.* Cambridge: Cambridge University Press, 2000.

McLoughlin, Kate. *Authoring War: The Literary Representation of War from The Iliad to Iraq.* Oxford: Oxford University Press, 2011.

McLoughlin, Kate. *Veteran Poetics: British Literature in the Age of Mass Warfare, 1790–2015.* Cambridge: Cambridge University Press, 2018.

McLoughlin, Kate, ed. *The Cambridge Companion to War Writing.* Cambridge: Cambridge University Press, 2009.

McLuhan, Marshall. *Understanding Media: The Extensions of Man.* London: Routledge, 2001.

McNeill, William H. *The Pursuit of Power: Technology, Armed Force, and Society since A.D. 1000*. Chicago: University of Chicago Press, 1982.

Mee, Jon. *Romanticism, Enthusiasm, and Regulation: Poetics and the Policing of Culture in the Romantic Period*. Oxford: Oxford University Press, 2003.

Meek, Allen. *Biopolitical Media: Catastrophe, Immunity and Bare Life*. New York: Routledge, 2015.

Meek, Allen. *Trauma and Media: Theories, Histories, and Images*. New York: Routledge, 2010.

Meek, Allen. 'Trauma in the Digital Age', in *Trauma and Literature*, edited by J. Roger Kurtz, 167–80. Cambridge: Cambridge University Press, 2018.

Menke, Christoph. 'A Different Taste: Neither Autonomy Nor Mass Consumption', in *Cultural Transformations of the Public Sphere: Contemporary and Historical Perspectives*, edited by Bernd Fischer and May Mergenthaler, 183–202. Oxford: Peter Lang, 2015.

Menke, Christoph. 'Aesthetic Nature: Against Biology'. *The Yearbook of Comparative Literature* 58 (2012): 193–95.

Menke, Christoph. *Force: A Fundamental Concept of Aesthetic Anthropology*. Translated by Gerrit Jackson. New York: Fordham University Press, 2012.

Menke, Christoph. 'Force: Towards an Aesthetic Concept of Life'. *MLN* 125, no. 3 (2010): 552–70.

Menke, Christoph. 'Two Kinds of Practice: On the Relation between Social Discipline and the Aesthetics of Existence'. *Constellations* 10, no. 2 (2003): 199–210.

Mieszkowski, Jan. *Watching War*. Stanford: Stanford University Press, 2012.

Milchman, Alan and Alan Rosenberg. 'The Aesthetic and Ascetic Dimensions of an Ethics of Self-fashioning: Nietzsche and Foucault'. *Parrhesia* 2 (2007): 44–65.

The Military Cabinet; Being a Collection of Extracts from the Best Authors, Both Ancient and Modern; Interspersed with Occasional Remarks, and Arranged under Different Heads. The Whole Calculated to Convey Instruction in the Most Agreeable Manner, and to Give to Young Officers Correct Notions in Regard to Many Subjects Belonging to or Connected with the Military Profession. In Three Volumes. By Capt. T.H. Cooper, Half Pay 56th Regt. Infantry, Author of a Practical Guide for the Light Infantry Officer. London: Printed by R. Wilks, Chancery Lane, for T. Egerton, Military Library, Whitehall; Sherwood, Neely, & Jones, Paternoster-Row; and B. Crosby & Co. Stationer's Court, 1809.

Mills, Catherine. *Biopolitics*. New York: Routledge, 2018.

Minca, Claudio and Rory Rowan. *On Schmitt and Space*. Abingdon: Routledge, 2015.

Mitchell, Robert. *Experimental Life: Vitalism in Romantic Science and Literature*. Baltimore: Johns Hopkins University Press, 2013.

Mitchell, Robert. *Infectious Liberty: Biopolitics between Romanticism and Liberalism*. New York: Fordham University Press, 2021.

Moheau, Jean-Baptiste. *Recherches et Considerations sur la Population de la France, 1778. Public Avec Introduction et Table Analytique par Rene Gonnard.* Paris: Libraire Paul Geuthner, 13, Rue Jacob, 13, 1912.

Monthly Military Companion, 1801–02.

Monthly Review, or Literary Journal, 1802–11.

Moorman, Mary. *William Wordsworth: A Biography. Vol. 1. The Early Years, 1770–1803.* Oxford: The Clarendon Press, 1957.

Moretti, Franco. *Distant Reading.* London: Verso, 2013.

Moretti, Franco. *The Way of the World: The Bildungsroman in European Culture.* Translated by Albert Sbragia. London: Verso, 2000.

Morley, Edith J., ed. *Henry Crabb Robinson on Books and their Writers,* 3 vols. London: Dent, 1938.

Morrison, Robert and Daniel Sanjiv Roberts. '"A Character So Various, and Yet So Indisputably its own": A Passage to *Blackwood's Edinburgh Magazine*', in *Romanticism and Blackwood's Magazine: 'An Unprecedented Phenomenon*', edited by Robert Morrison and Daniel Sanjiv Roberts, 1–19. Basingstoke: Palgrave Macmillan, 2013.

Muir, Rory. *Britain and the Defeat of Napoleon, 1807–1815.* New Haven: Yale University Press, 1996.

Musto, Marcello, ed. *Karl Marx's Grundrisse: Foundations of the Critique of Political Economy 150 Years Later,* foreword by Eric Hobsbawm. Abingdon: Routledge, 2008.

Nall, Catherine. *Reading and War in Fifteenth-Century England: From Lydgate to Malory.* Cambridge: D. S. Brewer, 2012.

Naval Chronicle, 1799.

Nealon, Jeffrey T. *Foucault Beyond Foucault: Power and Its Intensifications Since 1984.* Stanford: Stanford University Press, 2008.

Nealon, Jeffrey T. 'The Archaeology of Biopower: From Plant to Animal Life in *The Order of Things*', in *Biopower: Foucault and Beyond,* edited by Vernon W. Cisney and Nicolae Morar 138–57. Chicago: The University of Chicago Press, 2016.

Neocleous, Mark. '"O Effeminacy! Effeminacy!": War, Masculinity and the Myth of Liberal Peace'. *European Journal of International Relations* 19, no. 1 (2013): 93–113.

Neocleous, Mark. *War Power, Police Power.* Edinburgh: Edinburgh University Press, 2014,

Neocleous, Mark. 'Perpetual War, or "War and War Again": Schmitt, Foucault, Fascism'. *Philosophy Social Criticism* 22, no. 2 (1996): 47–66.

New Monthly Magazine, 1829.

Nielson, Caroline. 'Disability, Fraud and Medical Experience', in *Britain's Soldiers: Rethinking War and Society, 1715–1815,* edited by Kevin Linch and Matthew McCormack, 183–201. Liverpool: Liverpool University Press, 2014.

Nolan, Cathal J. *Wars of the Age of Louis XIV, 1650–1715: An Encyclopedia of Global Warfare.* Westport: Greenwood Press, 2008.

Norris, Margot. *Writing War in the Twentieth Century*. Charlottesville: University Press of Virginia, 2000.

O'Quinn, Daniel. 'Invalid Elegy and Gothic Pageantry: André, Seward and the Loss of the American War', in *Tracing War in British Enlightenment and Romantic Culture*, edited by Neil Ramsey and Gillian Russell, 37–60. Basingstoke: Palgrave Macmillan, 2015.

Observations on the Character and Present State of the Military Force of Great Britain. London: Published by J. Hatchard, Piccadilly; and by A. Constable & Co. Edinburgh, 1806.

Odysseos, Louiza and Fabio Petito. 'Introduction: The International Political Thought of Carl Schmitt', in *The International Political Thought of Carl Schmitt: Terror, Liberal War and the Crisis of Global Order*, edited by Louiza Odysseos and Fabio Petito, 1–17. Abingdon: Routledge, 2007.

Ong, Walter. *Orality and Literacy: The Technologizing of the Word*. London: Routledge, 2002.

Östling, Johan, David Larsson Heidenblad, Erling Sandmo, Anna Nilsson Hammar and Kari Nordberg. 'The History of Knowledge and the Circulation of Knowledge: An Introduction', in *Circulation of Knowledge: Explorations in the History of Knowledge*, edited by Johan Östling, Erling Sandmo, David Larsson Heidenblad, Anna Nilsson Hammar and Kari Nordberg, 9–33. Lund: Nordic Academic Press, 2018.

Owens, Patricia. *Between War and Politics: International Relations and the Thought of Hannah Arendt*. Oxford: Oxford University Press, 2007.

Oxford English Dictionary. Oxford: Oxford University Press, 2019.

Packham, Catherine. *Eighteenth-Century Vitalism: Bodies, Culture, Politics*. Basingstoke: Palgrave Macmillan, 2012.

Page, Anthony. *Britain and the Seventy Years War, 1744–1815: Enlightenment, Revolution and Empire*. London: Palgrave Macmillan, 2014.

Page, Anthony. 'The Seventy Years War, 1744–1815, and Britain's Fiscal-Naval State'. *War and Society* 34, no. 3 (2015): 162–86.

Paltrinieri, Luca. 'L'Emergence de la Population comme Objet de Gouvernement au XVIIIeme Siècle, en France'. *Colloque International Jeunes Chercheurs en Démographie*, University of Paris X, 17–18 November 2010.

Paret, Peter. 'The Genesis of On War', in Carl Von Clausewitz, *On War*, edited and translated by Michael Howard and Peter Paret, 3–25. Princeton: Princeton University Press, 1984.

Paris, Michael. *Warrior Nation: Images of War in British Popular Culture, 1850–2000*. London: Reaktion Books, 2000.

Parker, Geoffrey. 'The "Military Revolution," 1560–1660--a Myth?'. *The Journal of Modern History* 48, no. 2 (1976): 195–214.

Parker, Geoffrey. *The Military Revolution: Military Innovation and the Rise of the West, 1500–1800*, 2nd edition. Cambridge: Cambridge University Press, 1996.

Parkes, Simon. *Home from the Wars: The Romantic Revenant-Veteran of the 1790s*. PhD diss., University of Warwick, 2009.

Parrott, David. *Business of War: Military Enterprise and Military Revolution in Early Modern Europe.* Cambridge: Cambridge University Press, 2015.

Pasley, Charles W. *Essay on the Military Policy and Instructions of the British Empire.* London: Printed by D. N. Shury, Berwick Street, Soho; For Edmund Lloyd, Harley Street, 1810.

Pasley, Charles W. *The Military Policy and Institutions of the British Empire: An Essay by C. W. Pasley, Captain in the Corps of Royal Engineers,* edited by B. R. Ward, 5th edition. London: Printed for the Organisation Society by William Clowes and Sons, Limited,31, Haymarket, London, S.W., 1914.

Patton, Philip. *The Natural Defence of an Insular Empire, Earnestly Recommended; with a Sketch of a Plan, to Attach Real Seamen to the Service of Their Country.* Southampton: Printed by T. Nealon, 22, High-Street; Sold by J. Hatchard, Bookseller to Her Majesty, Piccadilly; and by Mottley, Harrison, and Miller, Portsmouth, 1810.

Pfau, Thomas. *Romantic Moods: Paranoia, Trauma, and Melancholy, 1790–1840.* Baltimore: Johns Hopkins University Press, 2005.

Pichichero, Christy. *Battles of The Self: War and Subjectivity in Early Modern France.* PhD diss., Stanford University, 2008.

Pichichero, Christy. *The Military Enlightenment: War and Culture in the French Empire from Louis XIV to Napoleon.* Ithaca: Cornell University Press, 2017.

Plassart, Anna. *The Scottish Enlightenment and the French Revolution.* Cambridge: Cambridge University Press, 2015.

Pocock, J. G. A. *The Machiavellian Moment Florentine Political Thought and the Atlantic Republican Tradition.* 2nd ed. Princeton: Princeton University Press, 2003.

Poovey, Mary. *Making a Social Body: British Cultural Formation, 1830–1864.* Chicago: University of Chicago Press, 1995.

Powel, Brieg. 'The Soldier's Tale: Problematising Foucault's Military Foundations'. *Review of International Studies* 43, no. 5 (2017), 833–54.

Priestly, Joseph. *Hartley's Theory of the Human Mind on the Principles of the Association of Ideas; with Essay Relating to the Subject of It.* London: Printed for J. Johnson, No. 72, St. Paul's Church-Yard, 1775.

Prozorov, Sergei. *Agamben and Politics: A Critical Introduction.* Edinburgh: Edinburgh University Press, 2014.

Quarterly Review, 1811–28.

Ramsey, Neil. 'De Lancey's Tour: Military Barracks and the Endo-Colonization of England in the 1790s'. *English Language Notes* 54, no. 1 (2016): 27–41.

Ramsey, Neil. 'Exhibiting Discipline: Military Science and the Naval and Military Library and Museum', in *Tracing War in British Enlightenment and Romantic Culture,* edited by Neil Ramsey and Gillian Russell, 113–31. Basingstoke: Palgrave Macmillan, 2015.

Ramsey, Neil. '"Making My Self a Soldier": The Role of Soldiering in the Autobiographical Work of John Clare'. *Romanticism* 13, no. 2 (2007): 177–88.

Ramsey, Neil. *The Military Memoir and Romantic Literary Culture, 1780–1835.* Farnham: Ashgate, 2011.

Ramsey, Neil. '"A Question of Literature": The Romantic Writer and Modern Wars of Empire', in *Stories of Empire: Narrative Strategies for the Legitimation of an Imperial World Order*, edited by Christa Knellwolf and Margarete Rubik, 49–68. Trier: Wissenschaftlicher Verlag Trier, 2009.

Rancière, Jacques. 'The Aesthetic Dimension: Aesthetics, Politics, Knowledge'. *Critical Inquiry* 36, no. 1 (Autumn 2009): 1–19.

Rancière, Jacques. 'The Aesthetic Revolution and Its Outcomes'. *New Left Review* 14 (2002), 133–51.

Rancière, Jacques. *The Aesthetic Unconscious*. Translated by Debra Keates and James Swenson. Cambridge: Polity, 2009.

Rancière, Jacques. *Aesthetics and its Discontents*. Translated by Steven Corcoran. Cambridge: Polity Press, 2009.

Rancière, Jacques. 'Aesthetics and Politics Revisited: An Interview with Jacques Rancière', interviewed by Gavin Arnall, Laura Gandolfi and Enea Zaramella, *Critical Inquiry* 38 (Winter 2012): 289–97.

Rancière, Jacques. *Aisthesis: Scenes from the Aesthetic Regime of Art. Translated by Zakir Paul.* London: Verso, 2013.

Rancière, Jacques. *Disagreement: Politics and Philosophy*. Translated by Julie Rose. Minneapolis: University of Minnesota Press, 2000.

Rancière, Jacques. *Dissensus: On Politics and Aesthetics*, edited and translated by Steven Corcoran. London: Continuum, 2010.

Rancière, Jacques. *The Emancipated Spectator*. Translated by Gregory Elliott. London: Verso, 2009.

Rancière, Jacques. *Figures of History*. Translated by Julie Rose. Cambridge: Polity, 2014.

Rancière, Jacques. *The Flesh of Words: The Politics of Writing*. Translated by Charlotte Mandell. Stanford: Stanford University Press, 2004.

Rancière, Jacques. 'From Politics to Aesthetics?' *Paragraph* 28, no. 1 (2005): 13–25.

Rancière, Jacques. *The Future of the Image*. Translated by Gregory Elliott. London: Verso, 2007.

Rancière, Jacques. 'Jacques Rancière and Indisciplinarity', interviewed by Marie-Aude Baronian and Mireille Rosello. Translated by Gregory Elliot, *Art and Research: A Journal of Ideas, Contexts and Methods* 2, no. 1 (2008), n. p.

Rancière, Jacques. *Mute Speech*. Translated by James Swenson, with an intro. by Gabriel Rockhill. New York: Columbia University Press, 2011.

Rancière, Jacques. *The Names of History: On the Poetics of Knowledge*. Translated by Hassan Melehy, foreword by Hayden White. Minneapolis: University of Minnesota Press, 1994.

Rancière, Jacques. *The Politics of Aesthetics: The Distribution of the Sensible*. Translated and introduction by Gabriel Rockhill, with an afterword by Slavoj Žižek. London: Continuum, 2004.

Rancière, Jacques. 'The Politics of Literature'. *SubStance* 33, no. 1 (2004): 10–24.

Rancière, Jacques. *The Politics of Literature*. Translated by Julie Rose. Cambridge: Polity, 2011.

Rancière, Jacques. 'The Reality Effect and the Politics of Fiction', Public Lecture at ICI Berlin. www.ici-berlin.org/events/jacques-ranciere/. Accessed 15 April 2022.

Rancière, Jacques. 'Thinking Between Disciplines: An Aesthetics of Knowledge'. Translated by Jon Roffe. *Parrhesia* 1 (2006): 1–12.

Rancière, Jacques. *On the Shores of Politics*. Translated by Liz Heron. London: Verso, 1995.

Randall, David. *Credibility in Elizabethan and Early Stuart Military News*. London: Routledge, 2015.

Ransom, John S. *Foucault's Discipline: The Politics of Subjectivity*. Durham: Duke University Press, 1997.

Rawson, Claude. 'War and the Epic Mania in England and France: Milton, Boileau Prior and English Mock-Heroic'. *The Review of English Studies* 64, no. 265 (2013): 433–53.

Redfield, Mark. *The Politics of Aesthetics: Nationalism, Gender, Romanticism*. Stanford: Stanford University Press, 2003.

Reid, Julian. *The Biopolitics of the War on Terror: Life Struggles, Liberal Modernity and the Defence of Logistical Societies*. Manchester: Manchester University Press, 2013.

Reid, Julian. 'Foucault on Clausewitz: Conceptualizing the Relationship Between War and Power'. *Alternatives* 28, no. 1 (2003): 1–28.

Reid, Julian. 'Life Struggles: War, Discipline and Biopolitics in the Thought of Michel Foucault', in *Foucault on Politics, Security and War*, edited by Michael Dillon and Andrew W. Neal, 65–92. Basingstoke: Palgrave, 2011.

Reid, Julian. 'Re-appropriating Clausewitz: The Neglected Dimensions of Counter-Strategic Thought', in *Classical Theory in International Relations*, edited by Beate Jahn, 277–95. Cambridge: Cambridge University Press, 2006.

Reide, Thomas. *The Staff Officer's Manual; in Which is Detailed the Duty of Brigade Majors and Aides de Camp, in Camp, Garrison, Cantonments, on the March, and in the Field; with a Preliminary Essay on the Education of Young Gentlemen intended for the Military Profession. By Brigade Major Thomas Reide, On the Staff of the London and Home District; Author of a Treatise on the Duty of Infantry Officers, Military Finance, &c. &c.* London: Printed for T. Egerton, Military Library, near Whitehall, 1806.

Reinert, Sophus A. '"One Will Make of Political Economy … What the Scholastics Have Done with Philosophy": Henry Lloyd and the Mathematization of Economics'. *History of Political Economy* 39, no. 4 (2007): 643–77.

Roberts, John. *Trauma and the Ontology of the Modern Subject: Historical Studies in Philosophy, Psychology, and Psychoanalysis*. New York: Routledge, 2018.

Roberts, Michael. *The Military Revolution, 1560–1660: An Inaugural Lecture Delivered before the Queen's University of Belfast*. Belfast: M. Boyd, 1956.

Robertson, John. *The Scottish Enlightenment and the Militia Issue*. Edinburgh: Donald, 1985.

Robertson, Lisa Ann. *The Embodied Imagination: British Romantic Cognitive Science*. PhD diss., University of Alberta, 2013.

Robinson, Henry Crabb. *Henry Crabb Robinson on Books and their Writers*, edited by Edith J. Morley, 3 vols. London: Dent, 1938.

Robinson, Henry Crabb. 'On the Spanish Revolution'. *The London Review* 2, no.4 (1809): 231–75.

Rockhill, Gabriel. 'Appendix I. Glossary of Technical Terms' in Jacques Rancière, *The Politics of Aesthetics: The Distribution of the Sensible*, intro. and trans. Gabriel Rockhill. New York: Continuum, 2004.

Rockhill, Gabriel. *Radical History and the Politics of Art*. New York: Columbia University Press, 2014.

Rockhill, Gabriel. 'The Silent Revolution'. *SubStance* 33, no. 1 (2004): 54–76.

Rothenberg, Gunther E. *The Art of Warfare in the Age of Napoleon*. Bloomington: Indiana University Press, 1980.

Rusnock, Andrea. 'Biopolitics: Political Arithmetic in the Enlightenment', in *The Sciences in Enlightened Europe*, edited by William Clark, Jan Golinski and Simon Schaffer, 49–68. Chicago: University of Chicago Press, 1999.

Russell, Gillian. *The Theatres of War: Performance, Politics and Society, 1793–1815.* Oxford: Clarendon Press, 1995.

Ryan, Dermot. *Technologies of Empire: Writing, Imagination, and the Making of Imperial Networks, 1750–1820*. Newark, University of Delaware Press, 2013.

Saakwa-Mante, Norris D. 'Jackson, Robert (bap. 1750, d. 1827), Military Surgeon and Medical Writer'. *Oxford Dictionary of National Biography*. 23 September 2004. https://doi.org/10.1093/ref:odnb/14547. Accessed 5 August 2021.

Sarafianos, Aris. 'Pain, Labor, and the Sublime: Medical Gymnastics and Burke's Aesthetics'. *Representations* 91, no. 1 (2005): 58–83.

Satia, Priya, *Empire of Guns: The Violent Making of the Industrial* Revolution. New York: Penguin, 2018.

Saxe, Maurice, Comte de. *Reveries, or Memoirs Upon the Art of War by Field-Marshal Count Saxe. Illustrated with Copper-plates. To Which are Added Some Original Letters, Upon Various Military Subjects, Wrote by the Count to the Late King of Poland, and M. de Folard, Which Were Never Before Made publick: Together with His Reflections Upon the Propagation of the Human Species. Translated from the French*. London: Printed for J. Nourse, at the Lamb, opposite Katherine-street, in the Strand, 1757.

Scarry, Elaine. *Body in Pain: The Making and Unmaking of the World*. Oxford: Oxford University Press, 1985.

Scheipers, Sibylle. *On Small War: Carl von Clausewitz and People's War*. Oxford: Oxford University Press, 2018.

Schmitt, Carl. *The Theory of the Partisan: A Commentary/Remark on the Concept of the Political*. Translated by Alfred C. Goodson. Berlin: Duncker & Humblot, 1963.

Schmitt, Carl. *Land and Sea*. Translated and foreword by Simona Draghici. Washington DC: Plutarch Press, 1997.

Schmitt, Carl. *The Concept of the Political. Expanded Edition*. Translated and with introduction by George Schwab, with foreword by Tracey B. Strong and notes by Leo Strauss. Chicago: University of Chicago Press, 2007.

Schmitt, Carl. *The Nomos of the Earth in the International Law of the Jus Publicum Europaeum*. Translated and annotated by G. L. Ulmen. New York: Telos Press Publishing, 2006.

Schoenfield, Mark. *British Periodicals and Romantic Identity: The Literary 'Lower Empire'*. Basingstoke: Palgrave Macmillan, 2009.

Schroeder, Paul. *The Transformation of European Politics, 1763–1848*. New York: Clarendon Press, 1994.

Schuurman, Paul. 'What-If at Waterloo. Carl von Clausewitz's Use of Historical Counterfactuals in his History of the Campaign of 1815', *Journal of Strategic Studies* 40, no. 7 (2017): 1–23.

Scott, Hamish. 'The Seven Years' War and Europe's Ancien Régime'. *War in History* 18, no. 4 (2011): 419–55.

Scott, Sir Walter. *Waverley; or, 'Tis Sixty Years Since*. 3 vols, 2nd ed. Edinburgh: Printed by James Ballantyne and Co. for Archibald Constable and Co.; and London: Longman, Hurst, Rees, Orme, and Brown, 1814.

Seltzer, Mark. 'Wound Culture: Trauma in the Pathological Public Sphere'. *October* 80 (Spring 1997): 3–26.

Shaw, Philip. 'Introduction', in *Romantic Wars: Studies in Culture and Conflict, 1793–1822*, edited by Phil Shaw, 1–12. Aldershot: Ashgate, 2000.

Shaw, Philip. 'Longing for Home: Robert Hamilton, Nostalgia and the Emotional Life of the Eighteenth-Century Soldier'. *Journal of Eighteenth-Century Studies* 39, no. 1 (2016): 25–40.

Shaw, Philip. *The Sublime*. London: Routledge, 2006.

Shaw, Philip. *Waterloo and the Romantic Imagination*. Basingstoke: Palgrave Macmillan, 2002.

Showalter, Dennis E. 'Information Capabilities and Military Revolutions: The Nineteenth-Century Experience'. *Journal of Strategic Studies* 27, no. 2 (2004): 220–42.

Shumway, David R. *Michel Foucault*. Boston: Twayne Publishers, 1989.

Shy, John. 'Jomini', in *Makers of Modern Strategy from Machiavelli to the Nuclear Age*, edited by Paret Peter, with contributions from Gordon A. Craig and Felix Gilbert, 143–85. Princeton: Princeton University Press, 1986.

Simpson, David. 'Virtual Culture', review essay of *The Fateful Question of Culture* by Geoffrey Hartman. *Modern Language Quarterly* 60, no. 2 (1999): 251–64.

Simpson, David. *Wordsworth, Commodification, and Social Concern: The Poetics of Modernity*. Cambridge: Cambridge University Press, 2009.

Siskin, Clifford. 'The Problem of Periodization: Enlightenment, Romanticism and the Fate of System', in *The Cambridge History of English Romantic Literature*, edited by James Chandler, 101–26. Cambridge: Cambridge University Press, 2009.

Siskin, Clifford. *System: The Shaping of Modern Knowledge*. Cambridge, MA: MIT Press, 2016.

Siskin, Clifford. *The Work of Writing: Literature and Social Change, 1700–1830*. Baltimore: Johns Hopkins University Press, 1998.

Siskin, Clifford and William Warner. 'This is Enlightenment: An Invitation in the Form of an Argument', in *This Is Enlightenment*, edited by Clifford Siskin and William Warner, 1–33. Chicago: University of Chicago Press, 2010.

Siskin, Clifford and William Warner, eds. *This Is Enlightenment*. Chicago: University of Chicago Press, 2010.

Slauter, Will. 'Periodicals and the Commercialization of Information in the Early Modern Era', in *Information: A Historical Companion*, edited by Ann Blair, Paul Duguid, Anja-Silvia Goeing and Anthony Grafton, 128–51. Princeton: Princeton University Press, 2021.

Smith, Adam. *An Inquiry into the Nature and Causes of the Wealth of Nations. By Adam Smith, LL.D and F.R.S. Formerly Professor of Moral Philosophy in the University of Glasgow.* 3 vols. Dublin: Printed for Messrs. Whitestone, Chamberlaine, W. Watson, Potts, S. Watson, Holy, Williams, W. Colles, Wilson, Armitage, Walker, Moncrieffe, Jenkin, Gilbert, Cross, Mills, Hallhead, Faulkner, Hillary and J. Colles, 1776.

Smith, Philip. 'Meaning and Military Power: Moving on From Foucault'. *Journal of Power* 1, no.3 (2008): 275–93.

Smith, William. *An Historical Account of the Expedition Against the Ohio Indians, in the Year 1764. Under the Command of Henry Bouquet, Esq: Colonel of Foot, and Now Brigadier General in America. Including his Transactions with the Indians, Relative to the Delivery of their Prisoners, and the Preliminaries of Peace. With an Introductory Account of the Preceeding Campaign, and Battle at Bushy-Run. To Which are Annexed Military Papers, Containing Reflections on the War with the Savages; a Method of Forming Frontier Settlements; Some Account of the Indian Country, with a List of Nations, Fighting Men, Towns, Distances and Different Routs. The Whole Illustrated with a Map and Copper-plates. Published from Authentic Documents, by a Lover of His Country.* Philadelphia: Printed and Sold by William Bradford, at the London Coffee-House, the corner of Market and Front Streets, 1765.

Soldiers' Pocket Magazine, 1798.

Somogyi, Nick de. *Shakespeare's Theatre of War.* Aldershot: Ashgate, 1998.

Sonenscher, Michael. *Before the Deluge: Public Debt, Inequality, and the Intellectual Origins of the French Revolution.* Princeton: Princeton University Press, 2009.

Southam, Brian. *Jane Austen and the Navy.* London: National Maritime Museum Publishing, 2003.

Southey, Robert. 'Review of *Essay on the Military Policy and Institutions of the British Empire*'. *The Quarterly Review* 5 (1811): 403–37.

Speelman, Patrick. *Henry Lloyd and the Military Enlightenment of Eighteenth-Century Europe.* Westport: Greenwood Press, 2002.

Speelman, Patrick. *War, Society and Enlightenment: The Works of General Lloyd.* Leiden: Brill, 2005.

St Clair, William. *The Reading Nation in the Romantic Period.* Cambridge: Cambridge University Press, 2004.

Stahl, Roger. *Militainment, Inc.: War, Media, and Popular Culture.* New York: Routledge, 2010.

Starkey, Armstrong. *War in the Age of Enlightenment, 1700–1789.* London: Greenwood Publishing Group, 2003.

Steffens, Karolyn. 'Modernity as the Cultural Crucible of Trauma', in *Trauma and Literature*, edited by J. Roger Kurtz, 36–50. Cambridge: Cambridge University Press, 2018.

Sterling, Edward. *Views of Military Reform. By Edward Sterling, Esq. Formerly Captain in the 16th Regiment of Foot,* 2nd ed. London: Printed by C. Roworth, Bell Yard, Temple Bar. For T. Egerton, Military Library, Whitehall, 1811.

Stoddard, John. Letter to Charles Pasley, 1 September 1811, cited in 'Introduction' to Charles Pasley, *The Military Policy and Institutions of the British Empire,* edited and introduction by B. R. Ward, 5th ed. London: W. Clawes and Sons, 1914.

Strabone, Jeff. *Poetry and British Nationalisms in the Bardic Eighteenth Century: Imagined Antiquities.* Cham: Palgrave Macmillan, 2018.

Strachan, Hew. 'The Lost Meaning of Strategy'. *Survival* 47, no. 3 (2005), 33–54.

Strick, Simon. *American Dolorologies: Pain, Sentimentalism, Biopolitics.* Albany: State University of New York Press, 2014.

Summerfield, Stephen and Susan Law. *Sir John Moore and the Universal Soldier. Volume 1: The Man, The Commander and the Shorncliffe System of Training.* Godmanchester: Ken Trotman Publishing, 2016.

The Talisman: Or, Singular Adventures of an Old Officer; With its Consequences. Written by Himself. London: Printed for R. Dutton, No.45 Gracechurch St; J. Cawthorn, Catherine St.; Chapple, Pall-Mall; and T. Hurst, Paternoster Row; By John Abraham, Clement's Lane, 1804.

Tarizzo, Davide. *Life: A Modern Invention.* Translated by Mark William Epstein. Minneapolis: University of Minnesota Press, 2017.

Terry, Jennifer. *Attachments to War: Biomedical Logics and Violence in Twenty-First-Century America.* Durham: Duke University Press, 2017.

Teschke, Benno. *The Myth of 1648: Class, Geopolitics, and the Making of Modern International Relations.* London: Verso, 2009.

Thomas, Hugh. *The Story of Sandhurst.* London: Hutchinson, 1961.

Tichelaar, Tyler R. *The Gothic Wanderer: From Transgression to Redemption: Gothic Literature from 1794–Present.* London: Modern History Press, 2012.

Tilly, Charles. *Coercion, Capital, and European States, AD 990–1990.* Cambridge, MA: Basil Blackwell, 1990.

Toremans, Tom. 'Deconstruction: Trauma Inscribed in Language', in *Trauma and Literature,* edited by J. Roger Kurtz, 51–65. Cambridge: Cambridge University Press, 2018.

Trumpener, Katie. *Bardic Nationalism: The Romantic Novel and the British Empire.* Princeton: Princeton University Press, 1997.

Turenne, Henri de La Tour d'Auvergne, Vicomte de. *Military Memoirs and Maxims of Marshal Turenne. Interspersed with Others, Taken from the Best Authors and Observations, with Remarks. By A. Williamson, Brigadier-General.* Dublin: Re-printed by and for George Faulkner, in Essex Street, 1740.

Turpin, Comte de Crissé. *An Essay on the Art of War. Translated from the French of Count Turpin, By Captain Joseph Otway. In Two Volumes.* London: Printed by A. Hamilton, for W. Johnston in Ludgate-Street. 1761.

United Service Journal, 1829.

Ussishkin, Daniel. Morale: *A Modern British History*. New York: Oxford University Press, 2017,

Urban, Mark. *Rifles: Six Years with Wellington's Legendary Sharpshooters*. London: Faber and Faber, 2003.

Van de Kolk, Bessel. *The Body Keeps the Score: Brain, Mind, and Body in the Healing of Trauma*. New York: Penguin Books, 2015.

Vermeulen, Pieter. *Geoffrey Hartman: Romanticism after the Holocaust*. London: Continuum, 2010.

Vermeulen, Pieter. 'The Biopolitics of Trauma', in *The Future of Trauma Theory: Contemporary Literary and Cultural Criticism*, edited by Gert Buelens, 141–56. New York: Routledge, 2014.

Vetch, Robert Hamilton, and John Sweetman, 'Pasley, Sir Charles William (1780–1861), Army Officer'. *Oxford Dictionary of National Biography*. 23 September 2004. https://doi-org.rp.nla.gov.au/10.1093/ref:odnb/21500. Accessed 25 May 2021.

Virilio, Paul. *Speed and Politics*. Translated by Marc Polizzotti, introduction by Benjamin H. Bratton. Los Angeles: Semiotext(e), 2006.

Virilio, Paul. *War and Cinema: The Logistics of Perception*. Translated by Patrick Camiller. London: Verso, 1989.

Virno, Paolo. *A Grammar of the Multitude: For an Analysis of Contemporary Forms of Life*. Translated by Isabella Bertoletti, James Cascaito and Andrea Casson, foreword by Sylvère Lotringer. Los Angeles: Semiotext(e), 2004.

Vranjes, Vlasta. *English Vows: Marriage and National Identity in Nineteenth-Century Literature and Culture*. PhD diss., University of California, 2009.

Walker, Eric C. *Marriage, Writing and Romanticism: Wordsworth and Austen After War*. Stanford: Stanford University Press, 2009.

Walsh, Robert. *A Letter on the Genius and Dispositions of the French Government, including a View of the Taxation of the French Empire. Addressed to a Friend, by an American Recently Returned from Europe*. Baltimore: Published by P. H. Nicklin and Co.; also by Hopkins and Earle, Phliadelphia; Farrand, Mallory and Co. Boston; E. F. Backus, Albany; Williams and Whiting, New York; J. Parker, Pittsburgh; and E. Monford, Wellington and Co. Charleston, South Carolina, 1810.

Wasinski, Christophe. 'On Making War Possible: Soldiers, Strategy, and Military Grand Narrative'. *Security Dialogue*, 42, no. 1 (2011): 57–76.

Watson, John R. *Romanticism and War: A Study of British Romantic Period Writers and the Napoleonic Wars*. Basingstoke: Palgrave Macmillan, 2003.

Webb, Henry J. *Elizabethan Military Science*. Madison: University of Wisconsin Press, 1965.

Weil, Simone. 'The Iliad, or the Poem of Force'. *Chicago Review* 18, no. 2 (1965): 5–30.

Wheatley, Kim. 'Introduction: Romantic Periodicals and Print Culture'. *Prose Studies: History, Theory, Criticism* 25, no. 1 (2002): 1–18.

White, Laura Mooneyham. *Jane Austen's Anglicanism*. Farnham: Ashgate, 2011.

Williams, Raymond. *Writing in Society*. London: Verso, 1983.

Wimpffen, Francis. *The Experienced Officer; or Instructions by the General of Division, Francis Wimpffen to his Sons, and to All Young Men Intended for the Military Profession: Being a Series of Rules Laid Down by General Wimpffen, to Enable Officers of every Rank, to Carry on War, in All Its Branches and Descriptions, Form the Least Important Enterprises and Expeditions, to the Decisive Battles, which Involve the Fate of Empires. The Corrected and Revised Edition of the Latest Date, Illustrated by Notes. With an Introduction, by Lieutenant Colonel Macdonald, of the First Battalion of Cinque Port Volunteers; the Translator of the French Tactics, F.R.S. & c.* London: Printed for T. Egerton, Military Library, Whitehall, by C. Roworth, Bell Yard, Fleet Street, 1804.

Windham, William. *New Military Plan. The Speech of the Rt. Hon. Wm. Windham, Secretary of State, & c. Relating to the Regular Army, Militia, and Volunteers. Delivered in the House of Commons, on Thursday, April 3, 1806.* Norwich: Printed and Sold by Stevenson and Matchett, and May be Had of All Other Booksellers, 1806.

Winthrop-Young, Geoffrey. *Kittler and the Media*. Cambridge: Polity Press, 2011.

Woodfine, Philip. '"Unjustifiable and Illiberal": Military Patriotism and Civilian Values in the 1790s'. *War: Identities in Conflict, 1300–2000*, edited by Bertrand Taithe and Tim Thornton, 73–93. Stroud: Sutton Publishing, 1998.

Woodworth, Megan A. *Eighteenth-Century Women Writers and the Gentleman's Liberation Movement: Independence, War, Masculinity, and the Novel, 1778–1818.* Farnham: Ashgate, 2011.

Wordsworth, William. 'Letter to Captain Pasley, Royal Engineers. March 28, 1811', *Memoirs of William Wordsworth*, edited by Christopher Wordsworth. London, Edward Moxon, 1851.

Wordsworth, William. *Letters of the Wordsworth Family from 1787–1855*. London: Ardent Media, 1969.

Wordsworth, William. *The Prelude: A Parallel Text*, edited by James C. Maxwell. Harmondsworth: Penguin, 1971.

Wordsworth, William. 'XXIII. To the Men of Kent. October, 1803', in *The Poetical Works of William Wordsworth … in Six Volumes … A New Edition* (London, 1849), 64. Literature Online.

Index

279

CAMBRIDGE STUDIES IN ROMANTICISM

General Editor
JAMES CHANDLER, *University of Chicago*